# HOCKEY 365

# MIKE COMMITO

# HOCKEY

# 365

## DAILY STORIES FROM THE ICE

## DUNDURN
TORONTO

Cover design: Laura Boyle and Ron Beltrame
Printer: Webcom

**Library and Archives Canada Cataloguing in Publication**

Commito, Mike Anthony, author
    Hockey 365 : daily stories from the ice / Mike Commito.

Issued in print and electronic formats.
ISBN 978-1-4597-4184-3 (softcover).--ISBN 978-1-4597-4185-0 (PDF).--
ISBN 978-1-4597-4186-7 (EPUB)

    1. National Hockey League--Anecdotes. 2. Hockey players--
Anecdotes. 3. Hockey--Anecdotes. 4. National Hockey League--
Miscellanea. 5. Hockey players--Miscellanea. 6. Hockey--Miscellanea.
I. Title. II. Title: Hockey three sixty-five. III. Title: Hockey three
hundred sixty-five.

GV847.C63 2018          796.962'6402          C2018-903104-2
                                              C2018-903105-0

1  2  3  4  5      22  21  20  19  18

We acknowledge the support of the **Canada Council for the Arts**, which last year invested $153 million to bring the arts to Canadians throughout the country, and the **Ontario Arts Council** for our publishing program. We also acknowledge the financial support of the **Government of Ontario**, through the **Ontario Book Publishing Tax Credit** and the **Ontario Media Development Corporation**, and the **Government of Canada**.

Nous remercions le **Conseil des arts du Canada** de son soutien. L'an dernier, le Conseil a investi 153 millions de dollars pour mettre de l'art dans la vie des Canadiennes et des Canadiens de tout le pays.

Care has been taken to trace the ownership of copyright material used in this book. The author and the publisher welcome any information enabling them to rectify any references or credits in subsequent editions.
— *J. Kirk Howard, President*

The publisher is not responsible for websites or their content unless they are owned by the publisher.

Printed and bound in Canada.

VISIT US AT

 dundurn.com  |  @dundurnpress  |  dundurnpress  |  dundurnpress

Dundurn
3 Church Street, Suite 500
Toronto, Ontario, Canada
M5E 1M2

For Zoe

# PRE-GAME WARM-UP

Behind every great hockey play is a piece of history. Every milestone goal, point, or shutout is measured and contextualized by how it compares to the feats achieved by players from previous eras. Understanding the history of hockey is important because it highlights the sport's most significant athletes and how the game has evolved and situates the contemporary game within its rich heritage. You may not think you're a hockey historian just yet, but every time you watch a game, you're invariably comparing the accomplishments of the current players on the ice with those of their predecessors.

Having a better understanding of hockey's history gives you a better appreciation of the sport and how far it has come — from its early days on frozen ponds and rivers when the game was played with a block of wood instead of a puck to the riveting crescendo of the NHL's three-on-three overtime — and it also makes you a better fan. Knowing the history of the sport gives you an insider's knowledge of the game, both on and off the ice. Moreover, sharing in these moments engages you with the game on an intimate level and connects you in a way that transcends the outcome on the scoresheet. For example, understanding how Bobby Orr's career revolutionized the role of defencemen not only properly situates him as one of the greatest players of all time but also provides you with a better appreciation for what players such as Erik Karlsson do on the blue line in today's NHL. While knowing the dates that Bobby Orr rewrote the league's record books may not help you make sense of why your favourite team's defence corps is currently struggling, it will help you better understand why he was such a special player and how his impact is still felt throughout the league today.

But Bobby Orr is just one example of the historical snapshots you will find in the pages of *Hockey 365: Daily Stories from the Ice*. As the title suggests, you're about to embark on a journey through hockey history, highlighted by 366 different stories (don't forget leap years), each one representing a significant hockey moment for every day of the year. Think of it as a Word of the Day calendar that packs a punch. Now, visualize that calendar barrelling down the ice and wallpapering you into the boards. That's *Hockey 365*. With every flip of the page, you're introduced to a new episode in hockey history. Although there are some familiar names throughout the book — it would be rather difficult not to mention Wayne Gretzky more than a few times — each entry captures a unique moment in the game.

As you might have guessed, there are 12 chapters, one for every month of the year. While there are threads that link some of the stories together throughout the narrative, *Hockey 365* is not your standard hockey book. Much like the game itself, there is no linear flow. You can read it from cover to cover (and hopefully you do), or you can pick it up at any point and start from there. It begins with Willie O'Ree's first goal on January 1, 1961, but you don't have to follow the puck to the next day. Instead, you can jump to September 23, 1992, when Manon Rheaume became the first woman to suit up for NHL action, without missing a beat. There's no penalty for skipping ahead. However you want to read the book is up to you. Read it in your bathroom. Read it to your daughter. Read it during intermission. There's no wrong way for you to read *Hockey 365*.

While *Hockey 365* traces the sport from the first indoor matchup in Montreal in 1875 to Auston Matthews's electrifying debut in 2016, it is not a definitive account of the game. Although I've tried to pack in as many details as I could, it is not meant to be a comprehensive hockey history. Moreover, while the book touches on some notable moments in women's hockey and international hockey, most of the inspiration is drawn from the NHL, where the sport is played at its highest level.

At this point, you're probably wondering how I selected these 366 stories. I wish I could tell you I developed a complex algorithm that calculated the most historically significant hockey moment for each day of the year, but that wasn't the case. Using a variety of primary and secondary sources, I carefully chose moments I felt were entertaining and important enough to merit analysis. Sometimes this process was painstaking. There were a few instances where I found some anecdotal information for a story but could not corroborate it with a primary source, so I had to scrap it and go with the next one. Occasionally, I opted to explore some of the game's lesser known moments rather than focus on an event that has been covered extensively. For example, Wayne Gretzky became the NHL's all-time leading goal scorer on March 23, 1994, but instead I wrote about how Chicago's Bill Mosienko scored a hat trick in 21 seconds on that day 42 years earlier. Part of the reason behind that decision was because racking up three goals in 21 seconds is pretty darn impressive, but also because Wayne Gretzky looms so large in hockey history. Even though I didn't dedicate an entire section to his 802nd career goal, it was brought up in other ways as he is a recurring figure throughout the book. That being said, I also took great care to avoid this book turning into *Gretzky 365* or *Orr 365*. Although you could quite easily write a book dedicated to their year-round accomplishments, it was important to give them their proper due but also spread the ice time around to other players. You may not agree with every player or episode I have chosen to highlight here, but I think we can agree that if you're reading this right now you're either my mother (hi, Mom) or you have a passion for hockey history. If it's the latter, and I'm hoping it is, these stories are just 366 glimpses into the rich heritage of the game we all love.

# JANUARY 1
## MILESTONE GOAL, 1961

While many people might have started 1961 off with a hangover, Boston's Willie O'Ree began his new year with a milestone. On January 1, 1961, he scored his first career National Hockey League goal. His tally proved to be the game-winner as the cellar-dwelling Bruins toppled the first-place Canadiens by a score of 3-2. The significance of O'Ree's goal, however, transcended the outcome on the scoresheet: it was the first NHL goal ever scored by a black player. O'Ree made his debut for Boston three years earlier, on January 18, 1958, becoming the first black man to play in an NHL game. Originally from Fredericton, New Brunswick, O'Ree almost didn't make it to the NHL. During his junior hockey days with the Kitchener Canucks of the Ontario Hockey Association, O'Ree sustained a serious injury that left him blind in one eye. As a result, he not only had to compensate for his limited vision but also had to keep the injury a secret if he hoped to crack the league's ranks.

Following his goal against the Canadiens, O'Ree would go on to play 33 more games for the Bruins, picking up three more goals along the way. In the off-season, he was traded to Montreal but never suited up for the club at the NHL level, instead playing for the Hull-Ottawa Canadiens in the Eastern Professional Hockey League before heading to the West Coast. O'Ree went on to play for nearly 16 years in the Western Hockey League, suiting up for teams such as the Los Angeles Blades and the San Diego Gulls. Although O'Ree's time in the NHL was brief, he paved the way for other black hockey players to ascend to the NHL ranks in the decades that followed. Since retiring from professional hockey, O'Ree has been a tireless advocate for greater diversity and inclusion in the game and has served as the NHL's Director of Youth Development and ambassador for NHL Diversity since 1998. Given his significant contributions to the sport, O'Ree finally received his long overdue call to the Hockey Hall of Fame on June 26, 2018.

## JANUARY 2
# UP IN FLAMES, 1918

The NHL's inaugural campaign in 1917–18 was full of ups and downs, but no team fared worse than the Montreal Wanderers. Their season went up in flames. Literally. On January 2, 1918, Montreal's Westmount Arena burned to the ground. According to historian J. Andrew Ross, the fire was caused by faulty wiring that ignited a blaze in a dressing room before it caused the boilers and ammonia tanks to explode. At the time, the facility was shared by both the Wanderers and the Canadiens, with both teams losing nearly $1,000 worth of equipment in the conflagration. Although the Canadiens were able to relocate to the city's Jubilee Rink in the east end, thereby drawing upon the considerable support they enjoyed from the francophone community in that district, the Wanderers could find no suitable alternative. The team's owner, Sam Lichtenhein, threatened to withdraw the club from play unless the NHL committed additional resources in the wake of the fire. The league refused. Although the league hoped Lichtenhein was bluffing, it proceeded with plans for a three-club schedule should it be needed. But where there's smoke, there's fire. With the Westmount Arena still smouldering, the Wanderers defaulted on their next match against Toronto.

In the end, the franchise lost its charter and, to pour salt on the wound, was fined $500 by the league. To help keep the league's remaining three clubs above water for the remainder of the season, a revenue-sharing model was introduced. Although the Wanderers had previously won the Stanley Cup four times as members of the Eastern Canada Amateur Hockey Association and National Hockey Association, their brief NHL tenure was a disaster. The team finished with a record of 1-5-0 and never returned to the league.

# JANUARY 3
# BROTHER TO BROTHER ... TO BROTHER, 1943

n a game against the Rangers on January 3, 1943, the Bentley brothers stole the show, with all three contributing to the Chicago Black Hawks' first goal of the game. It was also the first goal of Reg Bentley's career and, assisted by younger brothers Max and Doug, the first time in NHL history when all three points were awarded to the same family. Doug and Max were already stalwart players in Chicago, but the league was short on personnel because of the Second World War, so Reg had been called up just two days before the game. The marker proved to be Reg's only National Hockey League goal, but with both brothers assisting, it couldn't have been more special.

Reg played just six more games with the Black Hawks before putting his professional hockey career on hold to join the Canadian military. While serving in Calgary, however, he did get some ice time, suiting up for the Calgary Currie Army of the Calgary National Defence Hockey League. Following the conclusion of the Second World War, Bentley headed west to play for the New Westminster Royals of the Pacific Hockey League. In his second year with the club, he racked up 41 goals and 71 points. Meanwhile, in the NHL, Doug finished the season with the most goals and as the league's scoring leader with 73 points, becoming the first Chicago player to win a regular-season scoring title. The following season, Doug found the back of the net 38 times to lead the league in goal-scoring for the second straight year. Although Doug would play nearly another decade for the Black Hawks, the Bentley brothers' time in Chicago officially came to an end when Max was traded to the Maple Leafs in 1947.

# SALUTING SALMING, 1988

When Maple Leafs defenceman Borje Salming became the first European-born NHLer to reach the 1,000-game mark, it should have been a cause for celebration. After all, he was just the 62nd player in league history, and only the fifth Maple Leaf, to reach the milestone. The only other players to have reached the benchmark as members of the Maple Leafs were George Armstrong, Tim Horton, Dave Keon, and Ron Ellis. Despite the illustrious company that Salming was joining, his feting would have to wait. At the time, Toronto owner Harold Ballard was on respite because of poor health and insisted that his player not be honoured until he returned. So when Salming played his 1,000th game against the Vancouver Canucks on January 4, 1988, there was no pomp or ceremony. Sure, the Swedish blueliner had his brother Stig in the stands to watch the memorable game, and he was saluted by his teammates, but that was about it.

It was nearly two months later, when the Maple Leafs hosted the St. Louis Blues on February 27, that Salming was officially recognized by the club. During the belated tribute at Maple Leaf Gardens, Salming was presented with a sparkling blue Chevy S-10 Blazer. Emblazoned on the doors were the Maple Leafs logo, Salming's number, and the number 1,000 to signify his accomplishment. Even better than the keys to a new vehicle was who was inside. Behind the wheel was good friend and former teammate Inge Hammarstrom, who had signed with Borje to play for the Maple Leafs in 1973. In addition, Inge was chauffeuring Salming's brother, sister, and parents, Erland and Karin, who hadn't been to Canada in nearly a decade. Although the Maple Leafs lost the game on Salming's big night, the celebration proved to be worth the wait for the Swedish rearguard.

# JANUARY 5

## LANDMARK TV GOES LIVE, 1957

During the summer of 1956, the NHL and CBS struck a 10-game television contract. It was a big deal, as it signalled the first TV network coverage of hockey in the United States. As part of the agreement, CBS would televise 10 Saturday-afternoon games throughout the 1956–57 season beginning in the new year. So when the Bruins and Rangers squared off on January 5, 1957, it wasn't just simply another game. It marked the first time an NHL contest was televised from coast to coast in the United States. Aside from the broadcasting implications, it was also significant for the Rangers. Matinee games were nothing new to the NHL, but this was the first time the New York squad, affectionately known as the Blueshirts, had ever played one at Madison Square Garden.

The game proved to be an easy win for the Rangers, who opened the scoring in the first period, then potted the game-winner at the tail end of the second frame. Chicago got on the scoresheet 44 seconds into the final stanza, but the damage had been done. The Black Hawks kept it a one-goal game for most of the period, but the Rangers scored two quick goals, 20 seconds apart, in the final minute to put the game out of reach. While 9,853 fans were in attendance for the game, countless more viewers were watching the drama unfold from the comfort of their living rooms. With the contest being transmitted on more than 100 stations as far south and west as New Orleans and Los Angeles, respectively, there would have been no shortage of people tuning in to catch some afternoon hockey. The televised games proved to be very popular that season. As a result, the NHL and CBS both agreed to renew the television package for 1957–58, increasing the number of games to 21 and beginning the coverage earlier in the season.

## JANUARY 6
# UNDEFEATED, 1980

The Flyers seemed unbeatable. After losing to the Atlanta Flames on October 13, 1979, in just their second game of the season, Philadelphia would win or tie every contest until January 6, 1980, in what became the longest unbeaten streak not just in NHL history but in all professional sports. Over nearly three months, the Flyers racked up 25 wins and 10 ties as opponent after opponent failed to defeat them. During the course of the streak, which included nine straight victories, the Flyers later said they never felt any pressure except on the evening of December 22, 1979, when they faced Boston in a matchup that would determine if they would rewrite the league's record book. By defeating the Bruins 5-2 at the Garden, Philadelphia extended its streak to 29 games, eclipsing the mark that had been set by the Canadiens in 1976–77. The Flyers then closed out the calendar year with three more victories and a draw to keep the streak alive.

In the new year, they just kept on rolling. After vanquishing the Rangers on January 4, 1980, the Flyers travelled to Buffalo to take on the Sabres two nights later. After the Sabres took a 2-1 lead early in the second period, the Flyers fought back with a goal late in the frame from Dennis Ververgaert, who had parked himself in front of the net and wired the puck over the right shoulder of Buffalo goaltender Don Edwards. Heading into the third period, the Flyers simply needed to hang on to extend their record-setting streak to an unfathomable 35 games. With time winding down on the clock, Philadelphia's Bill Barber and Rick MacLeish each potted a goal to break a 2-2 deadlock and lift the Flyers over their opponents to extend the streak in convincing fashion.

# JANUARY 7
# THE FLYERS' STREAK
# COMES TO AN END, 1980

Unfortunately, all good things must come to an end. The very next night, the Flyers travelled to Minnesota to take on the North Stars. Before a crowd of 15,962 fans at the Met Center, the Flyers, along with their record, came crashing down. After Bill Barber opened the scoring for the Flyers early in the first period, the North Stars scored three goals in the final seven minutes of the frame to jump out to a 3-1 lead. When play resumed following intermission, Minnesota added two more goals in the second period to put the game out of reach for Philadelphia. Head coach Pat Quinn, who was behind the bench for his first full season, wished the streak could have lasted longer but was practical about the outcome. "We walked into a club that was fairly fresh and obviously well primed…. We didn't really care where the streak ended. I said all along that it was inevitable. We didn't lose — we got beat," he said. Speaking to reporters after the game with 11 stitches in his face from being struck by a puck, Bobby Clarke, who had won two Stanley Cups with the Flyers in 1974 and 1975, did not believe the end of the streak would negatively impact the team. "The loss isn't going to bother us. The wins didn't bother us when we were winning and the loss won't hurt us, either. The only time there was any pressure was the night we beat Boston to set the record," he said.

As for the North Stars, they also became part of history. In ending the streak on January 7, 1980, they became forever intertwined with the Flyers' incredible accomplishment. The Flyers would finish the season atop the regular-season standings with a record of 48-12-20. They advanced as far as the Stanley Cup Final before coming up short against the Islanders, who captured their first of four straight championships.

# BABE'S SIX HELPERS, 1944

Maple Leafs defenceman Walter "Babe" Pratt had himself quite the game on January 8, 1944. He not only assisted on half his team's goals but also did something no other blueliner had accomplished in NHL history: he recorded six assists in a single game. Pratt was instrumental in Toronto's 12-3 win over Boston, and he set a new gold standard for rearguards in the process. He would finish the season with 41 assists and 58 points to lead the league in scoring among defencemen. Moreover, it was the highest number of points registered by a blueliner in a single season, a benchmark that would stay on the books for another two decades. When Chicago's Pierre Pilote finally broke the record in 1965, he needed nearly 20 more games than Babe to accomplish the feat.

For his efforts in 1944, Pratt was awarded the Hart Trophy as the player most valuable to his team, making him the first Maple Leafs player to receive the award. He would play another two seasons in Toronto, scoring the Stanley Cup–winning goal in 1945, before finishing his NHL career with none other than the Bruins. Although he would continue to play professional hockey for another six years, nothing could top his January performance against Boston. In the decades since, other future Hall of Famers of the likes of Bobby Orr and Paul Coffey have matched Pratt's six-assist record-setting game, but no defenceman has surpassed Babe. In fact, among all NHL players, only Bill Taylor and Wayne Gretzky have recorded seven helpers in a game. Pratt was inducted into the Hockey Hall of Fame in 1966.

# JANUARY 9
## SHUTOUTS GALORE, 2004

When Phoenix's Brian Boucher recorded a shutout on New Year's Eve 2003, nobody — not even the goaltender himself — would've thought he was about to make history. The fact that he was even in net for the Coyotes was somewhat unexpected. Heading into the season, Boucher was third on the Coyotes' goaltending depth chart and was left unprotected in the league's annual waiver draft. But he started entering the lineup after the team's regular backup netminder, Zac Bierk, injured his groin in October. When Boucher made his eighth start of the campaign on New Year's Eve, it would mark the beginning of a magical run that set two modern NHL records: most consecutive shutouts and longest shutout streak. After picking up a shutout against the Kings, Boucher then collected three more.

Nine days later, on January 9, Boucher picked up his fifth straight shutout to pass Montreal's Bill Durnan, who had recorded four consecutive goose eggs in the 1948–49 season. Although Boucher had stonewalled the Wild to set the record on the road, even the faithful Minnesota crowd could not help but give the netminder a roaring ovation for his accomplishment. Two nights later, he was going for the league record of six straight shutouts, originally set by Alec Connell in 1927–28 before the NHL's modern era began with the introduction of the red line. But it wasn't meant to be. Boucher finally let a puck slip by, but he still made history by extending his shutout streak to 332:01 minutes, surpassing Durnan's mark of 309:21. While Boucher would finish his career as a journeyman goaltender, for nearly two weeks in January 2004, there was practically nothing that could get by him.

# THE UNLUCKY ST. PATRICKS, 1920

The St. Patricks certainly didn't have the luck of the Irish on their side when they met the Canadiens on January 10, 1920. That night, they were trounced 14-7. The combined total of 21 goals — six by Montreal's Newsy Lalonde — is still the most in NHL history, although some games have come close to beating it. On February 22, 1981, the Nordiques defeated the Capitals 11-7, a bit shy of the mark, but the teams did set an NHL record for most scoring points in a game with 53.

Sixty-five years after the St. Patricks' misfortune, the Oilers and Black Hawks scored 21 times in a matchup on December 11, 1985, that saw Edmonton defeat Chicago 12-9. While it matched the record for combined goals in a game, it also tied another league record for most goals in a single period, when both teams exploded for six goals apiece in the middle frame. This matched the mark set by the Maple Leafs and Sabres four years earlier when Buffalo outscored their opponents 9-3 in the second period of a game that would end in a 14-4 rout of Toronto. In addition to the records matched by the Oilers and Black Hawks, the game also surpassed the previous benchmark for most scoring points in a game, as 62 points were awarded to members of both teams. Besides the goaltenders, only five players from that game failed to find their way onto the scoresheet. Wayne Gretzky certainly had no such issues. He collected seven assists, extending his point streak to 20 consecutive contests.

# JANUARY 11
## KILLING TIME, 1983

Edmonton's Pat Hughes wasn't thinking about scoring goals when he was killing a penalty against the St. Louis Blues on January 11, 1983. "My first responsibility is to kill the penalty," he said, "not score goals." That night, however, Hughes set an NHL record by scoring the two fastest short-handed goals in league history. The Oilers were winning 2-1 in the second period when the winger's tallies, just 25 seconds apart, opened the game up. Edmonton went on to beat St. Louis 7-5 that night. More impressive, perhaps, was that Hughes had eclipsed the previous record holder, who happened to be none other than Wayne Gretzky, the Great One having scored a pair of short-handed goals 27 seconds apart on March 25, 1982, in a game against Calgary.

Two nights before Hughes had done his damage on the penalty kill, Philadelphia's Mark Howe and Bill Barber were just five seconds shy of equalling Gretzky's mark when they potted two short-handed goals in 32 seconds against the Whalers. With Hughes's two quick goals against the Blues, he became the first player to break a Gretzky record, a claim few players can make. In reflecting on that moment years later, Hughes said he remembers Gretzky coming up to him after the game and saying, "I thought that one was going to last a long time." Hughes would finish the season with five short-handed goals, a career high. He would win two Stanley Cups with Edmonton before finishing his career in Buffalo, St. Louis, and Hartford. Two years after Hughes hung up his skates, Esa Tikkanen, who was just starting his career in Edmonton when Hughes was on his way out, shattered the record, scoring two short-handed goals in 12 seconds against the Maple Leafs on November 12, 1988.

# JANUARY 12
## JOE MALONE MAKES HISTORY, 1918

oe Malone was no stranger to scoring goals. The forward, nicknamed "Phantom Joe" for his deceptive quickness and his uncanny ability to appear at the right time to tap home a goal, rightfully earned his moniker. During his days in the National Hockey Association, the precursor to the NHL, he lit the lamp nine times in Stanley Cup action against the Sydney Millionaires. When the NHL's first games were played on December 19, 1917, Malone scored five goals in his debut for the Canadiens. Less than a month later, on January 12, 1918, in just his seventh game of the campaign, he matched that output in a game against Ottawa to become the new NHL's first 20-goal scorer. By the time the season ended in March, Malone had racked up a remarkable 44 goals in just 20 games, establishing an NHL record for goals-per-game average in a single season, among players with 20 goals or more, that will likely never be matched.

Ottawa's Cy Denneny came close that season, scoring 36 goals in 20 games for an average of 1.80 goals per game, but even that doesn't come close to Malone's 2.20 in 1917–18. To put that number into perspective, if a player scored at that clip under the NHL's current 82-game format, it would amount to 180 goals, which would dwarf Wayne Gretzky's record-setting 92-goal campaign in 1981–82. In fact, Gretzky's output from that season only puts him 20th all-time among players in that category. The Great One's best average actually came from his 1983–84 season, in which he scored 87 goals in 74 games for 1.18 goals per game.

# JANUARY 13
## YOUNGEST 400 GOAL SCORER, 1985

By the tender age of 13, Wayne Gretzky had already scored 1,000 lifetime goals in his young career. So when he graduated to the NHL as an 18-year-old, there was plenty of reason to suppose he would topple record after record. He certainly didn't disappoint. When the Great One retired, he held or shared 61 NHL records, along with even more unofficial records, including the distinction of being the youngest player to score 400 goals. On January 13, 1985, just two weeks shy of his 24th birthday, Gretzky potted his 400th career NHL goal. With five seconds remaining in the second period, he scored his 44th of the season to tie the game 3-3. Early in the final frame, Buffalo's Dave Andreychuk scored to regain the lead, but Mark Messier would score the tying goal and the game-winner with less than a minute remaining in regulation. While most of the newspaper coverage focused on Messier's late-game heroics, Gretzky had quietly become the youngest player to score 400 goals.

Even more impressive is that he needed only 436 games to accomplish the feat. Gretzky would score 29 more goals that season and finish the campaign with 208 points to capture his fifth straight Art Ross Trophy and his sixth consecutive Hart Trophy, as the most valuable player to his team. In the playoffs, Gretzky's incredible play continued. He scored 47 points in 18 games, establishing a post-season record that will never be broken. To put that in perspective, the runner-up in scoring that post-season was teammate Paul Coffey, who piled up 25 assists but still trailed Gretzky by 10 points. The highest-scoring player in the playoffs who didn't play for the Oilers was Chicago's Denis Savard, who had an impressive campaign by his own standards but was still 18 points behind the Great One. For his efforts, Gretzky was once again recognized as an MVP, receiving the Conn Smythe Trophy for the first time in his career as he led Edmonton to back-to-back championships.

# JANUARY 14
## HATS OFF FOR ROOKIES, 1943

After Alex Smart scored his third goal in a game on January 14, 1943, he wasn't showered with porkpies and fedoras (the practice of throwing hats to mark a hat trick was a few years away), but it was still a feat worth celebrating. With his accomplishment, Smart became the first rookie in NHL history to score three goals in his debut. Smart had been playing in the Quebec Senior Hockey League and posting some respectable numbers when he got the call to suit up for the Canadiens. He had a brilliant debut, as he paced the Canadiens to a 5-1 victory over the visiting Black Hawks. Despite his extraordinary first game, however, Smart was not long for the NHL. He played just seven more games for the Canadiens, scoring twice, before he was sent back to the senior league.

Although Smart is often credited with being the first rookie to score a hat trick in his debut, that's not entirely accurate. On December 19, 1917, in the NHL's inaugural games, Joe Malone and Harry Hyland each scored five goals for their respective teams. But they were hardly rookies. Malone was just two months shy of his 28th birthday, and Hyland was mere weeks away from turning 29. Moreover, both were nearly 10-year veterans of the National Hockey Association, the predecessor to the NHL. Malone had long established himself as one of the most prolific scorers of his era, netting 43 goals in 20 games with the Quebec Bulldogs in 1912–13. Hyland, meanwhile, potted 30 markers in 18 games with the Wanderers in the 1913–14 season. While Malone and Hyland may have technically been NHL rookies, they were no greenhorns. Since Smart's debut, only four other players have recorded hat tricks in their NHL openers. Real Cloutier, Fabian Brunnstrom, and Derek Stepan all scored three goals in their first outing, but Toronto's Auston Matthews topped them all when he racked up four goals in his debut against the Ottawa Senators on October 12, 2016.

# JANUARY 15
## PATRICK ROY'S FIRST SHUTOUT, 1986

Patrick Roy's first taste of NHL action wasn't exactly memorable. On February 23, 1985, with the game between the Canadiens and the Jets tied 4-4, Roy came into the contest to start the third period in relief of goaltender Doug Soetaert. The young netminder had to stop only two shots in his 20-minute appearance, but it was enough for Montreal to score two goals, giving Roy his first career NHL victory. Then he was sent back to junior. The next season, after backstopping Montreal's American Hockey League affiliate to a Calder Cup championship, Roy returned to the Canadiens, where he assumed full-time duties. He picked up his first shutout on January 15, 1986, stopping all 19 shots he faced from the Jets, the same opponents he had faced in his first NHL game a year earlier. But that first shutout was just a preview of things to come.

By the time the post-season arrived, Roy had firmly wrestled the starting job from Soetaert. During an incredible playoff run, Roy guided his club to a Stanley Cup with a sterling .923 save percentage and picked up the Conn Smythe Trophy, the award for the most valuable player to his team during the playoffs. Three years later, Roy would earn his first Vezina Trophy, awarded annually to the best goaltender as judged by the league's general managers. He would add two more Vezinas to his trophy case with the Canadiens before collecting another Conn Smythe when he led the club to another Stanley Cup in 1993. Following an abrupt trade to Colorado in 1996, Roy would win two more championships and capture another Conn Smythe in 2001 with the Avalanche. When he retired in 2003, he had played in 1,029 career NHL games, a record at the time, and racked up 66 shutouts. He was inducted into the Hockey Hall of Fame in 2006.

# KEN DORATY'S OVERTIME HEROICS, 1934

After 60 minutes of play, the Senators and Maple Leafs were deadlocked 4-4. Early in the overtime period, Toronto's Ken Doraty scored. Less than a minute later he scored again, before adding another goal in the final minute of the extra frame to complete the overtime hat trick. On January 16, 1934, Ken Doraty became the first, and only, player in NHL history to record a three-goal performance in overtime. Prior to the league's introduction of sudden-death overtime in 1983, clubs used to simply compete in a supplementary 10-minute period that was played as straight time. As a result, teams could score multiple times in the additional frame, and games could still end in a draw if neither squad found the scoresheet in the extra period or scored the same number of goals. This format, first introduced for the 1928–29 season, persisted for over a decade until the NHL scrapped overtime at the height of the Second World War. On November 20, 1942, the league announced it would be cancelling extra time during the regular season in the face of growing concerns over wartime travel.

Although Doraty had won the game for the Maple Leafs and enshrined himself into hockey history lore with his three-goal performance, he was no stranger to playing the part of overtime hero. Just a year earlier, during his rookie season with Toronto, Doraty was a part of NHL history when the Maple Leafs took on the Bruins in the fifth and deciding game of their semifinal matchup on April 3, 1933. Following 60 minutes of regulation, the two teams were stuck in a scoreless stalemate. The first overtime period solved nothing. The second overtime period solved nothing. The third overtime period solved nothing. The fourth overtime period solved nothing. The fifth overtime period solved nothing. Finally, less than five minutes into the sixth additional frame, Doraty scored the winning goal to mercifully end the game. As of the end of the 2018 Stanley Cup Playoffs, it remains the second-longest game in league history.

# THE RUSSIAN ROCKET LEAVES VANCOUVER, 1999

After seven seasons with the Canucks, including two 60-goal campaigns, Pavel Bure's time in Vancouver came to an end. On January 17, 1999, he was traded to the Panthers as part of a blockbuster seven-player deal. Bure had been drafted in the sixth round by Vancouver in 1989 and made his NHL debut two years later, on November 5, 1991, in a game against the Jets. He finished his inaugural campaign with 34 goals, a Canucks rookie record, and became the first Vancouver player to win the Calder Trophy as the league's top rookie. Nicknamed the "Russian Rocket" for his incredible speed and innate ability to score goals, Bure instantly became a fan favourite in Vancouver. The next season, he continued to impress, scoring his 60th goal on April 11, 1993, setting a franchise record for most goals in a season. He would match the feat again the following year. Despite his success in Vancouver, by the end of the 1997–98 season, it was reported that Bure wanted out. He refused to shed light on the situation, simply stating that it was a personal decision. When a deal was not forthcoming, he refused to report to the Canucks' training camp before the start of the following season.

The drama was finally resolved on January 17, when he was traded acrimoniously to Florida, along with defencemen Bret Hedican and Brad Ference and a third-round draft pick, in exchange for defenceman Ed Jovanovski, goaltender Kevin Weekes, forwards Dave Gagner and Mike Brown, and Florida's first-round draft pick in 2000. The following season, his first full campaign in a Panthers uniform, Bure scored 58 goals, setting a new franchise record and winning his first Maurice "Rocket" Richard Trophy as the league's top goal scorer. The next season, he'd break his own Panthers record by scoring 59 goals, and for the second straight year, the Russian Rocket snagged the Rocket.

# YZERMAN PASSES LEMIEUX, 2000

After scoring 613 goals with the Red Wings through the first 16 years of his career, Steve Yzerman was chasing some history. With one more goal, he would vault past Mario Lemieux for sixth place on the NHL's all-time scoring list and also move into first place for the most goals in league history by a player who spent his entire career with one team. Before Detroit's game against the Flames on January 18, 2000, Yzerman spoke with Allan Maki from the *Globe and Mail* about reaching the milestone and whom he thought might be able to surpass him. "If [Jaromir] Jagr stays in Pittsburgh, he'll blow by me for sure," he told Maki. "I feel very lucky. This one will be more special than others, I guess, because it's kind of unique. There's luck involved in playing your career for one organization," he added. Yzerman's history-making moment did not happen on the ice but rather on the bench. Two minutes into the game against the Flames, the Red Wings opened the scoring, but the officials had initially credited defenceman Steve Duchesne with the goal, with assists going to Chris Chelios and Yzerman.

During the second period, however, a change was made. While Yzerman was sitting on the bench, it was announced that he had been awarded the goal, his 614th career tally. At the time, the two teams were tied 1-1 but the Flames quickly took control, scoring three more unanswered goals that period and two more in the final frame to trounce the Red Wings. Following the game, Yzerman's personal achievement was of little consolation. "We got beat 6-1 and we got beat easily 6-1, so the goal really doesn't have any significance to me right now," he told reporters. Yzerman would add another 78 goals in his final five years with the Red Wings. Although Lemieux came out of retirement the following season, Yzerman finished his career with two more goals than Super Mario and as of 2017–18 remains the NHL's all-time leading goal scorer among players who spent their entire career with one team.

# WHEN THE JETS FLEW THE COOP, 1996

When Winnipeg Jets fans heard the news that the NHL's board of governors had approved the sale of their team on January 19, 1996, it had been a long time coming. Over the preceding months, a tumultuous saga had dragged on that saw the Winnipeg faithful read their club its last rites and bury it several times over. The announcement might have been the team's official obituary notice, but the Jets had already been long dead heading into the 1995–96 season. Although the team's financial struggles had reached their nadir heading into that campaign, the Jets had been hemorrhaging cash for years. The club received a stay of execution in November 1991 when it received a significant injection from business leaders and from the municipal and provincial governments. Together, they provided the Jets' owners with a $10 million fund from which to draw annual management fees. It was believed that this new outlay from local businesses and the two tiers of government would mitigate the Jets' short-term troubles and get them on the runway toward financial stability.

Unfortunately, it never took off. While that deal should have kept the Jets in Winnipeg for the immediate future, the financial situation only got worse. In the years that followed, the Jets were losing millions of dollars each season and were projected to lose as much as $20 million by 1997 if the trend continued. Following the lockout-shortened season of 1994–95, things took a nosedive. With Winnipeg's aging arena crumbling and a struggling loonie in the face of rising player salaries, the Jets were feeling the pinch. Winnipeg finished the season, made the playoffs, and pushed the Presidents' Trophy–winning Red Wings to a six-game series before the franchise took flight for Arizona. Winnipeg's relocation story, however, came full circle in 2011 when the NHL moved the Atlanta Thrashers to Manitoba, where the Jets were relaunched.

# THE MAGNIFICENT ONE'S 50TH, 1989

Wayne Gretzky was the Great One, but there's a reason Mario Lemieux was known as the Magnificent One. On January 20, 1989, Lemieux became just the second player in NHL history to score 50 goals in fewer than 50 games. While Gretzky accomplished the feat on December 30, 1981, in an astonishing 39 games, Lemieux was not that far behind him. After scoring 49 goals through the first 43 games of the campaign, Lemieux and the Penguins travelled to Winnipeg to take on the Jets. It did not take him long to reach the milestone. Just over a minute into the game, Rob Brown dished Lemieux a cross-ice pass deep in the Jets' zone. After corralling the puck, Lemieux wired it past Winnipeg goaltender Pokey Reddick short side to notch his 50th goal of the season. As the game continued, Lemieux also picked up two assists to give him 638 career points, vaulting him past his assistant coach Rick Kehoe as the team's all-time leading scorer.

It should have been a magnificent evening for the 23-year-old goal scorer, but his achievement was overshadowed by the fact the Jets trounced the Penguins 7-3, handing Pittsburgh its third straight loss. Moreover, on the other side of the ice, Winnipeg rookie Pat Elynuik stole some of the limelight, recording a five-goal game much to the delight of the home crowd. Following the game, Lemieux, who had factored in on all three of his team's goals, sat dejected in the dressing room. While he should have been toasting his accomplishment, instead he was trying to find answers for the loss. "We didn't put any type of effort in out there…. I don't know what's going on," he told reporters. The Penguins quickly figured it out, snapping their skid the next night in Edmonton. Lemieux continued to find the back of the net down the final stretch of the season, adding 35 more goals to finish the campaign with 85 markers and 114 assists, narrowly missing the 200-point plateau by just a single point, to snag his second straight Art Ross Trophy.

# JANUARY 21
## THE KENORA THISTLES, 1907

The city of Kenora has a rich hockey history. The small community in far northwestern Ontario is home to just over 15,000 people, but it lays claim to something that has escaped the grasp of many large-market NHL cities: the Stanley Cup. The roots of hockey in Kenora can be traced back to the late 19th century when it was still known as Rat Portage. The town's first team, the Thistles, started playing in 1894 and competed in the Manitoba Hockey Association. Within a few years, the Thistles had garnered a loyal following. So much so that the team brokered an arrangement with the Canadian Pacific Railway so that fans could travel for games of note in Winnipeg at a discounted rate. By 1903, the Thistles were playing in the senior division of the Manitoba and Northwestern Hockey Association (MNHA) and made an impact in their inaugural season there by winning the league championship. While regional bragging rights were nothing to scoff at back in the day, the title also gave them the opportunity to issue a challenge for the Stanley Cup.

From 1893 to 1914, a period known as the challenge era, the Stanley Cup was contested among the champions of Canada's amateur hockey leagues. As a result, the Thistles issued a challenge to the Ottawa Hockey Club, the top team from the Canadian Amateur Hockey League. Although ice conditions were poor, reports from the *Globe* suggested that the Thistles were simply outmatched. Ottawa kept the Cup and Rat Portage returned to the Lake of the Woods empty-handed. On January 21, 1907, the Kenora Thistles had the chance to redeem themselves, this time defeating the Montreal Wanderers in another challenge series for the rights to Lord Stanley's mug. The Thistles had enshrined themselves in hockey lore. At the time, the lumber and mining town had a population just north of 5,000, making it the smallest community ever to win the Cup, a distinction that likely will stand the test of time.

# JANUARY 22
## SNOWED IN, 1987

The Garden State was snowed in. By January 23, 1987, over 16 inches of snow had fallen in just a couple of days and New Jersey stopped cold: traffic was bogged down, planes were grounded, and schools were closed. The only people who didn't seem to get the memo about the impending shutdown were the brave fans who showed up at the Meadowlands in East Rutherford the previous evening to watch the Devils take on the Flames. Although the Devils expected 11,247 patrons — the number of tickets sold — only 334 fans turned out because of the crippling winter storm, believed to be the record for the lowest-attended game in the NHL's modern era.

The game, scheduled to start at 7:35 p.m., was pushed back by nearly two hours because most of the New Jersey players and the team's physician were late because of the weather. Reflecting on the situation years later, Devils defenceman Ken Daneyko remembers the scene when he stepped out onto the ice after arriving late. "We rushed in and just got dressed. It was like a practice, there was nobody there. About 334 people — obviously diehards," he later recalled. When the puck was finally dropped, fans in the eerily quiet arena were treated to a pretty entertaining game. Heading into the third period, the Devils trailed 4-3 but scored three goals in a span of less than six minutes as they went on to ice the Flames 7-4. During the course of the game, a member from New Jersey's front office went around the arena and collected the names and addresses of all the patrons in attendance. A couple of months later, to commemorate the special occasion, the Devils sent a letter to each of the 334 fans, informing them they had been inducted into and given lifetime membership to the 334 Club.

# JANUARY 23
## BATTERED BLUESHIRTS, 1944

f you're a fan of the New York Rangers, you might want to skip to the next day. On January 23, 1944, the Blueshirts suffered the most lopsided defeat in NHL history: a 15-0 shellacking at the hands of Detroit. That night the Red Wings broke their own record, as they had previously vanquished the Montreal Canadiens 10-0 on January 4, 1942. Although the Rangers were unable to find the scoresheet against Detroit, their goaltender, Ken McAuley, performed admirably under the circumstances. He made 43 saves, but it simply wasn't enough to repel the relentless Red Wings. Even as the clock wound down in the third period, Detroit continued the onslaught. Forward Syd Howe, with just one assist after the first two frames, bagged three goals in the final minutes to record the game's only hat trick.

When the dust settled, four Red Wings had registered five-point performances. The only members of the team who did not factor in on the scoring were defenceman Cully Simon and goaltender Connie Dion. But the Detroit netminder didn't mind. He picked up his first career NHL shutout and added to a five-game unbeaten streak since his discharge from the Canadian military. Following the defeat, the Rangers lost their next two games but had the chance to redeem themselves when they travelled to Detroit again just over a week later. Unfortunately, it was much of the same. Although the Rangers found the scoresheet this time, scoring two goals, they gave up 12 goals at the Olympia. Looking back, the Red Wings' 15-0 dismantling of the Rangers may have been the nail in the coffin in the Blueshirts' abysmal season. The Rangers wouldn't win another game that year, posting a 21-game winless streak to close the campaign. They'd finish in the basement of the standings with a record of 6-39-5, the worst performance in club history, 26 points back of the next closest team, the Boston Bruins.

# MIKE BOSSY'S 50 IN 50, 1981

Maurice "Rocket" Richard made history on March 18, 1945, when he scored his 50th goal in his 50th and final game of the season. No one had ever done that before, and it would be nearly four decades before another player repeated the feat. By the 1980–81 season, the Islanders' Mike Bossy had firmly established himself as one of the league's pre-eminent goal scorers. In his rookie campaign, he had scored 53 goals and won the Calder Trophy. The following season, 1978–79, Bossy showed no signs of a sophomore slump, racking up 69 goals. Nice. But the most memorable moment in his early career happened on January 24, 1981.

Heading into the 50th game of the campaign, Bossy had 48 goals and was chasing down Richard's record. He hadn't made it easy for himself. Two nights earlier, with the Islanders holding a late lead in a game against Detroit, the Red Wings pulled their goaltender for an extra attacker. Bossy's teammates gave him the puck twice, but both times he failed to fill the yawning net from long range. Following the game, spectacled head coach Al Arbour said he should have given Bossy his glasses. Nevertheless, Bossy had one more opportunity to match the Rocket. With fewer than five minutes left in the contest against the Nordiques, he was still not on the scoresheet, and it looked as though he would fall short of matching Richard's record. He caught a break, however, when the Islanders were awarded a power play with 4:10 remaining. On the man advantage, Bossy wired home his 49th, then scored the record-tying goal with just 1:29 left on the clock. Nassau Coliseum erupted. Although Bossy's accomplishment was the toast of the league, the following season, Wayne Gretzky would eclipse both Richard and Bossy, scoring 50 goals in an unfathomable 39 games.

# JANUARY 25
# PHIL ESPOSITO'S FIRST GOAL, 1964

Phil Esposito unassumingly picked up his first career NHL goal in a 5-3 Black Hawks loss to Detroit on January 25, 1964. His tally, in the final minutes of the second period, tied the game, and Chicago would add another in the third. But the Red Wings would score three more to put the game out of reach. Esposito scored only two more goals that season, for a total of three over the course of his 27-game rookie campaign. Over the next three seasons, he established himself as a proficient scorer with the Black Hawks. In 1965–66 he scored 27 goals, and the following season he racked up 61 points to finish tied for seventh in league scoring, but it was only after he was traded to the Bruins in 1967 that he really made a significant impact in the NHL. After piling up 84 points in his first season in Boston, the Sault Ste. Marie, Ontario, native exploded in his sophomore campaign, scoring 49 goals and 126 points, becoming the first player in league history to reach the 100-point plateau.

Through the 1970–71 to 1973–74 seasons, Esposito would win the Art Ross Trophy four consecutive times as the league's top points scorer. Moreover, for six straight years, Esposito led the league in goals, including a record-setting 76-goal campaign in 1970–71 that went unmatched until Wayne Gretzky shattered it in the 1981–82 season. Over the next decade, Esposito established himself as one of the league's best players, while he and Bruins superstar defenceman Bobby Orr feasted on opponents. After being unceremoniously traded to the Rangers in 1975, Esposito continued to light the lamp. He scored his 600th career goal on November 4, 1977, becoming the first player to reach the milestone in a Rangers uniform. When Esposito hung up his skates in 1981, he had 717 career goals. At the time of his retirement, only Gordie Howe had more tallies.

# GORDIE HOWE'S LONGEVITY, 1966

When the *New York Times* recapped the Red Wings' game against the Rangers on January 26, 1966, it omitted a significant detail: 37-year-old Gordie Howe had played his 1,300th career NHL game, becoming the first player to reach that milestone. By then, Howe had been in the league for the better part of 20 seasons, but he would go on to play another 387 games with the Red Wings. By 1971, when arthritis forced him to retire, he had logged an incredible 1,687 regular-season games. But he wasn't done. After hanging up his skates for two years, Howe returned to professional hockey in 1973 when he was given the opportunity of a lifetime: to play with his children. The elder Howe joined sons Marty and Mark in the World Hockey Association as a member of the Houston Aeros.

At first, the 45-year-old seemed out of place. But younger son Mark remembers how quickly his father found his game. "It was a tough start for him, he had been retired two years, but after that two or three-week period it was hard to keep up to him. His endurance as a human being was the most incredible thing I've ever seen. That was the most impressive thing for me," he recalled. By the end of his first year in the WHA, Gordie had 100 points to his name and was given the Gary L. Davidson Award as the league's most valuable player. After playing in the rival league for six years, Howe, then 51, returned to the NHL for one final season. He ended his career as the all-time leading scorer and all-time leader in games played. Wayne Gretzky now holds the former distinction, but no one has played more regular-season NHL games than Mr. Hockey. Who knows ... if Howe hadn't taken that six-year sabbatical in the WHA and stayed in the NHL all those years, he might have suited up for more than 2,000 NHL contests — a record no one else would ever approach.

# JANUARY 27
## NO SWEDER DEBUT, 1965

When Swede Ulf Sterner was called up to play his first game for the New York Rangers on January 27, 1965, it wasn't just a milestone in his career; it was also a significant moment in European hockey history. Sterner's debut marked the entry of the first European-trained player into the National Hockey League. To be sure, a handful of other Europeans had played in the NHL, but they had learned the game elsewhere. Gus Forslund, for example, was born in Sweden, but after his family immigrated to Canada when he was still a child, he honed his skills in northwestern Ontario. After three seasons with the Duluth Hornets of the American Hockey Association, Forslund made his NHL debut, playing 48 games for the Ottawa Senators in 1932–33. Thirty-two years later, Sterner would get his opportunity. He had actually attended the New York Rangers' training camp in 1963 and impressed the team so much that they tendered him a five-game tryout. But with the Olympics being held in Innsbruck, Austria, in 1964, Sterner was concerned that the contract would affect his amateur status. As a result, he declined the offer in order to suit up for Sweden at the Winter Games.

After winning the silver medal, Sterner returned to New York the following year. He started the season with the St. Paul Rangers in the Central Hockey League but quickly earned a promotion to the Baltimore Clippers of the American Hockey League, finally making his way to Broadway in early 1965. Sterner lasted only four games with the Blueshirts before being sent back down to the minors. Although he was a smooth skater and seamless playmaker, he was unwilling to play the more physical brand of NHL hockey. He'd finish the year with Baltimore before returning to Sweden. Although his NHL tenure was short, Sterner's experience demonstrated what other European-trained players needed to do if they wanted to break into North America's top league.

# HOWIE MORENZ'S FINAL GAME, 1937

owie Morenz was the NHL's first superstar. Known as the Stratford Streak, he captivated fans with his incredible speed and goal-scoring ability. After breaking into the league with the Montreal Canadiens in 1923, Morenz established himself as one of the most dynamic players of his era. Over the next 11 seasons with the Canadiens, he captured the Hart Trophy three times as the most valuable player to his team and was instrumental in three championships. After spending a few years with the Black Hawks and Rangers, Morenz returned to the Canadiens for the 1936–37 season. By that point in his career, he wasn't the player from his high-flying days with the Canadiens, but he was given a hero's welcome in his return to Montreal. Thirty games into the campaign, Morenz had scored four goals and 20 points and was on pace for one of his most productive seasons since first leaving Montreal, when tragedy struck. On January 28, 1937, in a game against the Black Hawks, Morenz went into the boards awkwardly and fractured his leg. Following the game, the team's physician said, "The break is just above the ankle and is very bad. Morenz will be out of the game for at least six weeks."

Little did they know, he would never return. While recovering from his injury, at only 34 years of age, Morenz died when blood clots in his leg led to a coronary embolism. At his funeral, held on March 10, 1937, at the Montreal Forum, some 50,000 fans passed his coffin at centre ice to pay their respects, while thousands more lined the streets to get a glimpse of his cortège. At the beginning of the following season, players from the Maroons and Canadiens joined forces to challenge a team of all-stars to pay tribute to the league's fallen star and raise money in support of his family.

# SYD HOWE NIGHT, 1942

n a special evening, Syd Howe tickled the ivories at centre ice before tickling his fans with a two-goal performance. On January 29, 1942, the Red Wings winger was honoured by his team and its fans before stealing the show on the ice. Back in the day, it was common for NHL teams to honour their long-standing players with tribute nights. On St. Patrick's Day in 1934, for example, the Maple Leafs had honoured King Clancy, a fan favourite and the team's most beloved Irishman. Before the game began, Clancy, doing his best impersonation of St. Patrick, was heralded onto the ice on a throne while sporting a crown, beard, and green robe. As part of the festivities, Clancy wore a special green sweater for the first period. His usual number seven had been replaced by a shamrock. Years later, when Montreal hosted "Elmer Lach Night," the famed Canadiens centreman received an avalanche of gifts that included a television set, a radio-phonograph, and even a rowboat. Lach also took home dining room and kitchen sets, but those items were too cumbersome to be paraded out onto the ice.

But back to "Syd Howe Night." As man of the hour, the seven-year Red Wings veteran was showered with gifts from the organization and fans, including a grand piano. Before the game commenced, the piano was rolled out to centre ice where Howe played the keys, much to the delight of the 7,164 patrons at the Olympia. At the time, the *Globe and Mail* reported that players usually fared poorly on their tribute nights, but that proved not to be the case for Howe. He scored Detroit's only goals, picking up markers in the second and third periods, to power his team to a 2-0 victory over the Black Hawks. Howe played four more seasons with the Red Wings, winning his third Stanley Cup with the team in 1943. He was inducted into the Hockey Hall of Fame in 1965.

# THE OTTAWA FIREMAN'S RECORD-SETTING SHUTOUT, 1926

Alec Connell came by his nickname, the Ottawa Fireman, honestly. He was a fireman and he was from Ottawa. In addition to putting out blazes, Connell was also known for extinguishing shots by his opponents. Although he established himself as one of the premier goaltenders of his era, he almost didn't play hockey. Athletically gifted, Connell excelled in a number of sports, including baseball and lacrosse, but never took to the ice. It was only during the First World War, while stationed in Kingston, Ontario, that he was coaxed into playing the game. Since he could not skate, he took up duties in net. Following the conclusion of the war, Connell continued playing hockey, backstopping the Kingston Frontenacs of the Ontario Hockey Association before returning to Ottawa to tend the twine in the city's senior league. Connell made the jump to the NHL for the 1924–25 season, serving as the goaltender for his hometown Senators. In his inaugural campaign, he picked up 17 wins and recorded seven shutouts.

The following year, Connell made history on January 30, 1926, when he guided the Senators to a 1-0 victory over the New York Americans. It was Connell's 10th shutout of the year, making him the first goaltender in NHL history to record that many in a single season. He would finish the campaign with 15 shutouts — a benchmark that held up for a couple of years until Montreal's George Hainsworth held his opponents scoreless for half the games he played, registering 22 shutouts in 1928–29. As of the end of the 2017–18 season, Connell's 15 shutouts from 1925–26 are still tied for the second most shutouts by an NHL goaltender in one season, although it should be noted that forward passing was not completely permitted in the attacking zone until 1929–30. Connell entered the Hockey Hall of Fame in 1958 but died just two weeks before his induction ceremony.

JANUARY 31
# PHANTOM JOE SCORES SEVEN, 1920

Well before the NHL was formed in 1917, Joe Malone had already established himself as one of the most prolific scorers of his day. Playing for the Quebec Bulldogs of the National Hockey Association, Malone had racked up 43 goals in 1912–13, and on March 8, 1913, he found the back of the net nine times against the Sydney Millionaires of the Maritime Professional Hockey League in the first game of a series for the Stanley Cup. Although Quebec was a founding member of the National Hockey League, it did not ice a team until 1919. As a result, in the league's inaugural season, Malone suited up for the Canadiens. Despite changing uniforms, Malone, known for his deceptiveness and quick shot, continued his propensity for finding the back of the net with Montreal. In his NHL debut he scored five goals, and just seven games into the campaign, he became the league's first 20-goal scorer. He finished the season with 44 goals in just 20 games. The following year, however, he was limited to just eight games as he battled against an arm injury, but he still managed to rifle off seven goals.

When Malone returned to NHL action the next season, with the Quebec Bulldogs, the team with which he had begun his professional career, he returned to his scoring ways. After scoring 13 goals in his first 11 games, Malone exploded for seven goals in a meaningless game against the Toronto St. Patricks on January 31, 1920. At that point in the first half of the season, both teams were mired in the cellar of the standings, but Malone's performance was certainly not indicative of that. After scoring a goal in the first period, he added three more in the middle frame and scored another hat trick to close out the third period, as the Bulldogs defeated the St. Patricks 10-6. Although a handful of NHL players have scored six goals in a game in the decades that followed, nobody else, not even Wayne Gretzky or Mario Lemieux, has ever scored seven.

# FEBRUARY 1
## GRETZKY'S FIRST HAT TRICK, 1980

Heading into his 50th NHL game, Wayne Gretzky had already amassed 28 goals and 78 points that season, an incredible output for a player who had just turned 19. Although Gretzky had six multi-goal games on his bourgeoning NHL resumé, the hat trick still eluded him. That changed, however, on February 1, 1980, when Edmonton hosted Winnipeg at the Northlands Coliseum. In a game that included plenty of offence from the home team — the Oilers scored four goals in the first period to down the Jets 9-2 — Gretzky was the standout. The young phenom scored his first NHL hat trick in what would become a very long career of racking up three-or-more-goal games.

Over the next two decades, he would score 50 career hat tricks. When he hung up his skates in 1999, he had 37 three-goal games, 9 four-goal games, and 4 five-goal games. Those 50 hat tricks are the most in league history, a mark that is likely never to be broken. Even other dynamic and dominant scorers such as Mario Lemieux, Mike Bossy, and Brett Hull could not hold a candle to Gretzky when it came to three-or-more-goal outings. Although Lemieux is the runner-up with 40, being off by 10 is a significant gap when stacking up these types of individual offensive performances. Just one of the many reasons we call Gretzky the Great One.

## THE RED WINGS HEAD TO THE BIG HOUSE, 1954

The Red Wings went to jail. On February 2, 1954, Detroit played its first outdoor game in franchise history against a gang of inmates in a penitentiary. The origins of the game dated back to June 1953, when Red Wings general manager Jack Adams and captain Ted Lindsay were doing a promotional tour across Michigan, and one of their stopovers just so happened to be Marquette Branch Prison, better known as the Alcatraz of the North. As the two Red Wings strolled the grounds with warden Emery Jacques, the latter suggested to Adams that he should bring the whole team back for a game. The Wings GM initially shrugged it off, but after hemming and hawing, Adams eventually accepted the offer on the condition that Marquette finance the club's entire trip. The warden called his bluff and agreed. The Red Wings were going to the big house. At that point in the regular season, Detroit had just played its 59th game and was sitting atop the league standings. The Red Wings were coming off a dominant 5-1 victory in Chicago, and rather than getting a full three days' rest before hosting the Bruins at the Olympia, they were on their way to the southern shore of Lake Superior to face off against Marquette's hockey team, which was fittingly known as the Pirates.

On the morning of the game, the mercury was below zero, but that didn't dampen the enthusiasm among the prison's spectators. When it became clear just how outmatched the inmates were, they stopped keeping score and simply had some fun. To shake things up, some Red Wings switched teams, but the greatest thrill of the day undoubtedly went to the prisoner who had the chance to don a Red Wings jersey and centre a line flanked by Gordie Howe and Ted Lindsay.

# FEBRUARY 3
## SYD SCORES SIX, 1944

n a season where everything was going in the net for the Red Wings against the Rangers, Syd Howe personified that trend in a game on February 3, 1944. Less than two weeks earlier, Detroit dismantled New York 15-0. It is still a league record for the most lopsided victory and gave the club 38 goals in just six contests against their Broadway adversaries. So when the Rangers visited the Olympia in Detroit that evening in February, many Red Wings fans expected the thrashing to continue. They would not be disappointed. After two periods of play were in the books, the home team was up 6-0, and Howe had already potted four goals. Before the halfway mark of the third stanza, he had scored another pair, and New York's deficit had increased to nine. Although the Rangers would get on the board twice in the final frame, the damage was already done; the Red Wings cruised to a 12-2 victory over their opponents.

In the end, Howe did much of the heavy lifting and put on an individual performance that had not been seen for nearly a quarter-century. Although Howe finished just shy of Joe Malone's seven-goal benchmark, he still left his mark on the game's history. Only two other players have equalled his output since: Red Berenson of the St. Louis Blues in 1968 and Darryl Sittler of the Toronto Maple Leafs in 1976.

# LEMIEUX SCORES 600TH AT HOME, 1997

Mario Lemieux scored his 500th career goal on the road against the Islanders on October 26, 1995, but when his next major milestone came around, he had much better timing. On February 4, 1997, before the home fans at the Igloo in Pittsburgh, Lemieux notched his 600th goal, becoming just the seventh player in NHL history to reach the milestone. Playing in his 719th career game, Lemieux also became the second fastest player in league history to reach the benchmark, needing just one more contest than Wayne Gretzky to pull it off. With time winding down in a game against the Canucks, the Penguins were protecting a 5-4 lead when Vancouver pulled their goaltender in a last-ditch effort to even the score. With the net empty, Lemieux, who had not yet found his way onto the score sheet, took advantage of the situation and potted his milestone marker with just 56 seconds remaining. As the magnificence of the moment set in, the Igloo's 17,355 patrons rose to their feet and gave their hero a hometown ovation.

While the faithful crowd chanted "Mario" in unison as a highlight reel of his past exploits was displayed across the scoreboard, Lemieux embraced the celebration and saluted the fans with his stick. Following the game, Lemieux reflected on how important it was for him to achieve the feat at home: "That's why I wanted to do it tonight. To get a standing ovation like that is something special," he told reporters. The moment proved to be even more special because Lemieux, who had battled back from Hodgkin's lymphoma just a few years earlier and had been contending with an ailing back for quite some time, had indicated it would likely be his last NHL season. He made it official on April 6, when he announced he would retire following the playoffs, but not before finishing the season with 122 points, his 10th, and final, 100-point campaign.

## MR. HOCKEY, THE PERENNIAL
## ALL-STAR, 1980

No one has played in more NHL All-Star Games than Gordie Howe, and no one ever will. On February 5, 1980, Mr. Hockey made his 23rd All-Star Game appearance, furthering his legacy as one of the league's most enduring players. At the time, Howe was just two months shy of his 52nd birthday and had been playing in All-Star Games since 1948, meaning he had suited up for the NHL's annual celebration of the league's best players in five different decades. Although Howe had started his career with the Red Wings, he was finishing it with the Hartford Whalers. That year, the league's All-Star Game was held in Detroit, and there was no better swan song for Mr. Hockey than to make his final All-Star Game appearance in the city where the fans had supported and rooted for him since he became a Red Wing in 1946.

When Howe stepped onto the ice to start the game, he received a standing ovation that was unparalleled in the game's history. For Gordie, it seemed to last forever, and that certainly did not bother him. He reflected on that moment years later in his autobiography: "Standing on the ice that night was not only one of the great moments I enjoyed in the game of hockey but also one of the best feelings I've ever had in my life."

# FEBRUARY 6
## MAD DOG MAKES HIS DEBUT, 1973

Connie Madigan waited a long time to make his NHL debut. After a career in the minor leagues that spanned three decades, "Mad Dog" finally got the call he had been waiting for. In early February 1973, the Blues recalled him from the Portland Buckaroos of the Western Hockey League. While many of his colleagues had already retired, especially those who never attained the promotion they had been seeking, Madigan continued to relentlessly pursue hockey. His effort eventually paid off, and he made his first NHL appearance when the Blues hosted the Vancouver Canucks on February 6.

Although Madigan never found his way onto the scoresheet, he was still able to leave his mark on hockey history. At the time of his debut, Madigan was 38 years old, which made him the oldest rookie to ever play in the National Hockey League. In fact, the Blues' bench boss, Jean-Guy Talbot, was just a few years older than Madigan. Despite his age and years of punishment — Mad Dog had accumulated 2,474 penalty minutes in his minor career before joining St. Louis — the hard-hitting defenceman would stay with the Blues for the rest of the year and even see some action during the playoffs. That was, however, the extent of his time in the big leagues. The following season he was back in the minors and finished his career with the Buckaroos during the 1974–75 season, at the age of 40. Although Madigan's time in the NHL was fleeting, he reached the pinnacle of the sport, something many aspire to but few attain.

# FEBRUARY 7
## DARRYL SITTLER MAKES NHL HISTORY, 1976

or captain Darryl Sittler and the Toronto Maple Leafs, February 7, 1976, appeared as though it was going to be just another ordinary game against the Boston Bruins. At the end of the first period, Sittler had two assists and the Leafs were winning 2-1, but by all accounts, it seemed to be business as usual at the Gardens. After the first intermission, however, something transpired on the ice that changed the hockey world. In an offensive tour de force, Sittler scored three goals and added two assists in the second period, setting a new franchise record for most points in a period. More important, his performance in the middle frame also put him within striking distance of the NHL record for most points (eight) scored in a single game, originally set by Maurice "Rocket" Richard in 1945 and later tied by Bert Olmstead in 1954. Sittler had the chance to make history, and as the third period commenced, he did not disappoint. Within 44 seconds of the puck drop, he scored another goal to tie the record and later added two more tallies to set a new benchmark that remains unsurpassed to this day.

Was there a secret behind that incredible individual performance? In reflecting on that game 40 years later with VICE Sports, Sittler described how he had deviated slightly from his typical game-day routine. "Going home from the rink in the morning, Wendy [his late wife] would have a pregame meal ready for me, but she had been out doing a bunch of things and running errands and was behind schedule," he said. "I was also running late so I just went and grabbed some Swiss Chalet chicken and basically ate it out of my car on the way to my house so I could get a good nap in in the afternoon. So, changed my routine a little bit, but I'll always remember that change up." There you have it: it was all because of the Swiss Chalet. If you ask me, the rotisserie has missed out on some significant marketing opportunities by not offering a promotional "10-point chicken dinner" each year on February 7.

# FEBRUARY 8
## THE GREAT ONE'S ALL-STAR NIGHT, 1983

When Wayne Gretzky made his first NHL All-Star Game appearance in 1980, he was just 19 years old, making him the third-youngest player to ever appear in an All-Star Game at that time. Moreover, in that contest, Gretzky also had the opportunity to face off against his boyhood idol, Gordie Howe, who was appearing in his 23rd and final All-Star Game. While the Great One had no problem finding the back of the net during the regular season, he came up scoreless in his inaugural All-Star Game. In fact, Gretzky wouldn't score a goal in an All-Star Game until his third appearance in Washington on February 9, 1982. Although the annual matchup of the league's best is largely an exhibition for the fans, it still means something for the players, and Gretzky was looking to rebound from his previous performances.

Then, on February 8, 1983, the Great One made up for lost time. He dazzled the crowd at Nassau Coliseum with four goals in the third period to power the Campbell Conference to a 9-3 victory over the Prince of Wales Conference. In the process, his four markers set NHL All-Star Game records for most goals in a game and most tallies in a period. For his efforts, Gretzky received the game's Most Valuable Player award as well as the keys to a white Chevrolet Camaro. Afterward, Gretzky hinted that his breakout performance may have been the result of better preparing himself for the event. In previous years, he mentioned having gotten caught up in the festivities with his fellow players and how it threw off his whole schedule. "But last night ... I hit the sack early. This was the one game where I wanted to go out and play the best I could," he told reporters at the time. It certainly worked out for him.

# FEBRUARY 9
## THE NHL LANDSCAPE CHANGES, 1966

The hockey landscape was forever changed on February 9, 1966, when the National Hockey League officially expanded to 12 teams. For more than 20 years, it had operated a six-team loop, but now it would be doubling in size in what would become one of the boldest expansion moves in professional sports. A year earlier, on March 11, 1965, the NHL announced that it was committed to growing its operation. At the time, North America's other major leagues had already grown, and the NHL was the only organization without a West Coast team. For many of the existing club owners, tapping into new markets represented an important step toward landing a lucrative national television deal in the United States. As a result, the owners pushed for entry into the large markets of California, while others pushed for other locales in the northern United States that included Pittsburgh, Minneapolis-St. Paul, and even Baltimore.

By October 1965, the NHL had tapped Los Angeles, St. Louis, Vancouver, and San Francisco-Oakland as the most acceptable cities for expansion, which meant there were still two spots up for grabs for prospective cities that were hoping to land an NHL club. When the dust settled on February 9, 1966, franchises were awarded to successful bids from Pittsburgh, Minneapolis-St. Paul, Philadelphia, Los Angeles, San Francisco-Oakland, and St. Louis. When the puck dropped for the 1967–68 season, a new era of NHL history was ushered in as the Penguins, North Stars, Flyers, Kings, Seals, and Blues joined the ranks.

# THE KRAUT LINE IS CARRIED OFF THE ICE, 1942

During the Second World War, NHL players risked their lives and careers to serve in the Canadian or American military. No moment better personified the significance of this sacrifice than the game that was played between the Canadiens and Bruins on February 10, 1942. Among the Boston players who took to the ice that evening were Milt Schmidt, Woody Dumart, and Bobby Bauer, who were collectively known as the Kraut Line because of their German heritage. That night, the trio terrorized the Canadiens for 11 points as Boston easily cruised to an 8-1 victory. The significance of the game, however, was not that the Kraut Line had racked up so many points but that it was their final game before reporting for duty with the Royal Canadian Air Force. At the conclusion of the match, the three were presented with farewell gifts from management, including their full season's salaries, gold identification bracelets, and wrist watches. Boston general manager Art Ross reportedly referred to them as "the most loyal and courageous players in Bruins history."

More significant than the gifts, however, was the remarkable show of camaraderie and respect from their opponents. While the Bruins and Canadiens were fierce rivals on the ice, the seriousness of the assignment that Schmidt, Dumart, and Bauer had just signed up for was not lost on anyone. As a result, the Canadiens and Bruins joined forces and hoisted the three men on their shoulders and carried them off the ice. Although there are many touching moments in the NHL's long history, there are few that better attest to the respect and honour that has always undergirded the league. Following the conclusion of the war, the Bruins trio returned to the NHL but were likely unable to top the special moment they shared with their fans, teammates, and opponents before they had gone off to serve.

# FEBRUARY 11
## FIRST TIE GAME, 1922

When the matchup between the Toronto St. Patricks and Ottawa Senators concluded on February 11, 1922, the result was something that had never happened in the NHL: a draw. After regulation play had been completed, the two teams were tied 4-4. To break the deadlock, a 20-minute overtime period was played, but after it failed to produce the desired result, Toronto and Ottawa left the ice tired and tied. During the overtime period, it was reported that both squads put it all on the line in an effort to try and break the deadlock. Most impressive was that, even as the desperation increased as the matchup dragged on, neither team incurred a single penalty. According to the *Ottawa Evening Journal*, the additional frame was "a presentation of everything that makes hockey." Although the players were utterly exhausted, they "kept up a killing pace and stormed and re-stormed opposing goals with fierceness and abandon."

By the newspaper's estimate, when the game finally ended, Toronto goaltender John Ross Roach had stopped 76 shots, while his counterpart in the Ottawa crease, Clint Benedict, managed to turn aside 63. Although the hometown netminder may have faced fewer shots, the *Journal* was careful to note that his performance was no less noteworthy than his St. Patricks colleague. "Too much praise cannot be showered on Benedict who if less spectacular was no less effective than Roach," they wrote. In particular, during the third period and overtime, when it seemed like Ottawa was going to collapse, Benedict made some critical saves, keeping his team in the game. Less than two years later, Ottawa would find itself part of another historic stalemate when the goaltenders once again stole the show. On December 17, 1924, the Senators and Hamilton Tigers played to a scoreless tie, another first in NHL history.

# THE MOST LOPSIDED INTERNATIONAL HOCKEY GAME, 1949

When Canada squared off against Denmark in the opening game of the world amateur ice hockey championship in Stockholm, Sweden, on February 12, 1949, they didn't stand much of a chance. Denmark had only just recently joined the International Ice Hockey Federation (IIHF), not even two years earlier, and were still just honing their skills. When the puck dropped, Canada, represented by the Sudbury Wolves, a club from northern Ontario, ravaged the Danes. After the first period ended, the Wolves were up by a baker's dozen, and when the second frame concluded, it was 29-0. The Canadians, with their appetites not quite sated, added another 18 tallies in the third period. With the game already all but decided early on, the *Globe and Mail* reported that fans kept themselves entertained by placing bets on whether they thought Canada would reach 50 goals. They ended up falling just three goals shy in a 47-0 rout that set the record for the most lopsided international hockey game in history, easily eclipsing the mark set a year earlier at the 1948 Winter Olympics when the United States defeated Italy 31-1.

The Danes remained on the wrong side of the record books for nearly four decades until New Zealand's national team, the Ice Blacks, were shelled 58-0 by Australia at the world ice hockey championships in their first international hockey matchup. But just over 10 years later, New Zealand's embarrassing debut was overshadowed when Thailand was trounced by South Korea at the IIHF Asian Oceania U18 tournament. In the first period, South Korea registered 71 shots on net and went into the intermission with a 36-0 lead. Over the next 40 minutes, Thailand was outshot 105-1 as South Korea added another 56 goals to set a new international record and finish the game 92-0. When it was all said and done, the scorekeepers had to fill out a five-page game report just to record all of those goals.

# FEBRUARY 13

## FINAL GAME AT MAPLE LEAF GARDENS, 1999

or some, it was just another arena. For others, it was the last hockey cathedral from the NHL's Original Six era. On February 13, 1999, the Toronto Maple Leafs bid farewell to Maple Leaf Gardens, which had been the club's home for nearly 68 years. The origins of the famous building date back to Toronto's early Conn Smythe years. Although Canada was mired in an economic depression, the Maple Leafs owner was adamant about building a new home for his club. Incredibly, seven months after the first bricks were laid, the Gardens opened just in time for the Maple Leafs to host the Black Hawks, on November 12, 1931, for the first game of the regular season. Chicago spoiled the party, however, as they narrowly edged Toronto 2-1 in the Buds' debut in their new arena.

Nearly seven decades later, the Blackhawks (stylized as one word after the 1985–86 season) would take on the Maple Leafs in the last game at the Gardens. Once again, the outcome did not go Toronto's way. Although more than 100 former Maple Leafs players turned up for the festivities, it seems as though the current players did not. Toronto was trounced 6-2, with Bob Probert scoring the final goal in the historic building. While the outcome was not what the team or the fans had hoped for, the evening concluded with an Anne Murray rendition of "The Maple Leaf Forever," a fitting final tribute to the place that witnessed the club hoist eight of its Stanley Cups.

# ALL-STARS TURN OUT FOR ACE, 1934

During a game between Toronto and Boston on December 12, 1933, Irvine "Ace" Bailey was the victim of a vicious attack by Bruins defenceman Eddie Shore. After sustaining a hit from behind, the Toronto winger collapsed to the ice and fractured his skull. The impact was so jarring that Bailey was reportedly read his last rites while he lay bleeding on the ice. In hospital, doctors were able to save his life but his hockey career was finished. Two months later, on Valentine's Day, a team of NHL all-stars, consisting of representatives from the league's other eight teams, took on the Toronto Maple Leafs in order to raise money for Ace and his family. A capacity crowd of 14,074 turned out to see what would be the first game of its kind in the league.

Although the NHL would host its first official All-Star Game in 1947, none could compare to the meaning behind the exhibition held on February 14, 1934. The benefit raised more than $20,000 for the Baileys, and while the local crowd was certainly delighted to see their Maple Leafs skate off with a 7-3 victory over the all-stars, the most significant moment was when Ace and Eddie embraced before the game commenced. It was the first time the two had faced each other since the incident and the first time Shore had returned to Toronto. The Bruins defender received a warm welcome from the home crowd, which undoubtedly felt Shore's trepidation and unease as he skated onto the ice to shake hands with Bailey. Although Ace reportedly forgave Eddie for what had happened, a true testament to his spirit and sportsmanship, Shore was haunted by the incident for the remainder of his career, unable to reconcile his actions with their outcome.

# FEBRUARY 15
# BRODEUR NETS GAME-WINNER, 2000

Goaltender Martin Brodeur was always better known for keeping pucks out of the net than for putting them in. Although he scored his first goal by shooting the puck the length of the ice on April 17, 1997, during a playoff game against Montreal, the netminder, who is the NHL all-time leader in wins and shutouts, also has two career regular-season goals to his name. While that's still three more than nearly every goaltender who has played before or after him, Brodeur never went into games thinking he would find the back of the net. In fact, on February 15, 2000, in a game against the Philadelphia Flyers, the Devils goaltender was surprised to learn he had been credited with his first regular-season goal. More important, it held up to be the game-winner, which made Brodeur the first goaltender in NHL history to be credited with a game-winning goal.

The sequence happened when the Flyers pulled their goaltender, Brian Boucher, following a delayed penalty call against the Devils. As Philadelphia attempted to set up for a charge before a whistle initiated the power play, New Jersey's Sergei Brylin pressured the puck loose from Philadelphia's Daymond Langkow, and it rolled into the empty net. Since Brodeur was officially the last Devil to touch the puck before it crossed the goalmouth, he found his name on the scoresheet. Although much of the credit goes to Brylin's forecheck for knocking the puck loose, hockey's a team sport and one could imagine the Russian forward was happy to spot his netminder a goal.

# FEBRUARY 16
## ALEX DELVECCHIO REACHES 1,000-POINT CLUB, 1969

Although Gordie Howe may have been the one to watch in a game against the Los Angeles Kings on February 16, 1969, Alex Delvecchio was the Red Wings player who made history. While Mr. Hockey racked up a hat trick, including two goals in the final five minutes of the contest, Delvecchio picked up two assists on his linemate's tallies to make him the third player in NHL history to reach the 1,000-point club. With his performance that night, Delvecchio joined teammate Howe and Montreal's Jean Beliveau as the only other members of the league to reach the milestone.

Nearly two decades earlier, Delvecchio had joined the Red Wings as a fresh-faced youngster, centring the team's third line with Metro Prystai and Johnny Wilson. Although he was the youngest player on the team, Delvecchio had an immediate impact. Howe later wrote in his autobiography that Delvecchio played beyond his years. "At only nineteen, Delvecchio took over as the baby of the team. You wouldn't have known it by the way he handled the puck, though. He was magic," Howe wrote. After playing an important role in Detroit's Stanley Cup victory that season, Delvecchio was promoted to the club's top centre, following Sid Abel's departure to the Black Hawks in 1952. Filling in for Abel on the Red Wings' famed Production Line with Howe and Ted Lindsay was no small task, but Delvecchio seamlessly made the transition and provided the iconic wingers with plenty of nifty passes over the years. After notching his 1,000th career point with the Red Wings, Delvecchio added 281 more with the team before hanging up his skates in 1973. The only Detroit players with more goals and points than Delvecchio are Howe and Steve Yzerman.

# FEBRUARY 17
## FIRST MAPLE LEAFS GAME, 1927

When Toronto's NHL team hit the ice on February 17, 1927, to take on the New York Americans, they were sporting a new name and look. For nearly a decade, the club had been known as the St. Patricks. All that changed, however, when the team was purchased by a conglomerate on Valentine's Day 1927. Under this new ownership group, which included Conn Smythe at the helm, the team discarded its Irish roots and were rechristened as the Toronto Maple Leafs. Smythe, a veteran of the First World War, wanted the team to sport a symbol that would have meaning across the country. As a result, they went with a maple leaf, an ode to the insignia worn by Canadian military regiments and a nod to the emblem on the sweaters that Canada's hockey team had donned in the 1924 Winter Olympics. When the club faced off against the Americans for its first game under the new banner, they wore white sweaters with a green maple leaf and *Toronto* emblazoned across the chest.

The new look must have had an effect, as the newly minted Maple Leafs made short work of their opponents, beating them 4-1. For the remainder of the season, the team sported the green colour scheme that traced its antecedents back to the St. Patricks, but the following year, they would adopt the blue and white uniforms — reminiscent of the colours Smythe wore when he played hockey for the Varsity Blues as an undergraduate at the University of Toronto. Five years after adopting their new name, the team won their first championship as the Maple Leafs on April 9, 1932, after defeating the Rangers in three straight games in the Stanley Cup Final.

# FIRST NHL SHUTOUT, 1918

igh-flying offence was a hallmark of the NHL's inaugural season. When the pucks dropped on the first slate of games on December 19, 1917, the Montreal Canadiens beat the Ottawa Senators 7-4 and the Montreal Wanderers dusted the Toronto Arenas 10-9. The trend continued for the balance of the schedule. Of the 34 total regular-season games played from December to March, more than half saw teams combine for 10 or more goals. Moreover, in four of those contests, the nets were filled at least 15 times. Standing in the way of those would-be goal scorers were netminders like Georges Vezina.

Hailing from Chicoutimi, Quebec, Vezina earned the nickname the Chicoutimi Cucumber for being unflappable and remaining calm under pressure. The story goes that he was discovered by the Canadiens in 1910, when the team was still a part of the National Hockey Association (NHA), the precursor to the NHL. Montreal had travelled to Chicoutimi to play one of the local teams, and Vezina backstopped his club to victory. The Canadiens were so impressed with his play that they offered him a roster spot. Although he initially declined, Vezina eventually did take them up on the opportunity. Once in the NHA, Vezina established himself as one of the league's premier goaltenders and a cut above his peers. It's fitting that, when he continued his play in the NHL, he'd be the first netminder to record a shutout in the new league. On February 18, 1918, Montreal scored nine goals on the road against Toronto, but the Chicoutimi Cucumber remained calm and pushed aside all the shots he faced, making NHL history in the process.

# FEBRUARY 19
## CAPITALS FINALLY BEAT CANADIENS, 1980

When the Washington Capitals joined the NHL for their first season in 1974–75, it could not have gone any worse. The newly arrived expansion team finished the campaign with just eight wins and 67 losses. On the road, the club managed to eke out only one victory, while conceding 39 losses in enemy territory. Therefore, it's no surprise that the Capitals did not beat the Canadiens, one of the league's most storied and long-standing powerhouse teams, that year. Or the next year. Or the next year. Or the next year. Or the year after that.

Finally, after 34 failed attempts, Washington defeated Montreal for the first time in franchise history on February 19, 1980. With the game tied 1-1 with less than 10 minutes remaining in the third period, it seemed as though it was going to be business as usual for the Capitals. Washington forward Bengt-Ake Gustafsson, however, had other plans. As the clock ticked down, he wired a high shot over the shoulder of Montreal goaltender Denis Herron to break the deadlock. With less than a minute to go, rookie Mike Gartner scored the empty-net insurance goal for the Capitals to complete the upset. But the loss cost the Canadiens more than just bragging rights. Guy Lafleur, the club's star right wing, sustained a knee injury during the game and was sidelined indefinitely. The Flower, however, much like his play, made a speedy recovery and finished the season with 50 goals, his sixth straight 50-goal campaign with Montreal.

# THE NHL'S FIRST MASKED MAN, 1930

When NHL goaltender Clint Benedict returned to action on February 20, 1930, following a three-week absence, he was sporting a different look. He was wearing a mask. The last time he played, he had taken a puck to the face from Howie Morenz and broken his nose. At the time, goaltenders did not wear facial protection, so Benedict's injury was simply chalked up as a hazard of the job for those brave enough to be members of the goaltending guild. Hoping to protect his face from further aggravation, Benedict donned a leather mask that covered parts of his forehead, nose, and chin when the Montreal Maroons visited the New York Americans. The mask certainly afforded the goaltender more protection, but how would it affect his performance? Although the *Globe* reported that Benedict's facial protection was rather large, it did not hamper his play as he turned in a fine performance in a 3-3 tie.

Benedict would wear the mask for the next few games until he was injured in a game against the Ottawa Senators on March 4, 1930. A few days later, he watched his team take on the Maple Leafs from the stands while he shot down rumours he would be retiring. Calling his run of bad luck with injuries that season his "hoodoo year," Benedict hoped to return to the lineup the following season, but it never happened. He would never play another NHL game, and the league would not see another masked man for nearly three decades, when the Canadiens' Jacques Plante put on a mask after injuring his face during a game against the Rangers. Although Plante became the first NHL goaltender to regularly wear a mask, Benedict was the first in the league to buck the standards surrounding equipment.

# FEBRUARY 21
## TIM HORTON DIES, 1974

On the morning of February 21, 1974, the NHL awoke to tragic news. Just hours earlier, Buffalo Sabres defenceman Tim Horton had died after he lost control of his car on the Queen Elizabeth Highway near St. Catharines, Ontario. Following a loss on the road to the Maple Leafs, Horton had decided to drive home to Buffalo in his white Ford Pantera, a gift from Sabres general manager Punch Imlach, instead of taking the team bus. At the time of the crash, Horton had been cruising at speeds upward of 160 kilometres an hour, and was under the influence of alcohol. His death rocked the hockey world. He had been in the NHL for more than two decades and established himself as one of the game's premier defencemen.

Three years after his death, Horton was posthumously inducted into the Hockey Hall of Fame. While his on-ice accomplishments were legendary, including four Stanley Cups with the Maple Leafs and a stretch of 486 consecutive games with the club, his more lasting legacy is his eponymous coffee franchise, Tim Hortons. Motivated by an entrepreneurial spirit, Horton pursued a number of business ventures throughout his hockey career, particularly during the off-season. After he and his brother, Gerry, opened a restaurant in North Bay, Ontario, in the early 1960s, Horton went on to open a little donut and coffee shop in 1964 that was originally known as "Tim Horton." The rest is history.

# FEBRUARY 22
## BROTHER TO BROTHER, 1981

There was no stopping the Stastny brothers when the Nordiques visited the Capitals on February 22, 1981. Playing on a line with Michel Goulet, Peter and Anton combined for 16 points as Quebec blasted Washington 11-7. Peter, the elder Stastny, found the back of the net four times and added just as many assists, while Anton notched a hat trick and collected five helpers. Their efforts were both record setting in their own right as no NHL player had ever scored eight points in a road game. Two nights earlier, the duo had each scored three goals in the Nordiques' 9-1 trouncing of the Canucks. With their sticks still white-hot from their performance in Vancouver, Peter and Anton took their road show to Washington.

By the time the smoke had cleared from their outing in Maryland, the Stastny brothers had combined for 26 points in just two games and shared the NHL's player-of-the-week award. It was the first time in league history that two brothers shared that particular honour. Since then, plenty of players have come close to matching their production on the road. A year later, Peter himself was at it again when he scored three goals and assisted on four others in Quebec's 8-5 victory over the Bruins on April 1, 1982. Most recently, former Ottawa Senator Daniel Alfredsson scored seven points in Tampa Bay on January 24, 2008, but no one has yet to equal the incredible mark set by the travelling Stastnys.

# FEBRUARY 23
## THE SEALS BLOW IT, 1972

The Seals were golden halfway into the second period in a game against the Bruins on February 23, 1972. By that point, California had a commanding 6-1 lead after scoring three unanswered goals to start the middle frame. Boston responded by adding two markers, but heading into the second intermission, the Golden Seals were still up by three. It was in the bag. Besides, history was on their side. At that time, no NHL team had ever come back to win a game after trailing by five goals. Well, turns out the Bruins never got the memo. When the third period commenced, superstar defenceman Bobby Orr scored an early goal to move Boston to within two. Shortly thereafter, Fred Stanfield buried his 19th goal of the season, and suddenly the Seals were shaking in their white skates.

With less than six minutes remaining in the contest, Phil Esposito tied the game and then added another goal in quick succession that proved to be the game-winner. Boston's Derek Sanderson would put the final nail in the coffin, as the Bruins came all the way back from a five-goal deficit to beat the Seals 8-6. While that type of defeat would have stung anyone, for a pair of players on California, it was much worse. Earlier that day, Rick Smith, Reggie Leach, and Bob Stewart were actually members of the Bruins but had been traded to the Golden Seals in exchange for Carol Vadnais and Don O'Donoghue. When the game began, they found themselves squaring off against their former teammates in what proved to be a humiliating introduction to their new squad. If that wasn't bad enough, while Smith, Leach, and Stewart remained mired in California, Vadnais would prove to be an integral part of Boston's Stanley Cup victory later that spring.

# FEBRUARY 24
## GRETZKY MAKES HISTORY, 1982

When Wayne Gretzky tied Phil Esposito's mark for most goals in a single season, 76, the question was not if the record would fall but when. After equalling the benchmark in a game against the Red Wings, the Great One had the chance to make history in Buffalo on February 24, 1982. Then, before a crowd of 16,433 at the Memorial Auditorium, including movie stars Burt Reynolds and Goldie Hawn, it almost didn't happen. With seven minutes remaining in the contest and the score tied at three apiece, Gretzky still hadn't found the back of the net. But sure enough, right around the time some may have begun to wonder if they'd see the landmark goal that night, Gretzky scored his 77th of the season to a chorus of thunderous applause. The Great One, however, wasn't done just yet. He added two more goals to complete the hat trick and move himself into the conversation for a 100-goal season.

After the game, Gretzky was met by a cavalcade of well-wishers, including Phil Esposito, who had been in attendance to see his record get toppled. The young phenom even received a congratulatory telegram from Prime Minister Pierre Elliott Trudeau, who wrote, "Congratulations on another spectacular record-break. Canadians are all very proud of our young national asset." Despite the accolades, Gretzky was very modest, as he always was, about his accomplishment. During the press conference, newspapers reported that instead of focusing on the achievement, Gretzky predicted that his own record would be surpassed one day. Not likely. The Great One finished that season with 92 goals, and while Brett Hull came awfully close to equalling the mark in 1990–91, no player has come within sniffing distance since, and it's likely no one else will in the future.

# FEBRUARY 25
## RICHARD SCORES 45 IN 1945

At the conclusion of the NHL's inaugural season, Joe Malone had tallied 44 goals in a mere 22 games. It was an incredible accomplishment, and for nearly three decades, no other player would score as many goals in a campaign as the Phantom. By the start of the 1944–45 season, however, a fiery young winger out of Montreal was starting to turn heads and challenge Malone's goal-scoring propensity. His name was Maurice Richard. Although he saw limited action in his first NHL campaign, he began piling up goals in his sophomore season, filling the net 32 times in 46 games and establishing himself as a dynamic scorer. Heading into a game against the Maple Leafs at home on February 25, 1945, Richard was sitting at 44 goals on the year, and many suspected he would vault ahead of Joe Malone that night and become the first player in NHL history to score 45 goals in a season. Nearly 14,000 fans packed the Forum with the hopes of watching Richard make history.

While the record-setting crowd waited for the milestone marker, it was treated to a scrappy game. After 57 minutes, plenty of punches had been thrown but Richard had not yet found the scoresheet. Then, when it seemed as though time was running out, the Montreal winger had put the puck past Maple Leafs goaltender Frank McCool. The Forum erupted and showered their hero with a six-minute standing ovation. When the raucous chorus had dissipated, Joe Malone, who had been a member of the faithful that night, presented Richard with the puck from his historic goal. Following the game, Malone was reported as saying, "He is one of those players that comes along every once in a while, and I hope he goes on to even greater feats." The Phantom's words proved prophetic as Richard's record-setting season was not done yet. Less than a month later, Richard would score his 50th goal of the campaign, becoming the first player to reach the benchmark and the first to accomplish the feat in 50 games.

# FEBRUARY 26
# THE BENTLEY BROTHERS
# COMBINE FOR 10, 1947

Before the Stastny brothers had their way against NHL teams, Chicago's Doug and Max Bentley were leading their club to victories. While Doug was the older of the two, Max had demonstrated a superior scoring proficiency. The younger Bentley captured the league scoring title in 1945–46 and was well on his way to repeating the feat the following season. In a contest against the Rangers on February 26, 1947, however, it was the elder sibling who stole the show that night as part of an incredible Bentley family performance.

While Doug opened the scoring for the game, little brother Max closed out the first period with a goal of his own. When play resumed in the second period, however, it was all Doug. He scored his second goal of the night within 30 seconds of puck drop and completed his hat trick another 30 seconds later. Three minutes after that, Max picked up his second goal of the night, and the game was quickly getting away from the Blueshirts. By that point, it was 6-2 for the Black Hawks, and the Bentley brothers would add two more goals as they paced their team to a 9-7 victory. While the home crowd rained boos down upon their squad, the Bentleys basked in their performance. When the final buzzer sounded, Doug had four goals and two assists, while Max had three goals and one assist; the pair had scored as many goals as their opponents. Although Doug held the bragging rights over his little brother that night, Max would finish the season with 72 points to win the regular-season scoring title in back-to-back years.

# FEBRUARY 27
## THE WRITTEN RULES OF HOCKEY, 1877

The game of hockey would be almost unrecognizable today compared with when its first written rules were published in the *Montreal Gazette* on February 27, 1877. The publication came on the heels of a game that had taken place between the St. James and Metropolitan skating clubs, who had squared off at the Victoria Skating Rink. Evidently, a dinner was on the line between the two teams, so the matchup attracted some fanfare. When the rules were published the following day, the newspaper outlined the basic tenets of the game. A couple of rules are important to note:

> When a player hits the ball, any one of the same side who at such moment of hitting is nearer to the opponents' goal line is out of play, and may not touch the ball himself, or in any way whatever prevent any other player from doing so, until the ball has been played. A player must always be on his own side of the play.

At the time, hockey was not yet played with a puck, which was originally made of wood and introduced only in the late 19th century; prior to that time, players chased after a ball. The other notable regulation was that forward passing was prohibited. While some iterations of the game played in other locales allowed forward passing, the Montreal version limited players from passing the ball to their teammates who were ahead of the play. In fact, when the National Hockey League was formed in 1917, forward passing was still prohibited, and the league did not permit it in all three zones until 1929. While the rules surrounding gameplay have significantly evolved over the years, the 1877 instructions codified the game and provided it with structure for patrons to adhere to at rinks and on frozen ponds across Canada.

# RILEY'S RAIDERS WIN GOLD, 1960

Twenty years before Team USA's improbable championship at the Lake Placid Winter Games, another American squad defied the odds to win Olympic gold. On February 28, 1960, in Squaw Valley, California, the United States defeated Czechoslovakia 9-4 to win the country's first Olympic hockey championship. Prior to facing the Czechs in their final game, the Americans faced even fiercer competition in matches against Canada and the Soviet Union. In a stunning upset, the United States beat their rivals to the north and then also defeated the Russians in a match the *Globe and Mail* referred to as "spine-tingling." It was the first time in team history that the Americans had beaten the Russians, who also happened to be the reigning Olympic champions, so as a result, the club was pretty exhausted and weary heading into the final game against Czechoslovakia.

Feeling the effects of that previous tilt, the Americans were listless when the championship puck dropped and found themselves trailing 4-3 heading into the third period. So how did the team break out of its fatigue and go on to snag the gold? Well, the story goes that, noticing the plight of coach Jack Riley's players and knowing the Russians needed the United States to beat Czechoslovakia if they wanted a shot at silver, Russian defenceman Nikolai Sologubov went into the American dressing room and urged them to take whiffs from oxygen tanks to help with their recovery. It must have worked. When Team USA returned to the ice, they scored six unanswered goals to pry the crown from the Czechs and claim victory on home soil.

# FEBRUARY 29
## MR. HOCKEY HITS 800, 1980

Since the NHL's formation in 1917, the league's history has intersected with 25 leap years. During that time, there has not been a February 29 performance more significant than the one Gordie Howe turned in back in 1980. On that day, Mr. Hockey scored his 800th career NHL goal, becoming the first player in league history to reach the milestone. In reality, the 51-year-old had scored his 800th goal long before. If you include the goals from his six-season sabbatical in the World Hockey Association (WHA), along with all of his playoff tallies from both leagues, Howe's goal that night was actually his 1,069th. Nevertheless, it was an incredible accomplishment for hockey's elder statesman.

Just over a month later, Howe would score his final regular-season goal, his 801st, when his team, the Hartford Whalers, fittingly hosted the Detroit Red Wings, the club he had started his career with over a quarter-century earlier. For the next 14 years, Howe's mark stood as the league best until March 23, 1994, when Wayne Gretzky, who had grown up worshipping Mr. Hockey, scored his 802nd career goal to take the all-time lead. Today, Gretzky and Howe are still the only two NHL players to be members of the 800-goal club, but only Howe can claim to have punched his ticket on a leap day.

# THE FLYERS' ROOF BLOWS OFF, 1968

With just a month remaining in their inaugural NHL season, the Philadelphia Flyers found themselves without a home. On March 1, 1968, gale-force winds tore the roof off the Spectrum, the team's arena. The trouble actually began in mid-February when another windstorm had ripped open a large hole in the building. Construction crews were able to mitigate the destruction, but 80-kilometre-an-hour winds swept through again two weeks later and caused further problems. Complicating the situation was that, two days later, as crews attempted to patch up the holes, the wind wrought havoc once again, blowing fire across the roof from the boiling-hot tar pots. Although the damage from the fire was minimal, it had some wondering if the Spectrum was cursed.

With the Flyers and the National Basketball Association's Philadelphia 76ers tenants of the building, it certainly complicated both teams' travel schedules after the city's mayor, James J.H. Tate, closed the arena because of safety concerns. As a result, the Flyers were forced to play their final seven "home" games on the road at either Maple Leaf Gardens, Madison Square Garden, or le Colisée in Quebec. Despite adding significantly to their travel, the Flyers finished the month of March with a 5-7-2 record and were still able to win their division.

# MARCH 2
## ESPOSITO JOINS THE CENTURY CLUB, 1969

On the evening of March 2, 1969, the capacity crowd of 14,659 at the Boston Garden interrupted play between the Bruins and Penguins for nearly 15 minutes, and for good reason. The club's star centre Phil Esposito had scored a goal and, in the process, registered his 100th point of the season. No other player in NHL history had ever accomplished the feat. By the time the arena crew had cleared the ice of hats and debris, Esposito was at it again. Six minutes after his first tally of the game, he found the back of the net, his 40th of the campaign, and the crowd broke into ovation once again. Esposito would finish the season with 126 points and win his first Art Ross Trophy, awarded annually to the NHL player who finishes the regular season with the most points. It was the first time a Bruin had won the award, and the team would hold on to the trophy for the next five years.

Superstar defenceman Bobby Orr would win it the following season and Esposito would win it another four times from 1971 to 1974. Since becoming the first member of the century club back in 1969, Esposito has been joined by 106 more players, including Connor McDavid, who most recently became the first back-to-back winner of the award in nearly two decades. The Oilers' captain first won the award in 2017 when he finished his sophomore NHL season with 100 points, and followed up that performance with a 108-point campaign in 2018.

# MARCH 3
## THE FIRST INDOOR HOCKEY GAME, 1875

When the first indoor hockey game was played at the Victoria Skating Rink in Montreal on March 3, 1875, it changed not only how the sport was watched but also how it was played. The contest attracted considerable fanfare as it had been reported that the players, including some students from McGill University, were very proficient in wielding their sticks on the ice. Moving the game indoors presented an improved viewing opportunity and experience for spectators. Having a captive audience watching from inside the rink, however, presented some logistical challenges, which led to modifications that forever changed the game. When hockey was played outside on frozen ponds and rivers, a ball was used, but inside there were concerns that the often unwieldy projectile could leave the ice and endanger the spectators. In order to avoid any issues at the Victoria Rink, the organizers of the game opted to introduce a flat, circular piece of wood to limit the chance of its leaving the playing surface. As a result, we can trace the antecedents of the modern puck back to safety concerns when the game was brought indoors. In addition, the two teams also played with a prescribed number of players.

Outdoors, hockey was often played with as many players as the frozen body of water could accommodate, but because of the confined dimensions of the rink, each squad was limited to nine players. While that is still considerably more than you would find on a modern ice surface, it represented a shift toward more tightly organized teams. Although the organizers of that contest were just looking to bring the game indoors and enhance the viewing experience, they ended up having a profound impact on how the sport was played for years to come.

# MARCH 4
## LOPRESTI'S 83-SHOT BARRAGE, 1941

t was supposed to be just another day at the office for the Black Hawks' rookie goaltender Sam LoPresti, but it turned out to be anything but. When Chicago went to Boston to face the Bruins on March 4, 1941, they were squaring off against a squad that was eager to break its deadlock with the Maple Leafs and take sole possession of first place in the standings. That determination certainly manifested itself on the ice as the Bruins fired 83 shots on the Black Hawks' net. The only thing that stood in their way was Sam LoPresti, who valiantly turned aside all but three of those attempts, an NHL record that still stands to this day. In fact, before Boston tied the game at 1-1 early in the second period, LoPresti was working on a 42-save shutout. The Eveleth, Minnesota, native kept his team in the game, and if not for his incredible performance in net that night, who knows how high the Bruins could have run the score.

While LoPresti's 83-shot barrage was one for the books, he would face his greatest challenge two years later as a member of the United States Navy during the Second World War. On February 8, 1943, his ship, the SS *Roger B. Taney*, was torpedoed by a German submarine. LoPresti managed to flee the sinking vessel and piled into a lifeboat that contained 28 of his shipmates. They spent 42 days drifting at sea before they were rescued off the coast of Brazil, nearly 4,000 kilometres away from where their ship went down.

# MARCH 5
## MAYHEM IN PHILLY, 2004

When the Flyers hosted the Senators on March 5, 2004, it was just supposed to be an ordinary game. Although the two teams had some bad blood dating back to an incident a few games earlier when Ottawa's Martin Havlat high-sticked Philadelphia's Mark Recchi, there was little indication that they were sitting on a powder keg for their next matchup. In fact, during the first 40 minutes of the game, only five minor penalties were called, and it seemed as though what had transpired in their previous encounter was water under the bridge. All that changed, however, when Senator Rob Ray and Flyer Donald Brashear got into a donnybrook with less than two minutes remaining. From there, other melees ensued, and even after officials cleared the ice of the first round of combatants, more fighting continued when play resumed.

The referees handed out so many misconducts that some players weren't even sure if they were still in the game. One of those happened to be Ottawa's Todd Simpson. "I'm in the dressing room and one of the guys goes, 'Simmer, you didn't get a penalty, you can still go play.' So I actually went back to the bench without any shoulder pads or elbow pads, I just had my jersey on. And I'm just sitting on the bench and the linesman skates over and says, 'Hey Simpson, what the heck are you doing? Get outta here.' Because there were so many penalties, they didn't have time to announce them all, so I had received some bad information," he recalled to VICE Sports. When the dust settled, Ottawa and Philadelphia had combined for 419 minutes' worth of infractions, an NHL record that eclipsed the previous mark (406) set by the Boston Bruins and Minnesota North Stars back in 1981.

# MARCH 6
## DALE HAWERCHUK'S INCREDIBLE PERIOD, 1984

When the Winnipeg Jets selected Dale Hawerchuk first over-all in the NHL Entry Draft in 1981, it came with signifi-cant expectations. The club had just finished dead last in the league with an abysmal record of 9-57-14, and after parading the young centre to a celebratory party that summer in a Brink's truck, it was now up to Hawerchuk to turn things around. He certainly handled the pressure with aplomb. In his first season in Winnipeg, Hawerchuk finished with 103 points, becoming the youngest player in NHL history to reach the 100-point mark and taking home the Calder Trophy as the league's top rookie in the process. His efforts that season not only added to his trophy case but also guided the Jets to a 48-point improvement in the standings, an unprecedented and historic turnaround.

While Hawerchuk's inaugural season was certainly one for the books, he continued to make an impact in Winnipeg as his career progressed. During his third campaign with the club, he had a single-period performance for the ages. In a game against the Kings on March 6, 1984, Hawerchuk contributed on every single one of Winnipeg's five goals in the second period. His superb puck dishing powered the Jets to a 7-3 victory, and with five assists next to his name on the scoresheet, Hawerchuk once again enshrined himself into hockey history with another record-setting achievement.

# THE FLAMES TRADE BRETT HULL, 1988

Heading into the 1988 post-season, the Calgary Flames were determined to win the Stanley Cup. To bolster their chances and shore up the back end, the club made a significant gamble by trading rookie Brett Hull and Steve Bozek to the St. Louis Blues for defenceman Rob Ramage and goaltender Rick Wamsley. At the time, Hull was sitting third in rookie scoring with 26 goals and 24 assists in 52 games. A season earlier, while playing with Calgary's American Hockey League affiliate in Moncton, he had notched 50 goals. In addition to the early signs that he could be a prolific scorer at the big-league level, Hull also had the pedigree. His father was Hall of Famer Bobby Hull, the first NHL player to score more than 50 goals in a season. As a result, given Brett's trajectory and lineage, Flames general manager Cliff Fletcher knew he was taking a significant risk when he dealt the bourgeoning goal scorer. When he addressed the trade to the media, Fletcher said, "Hull is going to score a lot of goals in the NHL."

He was certainly right about that. During Hull's first full season in St. Louis, he scored 41 goals and really began to demonstrate that he was becoming one of the league's premier snipers. The following year, he left no doubt. That season was the first of three straight campaigns in which he registered 70 goals or more, including the 1990–91 season when he lit the lamp 86 times. He would finish his NHL career with 741 regular-season goals, good enough for fourth all-time. Although the Flames ended up winning the Stanley Cup the year after they dealt Hull, they had expended a generational talent in the process. If Hull had been given the chance to develop into one of the game's most dynamic scorers while still in Calgary, it's possible the Flames would have more than one championship banner hanging from the rafters, but we'll never know.

# MARCH 8
## JOE MALONE SCORES NINE, 1913

ong before Joe Malone scored five goals in his NHL debut or racked up seven in a game against the St. Patricks, he found the back of the net nine times during Stanley Cup action. On March 8, 1913, Malone's team, the Quebec Bulldogs of the National Hockey Association, squared off against the Sydney Millionaires of the Maritime Professional Hockey League in the first game to determine who would hold the rights to Lord Stanley's trophy. Although newspapers such as Quebec's *Daily Telegraph* praised Sydney for starting off strong, the team was heavily outmatched, particularly when it came to Bulldogs centre Joe Malone. At the first intermission, the Millionaires trailed by only two goals and the game was not quite out of reach. Things quickly changed, however, when the puck dropped for the second period. Malone scored early in the frame, completing the hat trick, but he wasn't done just yet. He would add four more goals that period. In the final stanza, Malone scored two more goals for good measure, bringing his evening total up to nine.

When it was all said and done, the Bulldogs had handily defeated the Millionaires 14-3. Without the coverage from the broadsheets of the day, you would probably think Malone's play was the stuff of legends. The next game proved to be much closer, largely because Malone was not in the lineup. Nevertheless, even without the era's most prolific scorer on the ice, Sydney was still unable to stop Quebec's onslaught. In the end, the Stanley Cup went to the Bulldogs, and we can only imagine how that last game would have gone if Malone had suited up for an encore performance.

# WINNING THE STANLEY CUP AND GIVING IT AWAY, 1895

ong before the National Hockey League was formed, Canada's Governor General, Sir Frederick Stanley, had taken a keen liking to hockey. In 1892, he announced he would be donating a trophy that was meant to be a "challenge cup, which should be held from year to year by the championship hockey club in the Dominion of Canada." While it's now known as the Stanley Cup, awarded annually to the last team standing in the NHL post-season, it was originally vied for by the top teams from across the nation's amateur hockey leagues. It was first awarded in 1893 to Montreal Hockey Club (MHC), the top club from the Amateur Hockey Association of Canada (AHAC). While they were the first recipients, the following year they had to face off against another squad to claim hockey's top prize.

This inaugurated what was known as the challenge era. As the name suggests, clubs across the country could issue challenges to the reigning champions of the trophy in order to try to win it. A group of trustees was appointed to oversee this process, but it could be tricky sometimes, which explains how the MHC once won a Stanley Cup challenge but had to cede the trophy to their crosstown rivals, the Montreal Victorias. On March 9, 1895, MHC handily defeated Queen's University in a contest that should have earned them the Stanley Cup. The only problem was that the Victorias had already been crowned champions of the AHAC that year and were slated to receive the trophy. The challenge between Queen's and MHC, however, predated those results, and the Cup's trustees agreed that the competition could still take place. The only stipulation was that if the Montreal Hockey Club won, the trophy would go to the Victorias, but if Queen's was victorious, they would then have to play the AHAC champions. As it turned out, MHC won the match and, as agreed upon prior to hitting the ice, were forced to cede the Cup to the Victorias.

# MARCH 10
# THE ISLANDERS ACQUIRE BUTCH GORING, 1980

utch Goring had a reputation around the NHL. He was known for sporting the same helmet he wore as a 12-year-old, and he was also regarded as one of the poorest dressers off the ice. The story goes that, during a game on the road, a thief entered Goring's hotel room and snagged all the clothes belonging to his roommate but left all of Goring's attire hanging in the closet. Of course, looks can be deceiving, as dress code notwithstanding, Goring had established himself as a dependable and fearsome centre as a member of the Los Angeles Kings. It was for that reason that New York Islanders general manager Bill Torrey acquired the shabby dresser just before midnight on March 10, 1980. The deal sent the club's first ever draft pick, Billy Harris, along with Dave Lewis to the Kings in exchange for Goring, who was expected to enhance the offensive prowess of the Islanders' second line.

The move certainly paid off for New York. Goring scored 11 points in the final 12 games of the regular season with his new club and helped them elevate their game heading into the post-season. Once in the playoffs, however, Goring found another gear and truly demonstrated his value to the team. Scoring 19 points in 21 games, he led the Islanders to their first Stanley Cup in franchise history and won the Conn Smythe as the post-season's most valuable player. While the move to Long Island didn't necessarily improve his style, Goring became an integral part of an Islanders' team that would win four consecutive championships in the 1980s.

# MARCH 11
# RANDY HOLT'S PENALTY-FILLED PERIOD, 1979

Over the course of 10 seasons in the National Hockey League, there were very few times that defenceman Randy Holt shied away from taking on a fight. Although he was not diminutive by hockey standards, he was often at a size disadvantage compared with some of the hulking opponents he took on. Nevertheless, Holt never backed down and earned a reputation as a scrappy and pugnacious player who was not afraid of anybody. As a result, given his propensity for dropping the gloves, Holt often spent more time in the penalty box than on the ice. In fact, during a contest against the Philadelphia Flyers on March 11, 1979, as a member of the Los Angeles Kings, he racked up more penalty minutes than any other player in NHL history.

Late in the first period of that game, a bench-clearing brawl erupted between the two teams. At the centre of the melee was none other than Randy Holt, who was engaged in a bout of fisticuffs with Paul Holmgren. By the time referee Wally Harris had everything under control, he had assessed 352 minutes in penalties to both teams, but nobody had more than Holt. The Kings blueliner was given nine penalties: one minor, three majors, two 10-minute misconducts, and three game misconducts, for a grand total of 67 minutes. It set league records for most penalties in one period, most penalty minutes in one period, and most penalty minutes in one game. By the end of the regular season, Holt had accumulated 282 penalty minutes, surpassing his previous career high. Not surprising, given that nearly a quarter of those infractions were incurred during his extracurricular activities in that infamous game against the Flyers.

# THE GUMP GETS EGGED, 1967

orne "Gump" Worsley was no stranger to stopping pucks. He had been occupying NHL nets since 1952 and had faced a battery of shots over the years, including a blistering slapshot from Bobby Hull that had hit him square in the head in 1965, knocking him unconscious. While Worsley valiantly blocked these projectiles on the ice without a mask, he never anticipated having to make a save against an object launched from the stands. In a game against the New York Rangers on March 12, 1967, however, that's exactly what happened.

Playing on the road at Madison Square Garden, the Montreal Canadiens goaltender was hit by an egg on the right temple early in the first period. The impact of the shot dazed Worsley, and he was forced to leave the game. The tosser, who had brought a bag of eggs to the contest, was apprehended by security not long after the incident occurred. While the shot had injured Worsley and taken him out of the evening's action, he opted not to press charges against the fan. Following the matchup, which ended in a tie, Worsley told reporters, "I didn't know it was an egg until I felt the gook." Although newspaper reports described his injury as a "minor concussion," he didn't see the ice for another six weeks. Good thing the egg wasn't hard-boiled.

## MARCH 13
# LARRY KWONG GETS THE CALL, 1948

When the New York Rangers were riddled with injuries toward the end of the 1947–48 campaign, it gave minor-leaguers the chance to get some ice time with the big club on Broadway. One of those players happened to be Chinese-Canadian winger Larry Kwong. The Vernon, British Columbia, native was playing with the New York Rovers of the Eastern Hockey League, a team he would lead in scoring by the end of the season, and he was eager to prove his worth to the Blueshirts. But the call-up was more than a big-league audition; it was a historic moment for the National Hockey League. When Kwong took to the ice for the Rangers' game against the Montreal Canadiens on March 13, 1948, it marked the first time a player of Asian descent had suited up for an NHL game.

While he had hoped to demonstrate to the Rangers' brass that he could play at a higher level, his big break never materialized. During that game, Kwong played just one shift in what would prove to be his first, and only, NHL stint. Years later, in reflecting on his fleeting moment playing at the game's highest level, he told the *New York Times*, "I didn't get a real chance to show what I [could] do." Despite the missed opportunity, Kwong was not deterred from pursuing his hockey career. He continued to play in the Quebec Senior Hockey League and even took his talents overseas, playing for teams in Great Britain and Switzerland. In one season with the Nottingham Panthers of the British National League, Kwong notched 39 goals in 31 games. Although he may not have received a fair shake at the NHL level, Kwong's breakthrough certainly blazed a trail for Asian players who made the league's ranks years later.

## MARCH 14
## THE BLACK HAWKS FORFEIT, 1933

To say that Black Hawks coach Tommy Gorman protested the overtime goal scored against his team on March 14, 1933, would be a significant understatement. Following a Bruins marker three minutes into the extra frame, the Chicago squad was up in arms as they felt it should not have counted. Immediately after the goal light emitted its familiar red glow, the Black Hawks rushed behind their net to shout their disapproval to the goal umpire, Louis Raycroft. Feeling his words were not enough, Chicago defenceman Johnny Coulter tried ramming his stick through the netting in an attempt to knock some sense into Raycroft. While the players tried to make their case on the ice, coach Gorman took his frustration too far when he reportedly struck referee Bill Stewart. The two were then said to have engaged in a fist fight that had to be broken up by some Bruins players.

Following the skirmish, Gorman was ejected but he did not go alone. Instead, he withdrew his entire squad and retired to the dressing room for the evening. With Boston still ready to conclude the 10-minute overtime period — teams did not play the sudden-death style until 1983 — Stewart had no choice but to declare a forfeiture. Apparently, after the Black Hawks' disappearance, play resumed with the Bruins adding another goal on an empty Chicago net. When Stewart realized that Gorman and his group were not returning to the playing surface, he officially called the game. Although the Wanderers had surrendered a pair of games in 1918 after their arena burned down, Chicago's was the first real forfeiture in the National Hockey League, and to date, there has been only one other since.

# MARCH 15
## BOBBY ORR SCORES 100, 1970

When Bobby Orr entered the National Hockey League in 1966, he revolutionized the way defencemen played the game. The league had seen puck-carrying defencemen before with players like Eddie Shore, but nobody had ever possessed the skating, scoring, and playmaking ability from the blue line quite like Orr. By his third season, he had proven why he was the best player of his era. On March 15, 1970, Bobby Orr became the first defenceman in NHL history to notch 100 points in a season. During a game against the Red Wings, the Parry Sound, Ontario, native picked up two goals and collected a pair of assists to reach the milestone. Orr's performance that evening certainly merited the standing ovation he received from the Bruins faithful at the Boston Garden, as it kept him firmly in the lead in the league scoring race.

The defenceman's performance also moved him into some illustrious company. The only other players who had reached that benchmark were his teammate Phil Esposito, Chicago's Bobby Hull, and Detroit's Gordie Howe, who had all accomplished the feat just a season earlier while feasting on the league's bourgeoning expansion clubs. Orr would add another 19 points in Boston's final nine games to finish the season with 120 points. For his efforts, he won his first Art Ross Trophy as the league's regular-season leading scorer and the Hart Trophy as the most valuable player to his team. As of the end of the 2017–18 regular season, Bobby Orr still remains the only defenceman in NHL history to win the Art Ross.

# MARCH 16
## THE AMERICANS HAVE A BAD DAY IN NET, 1939

The New York Americans' final game of the 1938–39 regular season couldn't have gone much worse. Halfway into the second period on March 16, they were losing 4-1 to their crosstown rivals, the Rangers, when their goaltender, Earl Robertson, left the contest with a serious injury. After dropping to the ice to stop a shot from Rangers defenceman Art Coulter, Robertson returned to his feet but then immediately signalled to his bench that something was wrong. Wincing in pain, the Americans' netminder retired to the dressing room for the evening, where it was later discovered that he had torn ligaments in his left thigh. With Robertson out indefinitely, the Americans had no choice but to fill the crease with one of their other players.

The unlucky individual happened to be "Broadway" Roger Jenkins, who was just one of a handful of American-born players in the NHL at the time. While he normally patrolled the blue line for the Americans, Jenkins valiantly stepped into the breach to occupy his team's net for the remainder of the game. At the conclusion of the second period, he had yet to let in a goal and his squad had actually closed the deficit to two. His flawless play, however, proved to be an aberration when the final frame commenced. Although Rangers general manager and coach Lester Patrick had instructed his team to take it easy on their opponents, the substitute goaltender was helpless against the onslaught. Jenkins let in seven goals and the Rangers easily cruised to an 11-5 victory, the second-highest-scoring game in league history at that time. Although Jenkins was in net for only 30 minutes, he finished his goaltending career with a goals-against average (GAA) of 14. It proved to be his first and only stint in goal and also his last regular-season game with an NHL club.

# MARCH 17
## THE RICHARD RIOT, 1955

A tomato sailed up over Clarence Campbell's head and landed on his fedora. More projectiles followed, including peanuts, pennies, programs, and even prophylactics. Patrons at the Forum were certainly doing their part to welcome the NHL president to Montreal's St. Patrick's Day game against Detroit. Not far from his section, a fan was nervously fiddling with a cannister of tear gas. When it eventually went off, it would trigger one of the most infamous episodes in hockey history, the Richard Riot. A day earlier, Campbell had suspended the Canadiens' star player, Maurice "Rocket" Richard, for the remainder of the regular season and the playoffs from an incident on March 13, 1955, when Richard got into a fight with Bruins' Hal Laycoe and landed a punch on linesman Cliff Thompson during the skirmish.

Canadiens fans were outraged by the suspension. For years they felt that Campbell treated Richard, a French Canadian, more harshly than his English counterparts. With tension running high in Montreal, Campbell, against his better judgment, attended the team's next game against the Red Wings. It didn't take long for things to turn ugly. After smoke started billowing through the arena when the tear gas canister erupted, officials called the game. As the mayhem spilled out into the streets, it turned into a riot. When the dust settled, hundreds of thousands of dollars of damage had been done across more than 15 blocks in downtown Montreal, and more than 100 people were arrested. Following the chaos, in an effort to dissipate the tension, Richard looked to calm the masses. "I will take my punishment and come back next year to help the club and the younger players win the Cup," he said. Richard was true to his word. He returned the following season and helped the Canadiens vanquish the Red Wings to win the first of five straight Stanley Cups.

# CANADIENS UNDEFEATED AT HOME, 1944

The Montreal Canadiens made NHL history at the Forum on March 18, 1944, but unfortunately, it was before their smallest crowd of the season, with many missing out on the milestone moment. For the 8,000 who turned out, however, they watched their team cruise to an 11-2 victory over the New York Rangers and etch its name into the record books by becoming the first NHL team to end its home campaign without a defeat. Over the course of 25 games at the Forum, Montreal recorded an incredible record of 22-0-3.

Technically, the Canadiens tied the undefeated home record set by the Ottawa Senators in 1922–23, but since the NHL's modern era did not begin until the 1943–44 season, with the introduction of the red line at centre ice, the Habs are the only team to have accomplished the feat. Moreover, the Canadiens were nearly just as good on the road that year, tying another NHL record for the fewest losses in one season with just five. It's no surprise then that, given how dominantly the club had performed over the course of the campaign, the Habs went on to capture their fourth NHL-era Stanley Cup. In recent history, the only team that has come within sniffing distance of the Canadiens' record was the Quebec Nordiques. Playing in their final campaign before relocating to Denver, Colorado, the Nordiques went 19-1-4 at home in the 1994–95 lockout-shortened season.

# MARCH 19
## AFTERNOON DELIGHT, 1933

When the Detroit Red Wings and Chicago Black Hawks squared off in the afternoon on March 19, 1933, it had never been done before. It was the first matinee game in NHL history. The matchup, which drew roughly 5,500 people, was reported as "one of the wildest, roughest games ever played in Chicago." Although the Black Hawks were mired at the bottom of their division, they still battled hard against the Red Wings, a team that would finish the regular season tied for the most wins. Moreover, the Black Hawks were also injury-riddled, an issue that was only exacerbated during the game when Billy Burch, who had suited up in replacement of an ailing Taffy Abel, crashed into the boards and broke his leg in two places.

Nevertheless, Chicago played rough and even deployed some new techniques in an effort to repel the Red Wings' onslaught. According to the *New York Times*, the Black Hawks tried sending out units of five forwards in the final period, but that tactic was abandoned after Detroit was easily able to sneak behind the forward corps and score another goal. Although Chicago ended up losing the game 4-2, it was a historic matchup for the NHL and the inaugural "afternoon delight" for hockey lovers.

# BROTHER VS. BROTHER, 1971

When brothers Dave and Ken Dryden played hockey together in their backyard, they both had big-league aspirations. Dave, the eldest, was the first to make the jump to the NHL in the 1965–66 season, backstopping the Black Hawks. Meanwhile, Ken was tending the nets for Cornell University, but it was only a matter of time before he joined his brother in the professional ranks. On March 20, 1971, with Dave playing for the Sabres and Ken playing in his third NHL game for the Montreal Canadiens, the two squared off, the first time in league history that two brothers faced each other in goal. But it nearly didn't happen.

Leading up to the game, both coaches were aware of the history to be made. Recognizing the opportunity, Buffalo bench boss Punch Imlach started Dave, who was the team's backup, hoping Montreal's Al MacNeil would reciprocate and put Ken in net. MacNeil did not bite, however, and opted to start the Canadiens' stalwart goaltender, Rogie Vachon. As a result, Imlach pulled Dave early in the matchup and replaced him with Buffalo's regular goaltender, Joe Daley. Things have a way of working themselves out, though. During the second period, Vachon left the game with an injury, which forced MacNeil's hand, bringing Ken into the fray. Seeing the switch in the Montreal goal, Imlach immediately yanked Daley and replaced him with Dave, giving fans and the Dryden family the brother matchup they had been anticipating.

# MARCH 21
# BOBBY CARPENTER REACHES 50-GOAL PLATEAU, 1985

eading into the 1981 NHL Entry Draft, American high school prospect Bobby Carpenter was referred to as the Can't-Miss Kid. His trajectory was so promising he even graced the cover of *Sports Illustrated* while still playing for St. John's Preparatory School in Danvers, Massachusetts, making him the first U.S.-born player to be featured on the magazine's cover. Given his potential to have an impact, the Washington Capitals chose him third overall that year, making him the second American player to be selected in the first round of the draft. Carpenter continued to turn heads when he cracked the Capitals roster the next season, achieving another milestone when he became the first player to join the NHL ranks right out of high school hockey. Four years later, after scoring 92 goals in his first three seasons with the Capitals, Carpenter was about to make history again.

The Can't-Miss Kid couldn't miss, and on March 21, 1985, in a game against the Canadiens, he became the first U.S.-born player to score 50 goals in an NHL season. Prior to his milestone marker, Carpenter had already smashed the record for most goals in a campaign by an American player, eclipsing Joe Mullen, who had scored 41 as a member of the St. Louis Blues just a season earlier. Nevertheless, the 50-goal plateau still loomed large for an American player, and Carpenter was more relieved than anything when he accomplished the feat. After the game, he confessed that the task had been weighing on him psychologically. "You don't make the good passes and the great plays when you're trying to do something like that. It seems that when you try not to think about it, that's when you end up thinking about it the most," he told reporters. Carpenter would add three more that year to bring his season total up to 53, but it would prove to be his only 50-goal campaign.

## MARCH 22
# EDDIE JOHNSTON THE MINUTE MAN, 1964

When Bruins goaltender Eddie Johnston vacated the crease at the end of the team's final regular-season game on March 22, 1964, it was a familiar feeling. Despite making 36 saves, Johnston's efforts were in vain. Boston picked up its 40th loss of the campaign as the team finished in the basement of the standings for the fourth straight year. In the early 1960s, the Bruins were the hallmark of futility, a trend that would continue until nearly the end of the decade. Nevertheless, despite his club's ineffectiveness, Johnston performed admirably in his second season with the Bruins. In fact, he played every minute of every game that year, making him the last goaltender in NHL history to do so.

Over the course of the league's 70-game schedule, Johnston logged 4,200 minutes of ice time and registered a record of 18-40-12. Of his 18 wins, six of them were shutouts. As the league expanded over the intervening decades, the number of games teams played increased. As a result, it gave goaltenders the opportunity to appear in more contests and bump up their ice time. Years later, Grant Fuhr played in 79 games for the St. Louis Blues in 1995–96, and Martin Brodeur logged 4,696 minutes of ice time in 2006–07, both league records in their respective categories. Although Johnston's numbers from his sophomore season with the Bruins pale in comparison, no goaltender since can claim to have played in every minute of every game for an entire NHL season.

# MARCH 23
# BILL MOSIENKO'S RECORD-BREAKING HAT TRICK, 1952

Chicago's Bill Mosienko saved his best for last. In the Black Hawks' final regular-season game against the Rangers on March 23, 1952, the right winger from Winnipeg, Manitoba, shattered the NHL record for the fastest three goals. In a span of merely 21 seconds in the third period, Mosienko scored a hat trick. His achievement easily eclipsed the previous record held by Detroit's Carl Liscombe, who scored three goals in one minute and 52 seconds back in 1938. Of course, Mosienko didn't do it alone. Contributing on each of his rapid markers was Gus Bodnar, who also etched himself into the NHL record books with the fastest three assists. Mosienko's performance initiated a Black Hawks comeback that saw the team score five unanswered goals in the final period to take a 7-6 victory over the Rangers.

While Mosienko would play another three seasons in the NHL, that ended up being his final career hat trick. He certainly went out on a high note. More than a half-century later, even if you include team efforts, Mosienko's individual feat is still one of the fastest three-goal performances in league history. Only the 1970–71 Bruins did it faster, scoring three goals in 20 seconds in the third period in a game against the Canucks. Boston, however, needed goals from three different players — Johnny Bucyk, Ed Westfall, and Ted Green — to make it happen. Mosienko's individual performance remains practically untouchable. In 1953, the great Jean Beliveau came the closest, but even then, Le Gros Bill still needed more than double the time to notch his hat trick.

# MARCH 24
## THE LONGEST NHL GAME, 1936

rying to be inconspicuous, a patron at the Montreal Forum carefully pulled out his pocket watch. As his eyes spotted the time, he gasped and thought to himself, *My wife must be worried sick.* "How much longer do you think this will last?" he asked his companion. "I don't know, but I've got to be at work in five hours," the friend replied. It was just after 2:00 a.m., and they, along with 9,000 others, had been watching the Red Wings play the Maroons since the puck dropped the previous evening. Both teams had been trading chances for hours, literally, but neither club had been able to find the back of the net. The game was now into its sixth period of overtime, and it seemed like the contest would never end. The players were exhausted. The fans, at least those who were awake, were growing restless as the matchup dragged on. Then, it happened.

Detroit's Modere "Mud" Bruneteau, who had recently been called up from the Olympics, the Red Wings' minor-league affiliate, scored the biggest goal of his career. As he released his shot on Montreal's goaltender, Lorne Chabot, the crowd collectively held its breath. Could this be it? Was it finally over? The puck bobbled up over Chabot's foot to break the scoreless deadlock, mercifully ending the longest game in NHL history. By the time the battle-weary players had cleared the ice, it was early morning on March 25, 1936. When it was all said and done, the Wings and the Maroons had duelled through six additional overtime periods, for a grand total of 176 minutes and 30 seconds of hockey, surpassing the previous mark of 164 minutes and 46 seconds set by the Bruins and Maple Leafs in April 1933. As of the end of the 2018 Stanley Cup Playoffs, it remains the longest game in NHL history.

# MARCH 25
## GRETZKY PASSES 200-POINT MARK, 1982

t seemed like it was only a matter of time. After scoring 164 points in his sophomore NHL season, many believed it would not be long before Wayne Gretzky became the first player in league history to surpass 200 points in a single season. After all, he had already established records for quickest 50 goals in a season, most goals in a season, most assists in a season, and most points in a season. Given all that Gretzky had accomplished by the age of only 21, there was little doubt he would reach the extraordinary 200-point plateau. Sure enough, on March 25, 1982, on the road in a game against the Calgary Flames, Gretzky scored two goals and added two assists to bring his season point total up to 203.

While Flames fans typically booed the Great One whenever he touched the puck because of the heated provincial rivalry with the Oilers, even they couldn't help but be in awe of what they had witnessed that night. Although they initially jeered after the goal that enshrined Gretzky into hockey lore, the heckling dissipated and turned into a standing ovation. Needless to say, Gretzky was surprised but appreciative of the response. "Every rink where I've got a record, I received a standing ovation, but it's a little more special here because the people always boo me," he told reporters after the game. Gretzky would finish the season with 212 points, 65 points ahead of runner-up Mike Bossy, for the first of his four 200-point seasons. Although Mario Lemieux came close to the benchmark in 1988–89 when he logged 199 points, Gretzky remains the only NHL player in the 200-point club.

# THE SEATTLE METROPOLITANS WIN THE STANLEY CUP, 1917

When Lord Stanley announced plans to donate a trophy in 1892, it was supposed to be a challenge cup that was to be awarded each year to "the championship hockey club in the Dominion of Canada." A quarter-century later, the Seattle Metropolitans put a wrinkle in his plan when they defeated the Montreal Canadiens, on March 26, 1917, to become the first club from the United States to capture the Stanley Cup. The champions of the Pacific Coast Hockey Association, the Metropolitans took on the Canadiens, of the National Hockey Association, and hosted them in a best-of-five championship series in Seattle. After Montreal won the first game, despite playing under Pacific Coast rules that included a seven-man format, they lost the next three straight, including a 9-1 blowout in the final and decisive matchup.

The Metropolitans would have the chance to win the Stanley Cup again in 1919, but they, along with their opponents, were denied the opportunity when the series was cancelled partway through the competition because of the influenza epidemic. Although the Metropolitans folded in 1924, Seattle may become more than just a footnote in Stanley Cup history. On December 7, 2017, NHL commissioner Gary Bettman announced that a Seattle ownership group had been granted permission by the league to file an application for an NHL expansion team that could take to the ice in time for the 2020–21 season.

# MARCH 27
## CHRIS CHELIOS'S REMARKABLE DURABILITY, 2006

When Chris Chelios stepped out onto the ice for the Red Wings on March 27, 2006, in a game against St. Louis, he did something no other player in the league had done. The durable defenceman had become the first player in NHL history to appear in 400 or more contests with three different clubs. Drafted by Montreal in 1981, Chelios played 402 games on the Canadiens' blue line, where he'd win his first Stanley Cup and Norris Trophy, before he was traded to the Black Hawks in exchange for Denis Savard. In Chicago, Chelios would establish himself as a stalwart player on the back end, winning two more Norris trophies and appearing in eight All-Star Games over the course of 664 games.

At the age of 37, Chelios was traded to the Red Wings, where he'd remain a productive player, finding success while taking on a more reduced role. By his 400th game with Detroit, Chelios had already won a Stanley Cup in 2002 and would add another with the club in 2008. When his tenure with the Red Wings came to a close, he had appeared in 578 games. After adding seven more games with the Atlanta Thrashers in the 2009–10 season, Chelios completed his NHL career with 1,651 regular-season games under his belt, which will likely keep him in the top 10 all-time for quite a while.

# JETS ROOKIES RULE, 1993

With five seconds left in regulation in a game against the Kings on March 28, 1993, Winnipeg Jets rookie Alexei Zhamnov scored his 20th goal of the season. The tally capped off a third-period comeback that saw the Jets rebound from a three-goal deficit and salvage a tie. Zhamnov's effort, however, was overshadowed by another Jets rookie, Teemu Selanne, who racked up his 69th and 70th goals of the campaign during that game, becoming just the eighth player in NHL history to record a 70-goal season. In anticipation of the milestone, the Jets game against the Kings was actually broadcast in Finland, and Selanne did not disappoint his homeland. While the broadsheets heralded the electrifying game from the Finnish Flash, Zhamnov's goal went under the radar.

Although his counterpart certainly had a performance to write home about, Zhamnov's marker made the Jets the first team in NHL history to have four 20-goal rookies; the others were Evgeny Davydov and Keith Tkachuk, who both finished the season with 28. Selanne, of course, finished his campaign with 76, setting an NHL rookie goal-scoring record and making him the unanimous choice for the Calder Trophy. Meanwhile, Zhamnov finished the season with 25 goals, good enough for eighth among a rookie class that year that also included Eric Lindros. The significance of the Jets' rookie contributions should not be underestimated. No team since has been able to match the goal-scoring output from Winnipeg's rookies, a testament to the rich crop of young talent the team had on its roster that year. Even the 2016–17 Toronto Maple Leafs, which boasted the likes of Auston Matthews, William Nylander, Mitch Marner, and Connor Brown, were unable to equal the mark, although they came awfully close. One more goal from Marner would have vaulted the Maple Leafs quartet into the same echelon.

# MARCH 29
## BOBBY CLARKE GETS 100, 1973

Four years after every NHL general manager passed on him in the first round of the 1969 NHL Amateur Draft, Philadelphia's Bobby Clarke continued to make the league's top brass regret their decision. The Flin Flon, Manitoba, native had established himself as a fearsome and offensively gifted player in junior hockey — playing for his hometown Bombers — but he had diabetes, and NHL general managers were concerned his illness would affect his big-league career. Flyers scout Gerry Melnyk, however, insisted that his club snag Clarke with its second-round selection. Apparently, Melnyk told his colleagues at the draft table, "I don't give a damn if this kid's got one leg; he's the best player I've seen at this level. He'll right away be our best player." The scout's words proved to be prophetic.

Clarke would have an immediate impact in Philadelphia. Establishing himself as the heart and soul of the team, he earned Calder Trophy and Hart Trophy consideration in his first and second years, respectively. Halfway through his fourth campaign with the Flyers, Clarke was named team captain — making him the youngest in NHL history at the time — an honour he would cap off with another notable milestone later that season. In a game against the Atlanta Flames on March 29, 1973, Clarke scored two goals to become the first player from a post-1967 expansion team to score 100 points in a season. He'd finish the year with 104 points, earning the Hart Trophy and the Lester B. Pearson Trophy. A year later, Clarke would be a part of history once again as he led the Flyers to the first of back-to-back championships, becoming the first expansion team to capture the Stanley Cup. If not for the sage advice from scout Gerry Melnyk, the Flyers could have missed the boat on Clarke, forever changing the history of the franchise.

# MARCH 30
## TORONTO WINS FIRST NHL-ERA STANLEY CUP, 1918

At the conclusion of the National Hockey League's inaugural season, the Arena Hockey Club of Toronto, simply known as the Arenas, defeated the Montreal Canadiens in a total-goals playoff series for the privilege of representing the NHL in a final show-down against the Pacific Coast Hockey Association (PCHA) champion for the Stanley Cup. On the West Coast, the Vancouver Millionaires had defeated the Seattle Metropolitans. No less than 24 hours after securing the Pacific Coast crown, the Millionaires were on a train bound for Toronto. When the series began on March 20 — only one day after the Millionaires' transcontinental trek — it wasn't simply a competition between two leagues; it was a clash of two brands of hockey.

Unlike the NHL, the PCHA still used six skaters and a goal-tender. The extra position was known as the rover, and as the name suggests, it afforded this player the ability to roam the ice as needed. The National Hockey Association eliminated the position in 1910, but it persisted in western leagues until the 1920s. But it wasn't just the rover that set the PCHA apart. The league also featured a lim-ited forward pass. In the centre-ice zone, PCHA players could make forward passes, while their NHL counterparts were still restricted to lateral plays. To account for such fundamental differences between the two leagues, each game of the series alternated between NHL and PCHA rules. As a result, a decided advantage was to be had each contest. And with NHL rules set for three of the five games, it was the Arenas' Stanley Cup to lose. After splitting the first four games of the series, the pivotal matchup was played on March 30, 1918, under NHL rules. In what would be the lowest-scoring game of the series, the Arenas edged the Millionaires 2-1 to claim the first NHL-era Stanley Cup.

# MARCH 31
## KING CLANCY DOES IT ALL, 1923

Few players have been more valuable to their team than King Clancy was on March 31, 1923. That evening, in the second game against the Edmonton Eskimos to determine the rights to the Stanley Cup, the versatile Ottawa Senators defenceman did it all. A couple of nights earlier, in the first contest of the series, Clancy had played brilliantly on the back end, leading the Senators on charges up the ice and stymying his opponents as they took the first game 2-1 in overtime, but he saved his best performance for the next game. Not only did Clancy play every position from the blue line out, he also occupied the crease for two minutes.

During the third period, Ottawa goaltender Clint Benedict drew a penalty after striking Edmonton's Joe Simpson in the legs with his stick. At the time, goaltenders were still required to serve their own penalties, leaving the Senators net vacant at a pivotal moment in the game. With Benedict serving time, Clancy valiantly stepped into the net. With the game tied 0-0, there was no better chance for the Eskimos to break the deadlock and even the series. Despite having a significant advantage, Edmonton was unable to put the puck in the back of the net. In fact, Clancy's colleagues up front were so effective that the Eskimos were not even able to get a shot off. Not long after holding down the fort, Clancy's Senators scored the only goal of the game, clinching the Stanley Cup. Although Clancy did not face any rubber during his brief foray in the crease, he became the first — and only — player in NHL history to play all six positions in one game. Following the championship series, the *Vancouver Daily World* reported that each Ottawa player took home $700 for each game, but on March 31, 1923, no one worked harder for their money than Clancy.

# APRIL 1
## SERIES NOT COMPLETED, 1919

While the world dealt with the outbreak of the Spanish influenza, not even the National Hockey League was immune to its devastation. Before the league's second season began on December 21, 1918, Ottawa's Hamby Shore, a versatile player who played both forward and defence during his career, succumbed to the illness. Following his death, a black cloud hung over the 1918–19 season. As the virus began reaching epidemic proportions, the situation only got worse. In the final matchup of the season, the NHL's Montreal Canadiens and the Pacific Coast Hockey Association's Seattle Metropolitans faced off once again for Lord Stanley's trophy. Heading into the sixth game of the series, the stakes could not have been any higher. The two teams were deadlocked. Each squad had two wins, and with a tie in the fourth contest, now they faced a winner-take-all sixth game for the Stanley Cup. But it never happened.

Five hours before the pivotal game, on April 1, 1919, it was announced that the series would be cancelled. Across the street from the Seattle Ice Arena, in the Georgina Hotel, five Canadiens players and manager George Kennedy were bedridden with fevers ranging between 38 and 40 degrees Celsius. There was no way Montreal would be able to ice a team. The Spanish flu had claimed the Stanley Cup, but the worst news was yet to come. A few days later, Canadiens defenceman Joe Hall, who had rightfully earned his reputation as one of hockey's toughest players, died from complications brought on by the virus. It was the first and only time that competition for the Stanley Cup was outright cancelled after play had begun. In the end, both teams had their names engraved on the trophy accompanied by the ominous words "series not completed," a grim reminder of what the league had lost.

# APRIL 2
## MEL "SUDDEN DEATH" HILL, 1939

Good nicknames are hard to come by, but Boston Bruins forward Mel Hill came by his moniker honestly during the 1939 post-season. In overtime during the seventh game of the semifinals against the New York Rangers, on April 2, 1939, Hill scored the game-winning goal to punch his team's ticket to the Stanley Cup Final. Hill's overtime heroics, however, were nothing new. In fact, they had come to be expected by that point in the series. The Glenboro, Manitoba, native, who was playing in only his first full season with the Bruins, had already scored two overtime winners before netting his decisive goal. As a result of his high-stakes virtuosic performances, Hill was given the nickname Sudden Death, a testament to his ability to come through in the clutch for his club.

His reputation had been established early in the series when he scored the triple-overtime winner in the first matchup. After he followed up that performance with an encore in the extra frame of the second game, the Bruins won the next contest in regulation to take a stranglehold on the series. The Rangers, however, were not finished. Boston would lose the next three straight games, setting the stage for a pivotal Game 7, the first of its kind in NHL history. Playing in the biggest game of his life, Hill once again lived up to his sobriquet and scored the sudden-death winner in the early morning hours of April 3. The Bruins went on to face the Maple Leafs in the Stanley Cup Final, during which Boston would capture its first championship in a decade.

# APRIL 3
## HAKAN LOOB GETS 50, 1988

After the Flames defeated the North Stars on the final day of the regular season, on April 3, 1988, all the talk surrounded the fact that the victory clinched Calgary the top spot in the league standings. Finishing with 105 points, the best performance since the franchise entered the league in Atlanta in 1972, the Flames were red-hot heading into the playoffs. They not only locked up home-ice advantage throughout the post-season by securing the Presidents' Trophy but also added an extra $200,000 to their wallets.

Lost in the commotion, however, was that Flames forward Hakan Loob scored his 50th goal of the season, becoming the first Swedish player to notch a 50-goal campaign. Fellow Swede Kent Nilsson, who had also played for the Flames, came awfully close in 1980–81 but missed the milestone by just a single marker. Although Loob's goal was an important moment in Swedish hockey history, it proved to be a bittersweet end to the regular season. By the end of the month, the Flames would be prematurely eliminated from the playoffs, once again, by their provincial rivals, the Oilers. The next year, however, the Flames redeemed themselves. Although Loob did not repeat his 50-goal performance, he did assist on Lanny McDonald's final NHL goal, one that would give Calgary its first Stanley Cup in franchise history. After the championship, Loob returned to Sweden to play out his hockey career, which culminated in an Olympic gold medal at the 1994 Winter Games in Lillehammer.

# APRIL 4
## THAT'S A DRAW, 2004

When Carolina defenceman Brad Fast was recalled for the final game of the regular season, he was eager to take advantage of the opportunity. The 24-year-old had been drafted by the Hurricanes in 1999 but finished his NCAA career at Michigan State University before moving on to Carolina's American Hockey League affiliate, the Lowell Lock Monsters. It was the promotion he had been waiting for. On April 4, 2004, Fast met his teammates in Florida, where they would be taking on the Panthers in the season finale. The game went off without a hitch. The Hurricanes opened the scoring with four straight, but their opponents responded emphatically with six unanswered goals. With the third period winding down, it seemed as though the game had gotten away from the Hurricanes. Then, after Carolina rookie Eric Staal picked up his 11th goal of the campaign to bring the Hurricanes to within one, Brad Fast received a pass from Rod Brind'Amour and wired it past Florida goaltender Robert Luongo to tie the game. Overtime solved nothing, and so the Hurricanes finished the regular season with a 6-6 draw against the Panthers.

Although no one knew it at the time, Fast had made history. There would be no 2004–05 NHL season because of the lockout. When the league resumed operations the following year, it instituted a number of rule changes, including the introduction of the shootout, which scrapped the tie format that had previously been a possible way for a game to end. As a result, this meant Brad Fast had scored the last game-ending tying goal in NHL history. It also proved to be his only big-league marker. Fast never had another opportunity to play at that level, which also made him one of the few in NHL history to score a goal in their only career game. Fast had certainly left his mark. In reflecting on his place in history, he told author Ken Reid in *One Night Only*, "It will be a great trivia question. And some people — they won't even understand why we were playing to a tie."

# APRIL 5
## MARCEL DIONNE SNAGS THE ART ROSS, 1980

At the end of his first regular season in the National Hockey League, 19-year-old Wayne Gretzky had amassed 51 goals and 86 assists, good enough for tops in league scoring. It also marked the beginning of his leading the league in assists for 13 straight seasons. The Art Ross Trophy, it seemed, was his to lose. Marcel Dionne, however, had other plans. The Los Angeles Kings' top-line centre was only two points back of Gretzky when he went into his final game of the season. Sure enough, in a 5-3 loss to the Canucks, Dionne picked up two assists to draw even with Gretzky for the league lead.

As a result, with both players tied at 137 points, the league invoked the tiebreaking formula, which placed a premium on goals. Since Dionne finished with 53 goals and 84 assists, he was awarded the trophy. It was just the second time in league history the Art Ross was determined by the tiebreaker. Back in 1962, Andy Bathgate and Bobby Hull both finished the season with 84 points, but since the Golden Jet had nearly double the number of goals, he was the recipient of the award. Although the Art Ross just escaped Gretzky's grasp in his debut NHL season, he would keep a firm grip on it in the coming years. The following season, the Great One won his first Art Ross Trophy and wouldn't let it go for seven consecutive seasons.

# APRIL 6
## MR. HOCKEY'S FINAL GOAL, 1980

After breaking into the National Hockey League in 1946, Gordie Howe headed into the final game of the 1979–80 regular season with 800 career goals under his belt. The 52-year-old had first retired from the NHL in 1971 and then took a two-year leave of absence before he was lured by the Houston Aeros of the World Hockey Association (WHA) to play with his sons, Mark and Marty. Following a six-season sabbatical in the rival league, Howe returned to the NHL when the New England Whalers, along with five other WHA clubs, merged with the National Hockey League. The following season, the Whalers rebranded their home city designation to Hartford, and Howe had another opportunity to leave his mark on NHL history.

On April 6, 1980, playing in his 1,767th, and final, regular-season game, Howe scored a nifty backhand goal, his 15th of the season, on Red Wings goaltender Rogie Vachon, lifting his career goal total to 801. It would be his last regular-season goal. Interestingly, when Vachon made his NHL debut 13 years earlier for the Montreal Canadiens, the first save he ever made was against Gordie Howe on a breakaway. Mr. Hockey always got the last laugh. Although Howe played three games for the Whalers in the post-season, he hung up his NHL skates for good and retired as the league's all-time leader in goals. His 801 tallies would hold up for another 14 years before Wayne Gretzky knocked off the last of his idol's scoring records.

# OILERS AND KINGS SHOOT IT OUT, 1982

The 1982 Smythe Division semifinal between the Edmonton Oilers and Los Angeles Kings started off with a bang. On April 7, the two teams nearly burned out the light bulbs in the goal lamps at the Northlands Coliseum when they combined for 18 goals, setting a new NHL record for most goals by two teams in a playoff game. The output easily eclipsed the mark of 15 goals set by the Montreal Canadiens and Chicago Black Hawks in the 1973 Stanley Cup Final and later equalled by the Boston Bruins and Minnesota North Stars in the first round of the 1981 post-season. While high-flying offence was a hallmark of the NHL in the 1980s, there was always the expectation that teams would clamp down in the post-season as the stakes got higher. Clearly, that was not the case when the Oilers and Kings took the ice for the first game of the series.

Before the midway point of the first period, Edmonton was already leading 4-1, but they squandered that advantage after Los Angeles answered with two goals to close the frame. The drama continued into the second period as the two teams continued to trade goals. The Kings tied it up early on and then took the lead, only to see the Oilers even it up before responding with two more goals. When the contest adjourned for the second intermission, Los Angeles was up 8-6, but their lead was short-lived. With less than 10 minutes remaining, the Oilers scored two more goals to draw even, but their comeback would end there. The Kings would add two more, including an empty-netter, to take the first game 10-8 in what was setting up as an offensive tour de force. While it would have been hard to top that opening contest, the two teams would do just that three days later.

# MIKKO LEINONEN ASSISTS THE RANGERS, 1982

f you were to look up Mikko Leinonen's statistics for the 1982 play-offs, you would see he racked up seven points in seven games for the New York Rangers. Pretty darn good, but if you were to zero in on his individual game efforts, Leinonen's post-season performance would be even more impressive. That's because, on April 8, 1982, the Finnish rookie contributed on every Rangers goal except one, registering six assists in a single game. Not bad for an undrafted player who had only recently made the jump to the NHL after establishing himself as one of the top players in Finland.

But once Leinonen arrived in New York, it was not a seamless transition. After starting the season with the big club, he had been banished to the team's American Hockey League affiliate for three weeks in December. Even after he returned to the Blueshirts, Leinonen spent considerable time watching his squad play from the press box as a healthy scratch. Nevertheless, the 24-year-old persevered, and after compiling an impressive 15-point campaign in March, he cemented his role with the Rangers heading into the post-season. While Leinonen's stretch of play was impressive, there was no indication he would have that breakout night in the playoffs. With that performance, he set a new league record for most assists in a playoff game. In rewriting the NHL history book, he moved into some exclusive company with players like Maurice Richard, Phil Esposito, and Wayne Gretzky, who had all previously shared the all-time benchmark with five assists. Five years later, when Leinonen was back in Finland continuing his hockey career, Gretzky equalled his feat with a six-assist outing of his own in a playoff game against the Kings. Although Leinonen ended up playing only 162 career NHL games, not many players can say they share a league record with the Great One.

# APRIL 9
## JUMBO JOE MAKES HISTORY, 2006

Joe Thornton was selected first overall by Boston in the 1997 NHL Entry Draft, but seven years into his tenure with the organization, there were creeping doubts about his future with the Bruins. Although he had established himself as a productive centre, including putting up a 101-point campaign in 2002–03, Boston's top brass had questions about his long-term fit in Beantown. Despite opening the 2005–06 season with 33 points in 23 games, Thornton was traded to the Sharks on November 30, 2005, in exchange for Marco Sturm, Wayne Primeau, and Brad Stuart. Once in San Jose, Thornton picked up right where he had left off, racking up points as one of the league's premier passers.

Heading into a game against the Dallas Stars on April 9, 2006, he was sitting at 111 total points on the season, with the chance to make NHL history. Thornton needed just two points to eclipse Bernie Nicholls's 1989–90 production and take sole possession of the league record for most points in a season by a player who had been traded. Sure enough, with two assists in a 4-1 victory over the Stars, Thornton did just that. Incredibly, he added 12 more points in the final five games of the regular season to bring his season total up to 125 and win the league scoring title, which made him the only player in NHL history to win the Art Ross after being traded in the same season. While the Bruins won the Stanley Cup in 2011, the trade has worked out for the Sharks as well. Thornton holds club records for most career assists, 745 at the end of the 2017–18 season, and most points in a season with 114 in his first full campaign with San Jose.

# APRIL 10
## MIRACLE ON MANCHESTER, 1982

You can't blame Kings owner Dr. Jerry Buss for leaving his team's game after just two periods on April 10, 1982. Los Angeles was trailing Edmonton 5-0 in the third game of their best-of-five opening-round playoff series and the L.A. Forum on Manchester Boulevard was eerily quiet. After defeating the favoured Oilers three nights in earlier in a high-flying contest that featured 18 goals, and losing the second game, it seemed as though the Kings had run out of magic.

Following 40 minutes of play, Edmonton was poised to take a 2-1 lead in the series, but with less than three minutes into the final frame, Los Angeles defenceman Jay Wells finally got his team on the board. After a goal by the Kings' Doug Smith, Charlie Simmer put the Kings within striking distance when he closed the deficit to just two. As they continued to swarm the Oilers, the Forum faithful rallied behind their team, praying for a miracle. With four minutes remaining, Mark Hardy brought Los Angeles to within one. As the clock ticked down the game's final seconds, it seemed as though the Oilers were going to skirt disaster. Wayne Gretzky simply had to clear the puck from his team's zone, but with 10 seconds remaining he had his pocket picked by Jim Fox, and the Kings regrouped for a final rally. Fox shovelled the puck to Hardy, who got a shot off that was stopped by Edmonton goaltender Grant Fuhr. As the rebound trickled out, with just five seconds remaining, Steve Bozek directed the puck into the net — and the Forum broke out into bedlam. The Kings had done the impossible. Heading into overtime, the Oilers were deflated following their third-period collapse. Less than three minutes into overtime, rookie Daryl Evans wired a shot over Fuhr's right shoulder to end the game. The Manchester Miracle was complete. It remains the largest single-game comeback in Stanley Cup Playoffs history.

# HEXTALL SHOOTS, HE SCORES, 1989

Ron Hextall was one of the best puck-handling goaltenders in NHL history. His ability to initiate a counterattack by directing the puck to one of his players or simply clearing the zone made him lethal on the ice, in more ways than one. Therefore, given his skillful stickwork, it's no surprise Hextall was the first goaltender in the league to score a goal by shooting the puck into the net in both the regular season and the playoffs. Although Billy Smith of the Islanders was the first goaltender to be credited with a goal, that was only because he was the last New York player to touch the puck before Colorado Rockies defenceman Rob Ramage put the puck into his own net during a delayed penalty sequence. Hextall, on the other hand, wired the puck into an empty net in a game against the Bruins on December 8, 1987.

A year later, Hextall would make history again when he scored in the post-season against the Capitals on April 11, 1989. In Game 5 of the Patrick Division semifinal against Washington, Hextall made good on another opportunity. With just over a minute remaining in the third period, the Flyers had a two-goal lead but found themselves on the penalty kill. With time winding down, the Capitals attempted to take advantage of the situation and pulled their goaltender, but unfortunately for them, Hextall was just waiting to make his move. He flipped the puck high up into the air and down the ice, straight into the Capitals' net. Although the stakes were higher than the first time he had scored a goal, the Flyers goaltender knew it was worth the risk. Following the game, he told reporters, "I knew we were short-handed and that it wouldn't be icing." Besides, it was another chance to score a goal. "I don't know how many I'll score, but it's always a thrill," he added. While a handful of goaltenders have scored in the years since, including Martin Brodeur, nobody has made it look as easy as Hextall did.

# RED WINGS GET THE MOST WINS, 1996

Trailing by two goals early in the second period in a game against the Blackhawks on April 12, 1996, the Red Wings were chasing history. One more victory at Joe Louis Arena would give them their 36th of the campaign, tying them with the 1975–76 Philadelphia Flyers for the most home wins in one season. There was, however, a more important milestone at stake. Heading into that game against Chicago, the Red Wings had 60 regular-season wins, which matched the all-time record set by the Montreal Canadiens in 1976–77. With two contests remaining in the regular season, Detroit needed another victory to vault ahead of the Canadiens.

With history on the line, the Red Wings proceeded to make an impressive comeback in the second period thanks to the performances of their special teams. After the club scored two straight goals on the power play, Paul Coffey scored a short-handed marker, his second goal of the evening, to give the Red Wings the lead heading into the final frame. They would hold on to the lead, with Coffey's goal standing as the game-winner and Kris Draper adding an empty-net insurance goal with just 45 seconds to play. The Red Wings had done it. Two days later, they'd travel to Dallas where they'd pick up their final victory on the season to push their campaign total to 62. For their efforts, the Red Wings would win their second straight Presidents' Trophy, but it was all for naught. Given the team's regular-season performance, they seemed destined to win the Stanley Cup that year, but they would fall to the Colorado Avalanche in the conference final. Of course, Detroit's time would come. The following year, the club would win its first championship since 1955, the first of back-to-back Stanley Cups.

# APRIL 13
# JOHN TONELLI SAVES THE DAY, 1982

The New York Islanders were the NHL's last true dynasty, winning four consecutive Stanley Cups from 1980 to 1983. But if not for John Tonelli's late-game heroics on April 13, 1982, that dynasty might never have happened. It was the fifth and deciding game of the Patrick Division semifinal between the Pittsburgh Penguins and the Islanders. With less than six minutes remaining in the contest, the Islanders trailed by two goals and seemed destined to become but a footnote in NHL history. Back-to-back Stanley Cups would be nothing to scoff at, but if the team's run had ended there, they wouldn't be uttered in the same breath as the Montreal Canadiens and Toronto Maple Leafs, clubs that had previously earned the dynasty label. The Islanders' time, however, was not up yet.

New York's Mike McEwen scored to cut the deficit in half, and with less than three minutes remaining, John Tonelli was in the right place at the right time in the Penguins' end. After the puck hopped over Pittsburgh defenceman Randy Carlyle's stick, it went straight to Tonelli, who wired the game-tying goal into the far side of the open net. But Tonelli wasn't done yet. Once overtime began, the Penguins swarmed the Islanders with all they had, but it wasn't enough. After Tonelli retrieved the puck deep in the Penguins' zone, he passed it to his teammate Bob Nystrom, who was parked in front of Pittsburgh goaltender Michel Dion. Although Nystrom's shot was denied, Tonelli made no mistake. As the rebound spurted out, he scooped up the puck and sent it over Dion's shoulder and into the back of the net. Tonelli was the Islanders' hero yet again, coming through in the clutch in overtime to power his club to the next stage of the post-season. The Islanders would make short work of their next three opponents en route to a third straight Stanley Cup.

# PITTSBURGH'S WINNING STREAK
# ENDS AT 17, 1993

All good things must come to an end. After piling up a remarkable 17-game winning streak, the longest in NHL history, the Penguins' run of luck and dominance halted on April 14, 1993, in a tie against the Devils. It was Pittsburgh's final game of the regular season, so the streak, which dated back to March 9, was going to come to an end one way or another. For most of the third period, it seemed as though it would end in a loss. New Jersey went into the second intermission with a 6-5 lead, and the Penguins trailed nearly all of the final frame, until Joe Mullen potted the equalizer with just 66 seconds remaining in the game. It was the Penguins' first non-winning effort since a 3-1 loss to the New York Rangers on March 5.

Since the match ended in a draw, it actually gave Pittsburgh an 18-game undefeated streak, but that was still a far cry from the 35 consecutive games without a loss that the Philadelphia Flyers assembled in 1979–80. Whether their run ended in a tie or a loss was of no consequence; what mattered was that the Penguins were going into the NHL's record books with the longest winning streak in league history, having bested the New York Islanders' previous mark by two games. Since then, other teams have come close, but none has been able to equal or better what the Penguins accomplished at the tail end of the 1992–93 campaign. Most recently, the Columbus Blue Jackets racked up 16 straight wins from November 29, 2016, to January 3, 2017, for the second longest streak in NHL history. While this accomplishment was certainly worthy of celebration, team captain Nick Foligno later lamented that he'd rather see the club do it in the post-season: "16 in a row in the playoffs is the Stanley Cup," he told the Athletic.

# APRIL 15
# DETROIT'S OCTOPUS-TOSSING TRADITION BEGINS, 1952

The tradition of throwing octopuses at Red Wings games is older than most of the teams in the National Hockey League. The custom of chucking cephalopods in the post-season began with the Cusimano brothers, Pete and Jerry. Owners of a local fish market in Detroit, the pair believed the octopus made for a natural good luck charm because its eight tentacles symbolized the number of wins needed to secure the Stanley Cup in the Original Six era. One day, while handling an octopus in the shop, Jerry supposedly picked up a leg and gestured to his brother. As Pete recalled in the *Detroit Free Press* years later, he remembers Jerry saying, "Here's the thing with eight legs. Why don't we throw it on the ice and maybe the Wings'll win eight straight?" The brothers first put the idea into practice on April 15, 1952, when the Red Wings hosted the Canadiens in what was potentially the last game in the Stanley Cup Final.

At that point, Detroit had a commanding 3-0 series lead, and it was time to put Jerry's theory to the test. After Gordie Howe scored the first goal of the contest, Pete hopped out of his seat and hurled his stowaway mollusc onto the ice. The Red Wings went on to complete the post-season sweep and nab Lord Stanley's mug. Although the ritual did not catch on immediately, by the 1990s, hurling octopuses became synonymous with Detroit playoff hockey. Many fans emphatically embraced the tradition, with some even going to great lengths to leave their mark. In 1995, Al Sobotka, the Red Wings' building manager and ice keeper, but better known for his octopus-wrangling skills, picked one up off the ice that weighed an estimated 30 pounds. While you're more likely to see the four- or five-pound variety hit the ice, chucking cephalopods in Detroit remains one of the most unique traditions in hockey.

# LEAFS BECOME FIRST NHL THREE-PEAT, 1949

The Maple Leafs' 1948–49 season was nothing to write home about. Although the team was the defending back-to-back Stanley Cup champions, they certainly weren't playing as such. After posting a 22-25-13 regular-season record, Toronto barely snuck into the playoffs, claiming the final spot over the Chicago Black Hawks. It seemed as though the Leafs would be an easy mark in the post-season. After all, they had won only three games in their final 10 contests. Few expected that the team would be able to make NHL history by becoming the first squad to win three straight Stanley Cups. Once the playoffs started, however, the Maple Leafs came alive. Their listless play from the previous months was gone, and they seemed to be returning to their championship form. After dispatching the Boston Bruins in five games in the semi-finals, the Maple Leafs faced a familiar foe in the Stanley Cup Final: the Red Wings. Toronto had previously wrestled Lord Stanley's mug from Detroit in 1942 and in the previous year's showdown, and they hoped to do the same once again.

After pushing the Maple Leafs to overtime in the opening game and coming up short, the Red Wings then lost the next two contests and found themselves facing a sweep on April 16, 1949. While the desperate Detroit squad opened the scoring in that game and kept pace with the Maple Leafs throughout the first period, the game was all but over before the middle frame concluded. After scoring two goals in the second period, Toronto outshot Detroit 25-10 in the final 40 minutes, adding another tally in the third period to put the Wings out of their misery. As the Red Wings skated off the ice in defeat, the Maple Leafs hung around waiting for their prize. For the third straight year, NHL president Clarence Campbell presented Toronto with the Stanley Cup.

# SID THE KID HITS 100 POINTS, 2006

When Sidney Crosby broke into the NHL for his rookie season, the hockey world knew it had something special on its hands. He had been a hockey sensation from an early age, so it was no surprise when the Pittsburgh Penguins selected the Cole Harbour, Nova Scotia, native first overall in the 2005 NHL Entry Draft. After years of disappointment in Pittsburgh, the team once again had a superstar who was poised to turn the franchise's fortunes around. When the 18-year-old made his league debut just over two months later, he picked up his first NHL point, an assist, and then notched his first goal in his third contest. His impact on his club and the league continued throughout his inaugural campaign.

With just two games remaining in the season, Crosby had 97 points and was on the verge of league history. Twenty-four years earlier, Dale Hawerchuk, just two days shy of his 19th birthday, became the youngest player in NHL history to reach 100 points. So when the Penguins faced off against the Islanders on April 17, 2006, Crosby had the opportunity not only to join Hawerchuk as the only other 18-year-old to score 100 points but also to become the youngest player to reach the milestone. At the time Crosby was 18 years and 253 days old, and with him piling up points at a pace of 1.23 per game, it seemed likely he'd edge out Hawerchuk. Sure enough, in that game against the Islanders, Crosby bagged three assists to join the centennial club. He'd pick up two more points in his final game of the season to finish his rookie campaign with 102 points. Although the Calder Trophy would go to Alex Ovechkin for his brilliant 52-goal performance, the best was yet to come from Crosby.

# APRIL 18

## MAPLE LEAFS CAP INCREDIBLE COMEBACK, 1942

The Red Wings should have won the Stanley Cup in 1942. After taking the first three games in the final against the Maple Leafs, the championship was theirs to lose. Although the league had adopted the best-of-seven format just three years earlier, no one anticipated that Toronto would be able to dig itself out of its hole; hockey writers were already penning their obituaries. The Maple Leafs, however, were not ready to be buried. They won the next three games, including two on the road in Detroit, setting the stage for an incredible comeback.

When the series shifted to Toronto for the decisive seventh game, 16,218 fans packed themselves into Maple Leaf Gardens. At the time, it was the largest crowd to ever attend a hockey game in Canada. Although the Red Wings opened the scoring in the second period, it would be the only goal they'd tally that evening. When play resumed for the final frame, Maple Leafs left winger Dave Schriner lit the lamp to tie the game. Just minutes later, centre Peter Langelle scored a dramatic goal to take the lead. According to the *New York Times*, the puck had flown 15 feet into the air and came down right on Langelle's stick. All he had to do was give it a nudge across the line. It held up as the game-winner, although Schriner would notch another with just four minutes remaining. As the buzzer sounded, a chorus of cheers filled the overcapacity crowd at the Gardens. Toronto had done the unbelievable; they reversed a three-to-none series deficit and won four straight games to capture the Stanley Cup. Since then, only three other NHL clubs in league history have pulled off a similar comeback, but none with the championship on the line.

## APRIL 19

# BRODEUR SETS PLAYOFF SHUTOUT RECORD, 2012

When New Jersey Devils goaltender Martin Brodeur was chased from his net after allowing three goals on just 12 shots in Game 3 of their Eastern Conference quarterfinal series, he knew he had to be better. Heading into the fourth contest on April 19, 2012, he told reporters, "We'll be tested tonight, so we just have to perform. That's the bottom line." When the puck dropped, Brodeur was ready. The veteran goaltender, who was appearing in his 185th post-season game, shook off the disappointment from the previous evening and was ready to redeem himself. He probably wasn't even thinking about the fact he was just one perfect game shy of gaining sole possession of the NHL's all-time record for playoff shutouts, which he currently shared with Patrick Roy.

At the time, however, none of that mattered. Brodeur's only task was to give his team the opportunity to win. Early in the second period, the game was still scoreless. The 39-year-old goaltender stopped everything that had come his way. His teammates took care of the rest. The Devils scored a power-play goal to take the lead and then added three more in the final period to put the game out of reach. Even as New Jersey's offensive onslaught continued, Brodeur fulfilled his duty as the last line of defence. When it was said and done, he had stopped all 26 shots he faced from the Panthers, setting a new league record with his 24th post-season shutout. Brodeur would backstop the Devils all the way to the Stanley Cup Final that year, but they'd come up short against the Kings. While the netminder would play two more seasons in New Jersey and seven games in St. Louis, he wouldn't see playoff action again.

# APRIL 20
## THE GOOD FRIDAY MASSACRE, 1984

aster is typically a time for solemn reflection, but that certainly wasn't the case at the Colisée on April 20, 1984. That evening, the Montreal Canadiens and Quebec Nordiques engaged in a melee that went down in NHL history as the Good Friday Massacre, and for good reason. Although the Nordiques had been in the league for only five years, following the merger with the World Hockey Association, they had already developed a fierce rivalry with their provincial counterparts. While the Battle of Quebec was often fuelled by political and ideological differences, and even which beer each team's fan base consumed — the Canadiens and Nordiques were at one time owned by rival breweries — what happened on the ice was always the driving force behind the animosity. Following a league realignment in 1981 that brought the Nordiques into the Canadiens' Adams Division, the rivalry intensified.

Heading into that fateful Good Friday matchup, the Nordiques were on the brink of elimination. Toward the end of the second period, with Quebec maintaining a 1-0 lead, things turned ugly when a skirmish erupted. Both benches cleared, and all but one player from each team became involved in a bloody altercation that resulted in a whopping 252 penalty minutes. Given all the infractions, the third period was delayed as the officials attempted to sort out the chaos. As the penalties were announced and the players learned their fate, those who'd been ejected felt they had nothing else to lose and tried to exact retribution before retiring to the dressing room for the evening. As a result, all hell broke loose again. Once the officials cleared the ice for the second time, they imposed an additional cool-down period before beginning the final frame. When the game resumed, Quebec added to its lead but Montreal stormed back and scored five unanswered goals to win. It was an incredible comeback, largely overshadowed by the fisticuffs and mayhem that preceded it.

# APRIL 21
## THE LAST GOAL HE EVER SCORED, 1951

The championship series between Toronto and Montreal was not for the faint of heart. It was a hard-fought battle, with each game decided by overtime. Heading into the fifth game, on April 21, 1951, the Maple Leafs had the chance to win their fourth Stanley Cup in five years. Meanwhile, the Canadiens were just hoping to stave off elimination.

With less than a minute remaining in regulation and Montreal holding a 2-1 lead, it seemed as though there would be a sixth game. But Toronto's Tod Sloan had other plans. With just 32 seconds to play, he tied it up to send the contest to sudden death. Less than three minutes into the extra frame, Maple Leafs winger Howie Meeker initiated an attack. After his initial advance was stopped by Montreal goaltender Gerry McNeil, Meeker captured the rebound and made a nifty pass to teammate Bill Barilko, who converted the set-up with a dramatic diving shot into the back of the net. It was Barilko's biggest goal, but it proved to be his last. That summer, Barilko went on a fishing trip in northern Quebec with his friend and dentist, Dr. Henry Hudson. On the way back, their plane went down just north of Cochrane, Ontario. The wreckage and their bodies weren't found for another 11 years, just a few months after the Maple Leafs won their first Stanley Cup since Barilko's triumphant goal. If the lyrics to the Tragically Hip's "Fifty-Mission Cap" are now dancing in your head, you're in good company. For me and countless other Canadians, Bill Barilko and Gord Downie are forever intertwined.

# APRIL 22
## SUNDSTROM SETS PLAYOFF RECORD, 1988

There aren't many post-season scoring records that Wayne Gretzky doesn't hold or share, but chief among them is for most points in a game. In 1983, the Great One scored seven points in a 10-2 win over Calgary — establishing a new league record that had once been shared by the likes of Phil Esposito, Darryl Sittler, and Guy Lafleur — but this benchmark stood for only five years, not long for a Gretzky record. Although Wayne equalled this output two more times throughout his career, New Jersey's Patrik Sundstrom did him one better on April 22, 1988. That night, the Swedish centre scored three goals and added five assists, setting a new NHL record, as the Devils trounced the Capitals 10-4.

Following the conclusion of the game, which turned out to be a penalty-filled match, one of Sundstrom's linemates, Mark Johnson, told the *New York Times* he was in awe of how much damage Sunny had done. "You're talking Wayne Gretzky class. We witnessed history. I was more excited than he was when he got the last goal," he said. While Johnson beamed, Peter Sundstrom sulked. That's right, Patrik's twin brother Peter was on the ice that night, but he was on the wrong side of history, playing for Washington. Sundstrom's Devils would eventually be eliminated in the Prince of Wales Conference final against the Bruins. Just a little over a year later, Mario Lemieux would score five goals and add three assists in a 10-7 victory over the Philadelphia Flyers to tie the record. Sundstrom would play only eight more NHL post-season games before returning to Sweden to finish his career, but none of those games were bigger than the night he was in a class with Gretzky.

## APRIL 23
# PETE BABANDO COMES UP BIG, 1950

Pete Babando saved his goals for when they counted the most. The stocky left winger from South Porcupine, Ontario, was not known for his scoring prowess. Although he notched 23 goals in his rookie season with the Boston Bruins, when he was traded to the Red Wings two years later, he was chiefly utilized in a checking role. In 56 regular-season games in the Motor City, Babando scored just six goals. That post-season, the Red Wings squared off against the New York Rangers in the Stanley Cup Final. Babando had been held scoreless in the team's earlier series against the Maple Leafs, but after dispatching the defending champions, he began to find his game. He snagged two assists in a pair of games, which both resulted in Detroit victories, but he really found another gear when the stakes were at their highest. In Game 7 of the final, just the third time the series had gone the distance, he scored the biggest goals of his career.

With the Red Wings trailing by two in the second period, Babando lit the lamp on the power play to close the gap. Just 21 seconds later, Sid Abel scored another goal on the man advantage to tie the game. The teams traded another pair of goals, and regulation play concluded in a 3-3 draw. As the Rangers and Red Wings prepared for sudden death, the players knew they would be part of history. It marked the first time the winner of the Stanley Cup would be decided in overtime in Game 7. After an extra 20 minutes solved nothing, both clubs prepared for another period of nerve-racking hockey. Just before the halfway mark of the second overtime, Detroit's George Gee won a faceoff near New York's net and corralled the puck back to Babando, who was set up behind him. With a 15-foot backhander, Babando broke up the marathon game and clinched Lord Stanley's mug for the Red Wings. Nearly 70 years later, no other Game 7 in Stanley Cup Final history has stretched into a second overtime period, making Babando's heroics that much more special.

# APRIL 24
## MAY DAY, 1993

t's rare that a play-by-play call eclipses a goal, but it has happened. There's no better example of this than Brad May's overtime winner for the Buffalo Sabres against the Boston Bruins in the 1993 Adams Division semifinal. Even if you're not a Sabres fan, odds are you're familiar with this piece of NHL history because of Rick Jeanneret's famous play-by-play. Jeanneret, who had been with the Sabres organization since its second season in 1971–72 when he began calling games on the radio, had made some big calls over the years, but none were more iconic than his accompaniment to Brad May's game-winning goal.

The atmosphere surrounding that playoff series undoubtedly set the stage for that moment. The Sabres had previously squared off against the Bruins five times in the post-season but always came up empty-handed. This time around, things were different. The Sabres took the first three games, including two overtime victories, with the chance to sweep Boston at home at the Memorial Auditorium on April 24, 1993. After 60 minutes of regulation, the two teams were deadlocked at 5-5. Five minutes into sudden death, the Sabres' Pat LaFontaine was tripped up in the neutral zone but was still able to pass the puck to Brad May as he fell to the ice. Breaking into the attacking zone, May snuck behind both Bruins defencemen, and from there, it's all Jeanneret: "Here's May going in on goal. He shoots, he scores! May Day! May Day! May Day! May Day! May Day! Brad May, wins it in overtime!"

# APRIL 25

## JOHNNY BOWER'S GAME 7 SHUTOUT, 1964

You've already read about how the Maple Leafs became the first NHL team to win three consecutive Stanley Cups in 1949, but they accomplished the feat again 15 years later. On April 25, 1964, Toronto defeated Detroit to capture the championship. If you recall, the Red Wings were on the wrong end of the Maple Leafs' last three-peat. But while the Maple Leafs swept the Red Wings in 1949, this time around, Detroit pushed their rivals to the limit, stretching the Stanley Cup Final to the full seven games. Although the Wings hoped to exact their revenge, it was not meant to be. Early in the game, Andy Bathgate scored for Toronto and the team never looked back. The Buds racked up three more goals to blank the Red Wings 4-0 and clinch Lord Stanley's silverware.

Although Detroit threw 33 shots on Toronto's net, veteran goaltender Johnny Bower, who was just months away from his 40th birthday, turned in a tremendous effort to deny them all. In fact, it was the first time in NHL history a shutout was recorded in Game 7 of the Stanley Cup Final. While Bower's teammates mobbed him in celebration, the more outstanding performance may have actually come from blueliner Bobby Baun. A game earlier, Baun had broken a bone in his ankle after blocking a shot from Gordie Howe. With the game set to go into overtime and Toronto's season on the line, Baun refused to go to the hospital. Instead, he instructed the team's trainers to tightly tape his ankle so he could return for the extra frame. Despite having only one good foot to skate on, Baun scored the overtime winner to send the series to the pivotal Game 7. After coming off one of the most legendary and heroic performances in Maple Leafs playoff history, there was no way Baun was going to miss the deciding game. Sure enough, despite the fractured ankle, Baun never missed a shift and, in the end, got to sip champagne alongside Bower in the dressing room.

# APRIL 26

## THE BRUINS EXORCISE THEIR DEMONS, 1988

After 45 years of playoff disappointment against the Montreal Canadiens, the Boston Bruins exorcised their demons on April 26, 1988. The last time Boston defeated Montreal in the post-season was in 1943. The United States was still fighting in the Second World War, the National Hockey League had only six teams, and Bobby Orr was still five years away from being born. The Bruins would lose 18 consecutive playoff series to the Canadiens. It didn't matter if they were at home or on the road. At the Boston Garden, their efforts were futile, and as visitors, the Montreal Forum was a veritable haunted house. However, the spectres of those past failings never materialized in the fifth game of the Adams Division championship in 1988. The Bruins would finally exact their revenge.

The ghosts were quieted relatively early in the game when Steve Kasper scored the opening tally halfway through the first period. Cam Neely added another marker a few minutes later to put the game out of reach for the Canadiens. Kasper put the final nail in the coffin when he potted his second of the night, increasing Boston's lead to 3-0. Although Montreal's John Kordic got his team on the board with nine minutes remaining in the middle frame, it wasn't enough. Neely would find twine again to open the final stanza, and that was it. For the first time in nearly five decades, Bruins fans could finally scream in celebration rather than curse their miserable fortunes. When the final buzzer sounded, the black and gold faithful thought not of how Ken Dryden halted the team's chance at back-to-back Stanley Cups in 1971 or how a penalty for too many men on the ice in 1979 still haunted them. Instead, they rejoiced. The long-standing and familiar suffering was finished. Following the game, Bruins head coach Terry O'Reilly told reporters he was glad it was over. "It's such a sigh of relief," he said.

# APRIL 27
## DUELLING GOALTENDERS, 1994

After 60 minutes of regulation, Martin Brodeur and Dominik Hasek were perfect. After a 20-minute overtime period, perfect. After another period of overtime, still perfect. Twenty more minutes of overtime and, you guessed it, perfect once again. It was Game 6 of the Devils' and Sabres' first-round matchup in the 1994 Stanley Cup Playoffs. With Buffalo facing elimination at home, Hasek turned in a goaltending performance for the ages. Following regulation and 60 minutes of overtime, the Czech goaltender had stopped all 66 shots he had faced, while his counterpart, rookie Martin Brodeur, had turned away 49 shots.

While the skaters in front of them combatted fatigue and the bleary-eyed fans in the Buffalo Memorial Auditorium struggled to stay awake, the tenders of the twine remained composed and flawless. The acrobatic artistry of their craft was on full display that evening, and it seemed as though neither team would find the back of the net. The Sabres came close in the second overtime frame when Dale Hawerchuk fired a shot that fooled Brodeur but struck a goalpost, rolled along the goalmouth, and hit the other post before it was scooped away to safety by Devils defenceman Scott Niedermayer. Finally, at 1:52 the following morning, Buffalo's Scott Hannon broke the scoreless deadlock five minutes and 43 seconds into the fourth overtime. It had been nearly six hours since the initial puck drop. At the time, it was the third-longest playoff game in league history. When it was all said and done, Hasek had stopped all 70 shots he faced, for arguably one of the greatest post-season goaltending efforts of all time.

# APRIL 28
## GORD STELLICK BECOMES YOUNGEST GM, 1988

Just a month before he turned 31 years old, Gord Stellick received one heck of an early birthday present. On April 28, 1988, he was appointed general manager of the Toronto Maple Leafs, making him the youngest general manager in National Hockey League history. Stellick, who had been with the organization for 13 years, had started as a press-box assistant at Maple Leaf Gardens before taking the reins as general manager of Toronto's American Hockey League affiliate, the Newmarket Saints. Following his promotion to the big club, Stellick had his work cut out for him.

At the 1988 NHL Entry Draft two months later, he drafted goaltender Peter Ing and the pugnacious Tie Domi, who would become a fan favourite. The newly minted GM, however, did miss out on the opportunity to take Jeremy Roenick or Rod Brind'Amour or Teemu Selanne with the sixth overall pick, instead selecting Scott Pearson, a player who would suit up for only 63 games in Toronto. Stellick's tenure with the Maple Leafs turned out to be short-lived. After a disastrous season that saw the club post a record of 28-46-6, Stellick resigned from his position, citing interference from Toronto's cantankerous and meddling octogenarian owner, Harold Ballard. Twenty-eight years later, on May 5, 2016, the Arizona Coyotes made history when the club hired 26-year-old John Chayka as its general manager, making him not only the youngest GM in NHL history but also the youngest in the history of major league sports. Although Chayka's tenure with the Coyotes has already surpassed Stellick's time with the Maple Leafs, only time will tell what kind of long-term impact the former will have on his franchise.

# DEREK PLANTE PLAYS OVERTIME HERO, 1997

You rarely get to play the part of playoff hero twice in one game, but that's exactly what Buffalo's Derek Plante got to do on April 29, 1997. It was Game 7 of the Eastern Conference quarter-final series between the Sabres and the Senators. It was Ottawa's first time in the playoffs since the NHL returned to the nation's capital a few years earlier, and the Sens had pushed the much higher-seeded Buffalo team to the brink. After 40 minutes of play, the game was knotted at 1-1. Within 45 seconds of puck drop in the third period, Ottawa defenceman Wade Redden scored a goal to take the lead. Buffalo was on the ropes. They needed to get on the board again if they hoped to keep their playoff dreams alive.

Less than six minutes later, Derek Plante emerged as the unlikely hero. He scored the equalizer to put Ottawa into a tailspin. For the remainder of the period, the Senators' play cratered as the Sabres out-shot them by nearly three to one. But Ottawa held on to send the game into overtime. Plante's goal had already prolonged his team's season, but he was not done yet. At 5:24 into sudden death, Plante wired a hard slapshot that just bounced off Senators goaltender Ron Tugnutt's glove and trickled into the net. While Tugnutt covered his face mask with his hands in disappointment, the Sabres' bench rejoiced. Plante, once again the hero, became the first player in NHL history to score the third-period tying goal and the overtime winner in a Game 7. When he reflected on his performance after the game, he said, "You can't score a bigger goal unless you win the Stanley Cup."

# APRIL 30
## THE COMEBACK KINGS, 2014

April is full of incredible comeback moments in NHL history. From the Leafs rallying to win the Stanley Cup in 1942 to the Miracle on Manchester 40 years later, this month highlights the resiliency and perseverance of NHL teams in high-pressure situations. As a result, there's no better way to end this chapter than with the Kings' triumphant victory over the Sharks on April 30, 2014.

After capturing the first three games of the series, San Jose needed just one more win to move on to the next round. The Kings, however, weren't ready to surrender. They'd win the next three straight contests to push the series to a decisive Game 7 finale. Los Angeles, not that far removed from its first Stanley Cup just two years earlier, proved to be insurmountable for San Jose. Despite being outshot, the Kings vanquished the Sharks 5-1 and eliminated them from the playoffs, becoming the fourth team in NHL history to win a series after losing the first three games. For Los Angeles forwards Mike Richards and Jeff Carter, it was a familiar experience. They were both part of the Philadelphia Flyers team that rallied from a three game-deficit against the Boston Bruins in 2010, making them the first two players in NHL history to be a part of two teams that won the final four games of a series. While both players came up short in 2010 — the Flyers would end up losing to the Blackhawks in the Stanley Cup Final — history did not follow a similar pattern four years later. Instead, the Kings captured their second championship in three years.

MAY

MAY 1

# JEAN BELIVEAU WINS FIRST CONN SMYTHE, 1965

As the clock ticked down in the seventh game of the Stanley Cup Final, anxious patrons at the Montreal Forum began ripping up newspapers and tossing the shreds into the air like confetti. Elsewhere, men lifted their fedoras off their heads and flung them from their seats with reckless abandon. It was a familiar scene; the Canadiens were about to win the Stanley Cup. After team captain Jean Beliveau opened the scoring just 14 seconds into the game, the Black Hawks were playing on borrowed time. Chicago threw everything they could at Canadiens goaltender Gump Worsley, but he stood on his head and turned in his second shutout of the series. When the final buzzer sounded, the crowd erupted into a raucous chorus of cheers.

The Canadiens had taken home their first championship in five years. When the Stanley Cup was brought out onto the ice, it conjured up memories of the five straight championships the team had won from 1956 to 1960, but another piece of hardware also accompanied the shimmering silver of Lord Stanley's mug. It was the Conn Smythe Trophy. Presented for the first time in league history, it was to honour the playoffs' most valuable player. Without hesitation, the trophy was presented to the Montreal captain. There couldn't have been a better inaugural winner. The six-foot-three Beliveau, who was known for his effortless skating, superb defensive skills, and tireless commitment to the game, was unquestionably the best performer of the post-season that year, particularly when it mattered most. Le Gros Bill scored five goals in the Stanley Cup Final to lead his team to yet another championship. For his efforts, Beliveau not only received the Conn Smythe but also filled his pockets with a $1,000 cheque for capturing the new trophy.

MAY | 145

## MAY 2
# THE OLD LEAFS, 1967

ntering the 1966–67 regular season, no one predicted the Maple Leafs would win the Stanley Cup. Many believed the team's best days had passed, and the fact that many of the players on the roster were well into their 30s only furthered this notion. As the club slumped through a 10-game losing streak during the winter, critics had all but written them off. Even when Toronto rebounded and put together a 10-game undefeated streak, many believed it was too little too late. That post-season, however, the Maple Leafs' old-timers proved they still had some fight left in them. After upsetting the first-place Chicago Black Hawks in the semifinals — a stacked team that boasted the likes of Bobby Hull, Stan Mikita, and Glenn Hall — hockey's elder statesmen went on to defeat the defending Stanley Cup champions, the Montreal Canadiens, to win it all on May 2, 1967.

In doing so, the Maple Leafs became the first team in league history with an average age of 30 or older to win the Stanley Cup. The final scoring sequence of that game really reveals the depth of age the team was carrying. With just 55 seconds remaining, Toronto's 41-year-old Allan Stanley won the faceoff draw and passed the puck to 39-year-old Red Kelly. From there, the veteran defenceman floated the puck up to 31-year-old Bob Pulford, who then dealt it to 36-year-old captain George Armstrong. With Montreal's net empty, Armstrong added an insurance goal to seal the deal. At the other end of the ice, 37-year-old goaltender Terry Sawchuk, who had split the series with 42-year-old Johnny Bower, celebrated the tally after stopping 40 shots that game. While the 1967 Maple Leafs' Stanley Cup is often pointed to as the last time the franchise won a championship, it's a poignant reminder that age is sometimes just a number.

# MAY 3
# MARTIN "THE ELIMINATOR" GELINAS, 2004

Martin Gelinas is often remembered as one of the players involved in the seismic trade that sent Wayne Gretzky to the Kings. Gelinas, who had been drafted in June 1988 by Los Angeles, was part of the package that was sent back to Edmonton, along with Jimmy Carson, three first-round draft picks, and $15 million. While Gelinas was just a footnote in that trade, he made NHL history of his own on May 3, 2004, when he became the first player ever to end three playoff series with overtime goals. In 2002, in Game 6 of the Eastern Conference final, as a member of the Carolina Hurricanes, he scored the series-clinching goal over the Maple Leafs in sudden death. The next year, Gelinas signed as a free agent with the Calgary Flames, but the team failed to qualify for the post-season. When his new team returned to the playoffs in 2004, he showed that perhaps his overtime heroics two years earlier were not a fluke.

During Calgary's opening series against Vancouver, the left winger finished the Canucks off with an overtime dagger in Game 7. As the Flames squared off against the Presidents' Trophy–winning Red Wings in the next round, nobody gave them much of a chance. Beating the team with the best regular-season record would be a tall order, even for a squad with the seemingly magical overtime powers of Martin Gelinas. Sure enough, in the sixth game of the series, he struck again. With less than two minutes remaining in the first overtime, Gelinas scored to eliminate Detroit. When the Flames went on to face the Sharks in the Western Conference final, he continued to come through in the clutch. Although not an overtime marker, he scored the game-winning goal that sent the Flames to the Stanley Cup Final, becoming the second player in NHL history to score the winning goal in three series-clinching games in one playoff year. It was rather fitting that, for his efforts, Gelinas earned the nickname the Eliminator.

MAY 4

## THE NHL BUYS THE WESTERN
## HOCKEY LEAGUE, 1926

The face of professional hockey in North America changed dramatically on May 4, 1926, when the National Hockey League purchased the contracts of all the players in the Western Hockey League (WHL). Founded five years earlier as the Western Canada Hockey League — later renamed the WHL — it was the only game in town for professional hockey on the prairies. As the league developed, its annual winners would square off against the champions of the Pacific Coast Hockey Association for the rights to challenge the NHL for the Stanley Cup. In 1925, the WCHL's Victoria Cougars actually defeated the Montreal Canadiens to win hockey's ultimate prize. As a result, when the league closed its doors the following year, this made the Cougars the last non-NHL club to win the Stanley Cup.

When the National Hockey League absorbed the WHL, it changed not only the competition for the Stanley Cup but also the hockey landscape in general. The biggest benefactors of the takeover would be the NHL's new teams in Detroit, Chicago, and New York, set to join the league the following year. Players from the Victoria squad were absorbed by Detroit, which influenced not only the makeup of the roster but also the identity of the team; it adopted the Cougars as its initial name. Elsewhere, many of the players from the WHL's Portland Rosebuds filled the ranks that would make up the Chicago Black Hawks. Although it was initially reported by the *New York Times* that the newly minted club from the Big Apple, the Rangers, had purchased the Saskatoon Sheiks, it never came to pass. Nevertheless, while the other expansion teams benefitted from the disbanding of the hockey circuit on the prairies, the Rangers did especially well. They won the Stanley Cup in just their second season in the league.

## MAY 5
# THE FLYERS BEAT THE RANGERS, 1974

After a hard-fought seven-game series that included a record-setting 405 penalty minutes, the Philadelphia Flyers had accomplished something that had eluded all of the league's other modern expansion teams: they had defeated an Original Six team in the post-season. Not only that, the victory also marked the first time an expansion team reached the Stanley Cup Final by beating an established team. When the six new clubs joined the NHL in 1967–68, they competed within their own division during the playoffs. After three straight years of a non-competitive Stanley Cup Final, which saw the St. Louis Blues get swept each time, the NHL changed course and altered its playoff format in 1971. While this improved the quality of play in the final showdown of the post-season, the league's expansion clubs still struggled and failed to make an appearance beyond the opening round of the quarter-finals.

But on May 5, 1974, all that changed. The Flyers, known throughout the hockey world as the Broad Street Bullies for their physicality, were a lethal team because, in addition to their thumping style of play, they also had tremendous skill up front in Bobby Clarke, who could play the game both ways. As a result, the Flyers' unconventional mixture of brutality and finesse in concert with the superb goaltending of Bernie Parent proved too much for the Rangers. The Blueshirts once again faltered in the post-season — they had last won the Stanley Cup in 1940 — bowing out in the seventh game of the semifinals. The Bullies went on to face the Big Bad Bruins for the championship and would eliminate Boston in six games, becoming the first modern expansion team to win the Stanley Cup.

## MAY 6
# THE WHALERS' EXODUS, 1997

On May 6, 1997, the horns of the "Brass Bonanza" fell silent. That day signalled the end of the NHL's era in Hartford and sounded the final note on the tune that was the Whalers' long-time theme song. After years of struggling as one of the league's small-market teams, the Whalers' ownership group announced that the franchise would be relocating to Raleigh, North Carolina, where it would be rebranded as the Carolina Hurricanes. The team would eventually discard not only its familiar green, blue, and silver colour scheme when it crossed state lines but also the popular theme song.

Dating back to its World Hockey Association days, the Whalers adopted the song, arranged by Jack Say, as a way to liven up the atmosphere at the Hartford Civic Center. It immediately became a fan favourite and one of the team's hallmarks throughout the league. It wasn't always a hit with everybody, though. During his tenure as general manager in Hartford, Brian Burke placed a moratorium on the song, explaining he felt it was an embarrassment to the team and players, much to the dismay of fans. Not all the players shared his sentiment. Pat Verbeek, who played for the Whalers for six seasons, looks back on the song with great memories. "You know, I did like it. I think every team has to have their thing, and that was kind of the Hartford Whaler's thing," he later recalled. After Burke left office in 1993, the tune was resurrected and the tradition continued until the Whalers were harpooned four years later. While there's always the possibility that the NHL could return to Connecticut in the future, "Brass Bonanza" will remain one of the Whalers' greatest legacies.

# GRETZKY'S GOAL-SCORING RECORD, 1993

As a member of the Los Angeles Kings, Wayne Gretzky made NHL playoff history twice on May 7, 1993. With the Kings leading the Canucks 4-2 in the third period of Game 3 of the Smythe Division final, the Great One buried his fifth goal of the post-season, increasing his team's lead to three. The tally didn't simply put the game out of reach for Vancouver; it also notched another NHL record for Gretzky. That goal happened to be his 100th career post-season marker, making him the first player in league history to reach the milestone.

More than that, after the Canucks scored twice in a futile rally, he was credited with the game-winning goal, giving him 19 game-winners in the playoffs, vaulting him ahead of Maurice Richard for the all-time record. As the clock ticked down, Gretzky added another marker with just one second remaining. He'd go on to score 10 more goals as Los Angeles advanced to the Stanley Cup Final. They would be his last as a King. Gretzky would pick up 12 more goals with the St. Louis Blues and New York Rangers, in his final two post-season appearances, to bring his career total up to 122, a league record that is unlikely to be broken. When Gretzky retired in 1999, he also held the all-time record for most game-winning goals in the playoffs at 24, but that mark was later matched by Brett Hull.

# BLACK HAWKS AND CANADIENS COMBINE FOR 15 GOALS, 1973

The Black Hawks and Canadiens put on a Stanley Cup Final offensive performance for the ages on May 8, 1973. With their championship dreams on the line, Chicago knew what was at stake. Montreal, meanwhile, was hoping to finish off their opponents on home ice and hoist the Stanley Cup in front of their fans. Those competing aims led to an offensive flurry that saw the teams combine for 15 goals, setting a new NHL playoff record at the time for most goals in a game. After Montreal's Frank Mahovlich opened the scoring less than three minutes into the first period, the Black Hawks remained calm and waited for their chances. They scored two quick goals near the halfway mark, but the Canadiens responded and the teams headed into intermission tied at two apiece.

The second period started off with a bang. Montreal's Claude Larose scored within the first minute, but Chicago answered back to knot it up again. The volley continued two more times as the clubs traded goals back and forth. The Black Hawks broke the deadlock for good when they scored two unanswered goals to close out the period. When the teams adjourned to their respective dressing rooms, they had combined for eight goals that period, an NHL record at the time. In the final frame, Montreal added one more goal to reduce Chicago's lead to one, but the Black Hawks scored two more to prolong their season and their slim chances of winning the Stanley Cup. But the Canadiens would have the last laugh. They would win the next contest to capture their second championship in three years. Since then, teams have combined for more goals in a playoff game, but as far as Stanley Cup Final games go, no teams have matched or surpassed what the Black Hawks and Canadiens did in 1973.

# MAY 9
## LUPUL LIGHTS THE LAMP, 2006

verything went Joffrey Lupul's way on May 9, 2006. Of the six shots he took that night, only a couple failed to find the back of the net. The opportunistic winger managed to score all four of Anaheim's goals, including the winner in overtime, in the third game of the Ducks' playoff series against the Avalanche, a feat that had never been accomplished in NHL post-season history. Lupul, who had already scored a pair of goals in the opening two games of that series, was certainly not expecting that type of production. "I don't know if I'd ever dream of four goals in a playoff game, including an overtime winner," he told the *Globe and Mail* following the game.

Lupul did all the heavy lifting that night, and his teammates certainly noticed. Teemu Selanne called it an incredible performance and even used it to motivate his teammates by saying Lupul and his linemates single-handedly won the game for Anaheim. "The rest of us played a pretty average game," he was quoted as saying. Selanne wasn't wrong. Next to an individual four-goal performance, even the efforts from a future Hall of Famer would seem mediocre by comparison. Lupul would score two more goals that post-season before the Ducks were eliminated by the Oilers. He would make just three more playoff appearances over the next decade, scoring just eight goals in 30 games. While Lupul was never able to recapture the magic he found that night with Anaheim, he would cherish the memory of that game. "I'll remember this as long as I live," he said.

## MAY 10
# BOBBY ORR LEAPS, 1970

t is the most iconic image in hockey history. Just as Bobby Orr scored the Stanley Cup–winning goal, on May 10, 1970, Blues defenceman Noel Picard tripped him, but it was too little too late. Orr had already put the puck past goaltender Glenn Hall, and as Picard's stick lifted Orr's feet into the air, he embraced the moment he had been waiting for his whole life. In that instant, he knew his Boston Bruins had become Stanley Cup champions. As he took flight, rather than letting gravity run its course, Orr resisted the forces that would inevitably bring him back down to earth. Instead, he jubilantly lifted his arms up in victorious celebration, and for a second, you could swear he was flying.

But before Orr hit the ice and was mobbed by his teammates, the flashbulb and shutter of Ray Lussier's camera captured the sequence and immortalized it. The image of Orr, the greatest defenceman of all time, soaring through the air has been engrained into our collective hockey memory. Even if you are too young to have experienced the moment first-hand, it has become something that transcends generations. That photograph is so perfect it almost makes you forget the beautiful symbolism behind the goal. Bobby Orr, who wore number four, scored Boston's fourth goal of the game, in the fourth game of the Stanley Cup Final, in the fourth period (overtime), to give the Bruins their fourth championship in franchise history. All the while being tripped by Noel Picard, who also wore number four.

# MAY 11
# TOE BLAKE'S LAST STANLEY CUP, 1968

anadiens head coach Toe Blake went out on top. After winning his eighth Stanley Cup behind Montreal's bench on May 11, 1968, he announced his retirement. Not long after the Canadiens defeated the Blues to win their third championship in four years, Blake made it clear he had coached his last team. Although he had talked about hanging it up in the past after previous victories, this time he meant it. In fact, when his retirement was reported in the newspapers the following day, Blake had mentioned that, before the outcome of the post-season was decided, he had already informed the Molson brothers, the owners of the Canadiens, that he was done. For Blake, it was time. "The tension is just too much. It gets tougher every year," he told reporters.

If anyone knew about post-season tension, it was Blake. During his 13 years as Montreal's coach, his team never failed to qualify for the playoffs and won the Stanley Cup eight times, including five consecutive championships from 1956 to 1960, a feat that is unlikely to ever be matched. When he walked away from the bench, Blake had a sterling coaching record of 500-255-159, and to this day he remains the winningest coach in Montreal Canadiens history. While many NHL coaches have since racked up more wins than Blake, only Scotty Bowman has more Stanley Cups. Bowman, who was actually Blake's protege before he caught his big-league break with the Blues, would go on to capture nine Stanley Cups with the Canadiens, Penguins, and Red Wings, surpassing his mentor's mark in 2002. Similarly, Bowman retired from coaching on the heels of his final championship in Detroit. While Bowman continued to remain active in hockey, taking on executive positions and winning three more championships in a front-office position with the Chicago Blackhawks, Blake took a different route. When he announced his retirement plans, Blake said he would be tending to the eponymous bar he owned in Montreal.

# THE MONDAY NIGHT MIRACLE, 1986

May 12, 1986, was just another manic Monday. While the Flames wished it were Sunday, it was nothing short of a fun day for the Blues. Heading into the sixth game of the Campbell Conference final at St. Louis Arena, the Flames had the opportunity to punch their ticket to the championship round. If successful, it would mark the first time a Calgary hockey team would compete for the Stanley Cup since the Tigers took on the Canadiens in 1924, and after 40 minutes of play, the Flames had built a 4-1 lead. By this point in the playoffs, St. Louis had already exceeded expectations. Although they had knocked off the North Stars and Maple Leafs in their previous matchups, they were still heavy underdogs, and no one gave them a fighting chance against the Flames.

While the St. Louis faithful never doubted their hard-working team, it seemed they were playing on borrowed time. But the Blues weren't ready to quit. Six minutes into the final frame, Doug Wickenheiser wired a 35-foot slapshot past goaltender Mike Vernon to cut the deficit in half. Although the Flames' Joe Mullen, who had spent the last five years with St. Louis, promptly scored to widen his team's lead again, Blues captain Brian Sutter quickly returned fire. As the Blues continued to battle back, the dogged determination that had become the team's hallmark that post-season seemed destined to spark a miraculous comeback. After Greg Paslawski scored with less than five minutes to play, the Blues furiously searched for the equalizer. With just over a minute remaining, Paslawski stripped the puck from Flames defenceman Jamie Macoun and wired it past Vernon to tie the game. As the game continued into overtime, St. Louis's last-ditch effort culminated with Wickenheiser scoring at the halfway point to force a decisive seventh game. Although St. Louis was ultimately eliminated two days later, the Monday Night Miracle still lives on in Blues' lore.

# MAY 13
## IT WAS 4-1, 2013

n 2013, the Maple Leafs qualified for the playoffs for the first time since 2004. After years of frustration, fans welcomed a return to the post-season, even if it was expected to be a brief appearance. Toronto was squaring off against the Bruins, a team that had won the Stanley Cup in 2011 and was in position to challenge for another championship. The Maple Leafs, on the other hand, had just squeaked into the playoffs in a lockout-shortened season of play. As a result, with the prognosticators handing the series to Boston, many Maple Leafs fans, myself included, were quick not to get their hopes up. Then everything changed. After falling behind 3-1 in the series, Toronto stormed back to win two straight nail-biting games in regulation to force a seventh game. The Maple Leafs seemed to be on the cusp of the type of comeback the franchise hadn't experienced since 1942. Nevertheless, expectations remained low heading into that fateful game. This was, after all, the Maple Leafs — a franchise mired in futility and one that hadn't won a championship since 1967.

While fans prepared for the worst, on May 13, 2013, little did they know that whatever scenarios they conjured up in their minds paled in comparison to the events that would transpire. Early in the third period, the Maple Leafs had a three-goal lead. They were actually going to pull it off, or so we thought. With less than 10 minutes remaining in regulation, Nathan Horton scored a goal that triggered a Bruins comeback. After a series of Toronto miscues and defensive lapses, Boston scored twice in 31 seconds to tie the game in the dying minutes. How could this have happened? It was 4-1! It was absolutely gut-wrenching. Although there was still overtime to be played, it felt like the game was already over. Given the collapse and how deflated the players appeared as they adjourned for intermission, it seemed unlikely they would be able to salvage a win. Sure enough, six minutes into sudden death, Boston's Patrice Bergeron put the Maple Leafs out of their misery and ended the game.

# PAUL COFFEY ASSISTS HIS TEAM, 1985

n a contest in which Wayne Gretzky had nearly half as many shots as the entire Black Hawks, the Great One was not the main storyline. The hero of the game on May 14, 1985, was actually Oilers defenceman Paul Coffey, who powered his team to a 10-5 victory over Chicago in Game 5 of the Campbell Conference final with his impeccable puck-dishing skills. Coffey assisted on half his club's goals, establishing a new league record for most assists by a defenceman in a playoff game. In addition, with a goal in the final frame, he finished the game with six points, setting another record for most points by a blueliner in a post-season contest.

Besides his contributions to the game's outcome, Coffey also tied a couple of other NHL records, moving him into some pretty illustrious company. His third-period goal, his ninth of the playoffs, tied the mark set by Bobby Orr in 1970. Moreover, his six points that evening also brought his post-season total up to 25, matching Denis Potvin's output in 1981. As the playoffs continued, Coffey added to those records. Although the most important outcome for him that season was that his team won back-to-back championships, Coffey carved his name into the record books in nearly every offensive category for defencemen. He finished that post-season with 12 goals, 25 assists, and 37 points. Along with his individual game performance, no other defenceman in league history has yet to match or equal those records.

# THE BLACK HAWKS TRADE ESPOSITO, 1967

n advance of the NHL's expansion draft in 1967, the Bruins and Black Hawks shook up their rosters with a seismic trade that would reverberate for decades. On May 15, 1967, Boston acquired centres Phil Esposito and Fred Stanfield and winger Ken Hodge from Chicago in exchange for blueliner Gilles Marotte, centre Pit Martin, and minor-league goaltender Jack Norris. At the time, Esposito was 25 years old, and although he had tied for seventh place in league scoring that season, the narrative behind the transaction focused on how the Bruins were hoping to get stronger and bigger up front. To do that, they had to give up hard-hitting defenceman Marotte. When the *Globe and Mail* reported on the trade, Boston's GM Milt Schmidt lamented the departure of his rearguard. "We gained needed strength up front as well as size. We hated to give up Marotte, a promising, tough young defenceman, but we had to give up something to get what we wanted," he said. The Bruins already had their blueliner of the future in Bobby Orr, so giving up Marotte to shore up their forward positions was a logical move.

As the next season unfolded, it became clear that the trade gave the Bruins much more than just size and strength. In Boston, Esposito took his game to a new level. After scoring 84 points in his first year in black and gold, the Sault Ste. Marie, Ontario, native became the first player in NHL history to score 100 points in a season, capturing his first Art Ross Trophy. Esposito established himself as one of the league's most formidable offensive players, winning the Art Ross four straight years while he and Orr terrorized opposing teams. Together, the tandem was the driving force behind Boston's two Stanley Cups in the 1970s. Meanwhile, in Chicago, although Pit Martin made significant contributions to the Black Hawks, including assuming the team's captaincy, Gilles Marotte stuck around for only three years before he was traded to the Kings. In the end, it proved to be one of the most lopsided trades in NHL history.

# THE RIVERTON RIFLE WINS THE CONN SMYTHE, 1976

Reggie Leach won the Conn Smythe Trophy, but he would have preferred the Stanley Cup. On May 16, 1976, the Flyers sniper was selected as the playoffs' most valuable player despite the fact his team was swept by the Canadiens in the championship round. Although Philadelphia came up short that post-season, Leach did not. The Riverton, Manitoba, native was one of the premier scorers of his era. Known for his incredible shot and accuracy, it's not surprising they called him Rifle. After scoring 61 goals in the regular season and establishing a new franchise record, Leach continued to find the back of the net in the post-season. On May 6, he scored five goals in a game against the Bruins, matching a league record that had originally been set by Maurice "Rocket" Richard in 1944 and equalled that post-season by Toronto's Darryl Sittler. As the Flyers advanced to the Stanley Cup Final, Leach's goal-scoring campaign was unparalleled.

In 16 games that post-season, he scored 19 goals, nearly a third of his entire team's production. As a result, Leach was presented the Conn Smythe and is still the only non-goaltender to win the award as the member of a losing team. Since then, no other player has surpassed Leach's post-season goal-scoring output. Although Jari Kurri scored 19 goals in 1985, it's worth noting that he needed two more games to do it. Despite Leach's incredible achievements, those individual accolades seemed hollow without the Stanley Cup. In 2016, he told the author, "It's nice to have these awards, but I don't think it means very much at [that] moment unless you've won the Stanley Cup." Nevertheless, with more than four decades now between him and that stellar performance, Leach has had time to reflect on what he accomplished. "I think that after you're out of hockey and you reflect back on a lot of stuff, you think 'My God, I won the Conn Smythe Trophy and I'm still the only forward from a losing club to win it,' but in the moment, you don't really think of that stuff."

# DINO CICCARELLI SETS ROOKIE SCORING RECORD, 1981

After setting the NHL rookie playoff scoring record on May 17, 1981, with his 21st point of the post-season, it should have been Dino Ciccarelli's night. The 21-year-old's feat, however, was overshadowed by the fact his North Stars had lost their third straight game to the Islanders in the Stanley Cup Final. For most, the writing was on the wall. Minnesota was going to have to wish upon a star if it had any hope of making a comeback. Given the fact that the Maple Leafs were the only team in league history to pull it off in the championship round, things didn't look so good. Nevertheless, while the odds were against the North Stars, in the meantime they had something worth celebrating. Although Ciccarelli established his record in a losing effort to the Islanders, it was still something for him to be proud of. "I'm really happy, personally, with my play in the playoffs," he told reporters after the game.

His performance surpassed the 20-point mark set just two years earlier by the Rangers' Don Maloney, who also happened to set his benchmark in a series against the Islanders. Although Ciccarelli was pleased about carving his name into the record books, he knew there was much more at stake as his team fought for their playoff lives. "I'd rather have my name on the Cup," he said. The dynamic rookie's performance may have propelled Minnesota to stave off elimination in the next game, but it wasn't enough. Ciccarelli and the North Stars would ultimately fall to the Islanders in Game Five on Long Island, forced to watch their opponents celebrate back-to-back championships. Since then, no one has surpassed Ciccarelli's mark. Philadelphia rookie Ville Leino matched his output in 2010, but he too fell short in capturing the ultimate prize, as the Blackhawks defeated his Flyers in the Stanley Cup Final. Most recently, Pittsburgh's Jake Guentzel also tied Ciccarelli's record in 2017, but he was on the winning side of history as the Penguins defeated the Predators to win their second straight championship.

## MAY 18

# BRIAN SKRUDLAND WASTES NO TIME, 1986

Deep into the 1986 post-season, Canadiens rookie Brian Skrudland was still searching for his first career playoff goal. He wouldn't have to wait too long once overtime commenced in Game 2 of the Stanley Cup Final against the Flames on May 18. Before you could even spell S-k-r-u-d-l-a-n-d, the upstart centre had found twine to end the game. Within nine seconds of puck drop, he and Mike McPhee found themselves streaking toward the Calgary net. With Flames defenceman Al MacInnis sprawled on the ice, McPhee made a nifty cross-ice pass to Skrudland, who promptly put it past an unprepared Mike Vernon. And just like that, the game was over. It was the fastest overtime goal in NHL playoff history, surpassing the previous mark of 11 seconds set by J.P. Parise of the Islanders in 1975.

Following the game, Skrudland attempted to capture the quick sequence in words. "I still hadn't seen the red light go on, but I knew the puck was in the net and it was just a great feeling," he told reporters. "I wouldn't have predicted this in 1,000 years," he was quoted in the *New York Times*. He elaborated that he "had good chances, but it was like I was playing with a rubber stick. I think that was the first time I'd gotten by one of their defencemen all night long." Skrudland not only made history with his speed but also became just the second NHL player to record his first playoff goal in overtime in the Stanley Cup Final. He'd score one more that post-season, in Montreal's championship-clinching game. Skrudland would actually break the 1-1 deadlock in the second period. The Canadiens would not give up the lead and went on to capture their first Stanley Cup in seven years.

## MAY 19
# EDMONTON WINS FIRST
# STANLEY CUP, 1984

n some ways, it was the passing of a torch. On May 19, 1984, the Oilers defeated the Islanders to win their first Stanley Cup. New York had been a powerhouse, winning their fourth straight championship after a bitter first encounter with Edmonton the previous year. The Oilers had been tapped as the team that would take the reins from the Islanders, but in 1983, they simply weren't ready. At the time, Edmonton played a free-wheeling, offensively oriented game that was colloquially known as "firewagon" hockey. While it was fun to watch, it lacked the more methodical and grinding defensive game clubs like the Islanders also had in their arsenal. So when the two teams first met in the Stanley Cup Final, these two versions of hockey collided.

It wasn't even close. The Islanders swept the Oilers in dominating fashion. The outcome was a revelation for superstar Wayne Gretzky. What stayed with him the most was not what he saw on the ice but what he caught a glimpse of as he and Kevin Lowe left the Coliseum. In his book *99: Stories of the Game*, Gretzky recalls walking past the Islanders' dressing room and noticing the team was not in a celebratory mood. "They were battered and bruised and had ice bags and heat packs all over their bodies. Meanwhile we were in great shape, ready to go another playoff round. Seeing them like that told us ... how hard the playoffs are, and how disciplined and focused you have to be. But to win the Stanley Cup, you have to take it to another level." For Gretzky, it was a turning point. The next year, the Oilers did indeed take their game to the next level. Although Edmonton could still seemingly score goals at will, the team clamped down defensively and stopped nearly everything the Islanders sent their way that series. While Gretzky continued to fill the net, the Oilers choked off their opponents and were able to pry away the Stanley Cup, a trophy the Islanders had judiciously held on to for four years. It was now time for a new dynasty to take shape in Edmonton.

## MAY 20
## FOG CLOGS FLYERS, 1975

The scene from the third game of the Stanley Cup Final series between the Flyers and Sabres was like something ripped from the pages of a horror novel. Early in the matchup, a bat floated through the Memorial Auditorium in Buffalo. As its flight path veered toward the faceoff circle, the Sabres' Jim Lorentz whacked it out of the air with his stick. Not long after the winged creature dropped to the ice with a thud, a fog rolled in. As the mist infiltrated the arena and hovered over the playing surface, you can't blame the superstitious fans for thinking Lorentz had inadvertently summoned a terrible demon. While the ghoulish narrative — that Lorentz had actually killed a vampire that, with its last dying breath, ushered in an evil curse, forever damning the Sabres franchise — is compelling, there's a more logical explanation.

That evening, May 20, 1975, the high temperatures in Buffalo and the humidity inside the Auditorium combined to create the fog. The opaque mist hung above the ice like pea soup. It was so thick that referee Lloyd Gilmour was forced to halt the action at least 12 times throughout the course of the game. When play was suspended, he even went as far as instructing the players to leisurely skate around the rink with the hopes they'd stir up the air and dissipate the fog. Sabres defenceman Jerry "King Kong" Korab felt the conditions were brutal. "With the heat so bad, plus the fog, it was hard to breathe," he told reporters after the game. For the masked goaltenders, it was a nightmare. The fog impaired their vision further as they attempted to track the puck and the shadowy figures that appeared and vanished like apparitions in the night. Although the Sabres ended up winning that game in sudden death, legend has it there are some who believe Lorentz's actions have cursed the team. After all, the Flyers went on to win the Stanley Cup that year, while the Buffalo franchise has yet to win a championship.

## MAY 21
# CANADIENS WIN FOURTH STRAIGHT CUP, 1979

O
n the evening before the 1979 Canadian national election, Prime Minister Pierre Elliot Trudeau was not nervously pacing around 24 Sussex Drive. In fact, he wasn't even in Ottawa. He was in Montreal, at the Forum, to watch the Canadiens host the Rangers in Game 5 of the Stanley Cup Final. The prime minister's entrance drew a raucous chorus of cheers from the crowd, and later in the game, when he caught a puck that had been deflected his way, he received another warm ovation. Perhaps Trudeau had been looking to take his mind off the upcoming polls by attending the game, but it's just as likely he, along with the 18,000 other patrons, was there in the hopes of witnessing Montreal win its fourth straight championship. Although the Habs had already won five Stanley Cups that decade, none of them were captured before a home crowd. The last time the Canadiens had hoisted Lord Stanley's silverware in the Forum was back in 1968 when Jean Beliveau was still team captain. With the Canadiens leading the series three games to one, the stage was set for a brilliant homecoming on the evening of May 21, 1979.

Meanwhile, the Rangers, who hadn't won a Stanley Cup since 1940, were simply hoping to shift the series back to Madison Square Garden. The Canadiens and Bob Gainey, however, proved to be too much for New York, and they handily dispatched the Rangers 4-1. Gainey, who had proven himself to be a workhorse on both sides of the puck throughout the playoffs, was awarded the Conn Smythe for his tireless efforts. While the Canadiens capped off the decade with the 22nd Stanley Cup in franchise history, Trudeau was not so lucky. When Canadians headed to the polls the next day, they voted to elect Joe Clark and the Progressive Conservatives. But that wasn't the last of Trudeau as he would return to power the following year and hold the Prime Minister's Office until he retired from politics in 1984.

## MAY 22

# DOMINIK HASEK TALLIES AN OVERTIME ASSIST, 2002

ominik Hasek wasn't too busy on May 22, 2002. Through three periods of regulation and nearly 13 minutes of overtime, the Red Wings goaltender faced only 21 shots. Meanwhile, his team peppered Avalanche netminder Patrick Roy with 42 shots, two of which snuck by him. Although Hasek's workload paled in comparison to his counterpart's, he still remained sharp, making some critical saves early in sudden death. His most brilliant play, however, was not in the crease. Instead, Hasek cleared a loose puck to Steve Yzerman at centre ice, where the Red Wings captain delivered it to defenceman Fredrik Olausson, who then deposited it into the back of the Colorado net to win the game. For his efforts, Hasek became the first goaltender in NHL playoff history to register an assist on an overtime goal.

While that would have been the headline on most nights, Olausson stole the show. The Swedish blueliner, who was normally overshadowed by defensive partner Nicklas Lidstrom, was the talk of the town because it was his first playoff goal in more than a decade. The last time Olausson scored in the post-season, it was as a member of the Winnipeg Jets against the Vancouver Canucks on April 18, 1992. In his assessment of his overtime dagger, Olausson was pretty modest. "The defence backed off and I just shot it. It might have surprised Patrick a little bit," he told reporters. The Red Wings went on to eliminate the Avalanche in seven games to face the Carolina Hurricanes in the Stanley Cup Final. Hasek wouldn't pick up another point that post-season and that proved to be Olausson's last NHL playoff goal, but by June 13 they would both be Stanley Cup champions.

# THE HOWES SIGN WITH
# THE WHALERS, 1977

After hanging up his NHL skates in 1971, Gordie Howe was lured out of retirement a few years later by the opportunity to play with his sons Mark and Marty for the Houston Aeros of the World Hockey Association. Although Gordie had a tough transition to the new league, having taken three years off, he found his stride in Houston and compiled 100 points in his first season to win the league's most valuable player award. Howe and the Aeros would capture the first of back-to-back Avco World Trophies that year. Despite the family's early success in Houston, by 1977 the situation had significantly changed. While the on-ice results remained the same, the team's financial position worsened and it struggled to pay many of its players.

As a result, on May 23, 1977, the Howes were on the move to New England, with Gordie, Mark, and Marty signing with the Whalers of the WHA. Before that deal was inked, however, another possibility could have brought the Howes into the NHL sooner. One of the offers Colleen Howe, the family's business manager, fielded was from the Bruins. Boston, which had drafted Mark 25th overall in 1974, was keen on signing him and was willing to make brother Marty and father Gordie a part of the deal if they were able to pry their NHL rights from the Red Wings. The deal was apparently so close to being done that Bruins general manager Harry Sinden was surprised when he learned the Howes had signed with the Whalers. He told the *New York Times*, "I'm surprised Colleen Howe didn't call me and tell me this was happening." In the end, it came down to family matters. Although Gordie said it wasn't a necessity that all three went to the same club, it was something they wanted to continue. Two years later, when the Whalers were one of the four WHA teams that joined the NHL, with his two sons in tow, Gordie returned to the league where it all started.

# THE NIGHT THE LIGHTS WENT OUT IN BOSTON, 1988

t was Boston's best effort in their Stanley Cup Final against Edmonton ... and then the lights went out. On May 24, 1988, facing elimination, the Bruins were playing a superb game against the Oilers when a power failure struck the Boston Garden with less than five minutes to go in the second period. With the matchup tied at three, Edmonton was hoping to break the deadlock and capture its fourth Stanley Cup of the decade, while Boston was just looking to extend the series. The scene that evening was similar to the conditions the Sabres and Flyers had played in 13 years earlier. Before the arena darkened, fog filtered into the Gardens, and referee Denis Morel, taking a page out of Lloyd Gilmour's book, asked that the players skate around the rink in an effort to dispel the mist. But unlike the situation in Buffalo, the steamy weather in Boston not only wreaked havoc with the playing surface but also blew out the electricity.

After heated deliberations between the officials and top brass from both clubs, it was agreed the game would be suspended and replayed in its entirety if necessary. All the statistics from the contest, such as points and saves, were logged in the NHL's record books, but it would be as if the game never happened. The contingency was that, if the series became deadlocked at 3-3, the lost fourth game would be replayed as the seventh and deciding game in the series, which meant Boston would end up with home ice for the pivotal conclusion, assuming they got that far. The Oilers, however, quickly dispelled any plans of going back to Massachusetts. When the series shifted to Edmonton for the next game, the Oilers doubled up the Bruins 6-3 to win their fourth Stanley Cup in franchise history.

## MAY 25
# MESSIER'S GUARANTEE, 1994

With the Rangers facing elimination by the Devils in the Eastern Conference final, captain Mark Messier had a few choice words for reporters heading into that contest. "We know we are going to go in there and win Game 6 and bring it back to the Garden," he said. All eyes were now on Messier to back up his guarantee, and he certainly did not disappoint. Trailing by two goals late in the second period, the Rangers captain ignited a comeback when he set up Alexei Kovalev to pull the Blueshirts within one. When the puck dropped for the final frame, it was all Messier. He scored three goals, including the game-winner, to put his money where his mouth was and extend the series. After the game, his teammates praised his confidence. "Mark set a great example of not panicking. He's a great student of the game. He knows strategy, but more important, he knows the psychology of the team. He has his finger on the pulse of everybody in here. He can lead everybody," said Rangers goaltender Mike Richter.

For Messier, he didn't put much stock in his statement but instead focused on his play on the ice. "It wasn't about being cocky or arrogant. It was one of those things you have to do to get the team to believe in itself," he reflected afterward. Even his opponents were in awe of his performance. "He's the best clutch player," said Devils forward Bernie Nicholls. While many have focused on Messier's assertion, his three-goal effort is what really made his words a guarantee. Messier knew what needed to be said to motivate his teammates, but more important he knew what had to be done. His assurance and subsequent performance that game cemented his place as one of the game's greatest leaders. Those words, however, would have been hollow without hockey's ultimate prize. Fortunately for Messier and the Rangers, they ended up beating the Devils in Game 7 to punch their ticket to the Stanley Cup Final, where they went on to defeat the Vancouver Canucks to capture the club's first championship since 1940.

## MAY 26
# EDMONTON SAYS CHEESE, 1988

By 1988, the Oilers winning the Stanley Cup had become a familiar sight. But on May 26, the scene looked a little different. It was the club's fourth championship of the decade, and while winning never gets old, Wayne Gretzky wanted to make sure they savoured the moment. Following previous championships, the team had allowed spectators to come out onto the ice to celebrate the victory. This time around, the Edmonton captain wanted just the team on the ice should they defeat Boston that night. The Great One hadn't made his plans known, but he had something up his sleeve. When the Oilers completed the sweep against the Bruins that evening, the usual laps around the ice with Lord Stanley's mug followed, but Gretzky had other plans. Amid the chaotic celebratory hooting and hollering from his teammates, trainers, equipment staff, and managers, Gretzky grabbed the trophy and brought it to centre ice where he then began corralling the organization for a team picture.

Unbeknownst to most of the Oilers, Gretzky wanted to capture the moment the way other clubs in the 1950s and 1960s had taken team portraits with the Cup. In reflecting on that decision many years later with Sportsnet, Gretzky recalled how he felt it was such a poignant moment with just the team on the ice that it needed to be preserved with a photograph. "It has to do with the pictures that Kevin and I and Mark had cut out in 1980 of the teams in the '60s. We wanted to sort of get a picture to put with the pictures that we had hanging when we were first in the NHL," he said. While Gretzky and the Oilers may have revived an old custom from the Original Six era, they were the first team to pose for a picture with the Stanley Cup on the ice. Although they didn't know it at the time, Edmonton inaugurated a tradition that has become synonymous with the Stanley Cup.

# MATTEAU, MATTEAU, MATTEAU, 1994

ollowing Mark Messier's heroics from two days earlier, the Rangers were not yet out of the woods. They had forced a Game 7 against the Devils, but they'd still need another victory if they wanted a chance to exorcise their playoff demons. At the time, New York had the longest Stanley Cup drought in the league, having last won the trophy in 1940. In the intervening years, the Blueshirts made it to the Final three times but came up empty-handed in each visit. In fact, the last time the Rangers had a shot at Lord Stanley's silverware, it was 15 years earlier against the Montreal Canadiens. To say they weren't feeling the pressure was an understatement. And while Messier had delivered on his promise in Game 6, someone else would have to step up if the team hoped to keep its Stanley Cup dreams alive.

Enter Stephane Matteau. The left winger from Rouyn-Noranda, Quebec, had only recently joined the Rangers, after having been acquired from the Chicago Blackhawks just before the trade deadline that year. In 12 regular-season games with the Blueshirts, Matteau scored four goals and added another five through 15 games in the post-season. His biggest goal came on May 27, 1994. After New Jersey's Valeri Zelepukin scored with 7.7 seconds remaining to force overtime, the Rangers were headed to sudden death. After the first overtime period solved nothing, Matteau intercepted a loose puck in the Devils end, swung the puck in front, and put it into the back of the net. The goal sent the Rangers to the Stanley Cup Final, but it was immortalized by Howie Rose's incredible play-by-play call that transcended the tally. After the puck went into the net, Rose worked his magic. "He scores! Matteau, Matteau, Matteau! Stephane Matteau.... And the Rangers have one more hill to climb, baby, but it's Mount Vancouver! The Rangers are headed to the finals!"

# MR. GAME SEVEN, 2013

O n May 28, 2013, the legend of Justin Williams began to grow. Prior to his Kings taking on the Sharks in Game 7 of the Western Conference semifinal that day, there were rumblings that Williams had a reputation for turning in clutch performances, particularly in Game 7 matchups. Williams had already proven he could win, having won Stanley Cups in 2006 with Carolina and in 2012 with Los Angeles, but there were whispers he had an uncanny ability to elevate his game when everything was riding on it. In his previous three Game 7s, with the Flyers and Hurricanes, Williams scored three goals — including one in Game 7 of the Stanley Cup Final — and added four assists as his teams went undefeated. While that's an impressive stat line, none of that was on the Kings' radar when they acquired Williams in 2009.

At the time, the Cobourg, Ontario, native was in the midst of an injury-plagued season, and while he had already proven to be a consistent scorer at the NHL level, Los Angeles was simply looking to make a change and buy low on Williams, hoping his production would rebound once he became healthy. Sure enough, Williams found his game again with the Kings and helped the team win its first Stanley Cup in franchise history in 2012. A year later, with the team looking to defend its crown, Williams found himself in another Game 7. He did not disappoint. Williams scored both his team's goals as Los Angeles staved off elimination. He now had five goals in four Game 7 contests. Since then, his reputation has only grown. Prior to the 2016–17 post-season, Williams was 7-0 in Game 7s with 14 points, including seven goals, which matched a league record previously set by Glenn Anderson. Williams's seemingly supernatural talents, however, were not enough to save the Capitals from the Penguins on May 10, 2017. For the first time in his career, Williams was on the wrong side of a Game 7 result. Although his record no longer has the same undefeated ring to it, Williams remains one of the most clutch playoff performers in NHL history.

## GRETZKY GETS THE KINGS
## TO THE FINAL, 1993

Through the first five games of the conference final series between the Kings and Maple Leafs in 1993, with Wayne Gretzky still feeling the effects of a nagging back injury, some said the Great One was good, but he wasn't *great*. For *Toronto Star* columnist Bob McKenzie, it looked like Gretzky "was skating with a piano on his back." Toronto's Doug Gilmour, who battled the Great One hard throughout the series, believes those words were likely music to Gretzky's ears. "You'd better believe Gretzky read the article. If I had been his coach, I'd have posted it in the dressing room. If somebody has to say something about your team or your players, you post that up," he wrote in his autobiography with Dan Robson. Whether or not Gretzky read the column is unclear, but his efforts in Game 6 seemed to indicate he had been motivated by the criticism. In response, he notched the overtime winner to keep the Kings' playoff dreams alive and then headed into the deciding contest with unwavering determination.

On May 29, 1993, with the piano firmly off his back and shattered into thousands of pieces, Gretzky turned in a performance that would have knocked Beethoven's socks off. He opened the scoring with a short-handed effort and then set up Tomas Sandstrom to give the Kings a 2-0 lead before the first intermission. With the Kings leading 4-3 late in the third period, the Great One completed a hat trick to put the game out of reach for the Maple Leafs. It was his eighth career post-season three-goal game, an NHL record that vaulted him ahead of Maurice "Rocket" Richard and teammate Jari Kurri, who both had seven. Since joining the Kings in 1988, Gretzky had promised he'd lead his club to a championship, and now he had the chance to deliver. For the first time in franchise history, Los Angeles was going to the Stanley Cup Final to compete for hockey's crown.

# MAY 30

## OILERS REPEAT AS STANLEY CUP CHAMPIONS, 1985

After prying the Stanley Cup from the dynastic Islanders in 1984, the Oilers repeated as champions the following year in spectacular fashion. On May 30, 1985, Edmonton defeated the Flyers 8-3 to win hockey's ultimate prize for the second straight year. While the fans at the Northlands Coliseum spilled out onto the streets to continue exalting their heroes, champagne bottles popped in the Oilers' dressing room as the club and its well-wishers toasted their success. Although they were back-to-back champions, it was hard not to already vault the team into the dynasty conversation, even if they were still a long way off from matching the Islanders' four straight Stanley Cups from 1980 to 1983.

When the post-season had finished, the *Globe and Mail* estimated that Edmonton had set or tied 24 NHL playoff records. While Wayne Gretzky turned in one of his most dominating performances, racking up a record-setting 47 points in 18 games to take home the Conn Smythe as the most valuable player of the playoffs, Jari Kurri made history as well. By the third round of the playoffs, Kurri was shooting the lights out. In six games against the Black Hawks in the conference final, the crafty Finnish winger scored 12 goals, including a four-goal performance in the contest that punched Edmonton's ticket to the Final. By that point, he had 18 goals and was just one tally away from knocking off Reggie Leach's record for the most goals in a single post-season. After failing to score in the first four games of the Final, however, it seemed Kurri would fall short. But in the fifth — and deciding — game, he bagged his 19th to match Leach. Although the scoring slump cost him the record, at the end of the day it didn't matter — the Oilers were on top of the world.

# RAY BOURQUE'S LAST GOAL, 2001

ay Bourque had scored 40 career goals in the post-season but none bigger than the slapshot he wired over Martin Brodeur's glove in Game 3 of the Stanley Cup Final on May 31, 2001. Thirty-one seconds into the third period, Bourque connected on a shot when Joe Sakic knocked the puck toward the premier defenceman after winning a faceoff draw. It held up as the game-winner and moved him closer to the Stanley Cup than ever before, as the Avalanche took a 2-1 lead in the series. Bourque, who had played nearly 21 seasons with the Bruins, had been in the Final two times previously but had come up short both times against the Oilers. A season earlier, in an effort to finally try to capture a championship in the twilight of his career, Bourque was traded from Boston to Colorado. The Avalanche advanced as far as the Western Conference final that year but were stymied by the Stars in a hard-fought seven-game series.

A year later, with Bourque now 40 years old, many believed it might be his last shot at winning the Cup. With Bourque's decisive goal, which would prove to be his only tally that post-season, the Avalanche were now just two wins away from a championship. After the game, Bourque revelled in the importance of his contribution. "For me, that goal was awesome. Yes, I can probably say it was the biggest goal I've ever scored," he told reporters. It not only brought him that much closer to sipping champagne from Lord Stanley's mug but also moved him into the record books. With that goal, Bourque became the oldest player to score a goal in the Stanley Cup Final, surpassing Jean Beliveau, who previously held the benchmark as a 39-year-old. Just over a week later, Bourque finally won his championship, and retired on a high note.

# JUNE 1
## PENGUINS WIN BACK-TO-BACK STANLEY CUPS, 1992

When the 1991–92 season began, the Penguins should have been on top of the world. They were the reigning Stanley Cup champions. It should have been a cause for celebration. Instead, it was a time of mourning. During the off-season, head coach Bob Johnson had been diagnosed with brain cancer, forcing him to step down from his position. Johnson valiantly battled the disease but passed away just a few months into the next season; he was only 60 years old. For the remainder of the year, the Penguins honoured Johnson by wearing a patch with his nickname, Badger, adorning their jerseys. Although they played with heavy hearts, the Penguins kept Johnson in their thoughts and hoped they would be able to win another Stanley Cup for Badger Bob. By season's end, the Penguins did just that.

On June 1, 1992, Pittsburgh defeated Chicago four games to none to win its second straight championship. For many of the players, it was a bittersweet moment and the perfect way to finish the season. While the victory provided the team with some measure of closure, it was also punctuated by plenty of history. Mario Lemieux, who battled chronic back problems all season, won the Conn Smythe to become the first player since Bernie Parent in 1975 to win the trophy in back-to-back years. It was also the first Stanley Cup Final sweep in four years. Moreover, for reasons beyond the Penguins' control, the culmination of the series marked the first time an NHL game was played in the month of June. Following a 10-day players' strike in April, the first work stoppage in league history, the NHL's schedulers were forced to extend the season later into the year. Although it cut into the Penguins' summer vacation, it's doubtful anyone had any complaints once they hoisted the Stanley Cup.

# JUNE 2
## AVALANCHE HIRE BOB HARTLEY, 1998

Before Bob Hartley was a Stanley Cup champion, he worked at a windshield factory in his hometown of Hawkesbury, Ontario. While employed at the plant, Hartley picked up some duties on the ice, serving as a goalie coach for the local junior A club. After assuming the role of head coach in Hawkesbury, he later moved on to the Laval Titan of the Quebec Major Junior Hockey League. With Hartley at the helm, Laval won the league championship in 1993 and vied for an opportunity to capture the Memorial Cup. Hartley's successful tenure with the Titan caught the eye of the NHL's Nordiques, and he was hired as the assistant coach of their American Hockey League (AHL) affiliate.

After the Nordiques relocated to Denver and became the Avalanche, Hartley continued his duties behind the bench in the AHL, guiding Colorado's farm team, the Hershey Bears, to a Calder Cup in 1997. He was just coming off his second season in Hershey when Avalanche head coach Marc Crawford suddenly resigned from the club. A few days later, Hartley got a telephone call that changed his life. As he recounted to Craig Custance in the book *Behind the Bench*, he and his wife were entertaining friends on a Sunday afternoon in May when the phone rang. On the other end was Avalanche assistant general manager Francois Giguere, who invited Hartley to travel to Colorado to discuss the possibility of a significant promotion. Hartley wasted no time. He grabbed his best suit and hastily made travel arrangements to Denver. There, on June 2, 1998, Hartley inked a deal to become head coach of the Avalanche, taking over an incredibly talented team with a nucleus that included Patrick Roy, Joe Sakic, and Peter Forsberg. It was the opportunity of a lifetime. "It's not every day you can start your coaching career on a team that can win a Stanley Cup," Hartley later told Custance. Three years later, Hartley and the Avalanche did just that.

# JUNE 3
## HABS STICK IT TO KINGS, 1993

With less than two minutes remaining in the third period of Game 2 of the Stanley Cup Final, the Canadiens were in jeopardy of falling 0-2 in the series against the Kings. Thinking outside the box, head coach Jacques Demers took a gamble and called for a stick measurement on the curve of Los Angeles defenceman Marty McSorley. The Montreal bench boss suspected it was more than the half-inch allowed under league rules, but if he was wrong, his team would incur a two-minute penalty for delay of game. As luck would have it, McSorley's blade exceeded the NHL threshold, and the Canadiens were awarded a power play. On the man advantage, Habs defenceman Eric Desjardins, who had previously potted his team's lone goal, scored his second of the night to tie the game and send the contest to overtime. Just 51 seconds into sudden death, Desjardins reprised his role as hero, scoring his third goal of the game to even the series for the Canadiens. Although Desjardins scored every one of his team's goals and became the first defenceman in league history to score a hat trick in the Stanley Cup Final, the focus remained on Demers's tactics.

Some cried foul, even going as far as suggesting that members of the Canadiens staff were sneaking around the Forum, nabbing Kings' sticks to get a sense of whether any of the lumber was not regulation. Others, like Kings coach Barry Melrose, derided the move, stating he didn't believe in winning that way. Nevertheless, many believed Demers was just doing everything in his power to give his team an advantage. Even in defeat, Wayne Gretzky acknowledged Demers's acumen. "[Demers] is a smart coach.... they have 23 [Stanley Cup] banners for a reason," he told the *Globe and Mail*. In the end, McSorley didn't make any excuses. "Every team in the league has one stick on the bench that's illegal. I feel bad about it, but this isn't going to kill us," he told reporters. But you can bet that before the third game of the series, McSorley and the Kings gave his twig a second look.

# JUNE 4
## LIDSTROM MAKES HISTORY, 2008

When Nicklas Lidstrom hoisted the Stanley Cup above his head on June 4, 2008, it was a historic moment; the Swedish rearguard became the first European-trained captain of a championship-winning team. Five years earlier, when Detroit won its 10th championship, Lidstrom had also made history when he was named playoff MVP, becoming the first European player to win the Conn Smythe Trophy. This time around, although Lidstrom played brilliantly throughout the playoffs, it was his fellow countryman Henrik Zetterberg who took home the Conn Smythe, which, at the time, made them the only two Europeans to have nabbed the trophy. When Lidstrom was drafted 53rd overall by the Red Wings in the 1989 NHL Entry Draft, it had not been that long since European players had been forced to combat the stereotypes of the day, which posited they were not suited or equipped to play the North American style of game in the NHL.

When Swedish players Borje Salming and Inge Hammarstrom broke into the league in 1973 with the Maple Leafs, they faced scrutiny and had to defy the pejorative label of "chicken Swede." Salming, in particular, proved not only that he was one of the league's premier defencemen but also that he was tough as nails and could play a rough game. While Salming shattered some of the misguided preconceptions about European players, these mischaracterizations continued, and even into the 21st century, there were still some circles in the league that questioned whether you could win with European players. Although players like Lidstrom and Zetterberg have dispelled this myth, the truth could not be denied on the evening the Red Wings celebrated their 11th Stanley Cup in franchise history.

# FIRST NHL AMATEUR DRAFT, 1963

The Boston Bruins inked Bobby Orr to a professional services contract just before his 14th birthday. Given his age, Orr was not old enough to sign on the dotted line, so his parents did so on his behalf. The story goes that, in exchange for his committing to play for the Bruins as an 18-year-old, the Orrs received a cash bonus, a new automobile, and assurance that the team would pay to stucco the family home. This was the era before the league held an amateur draft. At this time, NHL clubs competed for the services of young players by sponsoring junior hockey clubs and reserving the rights to sign those players. It was not uncommon for NHL teams to have dozens of junior clubs under their purview in order to ensure a rich supply of talent. In addition to the sponsorship system, NHL teams could also secure players directly through a tier of contracts, the most common of which was the C form, which secured the professional services of a player indefinitely.

In an effort to do away with this model and give clubs the opportunity to uniformly compete for the newest crop of talent, the league instituted an amateur draft on June 5, 1963. Held in Montreal, the league's six clubs took turns drafting players who were over the age of 16 and not members of an NHL-sponsored team. Garry Monahan had the distinction of being the first player to be drafted when he was taken by the Montreal Canadiens. Twenty-one players were selected that day, and Monahan was one of the five who would go on to have big-league careers. Given that the most coveted players had already been signed to C forms or belonged to NHL-sponsored junior clubs, the crop of talent was rather thin that day, as evidenced by the fact that some teams opted to forgo making selections in the third or fourth rounds. Although the first draft left much to be desired, the process improved as the NHL discontinued the contract form system in 1968 and the sponsorship model a few years later, leading to the more modern incarnation of the amateur draft we are familiar with today.

# JUNE 6
## MESSIER SNAGS THE HART, 1990

For the first time in a decade, the Hart Trophy went to someone other than Wayne Gretzky or Mario Lemieux. On June 6, 1990, Edmonton's Mark Messier took home the award, just narrowly nosing out Ray Bourque. Awarded annually by the Professional Hockey Writers Association, the Hart is given to the player judged most valuable to his team. Each year, as part of the adjudication process, the writers assign weighted votes to players they feel are most deserving of the trophy. After the balloting is completed, three finalists are named and the winner is later revealed at the league's annual award presentations. Before Messier took home the Hart, the award had been synonymous with Wayne Gretzky. From 1980 to 1987, Gretzky won the award eight consecutive times, an incredible league record that is unlikely to be matched. In 1988, he was runner-up to Mario Lemieux, who bagged his first Hart after topping the Great One in league scoring by nearly 20 points.

The next year, after his first campaign with the Kings, Gretzky was once again named league MVP. The following season, however, for the first time in his career, Gretzky wasn't even named a finalist. The Great One openly admitted he didn't do enough to warrant inclusion. "I definitely did not deserve to be among the top three. It's not unfair to say I didn't deserve to be there," he said. Instead, top consideration went to Messier, Bourque, and Brett Hull. It couldn't have been a closer vote. In fact, it was the tightest margin of victory in league history. Messier received 227 out of a maximum of 315 points, while Bourque finished with 225. The results were a surprise for Messier but also an incredible honour. "I never thought that, aside from the Conn Smythe Trophy [which he won in 1984], I had a chance to win," he later told reporters. Gretzky, who was very close to Messier after spending almost 10 years with him and winning four Stanley Cups in Edmonton, couldn't have been happier for his friend. "He does everything from his heart. He's a great athlete," Gretzky said at the awards ceremony.

# DENIS POTVIN WINS THE NORRIS, 1976

After missing most of the 1975–76 season due to a nagging knee injury, Bobby Orr failed to take home the Norris Trophy for the first time in eight years. Awarded annually to the league's best all-around defenceman according to the Professional Hockey Writers Association (PHWA), Orr had captured the Norris eight consecutive times for his outstanding play before ceding it to Denis Potvin on June 7, 1976. That year, Potvin led the league in scoring among defencemen, finishing with 31 goals and 67 assists, making it easy for the PHWA to cast its votes. The Islanders blueliner finished atop the voting with 141 more points than runner-up Brad Park.

Potvin, who had been selected first overall by New York in the 1973 Amateur Draft, had been expected to turn the franchise around. Many believed that, with his nose for scoring and natural ability to join the rush, the highly touted prospect could be the next Bobby Orr. Although these were impossible expectations, Potvin made an immediate impact, capturing the Calder Trophy in his rookie season. While he never dominated the game like Orr — few could have — Potvin would establish himself as one of the league's premier defencemen and anchored the Islanders' back end to four straight Stanley Cups. A decade before Potvin accepted the Norris, a 35-year-old Harry Howell took home the award for the first time in his established career. Although it took him more than 10 years, Howell's timing could not have been better, as Bobby Orr had just finished his rookie season. At the NHL's awards luncheon, Howell spoke to that fact. "I'm glad I won it this year, because I think some other guy is going to win it for the next decade," he told his colleagues. Although Howell was off by a couple of years, his words were prophetic. Had knee injuries not shortened Orr's brilliant career, he may have exceeded Howell's expectations and held on to the Norris for even longer.

# FIRST STANLEY CUP FINAL GAME IN FLORIDA, 1996

The rats had been raining down in south Florida all throughout the post-season, but this time it was different. After Ray Sheppard scored a power-play goal to tie the game against the Avalanche, fans at Miami Arena showered the ice with plastic rats. It was June 8, 1996, the night of the first Stanley Cup Final game ever played in Florida. Two minutes later, the Panthers scored another goal to take the lead, this time triggering an even greater deluge of rats. With the playing surface littered with replica vermin, the game was delayed by approximately three minutes as crews worked to clear the ice.

The rat-throwing custom dated back to earlier in the regular season when Panthers forward Scott Mellanby killed a rat with his stick after it snuck into the team's dressing room prior to a game. After Mellanby went out and scored two goals with his bludgeon, news of his exploits prior to the game struck a chord with the fans, and the rest is history. The rat tossing became so popular that the Panthers even brought on Orkin, a pest control company, as a sponsor and referred to its ice crews as exterminators. While some members of the opposition despised the tradition, others welcomed it. Colorado's Claude Lemieux felt it actually worked in favour of the visiting team because it robbed the home squad of any momentum it garnered by scoring a goal. With the game on hold, opponents could use the hiatus to regroup and gather themselves before play resumed. It certainly seemed to work that way that evening in Florida. There would be no rat trick for the Panthers. The Avalanche would score two more goals to win the game 3-2 and take a stranglehold on the series. Two days later, Colorado would hoist the Stanley Cup. Before Florida returned to the ice for the next season, in an effort to curb the rat tossing, the NHL amended its rules so that referees could penalize home teams for delay of game when fans tossed debris onto the ice. The year of the rat was officially over.

# BLACKHAWKS WIN THE CUP, 2010

After 49 years, the Blackhawks were Stanley Cup champions. The last time they had claimed hockey's ultimate prize it was 1961; John F. Kennedy was in the White House, and the club still stylized its name as two words. While the nearly five-decade drought was over, the celebration was belated. It seemed that, despite the significance of the moment, the only person on the ice who was aware of what transpired was Chicago forward Patrick Kane.

It was June 9, 2010, Game 6 of the Stanley Cup Final. The Blackhawks held the advantage in the series, but with the game now in overtime, they had the opportunity to close out the Flyers on the road and bring Lord Stanley's mug back to Chicago. Four minutes into sudden death, Kane skillfully deked his way around Philadelphia defenceman Kimmo Timonen. As he approached the Flyers net, he fired a shot at goaltender Michael Leighton from a sharp angle. The puck disappeared from view. The crowd at the Wachovia Center barely reacted to the play, assuming Leighton had either stopped the puck or it had simply vanished from their field of vision. Kane, however, knew exactly where the puck was. It was in the back of the goal, stuck in the netting. As the Flyers faithful collectively held their breath, Kane raised his arms in celebration and began wildly sprinting toward his own end. As he entered the neutral zone, he flung his gloves into the air in a fit of euphoric disregard. While the officials and fans were still trying to sort out what had happened, the Blackhawks were in full celebration mode. Although Kane had initiated the festivities, there was no one more overjoyed than Chicago's Marian Hossa. After the Stanley Cup eluded his grasp with the Penguins in 2008 and the Red Wings in 2009, he became the first player in league history to reach the Final in three straight years with three different teams. This time, however, with the Blackhawks, he didn't go home empty-handed.

# GUY LAFLEUR GOES FIRST OVERALL, 1971

"With the first overall pick in the 1971 NHL Amateur Draft, the California Golden Seals are proud to select, from the Quebec Remparts, Guy Lafleur." That should have been what general manager Frank Selke Jr. said on June 10, 1971, but it never came to pass. In 1970, the Seals traded defenceman Francois Lacombe and their first-round selection in the 1971 draft to the Canadiens for forward Ernie Hicke and their first-round selection. At the time, it seemed like an innocuous trade, but Montreal general manager Sam Pollock was already looking to the future.

He had his sights set on Quebec Remparts superstar Guy Lafleur. Pollock knew the highly coveted junior player would be at the top of the draft heap, but he needed to hold the first overall selection if he was going to nab him. As a result, Pollock convinced Selke to make the trade, but he didn't stop there. The following year, when it seemed as though the Seals weren't going to finish at the bottom of the standings, and therefore not fetch him his first overall pick, Pollock made a trade with the struggling Kings. He figured that if he bolstered Los Angeles's roster, it would strengthen the team just enough to ensure they didn't land below the Seals in the standings. So Pollock sent centre Ralph Backstrom to the Kings for Gord Labossiere and Ray Fortin. It didn't matter what the Canadiens received in return; Pollock kept his eyes on the prize. Sure enough, California finished dead last in the league, which meant their first overall pick went to Montreal. Lafleur, who scored 130 goals in his last season of junior, went on to enjoy six consecutive 50-goal seasons in Montreal and win three Art Ross trophies, two Hart trophies, five Stanley Cups, and the Conn Smythe. For a team like the Seals, who had struggled mightily since entering the league in 1967, drafting a dynamic superstar like Guy Lafleur could have turned the franchise's fortunes around. Instead, the Seals missed a golden opportunity.

# KINGS TASTE FIRST STANLEY CUP, 2012

They say nothing tastes sweeter than champagne sipped from the Stanley Cup. Former Kings trainer Pete Demers, however, may tell you otherwise. Demers had been with the organization from almost the beginning. He got his start as the athletic trainer for the team's American Hockey League affiliate in Springfield. After spending three years down on the farm, he made the jump to the big club and became the head athletic trainer for Los Angeles, working with the team for the next 34 years. By the time he retired at the end of the 2005–06 season, Demers had logged 2,632 consecutive games and had treated Hall of Fame players from Rogie Vachon to Marcel Dionne and Wayne Gretzky to Rob Blake.

Following the Kings' loss to the Canadiens in the 1993 Stanley Cup Final, some bottles of Budweiser had been delivered to the team's dressing room. Given the circumstances, nobody felt like drinking — even if it was to drown their sorrows — so much of the beer was never consumed. One unopened bottle, however, made it back to Los Angeles. After sitting in an office at the Forum, it made its way to the Kings' new home at Staples Center before ending up in Demers's garage, where it collected dust for years. When Los Angeles won its first championship in franchise history on June 11, 2012, Demers had more than enough reason to finally crack open that antique Budweiser. Celebrating in the Kings dressing room following the victory, the former trainer poured the suds into Lord Stanley's chalice and chugged the fermented nectar. While you might think the contents of a nearly two-decades-old bottle of Bud would turn your stomach, drinking it out of a championship mug undoubtedly improved the taste. "And that old rotten beer tasted great," Demers later wrote on his Facebook page. Sweeter than the beer, however, was the celebration itself. Demers had lived through the heartache of 1993 but now finally had the chance to toast the team's success.

# BOBBY ORR IS CALLED TO THE HALL, 1979

When Bobby Orr got the call on June 12, 1979, that he'd be inducted into the Hockey Hall of Fame, he should have still been playing hockey; he was only 31 years old. The Parry Sound, Ontario, native burst onto the scene in 1966 with the Boston Bruins and took the league by storm. Orr revolutionized the role of the defenceman with his high-octane end-to-end rushes and his incredible playmaking. Although the league had seen plenty of skilled puck-moving blueliners, such as Eddie Shore and Doug Harvey, Orr truly changed the game.

In Boston, he won the Norris Trophy eight consecutive times and became the first player to be awarded the Hart Trophy three times. Moreover, he finished atop the league scoring twice in his career and remains the only defenceman in league history to capture the Art Ross Trophy. Of course, Orr was also best remembered for his integral role in two Bruins Stanley Cups, particularly his gravity-defying championship-winning goal celebration against the St. Louis Blues in 1970. Despite Orr's dominant play, his career was limited and ultimately cut short by chronic debilitating knee injuries. After more than a dozen surgeries throughout his NHL career, his knees finally betrayed him for the last time at the age of only 30. By the time Orr departed Boston and signed with Chicago in 1976, his joints had already gotten the better of him. He managed 26 games with the Black Hawks over three seasons, and after attempting a final comeback in 1978, he suited up for just six contests before hanging up his skates for good. That following June, the Hall of Fame waived its mandatory three-year waiting period and announced that Orr would be joining hockey's pantheon, making him the youngest player ever to be inducted. Three months later, in a bittersweet ceremony, Orr entered the Hall with Harry Howell and Henri Richard.

# RED WINGS INJURED IN CAR CRASH, 1997

The Red Wings were on top of the world. On June 7, 1997, the club had ended a 42-year championship drought to bring the Stanley Cup back to Detroit. The celebrations should have lasted all summer, but they were cut short when tragedy struck the team less than a week later. Six days after the victory, Red Wings players Vladimir Konstantinov and Slava Fetisov were out with the club's masseur, Sergei Mnatsakanov, following a team golf outing and party. When the evening's festivities concluded, the trio arranged for a limousine to take them home. On the ride home, the driver, Richard Gnida — whose licence was actually suspended because of a drunk driving incident — jumped a curb and slammed into a tree. All three members of the Red Wings organization were rushed to hospital, with Konstantinov and Mnatsakanov both in serious condition.

When the news broke the next day, it was reported that Fetisov — one of the best Russian defencemen of all time — had escaped with minor chest injuries. His companions, however, were not so lucky. Doctors at William Beaumont Hospital in the Detroit suburb of Royal Oak said it would take days to assess the extent of their head injuries, but with both Konstantinov and Mnatsakanov still in comas, the preliminary news was grave. In the coming weeks, it would be revealed that Konstantinov — who was one of the finalists for the Norris Trophy that year — had suffered a debilitating head injury and paralysis. He would never play hockey again. After awaking from his coma, Mnatsakanov also had significant head trauma. As the two embarked on a long road of rehabilitation, the Red Wings rallied around them. The next season, with the club now more determined than ever to defend its Stanley Cup title, Detroit emblazoned its jersey with a patch that featured Konstantinov's and Mnatsakanov's initials and the word *believe* written in both English and Russian.

# OILERS KEEP STANLEY CUP DREAMS ALIVE, 2006

At the end of the 2005–06 regular season, Fernando Pisani had 18 goals. Although it was a career high for Pisani, 137 players finished the season with more goals than him. The Edmonton native had been drafted a decade earlier by his hometown club but had only recently become an NHL regular. While expectations may have been low for the Italian-Canadian winger heading into the playoffs, they were probably even lower for the Oilers. Edmonton had finished eighth in the Western Conference and were slated to square off against the powerhouse Detroit Red Wings, who had finished atop the league with 124 points and won the Presidents' Trophy. No one gave the Oilers much of a chance to make it out of the first round. Pisani and his teammates, however, never got the message. Edmonton went on to defeat the Red Wings in six games, with Pisani racking up five goals in the process. Following the upset against Detroit, the Oilers went on an improbable Cinderella run.

By the time they faced off against the Hurricanes in Game 5 of the Stanley Cup Final on June 14, 2006, Pisani had 10 goals, more than half his regular-season output. Although the Oilers and Pisani had shattered their post-season expectations, they were now on the brink of elimination. Down in the series, and with the Hurricanes on a power play in overtime, it seemed as though Edmonton's luck was about to run out. As the clock ticked down on the penalty, Pisani took matters into his own hands. After intercepting an errant pass from Carolina's Cory Stillman to Eric Staal, Pisani skated in on goaltender Cam Ward and wired a shot over the top of his blocker. Pisani's 12th goal of the post-season made history; it was the first short-handed overtime goal ever recorded in the Stanley Cup Final. He had already racked up three game-winners that post-season, but none bigger than that one.

# BRUINS WIN THE STANLEY CUP, 2011

ruins captain Zdeno Chara took the Stanley Cup to new heights. Literally. On June 15, 2011, the six-foot-nine Slovakian lifted hockey's Holy Grail high above his head with such vigour that he knocked his hat right off. The celebration capped the conclusion of a hard-fought series against the Canucks that went the full seven games. For Boston, it marked the end of a championship drought that dated back to 1972. While Chara and the Bruins rejoiced, Vancouver mourned. They had come so far, but for the second time in franchise history, they had finished one victory shy of capturing the Stanley Cup. Back in 1994, the Canucks went the distance with the Rangers, only to come up short against a team that had finally managed to break a spell of playoff futility that spanned over five decades.

After taking the first two games of the Final at home in Vancouver in 2011, including a shutout to open the series, the Canucks simply had no answers for the Bruins once the series shifted to TD Garden. In Boston, the Canucks managed to eke out just a single goal in two contests while allowing 12 goals against, including eight in Game 3 on June 6. Despite the difficult road trip, the series was still tied, and both teams had a long way to go. Back in Vancouver, the Canucks rebounded. Goaltender Roberto Luongo stopped all 31 shots he faced to pick up his second shutout of the series. In fact, with that performance, he joined Frank McCool as the only other goaltender in league history to earn two 1-0 shutouts in the Stanley Cup Final. While some might have taken that as a good sign for Vancouver, considering McCool's Maple Leafs won the championship when he pulled off the feat 66 years earlier, Boston netminder Tim Thomas proved to be the superior goaltender in the final two games of the series, and I'm not just writing that to pump his tires. After stopping all 36 shots in Game 6 to stave off elimination, Thomas followed up that performance by turning aside every shot he faced in the decisive seventh game as the Bruins captured the Stanley Cup.

# JUNE 16
## KONSTANTINOV GETS THE CUP AGAIN, 1998

t had been a tough year for the Red Wings. Following the tragedy that struck the club in the summer of 1997, the team was determined to win another Stanley Cup to honour defenceman Vladimir Konstantinov and masseur Sergei Mnatsakanov. Their loss was irreplaceable. On the ice, Konstantinov was one of the toughest defencemen in the league to play against, but more than that, he was a teammate and friend. Throughout the season, the team maintained their former star blueliner's dressing room stall, including all of his equipment and gear, to serve as a reminder of what the team was playing for. As Detroit advanced through the playoffs, the culmination of the post-season would lead to one of the most poignant moments in Stanley Cup Final history.

With Konstantinov in the building on the road in Washington, the Red Wings defeated the Capitals on June 16, 1998, to complete the sweep and win back-to-back championships. After Red Wings captain Steve Yzerman received the Stanley Cup from league commissioner Gary Bettman, he immediately brought it over to his former teammate. Konstantinov, who had been watching the proceedings from a private box and had received a standing ovation from the crowd earlier in the game, had now joined the Red Wings on the ice. He was not going to miss out on the celebration. As Yzerman gently placed the Cup on Konstantinov's lap, he was joined by several teammates, who carefully helped hold the trophy up as they pushed him along the ice in his wheelchair. As Konstantinov paraded around the ice with hockey's ultimate prize, he raised two fingers to signify that the Red Wings had just won back-to-back championships. It was a touching moment and a testament to the unbreakable bonds forged between teammates. Afterward, Detroit sought and received permission from the league to engrave Konstantinov's name on the Stanley Cup. Although he never suited up for the Red Wings that season, he was a significant part of that victory.

# SUNDIN GOES FIRST OVERALL, 1989

The ill-fitting Nordiques hat may not have conveyed the proper look, but when Mats Sundin slipped it onto his head on stage at the NHL Entry Draft on June 17, 1989, it was a watershed moment in hockey history. Taken number one by Quebec that year, Sundin, an 18-year-old from Sweden, became the first European player to be selected first overall in the draft. Although plenty of talented Swedish and European players had already made their mark in the NHL, none had ever been drafted atop the annual pile of incoming big-league prospects. According to Pierre Gauthier, the Nordiques chief scout who was on stage to greet Sundin and present him with his new team's jersey and ball cap, the club was very confident in its selection. "He was the best talent available," he said. "We think this guy's got the exceptional hands and great talent. It gives us a chance to have a very good hockey player down the line," Gauthier added.

While Sundin was unquestionably the best available player in the draft, he and the Nordiques still had to combat the perceived notion back then that European players had the tendency to repatriate after just a handful of NHL seasons. Although he wouldn't be available to the Nordiques for a couple of years because of commitments in Sweden, Sundin immediately made an impact once he arrived in Quebec. As a rookie, he scored 59 points, and by his third season, he led his team in scoring with 47 goals and 67 assists. His time in Quebec, however, was short-lived. After another season with the Nordiques, Sundin was part of a blockbuster trade that sent him to Toronto, where he'd become the face of the franchise — and all-time leading scorer — for the better part of two decades. By the time Sundin retired from the NHL in 2009, he had racked up 1,349 career points in 1,346 games, making him the highest-scoring Swedish player in league history. He was inducted into the Hockey Hall of Fame in 2012.

## JUNE 18

# COACH TRADED FOR A FIRST-ROUND PICK, 1987

When Rangers general manager Phil Esposito jokingly approached Maurice Filion of the Nordiques about trading him his coach at the 1987 NHL Entry Draft, he expected his half-hearted proposal would be rebuffed. Instead, rather than snickering at the idea, Filion reportedly said, "Let's talk." Although it may have started off as a joke, it was no laughing matter for either organization. Esposito and the Rangers were in desperate need of a coach. After Tom Webster replaced Ted Sator as New York's bench boss during the 1986–87 season, he had to give up his coaching duties following a debilitating inner-ear infection that left him unable to travel. As a result, Esposito pulled double duty and coached the team's final 43 games of the year.

Meanwhile, in Quebec, it seemed as though head coach Michel Bergeron and the Nordiques were ready to part ways. Although he was an exceptional coach, he had been with the organization for seven years. Bergeron, who had guided the Nordiques to an Adams Division title, was well known for his coaching acumen but also for his fiery temper, which earned him the sobriquet Le Petit Tigre. While that may have rubbed some people the wrong way, that was the emotion Phil Esposito wanted instilled in his team. As a result, after some back-and-forth negotiations on the draft room floor on June 18, 1987, the Rangers agreed to send their first-round draft pick, along with $75,000, to the Nordiques in exchange for Bergeron. Quebec used the pick the following year to select Daniel Doré fifth overall, who appeared in only 17 NHL games. It was the first transaction of its kind in the league, and since then, no other coach has been traded. At the time, it seemed like a good deal, but it was short-lived. Less than two years into his tenure with the Rangers, Bergeron had drawn Esposito's ire and was dismissed midway through the 1988–89 campaign.

# STARS WIN STANLEY CUP, 1999

Brett Hull scored 844 career NHL goals (including playoffs), but one stands out above the rest. Of course, when you score the most infamous goal in Stanley Cup Final history, it tends to rise to the top. On June 19, 1999, with his skate in the crease, Hull scored a goal in the third overtime period against the Sabres in Game 6 of the Final, clinching the Stanley Cup for Dallas. While the Stars were popping champagne bottles in their dressing room, celebrating the first championship in franchise history, the Sabres demanded a meeting with the NHL's director of officiating, Bryan Lewis. Buffalo management, like many of the fans who had been watching the game live at Marine Midland Arena or on television, were flabbergasted over what had unfolded. At the time, the league had a rule stating that "unless the puck is in the goal crease area, a player of the attacking side not possessing the puck may not stand in the goal crease. If the puck should enter the net while such conditions prevail, the goal shall not be allowed."

Throughout the regular season and playoffs, in order to enforce this rule, the NHL had been using video replay to overturn a number of goals once it was determined a player had been standing in the crease. With Hull's skate clearly in Dominik Hasek's blue paint, many assumed the goal should not have counted. However, there was no formal review of the goal. But given what was at stake, Lewis and his team painstakingly scanned the sequence dozens of times. As stated in the rulebook, an attacking player could be in the crease if he had possession and control of the puck before entering the area. In this case, the league officials determined that, following the rebound from Hasek, Hull maintained possession of the puck and therefore the subsequent goal was permissible even if his skate was in the crease. Despite the NHL's explanation, many were frustrated with what appeared to be an inconsistent application of the rules at the most critical juncture of the season.

# ERIC LINDROS IS TRADED SOMEWHERE, 1992

Coming out of junior hockey, Eric Lindros was expected to have an impact on the NHL that hadn't been seen since the days of Wayne Gretzky and Mario Lemieux. He was the complete package at six foot four and 225 pounds, with the hands and playmaking ability to go along with that size. In his second year with the Oshawa Generals, the hulking centre had racked up 149 points. Heading into the 1991 NHL Entry Draft, there was no question he would go first overall. There was just one issue. Quebec held that pick, and even before he had been selected, Lindros made it clear he would never suit up for the Nordiques. Nevertheless, determined to make Lindros the centrepiece of a franchise rebuild, Quebec drafted the London, Ontario, native. When Lindros refused to put on the Nordiques sweater presented to him by team president Marcel Aubut, that was just the tip of the iceberg. It soon became clear he had no intention of reporting to Quebec. Given the immense value Lindros held as a player, the Nordiques wanted to get a return on him before he'd be eligible to re-enter the draft in 1993.

On June 20, 1992, Quebec traded Lindros to Philadelphia. The only problem was the Nordiques had also traded him to New York that same day. Lindros was going to the Patrick Division; it just wasn't clear if he'd be a Flyer or a Ranger. With both clubs adamant they had made legitimate deals with the Nordiques, an independent arbitrator was brought in to end the saga. Following a week-long arbitration process, it was determined that Lindros's rights would be awarded to Philadelphia. In one of the biggest trades in league history, the Flyers acquired him in exchange for Steve Duchesne, Peter Forsberg, Ron Hextall, Kerry Huffman, Mike Ricci, Chris Simon, two first-round draft picks, and $15 million. Two years later, in the lockout-shortened season, Lindros tied for the league lead in scoring and took home the Hart Trophy as the player deemed most valuable to his team.

# THE NHL REVAMPS RULES AFTER CONTROVERSIAL GOAL, 1999

ess than 48 hours after Brett Hull's controversial Stanley Cup–clinching goal, the NHL ripped some pages out of its rulebook. On June 21, 1999, the league announced that video review would no longer be used to overturn goals because a player was in the crease. For the Sabres and their incensed head coach Lindy Ruff, it was of little consolation. While it may have been too little, too late for some, the league maintained the change was unrelated to what had transpired just two nights earlier. According to NHL commissioner Gary Bettman, it was merely a coincidence. He claimed the league was changing course because it wanted to avoid further delays in the game, which had been all too commonplace that season. "We're relying too much on replay," he told reporters.

Although Bettman focused on avoiding delays and belated goal celebrations, it's difficult not to see how the sudden rule change was unquestionably linked to the outcome in Buffalo. While the league insisted the rule was applied correctly to Hull's goal, for most of the hockey world, the NHL blew it. In order to mitigate the fallout from the divisive goal, and to ensure it never happened again, especially on hockey's largest stage, the league divested that authority from the video review committee. On-ice officials still had the ability to determine if an attacking player in the crease interfered with the goaltender, but by taking it out of the hands of video replay judges, the league moved those decisions out of the spotlight. While the announcement eliminated crease replays, Brett Hull's goal continues to live in infamy to this day.

# ZIEGLER NAMED FIRST AMERICAN NHL PRESIDENT, 1977

After three decades of Clarence Campbell at the helm, the NHL elected a new president. On June 22, 1977, John Ziegler Jr. was confirmed as the league's top executive. The 43-year-old, the first American to assume the role, stepped into the position following Campbell's illustrious 32-year career. Although Campbell is often remembered for his role in inciting the Richard Riot in 1955, his legacy includes presiding over the 1967 expansion, which saw the league double in size, and establishing the All-Star Game and a permanent home for the Hockey Hall of Fame. Ziegler, an alternate governor and counsel for the Red Wings since 1966, had some big shoes to fill.

As Ziegler assumed the presidency, he would be confronted with significant challenges, including the proposed merger with the rival World Hockey Association (WHA) and the economic issues confronting the league, as storied franchises such as the Black Hawks, Red Wings, and Bruins struggled with dwindling gate receipts. He immediately set to work on tackling the WHA question, and two years to the day after becoming president, Ziegler presided over a successful merger with the WHA as the league added new teams in Edmonton, Winnipeg, Quebec, and New England (Hartford). Following a 10-day players' strike in April 1992, over issues such as a new collective bargaining agreement and the sharing of hockey card revenue, Ziegler was forced out of office by the league's owners. While he ushered in a new NHL era, his critics have argued he did little to market the sport and nothing to promote its development in the United States.

# JUNE 23
## BRUINS HIRE SULLY, 2003

J
ust a season removed from a hockey career that spanned more than a decade, Mike Sullivan found himself behind an NHL bench coaching some of the players he had only recently squared off against on the ice. On June 23, 2003, the Bruins named Sullivan the team's new head coach. Drafted 69th overall by the Rangers in 1987, he recorded 136 points in 709 games before retiring at the end of the 2001–02 season. Not long after hanging up his skates, the Marshfield, Massachusetts, native was tapped as the head coach of the Providence Bruins, Boston's American Hockey League (AHL) affiliate. Near the end of his inaugural campaign, Sullivan found himself doing double duty, also serving as an assistant coach of the Bruins. With just nine games remaining in the NHL regular season, Boston general manager Mike O'Connell sacked head coach Robbie Ftorek. Although O'Connell begrudgingly assumed the duties behind the bench, he brought Sullivan with him. In the offseason, he was appointed head coach. It was the perfect fit.

Sullivan was a hometown boy. He grew up in a suburb just outside Boston and had one of his most productive NHL seasons with the Bruins in 1997–98. At age 35, Sullivan was the youngest coach in the league at the time. Nevertheless, despite being a little wet behind the ears, his first season with the Bruins was a rousing success. With Sullivan at the helm, Boston finished atop the Northeast Division. But when the league resumed operations following the 2004–05 lockout, the Bruins struggled mightily and Sullivan was dismissed just two years into his tenure. After a number of stints as an NHL assistant coach and as head coach in the AHL for Wilkes-Barre/Scranton, Sullivan returned to the big leagues in December 2015, when he took over the coaching duties for the Penguins. Later that year, he became just the sixth head coach in NHL history to win the Stanley Cup after being hired midseason. He's since led the Penguins to back-to-back championships and is the only American coach to have won the Stanley Cup more than once.

# FLAMES MOVE TO CALGARY, 1980

Although the Flames were extinguished in Atlanta, they would reignite in Calgary. On June 24, 1980, the NHL franchise officially relocated to southern Alberta. Less than a month earlier, the team had been purchased by Nelson Skalbania — who had infamously sold Wayne Gretzky to Peter Pocklington's Oilers in the World Hockey Association in 1978 — and a group of Calgary businessmen. As soon as the acquisition was announced, the consortium made abundantly clear its intention to relocate the club to Canada. Although the team's home city changed, its name would stay.

When the franchise had originally joined the NHL in 1972, as part of the league's expansionist efforts to stymie and block the growth of the WHA, the team had been named after the siege of Atlanta in 1864, a significant moment in the American Civil War, when Union troops commanded by General William Tecumseh Sherman razed the city. While that history would not necessarily resonate with Albertans, the new owners kept the moniker as a nod to the province's rich oil and gas industry. The Edmonton Oilers had made this connection explicitly with their name, but Calgary evoked subtler imagery by referencing the controlled burning of excess natural gas in oil and gas production operations by flaring it off: a nod to the flames that could be seen emitting from the refineries that dotted the landscape in southern Alberta. As an homage to the club's roots in Atlanta, Calgary later stylized its alternate captain letter after the franchise's original A-shaped logo. Although the Flames fizzled out in Atlanta, they would thrive in Calgary. After playing their first three seasons in the Stampede Corral, the Flames moved to the Olympic Saddledome (now Scotiabank Saddledome), where the team captured its first Stanley Cup in franchise history in 1988.

# NHL ADOPTS RICHARD TROPHY, 1998

The NHL added some new hardware to its trophy case on June 25, 1998. At the board of governors meeting in Toronto that summer, the league announced it would create a new award for the league's top regular-season goal scorer. It would be named after Maurice Richard, the fiery winger who was the first player in NHL history to score 50 goals in a season and finished his career with 544 tallies. The new trophy would not only honour the league's annual top sniper but would also pay tribute to Richard, one of the best goal scorers of all time. The impetus behind adopting the trophy came from the Montreal Canadiens, who proposed the idea during the winter while Richard, the franchise's all-time leading goal scorer, was battling abdominal cancer.

The trophy, which was the first award to be named after a player who was still alive, was first revealed at the NHL's All-Star Game in Tampa Bay in 1999, but it was formally unveiled by Richard himself on February 6, 1999, in a pre-game ceremony at the Molson Centre in Montreal. A year after the initial announcement that the league would add the trophy to its annual awards banquet, Maurice Richard presented it to the league's inaugural winner, Teemu Selanne, who racked up 47 goals that season with the Ducks. Since then, 11 different players have won the award, but no one has snagged it more times than Alex Ovechkin. Following his first win in 2008, when he scored 65 goals, the Russian sharpshooter has captured the trophy six more times, including four consecutive victories from 2013 to 2016. Unlike other NHL trophies, such as the Art Ross, there is no tiebreaker for the Richard, which means multiple players can share the award, as was the case with Rick Nash, Ilya Kovalchuk, and Jarome Iginla in 2004 and Steven Stamkos and Sidney Crosby in 2010.

# "NO ONE REMEMBERS NUMBER TWO," 1993

After scoring 45 goals and 137 points in his sophomore season with the Victoriaville Tigers, Alexandre Daigle was considered the consensus number one selection heading into the 1993 NHL Entry Draft. With the draft being held in Quebec City, all eyes were on Daigle. The highly touted prospect had grown up in Montreal before taking the Quebec Major Junior Hockey League by storm, and was expected to be the first French-Canadian player drafted number one since Pierre Turgeon in 1987. On June 26, 1993, with the first overall pick, the Ottawa Senators made it happen. Immediately after joining the organization, Daigle signed a five-year deal worth $12.5 million, making him one of the highest-paid players in the league. When Daigle was asked about the significance of being drafted first overall, he infamously said, "I am glad I got drafted first, because no one remembers number two."

Those words would come back to haunt him. Although he scored 20 goals and 51 points in his rookie season with Ottawa, those statistics didn't align with the heavy expectations set for a future franchise player. After four more disappointing seasons with the Senators, Daigle found himself with a one-way ticket to Philadelphia. Four years later, he was out of the league at just the age of 25. After taking a sabbatical from hockey, he made a comeback several years later. In 2003–04 with the Minnesota Wild, he matched his career high of 51 points and earned consideration for the Masterton Trophy. Although he has been unfairly characterized by some as the greatest bust in NHL history — Daigle still recorded 327 points during his big-league career — he failed to live up to the lofty expectations set for a first overall pick. While he predicted that no one would remember who was selected after him, it turns out the number two pick from that draft ended up being defenceman Chris Pronger, who went on to a Hall of Fame career.

# THE GOLDEN JET BECOMES A JET, 1972

After 15 years as a Black Hawk and 604 career goals — more than any other NHL player at the time — Bobby Hull was leaving the National Hockey League. On June 27, 1972, it was announced that the Golden Jet had been lured to the Winnipeg Jets of the upstart World Hockey Association (WHA) to the tune of $2.5 million. At the time, it was an unprecedented sum of money, making Hull one of the highest-paid athletes on the planet. The deal with the Jets was structured for 10 years, paying Hull for five years at $250,000 as a player and five years at $100,000 in a front-office position. In addition, he also received a $1 million signing bonus that was to be split among the WHA's 11 clubs, as Hull was a drawing card that would benefit the entire association.

Prying the Golden Jet out of the NHL was a watershed moment for the neophyte league. When it was established in 1971, the founders of the WHA envisioned that it would rival the NHL and compete for the services of hockey's premier talent. As the league geared up for its inaugural season, however, its ranks were filled with career minor-leaguers and college players. Very few had top billing. That is, of course, until Bobby Hull came along. According to Ed Willes, author of *The Rebel League*, "Hull didn't just give the league instant credibility; without him, it is doubtful the league would have survived its first year, and the NHL would have gone about its business of printing money and exploiting players." As NHL players watched Hull accept an oversized cheque for $1 million at a press conference in Winnipeg, the wheels started turning. Following Hull's signing, other NHLers, including premier players such as Derek Sanderson, also jumped ship for the new league. In a few short years, largely due to Hull's defection and presence in the league, the WHA became a bona fide competitor of the NHL in terms of both talent and fans.

# MAPLE LEAFS MAKE A BLOCKBUSTER, 1994

There have been few Maple Leafs more popular than Wendel Clark. Drafted first overall by the club in 1985, the Kelvington, Saskatchewan, native immediately endeared himself to the fans with his hard-hitting style of play. While Clark was well known for his bone-crunching body checks, he also had a flair for putting the puck in the net. He racked up 34 goals in his rookie season and followed up that performance with 37 in his sophomore year. By 1991, he had been named team captain. Three years later, he was coming off his most productive season with the Maple Leafs, netting 46 goals and leading the team to its second straight conference final appearance in the post-season. Despite Clark's immense popularity with Toronto's passionate fan base, because of his rough approach to the game, he was frequently on the shelf. As a result, in the eyes of the team's brass, there were concerns among management that he was not durable enough to be part of the club's long-term plans.

So on June 28, 1994, general manager Cliff Fletcher pulled the trigger on a blockbuster deal that sent Clark, along with defence-man Sylvain Lefebvre, prospect Landon Wilson, and the team's first-round pick, to the Nordiques for Mats Sundin, Todd Warriner, defenceman Garth Butcher, and a first-round pick. The deal sent shockwaves through the core of the Toronto faithful, but for the Maple Leafs, it was about succession planning. With centre Doug Gilmour getting long in the tooth, the team needed to land another top-line pivot. Sundin, who had just turned 23 and was a season removed from a 114-point performance, seemed to be the perfect fit. He'd go on to become a franchise player and the team's all-time leading scorer. While Clark was devastated by the transaction, he would return to Toronto in just a couple of years, scoring 30 goals with the Maple Leafs in 1996–97.

# JUNE 29
## THE BOYS ARE BACK IN TOWN, 1990

t was a swap of two hometown boys. On June 29, 1990, the Canadiens and Blackhawks swung a major deal that shook up both franchises. In return for sending Norris Trophy–winning defenceman Chris Chelios and a second-round draft pick to the Windy City, Montreal received high-scoring centre Denis Savard. Born in Pointe Gatineau, Quebec, Savard had grown up in Montreal and played junior hockey for, well, the Montreal Juniors of the Quebec Major Junior Hockey League. After the Canadiens took Doug Wickenheiser first overall in the 1980 NHL Entry Draft, the Blackhawks selected Savard with the third selection. He had an immediate impact in Chicago, recording three assists in his first NHL game and setting a club record at the time for most points in a season by a rookie. Savard went on to lead the Blackhawks in scoring in seven consecutive seasons. Despite his individual success in Chicago, getting the chance to play for his hometown team was a dream come true for Savard.

Similarly, it was also a homecoming for Chelios, who had grown up in Chicago and played high school hockey at Mount Carmel before he was drafted by the Canadiens in 1981. Chelios would win a Stanley Cup in Montreal and establish himself as one of the league's premier defencemen, capturing the Norris Trophy in 1989. Chelios would have some of his best years in Chicago, winning the Norris twice before moving on to Detroit and capturing Lord Stanley's mug in 2002 and 2008. Meanwhile, the trade did not work out as well for Montreal. Savard's production dipped with the Canadiens, and he stuck around for only three seasons before pursuing free agency with the Tampa Bay Lightning. Twenty-six years to the day that Montreal traded away Chris Chelios, they shipped out another franchise defenceman, the charismatic and fan favourite P.K. Subban, to the Nashville Predators for Shea Weber. Although Weber is no slouch on the blue line, time has already shown that the Canadiens were once again on the wrong end of a one-sided deal.

# FUTURE CONSIDERATIONS, 1993

t would turn out to be the biggest bargain trade in NHL history. On June 30, 1993, the Jets traded forward Kris Draper to the Red Wings for future considerations. Draper, who had been drafted 62nd overall by Winnipeg in the 1989 NHL Entry Draft, had seen limited action with the big club during his first few seasons. Although he scored a goal in his NHL debut, it wasn't enough to make him a regular with the Jets, and he spent most of the campaign with the club's AHL affiliate, the Moncton Hawks. Over the next three years, Draper suited up for just 20 games with Winnipeg. So when the Jets shipped him to the Red Wings for future considerations, it was an innocuous deal. It's not uncommon for clubs to refer to future considerations if the terms of the trade are not finalized at the time of the swap. Those final details are simply sorted out down the road, whether it's a player to be named later or a conditional draft pick. In some situations, cash is involved, even if it's just a nominal amount to make the deal work for both clubs.

In Draper's case, it turned out to be just a dollar. On the surface, the amount wasn't necessarily that odd. The greenback simply completed the exchange, but it was the return on investment for the Red Wings that made it one of the best deals in league history. Once in Detroit, Draper established himself as one of the NHL's premier checkers and penalty killers, playing an integral part in the team's back-to-back championships in 1997 and 1998, and two more in 2002 and 2008. All told, he'd play 1,137 games for the Red Wings and even win the Frank J. Selke Trophy as the league's best defensive forward in 2004. Following his first Stanley Cup victory in 1997, Draper wanted to have a little fun with the team's owner, Mike Ilitch. At a fan appreciation event, Draper handed him $1 to square the deal. In response, Ilitch smiled, shook his hand, and kept the bill, sliding it into his pocket. Money well spent.

# JULY 1
## HOSSA SIGNS WITH THE BLACKHAWKS, 2009

ollowing his second straight year of playoff heartache, Marian Hossa seemingly made up for it by cashing in with the Blackhawks. On July 1, 2009, the veteran two-way forward inked a 12-year deal with Chicago worth $62.8 million. At the time, it was the most lucrative contract in franchise history. Prior to signing in the Windy City, Hossa was coming off back-to-back trips to the Stanley Cup Final. Leading up to the 2008 trade deadline, the Slovakian winger was acquired by the Penguins, where he was an integral part of the team's post-season run. Hossa racked up 26 points in 20 contests, but Pittsburgh faltered to Detroit in six games in the Final. Following the defeat, with Hossa approaching free agency, the Penguins offered him a long-term deal in the hopes of retaining his services. He rejected the offer, opting to pursue a one-year deal with the Red Wings. Hossa believed signing with Detroit gave him the best chance of winning the Stanley Cup. In the Motor City, he was a key contributor, logging 71 points during the regular season and adding another 15 during the playoffs. He again advanced to the Stanley Cup Final but came up empty-handed against his former team, the Penguins.

Although Hossa said he had no regrets about leaving Pittsburgh, it was clear that, by signing a long-term deal with the Blackhawks, he was going all-in on his Stanley Cup chances. As luck would have it, the following spring, Hossa was battling for Lord Stanley's mug yet again. This time, however, things would end differently. Hossa finally got his Stanley Cup. He would make up for those missed opportunities in Pittsburgh and Detroit by collecting two more championships with Chicago. Hossa's contract with the Blackhawks expires in 2021, but after missing the 2017–18 season because of a progressive skin disorder exacerbated by his equipment, he announced in May 2018 he will not play hockey anymore.

## JULY 2
## EDDIE BELFOUR SIGNINGS, 1997 AND 2002

ddie the Eagle flew the coop for Dallas. On July 2, 1997, following an unsuccessful end to the season with San Jose, Ed Belfour signed with the Stars. Although the Sharks had reportedly tabled a more lucrative offer to retain the veteran goaltender's services, he declined in favour of heading to Dallas. Prior to his stint in San Jose, Belfour had been a three-time all-star in Chicago, where he won two Vezina trophies and three William M. Jennings trophies for his superb goaltending. For Dallas, already boasting a core that included Mike Modano, Joe Nieuwendyk, and Sergei Zubov, adding Belfour would bring them one step closer to capturing the Stanley Cup. In his first season in the Lone Star State, Belfour backstopped the club to 37 wins as the Stars secured their first Presidents' Trophy. Although they faltered in the conference final that year to the Red Wings, the reigning champions, it was the furthest the Stars had advanced in the post-season since relocating to Dallas in 1993.

Belfour continued to deliver the following season. After racking up 35 regular-season wins, he outduelled Grant Fuhr, Patrick Roy, and Dominik Hasek as the Stars won their first Stanley Cup in franchise history. The next year, they nearly repeated as champions but fell to the Devils in double overtime in Game 6 of the Stanley Cup Final. Although Belfour continued to put up sterling numbers in Dallas, by 2001 he found himself at loggerheads with head coach Ken Hitchcock, who decreased his workload in favour of rising star Marty Turco. As the rift continued to widen, Belfour requested a trade out of Dallas and his play declined. Five years to the day after signing with the Stars, Belfour signed a multi-year deal with the Maple Leafs. Although things may not have ended well in Dallas, his first season in Toronto was a rousing success. He established a franchise record for most wins (37) in the regular season and picked up his 400th career victory over the Devils on April 1, 2003.

# SELANNE AND KARIYA JOIN FORCES IN COLORADO, 2003

Searching for their best opportunity to win the Stanley Cup, former teammates Teemu Selanne and Paul Kariya landed in Colorado. The Avalanche were just a season removed from their second championship, and although Patrick Roy had recently retired, the squad still boasted future Hall of Famers such as Joe Sakic and Peter Forsberg, along with a cadre of impact players that included Adam Foote, Milan Hejduk, and Alex Tanguay. Selanne and Kariya had played together in Anaheim from 1995 until the Mighty Ducks had sent the Finnish Flash to the Sharks before the 2001 trade deadline. With both players hitting the open market that summer, they teamed up to reunite with their best chance of winning a championship together.

On July 3, 2003, in a move that reverberated throughout the hockey world, Teemu Selanne and Paul Kariya both signed one-year deals with the Avalanche. Speaking on behalf of both of them, Kariya told reporters how thrilled they were about reuniting. "We think we have a terrific opportunity to win the Stanley Cup, and that's why we came here," he said. Money was certainly not a factor. Both players, but particularly Kariya, lightened their wallets in order to squeeze their star power onto Colorado's payroll. Kariya, who had made $10 million in his final season with the Mighty Ducks, inked a $1.2 million contract with the Avalanche, well below the league minimum. Although they left cash on the table, it gave the duo their best chance to win a Stanley Cup that season. The hockey gods, however, are remarkably fickle. That year, Selanne had his most unproductive campaign ever, while Kariya performed admirably despite being limited to 51 games because of injury. The Avalanche were eliminated in the first round of that post-season. Afterward, Selanne and Kariya went their separate ways. Kariya settled on Nashville, while Selanne returned to Anaheim, where he would win the Stanley Cup three years later.

# JULY 4
# TYLER SEGUIN IS TRADED TO THE STARS, 2013

ollowing a disappointing playoff run where he scored just eight points in 22 games, the Bruins traded Tyler Seguin to the Stars as part of a seven-player deal. Just the season before, Seguin had lit the lamp 29 times and racked up 67 points as a 20-year-old. As the young centre struggled to find a proper fit in a Bruins organization that already boasted Patrice Bergeron and David Krejci down the middle, there were apparently concerns within the organization that Seguin was not yet mature enough to handle the rigours of being an NHLer. While Boston's top brass may have misguidedly felt that cutting ties with Seguin so early in his career was the right move for the franchise, it was an extraordinarily short-sighted decision.

In his first season in Dallas, Seguin recaptured those flashes of brilliance he displayed as a sophomore, scoring 37 goals and 84 points, the fourth most in the league that year. While Boston received Loui Eriksson, Joe Morrow, Reilly Smith, and Matt Fraser in the swap, less than five years later, they have nothing to show for the trade. In December 2014, after being placed on waivers, Fraser was picked up by the Oilers. Later that summer, Smith was traded to the Panthers in exchange for Jimmy Hayes. After putting up just five points in 58 games in his second season with the Bruins, Hayes's contract was bought out. While Eriksson became a key contributor with the club in the 2015–16 season, racking up 63 points while flanking Krejci, he left the organization that off-season, joining the Canucks in free agency. Finally, Morrow, a former first-round draft pick, lasted just four seasons with the Bruins organization before signing with the Canadiens in 2017. Meanwhile, in Dallas, Seguin has matured into the star centre the Bruins hoped he would be when they drafted him second overall in 2010.

# ISLANDERS HIRE MIKE MILBURY, 1995

When the Islanders hired Mike Milbury as head coach on July 5, 1995, they hoped an outside perspective would alleviate the club's struggles. Although the team had previously won four consecutive Stanley Cups in the 1980s, New York had qualified for the playoffs only three times since 1988. While it would be a daunting task to step behind the bench Al Arbour had occupied for nearly two decades, the Islanders believed Milbury was up to the challenge. As a defenceman for Boston during his playing days, he was known for his hard-nosed attitude on and off the ice. Following a game against the Rangers at Madison Square Garden in 1979, Milbury was embroiled in controversy when he and some of his Bruins teammates were involved in an altercation with some fans. Milbury climbed into the stands and proceeded to whack a raucous spectator with his own shoe.

Beyond bringing that fiery spirit to the team, the Islanders coveted Milbury's hockey savvy behind the bench. As a former coach of the Bruins, he led the club to back-to-back divisional titles and an appearance in the Stanley Cup Final in 1990. Following his stint with his former team, Milbury accepted a coaching job at Boston College before abruptly leaving that position to work as an analyst at ESPN for a year. Back in the NHL's coaching ranks, Milbury planned to bring an old-school attitude to the Islanders. Within three months of his tenure on Long Island, Milbury also assumed general manager duties, where he'd go on to preside over some of the worst trades and deals in NHL history, transactions that had a long-lasting detrimental impact on the franchise. His coaching record wasn't any better. During Milbury's time as the Islanders' bench boss, the club went an abysmal 56-111-24 and failed to qualify for the post-season in any of those campaigns. He resigned from his coaching duties in 1997 and stepped down as general manager in 2006.

# RED WINGS SIGN KEN HOLLAND, 1983

t was an innocuous signing that didn't make front-page news. On July 6, 1983, the Red Wings organization signed goaltender Ken Holland. The diminutive netminder had been taken in the 12th round of the NHL Amateur Draft nearly a decade earlier by the Maple Leafs but had not been able to establish himself as a big-league goaltender. Spending most of his time in the American Hockey League (AHL), Holland had just one NHL game under his belt — with the Hartford Whalers — when he joined the Red Wings organization that summer. He started the season with Detroit's AHL affiliate, the Adirondack Red Wings, but got his first taste of action with the big club when he was called in to relieve goaltender Greg Stefan, whose night had gone off the rails in a game against the North Stars.

Less than two weeks later, Holland would get his first start with the Red Wings. He would stop 23 shots against his former club, the Whalers, in a 6-6 tie. Despite the uninspiring performance, he would get one more opportunity between the pipes for Detroit. On February 4, 1984, in his final NHL appearance, Holland squared off against the team that had drafted him, the Maple Leafs. Following a 6-3 loss to Toronto, in which Holland was yanked from the net, he was returned to the Adirondacks, where he'd finish his professional hockey career a year later. Although Holland didn't make his mark on the ice as a member of the Red Wings, he would have a significant impact on the club from the front office years later. After hanging up his skates, Holland joined Detroit as a scout and climbed the ranks to director of amateur scouting and later assistant general manager. On July 18, 1997, he was promoted to general manager, a position he has held for more than two decades. With Holland at the helm, the Red Wings repeated as Stanley Cup champions in 1998 and added two more championships in 2002 and 2008.

# GERRY CHEEVERS BECOMES COACH, 1980

The same day Bruins goaltender Gerry Cheevers hung up his pads, he took on a new role with the organization. On July 7, 1980, after announcing his retirement as a player, the 39-year-old netminder was appointed as Boston's next head coach. Known for his aggressive playing style and his trademark stitch-pattern mask, Cheevers backstopped the Bruins to Stanley Cups in 1970 and 1972 and was regarded as one of the best goaltenders of his era. While the club was disappointed to lose his services in net, Bruins general manager Harry Sinden said he was pleased that Cheevers "will still be around in a capacity where he will be controlling things just as he did in goal."

Early into his first season behind the bench, Cheevers was forced to undergo an emergency appendectomy but made a speedy recovery to guide the Bruins to a second-place finish in the Adams Division with a 37-20-13 record. The next year, with Cheevers settled into his role as coach, Boston improved to 43 wins but fell to the Nordiques in a hard-fought seven-game series in the second round of the play-offs. In 1982–83, the Bruins piled up 50 regular-season victories and finished atop the league standings with 110 points. In the post-season, the team took the defending Stanley Cup champions, the Islanders, to six games in the conference final but came up short. New York would go on to sweep the Oilers to win their fourth consecutive championship. Much like his reputation on the ice for being a fiery competitor, Cheevers brought that fighting spirit to the bench, sometimes to his own detriment. In a game against the Black Hawks on December 18, 1983, an irate Cheevers received a gross misconduct penalty and a $100 fine for throwing a water bottle at referee Ron Hogarth. Despite Cheevers's regular-season success, Sinden asked him to step down partway through the 1984–85 season. He never coached again and finished his career with a sterling record of 204-126-46.

# MARK HOWE SIGNS WITH THE RED WINGS, 1992

When Mark Howe signed with the Red Wings, it was a homecoming. On July 8, 1992, the five-time all-star defenceman signed with Detroit, the club for which his Hall of Fame father, Gordie, had played for a quarter-century and racked up 786 goals. Putting on a Red Wings sweater not only gave Mark the opportunity to take up his father's mantle but also brought him back to his roots and closer to his family. After spending the last decade in Philadelphia, moving to Detroit would bring him closer to his parents, who lived in nearby Traverse City. Moreover, his brother Marty was just up the road in Flint, coaching the Bulldogs of the Colonial Hockey League. In addition, Mark's oldest son, Travis, was a bourgeoning hockey player, and the family felt that being able to enroll him in a junior hockey program in the Michigan area would give him greater opportunities than would be available to him in Philadelphia.

At his introductory press conference, Mark also joked that signing with the Red Wings gave him the opportunity to settle some old debts. When he was younger and his dad was playing for the team, Mark went to as many of his father's games as he could. It turns out that, toward the end of Gordie's tenure in Detroit, he was usually the only one from the Howe family who attended games. Mark later told the *Detroit Free Press* that, since he'd sit upstairs in the press box to take in the action, he would sell the four or five complimentary tickets his father received for every home game. It was a good scam for the youngster, but eventually his parents caught on and put a stop to it. With Mark signing with Detroit, he could return the favour to his dad and pay him back for all those tickets he had sold.

# JULY 9
## PREDATORS HIRE DAVID POILE, 1997

Before the Predators even had a name, they had a general manager. On July 9, 1997, Nashville hired David Poile to serve as the club's chief architect while it prepared for its inaugural season as one of the league's newly minted expansion teams. Although Poile may have been new to Nashville, he was no stranger to the NHL. As a 22-year-old, he had cut his teeth with the Flames organization as an administrative assistant. After spending 10 years in Atlanta and Calgary, where he rose to the rank of assistant general manager, he took the reins of the fledgling Capitals franchise. Not long after assuming the GM role in Washington, Poile made a transformational trade with Montreal, acquiring defenceman Rod Langway along with Doug Jarvis and Craig Laughlin. The addition of Langway would shore up Washington's blue line for years to come. With Poile at the helm, the Capitals qualified for the post-season for 14 straight years. After the club failed to clinch a playoff berth in 1997, however, he was dismissed by the organization.

Poile was not out of work for long. A few months later, he was snatched up by the Predators. In Nashville, Poile has presided over a number of key trades that have improved the franchise significantly. In 2013, he acquired Filip Forsberg from Washington in exchange for veteran Martin Erat and Michael Latta, and on June 29, 2016, Poile sent Shea Weber to Montreal in exchange for the dynamic P.K. Subban. While Poile continues his engineering with the goal of capturing a championship, he has already cemented his legacy as one of the league's greatest general managers. On March 31, 2018, when the Predators defeated the Oilers 4-2, Poile picked up his 1,320th career victory, the most ever by an NHL GM.

## JULY 10
## THE CLARKSON CUP, 2006

When the lockout wiped out the 2004–05 NHL season, Canada's Governor General Adrienne Clarkson made the bold suggestion that, with the Stanley Cup sitting idle, women's teams should compete for hockey's Holy Grail. Although that idea never got off the ground, it opened the door for a discussion about creating a trophy exclusively for women's hockey. The proposal was certainly in keeping with the traditions of the Governor General's office. After all, Clarkson's predecessors, Lord Stanley and Lord Grey, had both donated trophies to hockey and football, respectively, forever linking their names to the ice and gridiron. In September 2005, Clarkson announced that a trophy would be commissioned for women's hockey. Renowned Canadian silversmith Beth Biggs, who was teaching at Nunavut Arctic College in Iqaluit, was tasked with bringing the trophy to life. Working with three Inuit artists, Okpik Pitseolak, Therese Ukaliannuk, and Pootoogook Qiatsuk, Biggs designed and created hockey's newest piece of silverware.

On July 10, 2006, the former Governor General presented the Canadian national women's hockey team, who had just won the gold medal at the Winter Olympics in Torino, with the Clarkson Cup. When team captain Cassie Campbell received the trophy, she was overcome with emotion. "This, to me, completely legitimizes women's hockey. This is our Stanley Cup — there's no turning back now," she said. While Campbell was right about the significance of the trophy to the women's game, it would be years before a team would hoist the Clarkson Cup again. Because of a legal battle between the trophy's artists and Hockey Canada over licensing rights, it was not awarded until 2009, when the dispute was finally settled. On March 21, 2009, the Montreal Stars (now Les Canadiennes de Montreal) of the Canadian Women's Hockey League were awarded the Clarkson Cup. They've since won it three more times as the top women's hockey club in the country.

# JAGR BECOMES A CAPITAL, 2001

After more than a decade with the Penguins, a team he won two Stanley Cups and five Art Ross trophies with, Jaromir Jagr felt it was time to move on. On July 11, 2001, Pittsburgh dealt the dynamic right winger to Washington, along with defenceman Frantisek Kucera, in exchange for three prospects, Kris Beech, Michal Sivek, and Ross Lupaschuk, and future financial considerations. Although Jagr had just captured his fifth Art Ross and was coming off his fourth consecutive season as the league's leading scorer, behind the scenes he was unhappy. Although it was not evident by his performance on the scoresheet, at one point in the season Jagr had reportedly said he was "dying alive." While teammates noticed a change in Jagr's demeanour, there were also reports he had struggled with Penguins' bench bosses Kevin Constantine and, more recently, Ivan Hlinka.

As a result, Jagr had requested several trades out of Pittsburgh. Even the comeback of Mario Lemieux, with whom Jagr had won back-to-back championships, was not enough to convince the discontented winger to stay. At the end of the 2000–01 season, Jagr still had two years remaining on his contract, and although the return of superstar player-owner Lemieux made it tricky to keep Jagr's deal on the books, general manager Craig Patrick told the Czech winger he'd find a way to afford him. In response, Jagr reportedly told him, "You don't understand, I don't want to be here." Not long after, Jagr got his wish. Once in Washington, he signed a then-record-setting contract for seven years, worth $77 million. Although he led the team in scoring in his first season with the Capitals, racking up 31 goals and 69 points, he was well out of contention for the Art Ross. The next year, Jagr failed to finish in the top 10 in league scoring for the first time since 1994. With his play not meeting expectations, Jagr was traded to the Rangers in 2004.

# JULY 12
## TEAM CANADA SUMMIT SERIES ANNOUNCEMENT, 1972

Dressed in their finest suits, some of the NHL's best players paraded out onto a stage at Sutton Place in Toronto. They would form the nucleus of the Canadian roster that would take on a Soviet team in an eight-game exhibition hockey series to be held that September. On July 12, 1972, Team Canada coach Harry Sinden unveiled a list of 35 players who would be invited to camp. It included the NHL's brightest stars such as Phil Esposito, Marcel Dionne, and Bobby Orr. Also on the list that day was Bobby Hull. The Golden Jet, who was the first player in league history to score 50 goals in a season more than once, made waves earlier that summer when he signed a lucrative $1 million contract with the Winnipeg Jets of the upstart World Hockey Association (WHA).

When the idea for the tournament was initially conceived in April 1972, it was determined that the squads would be made up of the country's best players, which invariably meant the NHL, but after Hull signed with the WHA, this put Team Canada in a bind. As part of an agreement with the NHL, Hockey Canada had agreed to fill its roster only with players signed with NHL teams. As a result, although his name was included in the preliminary announcement of names, Hull would be barred from suiting up for the tournament. When the news hit that Hull would be ineligible, the hockey world was livid. Maple Leafs owner Harold Ballard opposed the move, and even Prime Minister Pierre Trudeau lobbied to get him onto the roster. In addition to Hull, goaltender Gerry Cheevers, defenceman J.C. Tremblay, and forward Derek Sanderson would also be ruled out of the tournament, as they would all sign contracts with the WHA later that summer.

# THE LOCKOUT ENDS, 2005

After 310 days, the NHL and its players broke the ice. On July 13, 2005, they reached a tentative deal that would end the longest lockout in professional sports history. When the league and the players failed to reach a new collective agreement before the start of the 2004–05 season, the NHL locked the doors. As days turned to weeks, and weeks turned to months, fans and players feared the worst. With the lockout dragging on, there were often rumblings that an agreement would be reached, but when both sides failed to come together at the eleventh hour on February 16, 2005, all hope was lost. On that day, the season was officially cancelled, making the NHL the first professional sports league in history to scratch an entire season.

The players were disheartened. The fans were furious. For the first time since 1919, when influenza halted the championship series between the Montreal Canadiens and Seattle Metropolitans, the Stanley Cup would not be awarded. Instead, it would remain tucked away in the Hockey Hall of Fame, collecting dust. Although a number of groups petitioned to have the trophy brought out of hibernation by allowing other leagues to compete for it — hearkening back to its origins as a challenge cup — it remained under lock and key. By July 2005, there was growing concern that, with no agreement in hand, another season was in jeopardy. But a tentative deal was ratified by the players and the league. The new collective bargaining agreement instituted a salary cap and a number of rule changes to speed up the game, including the promise to crack down on obstruction and the elimination of the red line. Other changes included the introduction of a trapezoid-shaped area behind the net and the shootout to resolve overtime stalemates. Although the game had significantly changed when play resumed for 2005–06, hockey was back.

## JULY 14

# GRANT FUHR SIGNS WITH THE BLUES, 1995

By 1995, some believed Grant Fuhr's best days were behind him. The veteran goaltender was coming off a season during which he had been utilized in a limited backup role, splitting time between the Sabres and Kings. While some felt the 32-year-old Fuhr was washed up, Wayne Gretzky thought otherwise. During the 1995 off-season, St. Louis Blues general manager and coach Mike Keenan reportedly had a chance encounter with the Great One at a café in Manhattan. As Gretzky sat down with Keenan and assistant coach Bob Berry, they got to chatting and Fuhr's name popped into the conversation. While Gretzky had won four Stanley Cups with the netminder in Edmonton, he didn't revisit the glory days. Instead, he talked about how much he had been impressed with Fuhr's play during the 1994–95 lockout, when he organized a travelling exhibition squad known as the Ninety-Nine All-Stars. The team played eight exhibition games in five countries, and Fuhr had been along for the ride. Although the veteran goaltender may have lost a step later that regular season, shuffling between Buffalo and Los Angeles, in the eyes of the Great One, he still had plenty of game left in him. That was all Keenan needed to hear.

A month later, on July 14, 1995, St. Louis signed Fuhr to a multi-year contract. Although he initially arrived at the Blues' training camp out of shape, much to the chagrin of Keenan who promptly suspended him, he returned in peak condition and put together a season for the books. In his inaugural campaign in St. Louis, he played in 79 games, including 76 consecutively, both of which remain single-season records that are unlikely to be broken. Fuhr's superb play on the ice that season certainly lived up to Gretzky's billing. Funnily enough, the Great One was traded to the Blues the following year, where he would be reunited with Fuhr once again.

# JULY 15
# KEENAN RESIGNS FROM
# THE RANGERS, 1994

ust a month after kissing the Stanley Cup, Mike Keenan kissed the
Rangers goodbye. On July 15, 1994, the New York coach abruptly
resigned from his position, just weeks after bringing the Blueshirts
their first championship since 1940. Keenan, who had just completed
the first year of a five-year deal with the Rangers, cited a breach of con-
tractual obligations as his reasoning for leaving the club. Apparently, the
dispute stemmed from Keenan's insistence that the club had been a day
late in paying out his playoff bonus. Although news of his departure was
jarring at the time, it may not have been all that unexpected. During
the season, Keenan had developed a rancorous relationship with general
manager Neil Smith. There were even reports that the two were not on
speaking terms as New York made its deep post-season charge.

In addition, while Keenan and the Rangers were battling the
Canucks for the championship, he was fielding questions about
rumours of him leaving to join the Red Wings organization. In fact,
even on the night the Blueshirts hoisted the Stanley Cup and sipped
champagne from the silver mug in the bowels of Madison Square
Garden, Keenan could not avoid inquiry about a prospective Detroit
deal. Although he dismissed it as nonsense, on the biggest night of
his career and for the Rangers in their last 54 years, Keenan could
not escape the notion he was looking to bolt. Moreover, a sudden exit
would not have been out of keeping for Keenan. Before joining New
York, his tenure with the Blackhawks had ended in a huff following a
dispute with the club's top brass, which led to him taking a sabbatical
as a broadcaster for the 1992–93 season. After bringing the Rangers
their first hockey championship in more than five decades, Keenan
could have stayed on Broadway and been a hero for years to come.
Instead, he opted to play the villain.

## JULY 16

# THE GREAT ONE TIES THE KNOT, 1988

Although the Great One won only four Stanley Cups with Edmonton, he still picked up five rings in Alberta. On July 16, 1988, Wayne Gretzky and Janet Jones were married in a lavish ceremony at St. Joseph's Basilica in Edmonton. Although neither were Catholic, they had requested to tie the knot there because no other church in the city could accommodate their bulging guest list of 650 people. It was Canada's unofficial royal wedding. The nation's most beloved son was marrying his beautiful princess in a glamorous ceremony. As Janet gracefully walked down the aisle, she had on a $40,000 designer wedding dress that paled in comparison only to the diamond engagement ring on her finger, for which Gretzky had reportedly paid $250,000. Flanking the Great One at the altar was a cast of groomsmen who could have formed a formidable line on the ice. They included his brothers, Brent, Keith, and Glen, and Oilers teammates Mark Messier, Kevin Lowe, and Paul Coffey. Gretzky's best man was Eddie Mio, the goaltender he had started his professional hockey career with as a member of the Indianapolis Racers of the World Hockey Association.

After the Great One and Janet exchanged their vows, it was time to party. The story goes that, at the reception, Mio got the biggest ovation with his best man's speech. With microphone in hand, the former netminder asked Gretzky's past girlfriends in the audience to return the keys to his apartment now that he was a married man. One by one, they filed up. Of course, Mio had distributed the keys in advance as a gag, and the procession included the wife of one of Gretzky's teammates and Paul Coffey's mother. But he saved the best for last. After some coaxing, the holder of the final key was revealed: it was none other than Gordie Howe.

# MIKE KEENAN JOINS THE BLUES, 1994

Mike Keenan was not out of work for very long. Just days after announcing he was leaving the Rangers, reportedly as a free agent because the team had breached his contract, he had a new job. On July 17, 1994, Keenan was named head coach and general manager of St. Louis. Although it was widely speculated he would be heading to Detroit, as those had been the rumours swirling throughout the post-season, Keenan had reportedly spurned a more lucrative offer from the Red Wings in favour of the Blues. In a restaurant in suburban St. Louis, Keenan and Blues chairman Mike Shanahan supposedly ironed out the details of a five-year contract. Meanwhile, in New York, the Rangers still considered Keenan an employee, as he still had four years remaining on his contract with the team, and they were prepared to bar another team from retaining his services.

The following day, true to their words, the Rangers requested that NHL commissioner Gary Bettman formally investigate the matter. That same day, after enlisting the help of the league's top brass, the Rangers filed a lawsuit against Keenan to bind him to the contract he had recently ditched with the club. Just as both parties were preparing to dig in for a lengthy legal battle, Bettman resolved the situation. The commissioner allowed Keenan to assume his post in St. Louis as part of a settlement that left no one unpunished. It included a trade that sent Petr Nedved to the Rangers in exchange for Esa Tikkanen and Doug Lidster. Bettman also ordered the Rangers to pay Keenan a $608,000 bonus, of which Keenan would return $400,000 to the team. Moreover, he fined Keenan $100,000 and suspended him from his duties in St. Louis for 60 days for "conduct detrimental to the league." Bettman also levied fines against the Blues and Red Wings for tampering and even fined the Rangers $25,000 for taking legal action despite asking the commissioner for an investigation earlier that day. In the end, Keenan's tenure with the Blues lasted less than three seasons.

# JONATHAN TOEWS BECOMES CAPTAIN, 2008

When Jonathan Toews was informed he would become the Blackhawks' next captain at the end of his first season with the club, it caught him by surprise. Although he had led all rookies in goal-scoring that year and finished third in Calder Trophy voting, he was still only 20 years old. While it was an incredible honour, Toews couldn't help but think that perhaps the captaincy should have gone to one of the club's more established veteran players like Brent Seabrook or Duncan Keith. Instead, on July 18, 2008, the Blackhawks named Toews captain, making him the third-youngest captain in NHL history. Only Tampa Bay's Vincent Lecavalier and Pittsburgh's Sidney Crosby had been younger, both 19, when they had assumed the captaincy of their respective clubs.

Just a few months removed from his 20th birthday, Toews was the second-youngest player on the Blackhawks roster heading into the season. But despite his youthfulness, there was no doubt in the organization that Toews was the best fit for the position. General manager Dale Tallon said he was "a tremendous individual and a wonderful leader on and off the ice." In the dressing room, where the opinions of players and colleagues mean more than the words of management, Toews's teammates embraced his new role. In reflecting on the appointment with author Mark Lazerus for the book *If These Walls Could Talk: Chicago Blackhawks*, former Blackhawks forward Troy Brouwer said, "For management, it was an easy decision. And for players, it was easy to get on board with. I didn't know he was going to turn out as good as he is now, and as a good a leader as he is now, but we knew he was special." Two years later, Toews would lead Chicago to its first Stanley Cup in 49 years and pick up the Conn Smythe Trophy as the most valuable player to his team in the playoffs. By 2015, he had guided the Blackhawks to two more championships, and he remains among the most revered leaders in the league.

# KOVALCHUK SIGNS WITH THE DEVILS, 2010

hey say the devil is in the details. That was certainly the case when Ilya Kovalchuk signed with New Jersey. On July 19, 2010, Kovalchuk, the league's most coveted free agent, inked a massive deal with the Devils, worth $102 million over 17 years. At the time of the signing, it was the longest contract in league history. Kovalchuk, who had joined the Devils via a trade earlier in the season, was taken first overall by the Atlanta Thrashers in the 2001 NHL Entry Draft. In eight NHL seasons, he had racked up 338 goals, including two 52-goal campaigns. Given the Russian sniper's propensity for putting the puck in the net, there was little doubt about his prolific goal-scoring abilities, but there were concerns about whether he would fulfill the contract. When the pact was set to expire in 2027, Kovalchuk would have been 44 years old, making him one of the oldest players to ever play in the NHL.

As a result, before the ink was even dry, the league intervened. The NHL blocked the deal, arguing that its length and structure circumvented the salary cap. When the NHL Players' Association grieved the decision on Kovalchuk's behalf, an arbitrator was called in. On August 9, arbitrator Richard Bloch sided with the league and ruled that the contract had indeed sidestepped the salary cap, making Kovalchuk an unrestricted free agent yet again. Less than a month later, after hammering out a new deal, the Devils announced they had signed Kovalchuk to a 15-year contract worth $100 million. Although it seemed as though the saga was complete, the matter was far from over. The league imposed sanctions against the club for salary cap circumvention, which included a stiff fine and forfeiture of draft picks. The punishment was later amended in 2014 when the league awarded the Devils a first-round pick that year. Meanwhile, after three seasons in New Jersey, Kovalchuk longed to return to his family in Russia. In 2013, he retired from the NHL and his contract was terminated. But after five years away, Kovalchuk will be returning to the NHL for the 2018–19 season as a member of the Los Angeles Kings.

# JULY 20
## SHARKS HIRE DEBORAH WRIGHT, 1992

The Sharks made waves on July 20, 1992. On that day, the team hired Deborah Wright as a part-time scout, making her the first woman to scout for an NHL team. Wright, who was 26 years old at the time, had been working for the Drummondville Voltigeurs of the Quebec Major Junior Hockey League when San Jose recruited her to evaluate talent for the club at the junior and collegiate levels in Quebec, along with the eastern portions of Ontario and the United States. Following her hiring, the Sharks' eastern scouting supervisor, Ray Payne, told the press that Wright was "clearly our best candidate. Because of her ability, we were not afraid to make this move."

A year later, Wright would be joined in the league by Angela Gorgone, who had been hired as the inaugural scouting coordinator for the Mighty Ducks. Before making the move to Anaheim, Gorgone had been with the Devils as a hockey assistant, where she did everything from stat tracking to working on arbitration briefs, including the case that awarded New Jersey Scott Stevens from the Blues in 1991. When she arrived in Anaheim, Gorgone had her work cut out for her. One of her first duties was getting the club's grizzled scouts on board with adopting a computerized system for the scouting process. At that time, most of them were still mailing reports and using rotary telephones, but she won them over. She quickly rose to the rank of assistant to the general manager and went on to become manager of hockey operations for the Predators. But after a couple years in Nashville, Gorgone (now Swartz) retired from the hockey world. She now runs a successful bakery in the Bay Area called Bake My Day. Although Wright and Gorgone were trailblazers, the gendered landscape of the league has been slow to change. Women continue to be under-represented in hockey operations positions at the NHL level.

# JULY 21
# THE GREAT ONE GOES
# TO THE BIG APPLE, 1996

The Great One was heading to the Big Apple. On July 21, 1996, Wayne Gretzky signed with the New York Rangers. After finishing the season with the Kings and Blues, for the first time in his illustrious career, the Great One was a free agent. Although he had been in discussion about returning to St. Louis or even going to Vancouver, Gretzky decided that Broadway was the better fit for him. In order to squeeze Gretzky onto a roster that already included some high-priced talent, he'd have to take less money than he had previously been paid, something he acknowledged at his introductory press conference. "I'm probably the only free agent to come to New York for less money," he said. "Don't get me wrong — I'm still being paid very nicely. But my gut feeling was that I wanted to come here. I was always intrigued by New York. I always thought it was a great place to play," he added.

For Gretzky, the money wasn't all that important. What mattered most was that going to the Rangers gave him the chance to be reunited with his former Oilers teammate and best friend, Mark Messier, and one last opportunity to win the Stanley Cup. "I guess what probably tipped the scale was the chance to play with Mark and the opportunity to get a chance to play with a team that is really focused on trying to win a championship," he told reporters. In his first campaign with the Blueshirts, Gretzky dished out 72 assists and led the team in scoring with 97 points. In the playoffs, with Gretzky scoring 10 goals and 20 points, the Rangers advanced as far as the Eastern Conference final but came up short against the Flyers. It proved to be the Great One's final post-season appearance. Although Gretzky would play two more seasons in New York, finishing his brilliant career in the Big Apple, the Blueshirts would not qualify again for the playoffs for another decade.

# SUITCASE TRADED TWICE IN
# ONE DAY, 2003

Mike Sillinger's nickname was Suitcase, and for pretty good reason. A touted prospect coming out of junior hockey, Sillinger was selected 11th overall by the Red Wings in the 1989 NHL Entry Draft. Although he had recorded three consecutive seasons of 50 or more goals with the Regina Pats, that scoring touch didn't follow him to the NHL. As a result, after just a few years in Detroit, Sillinger was traded to the Mighty Ducks. After playing 77 games in Anaheim, he was dealt to the Canucks. Sillinger stayed in Vancouver for the better part of two years but once again found himself on the move, this time to Philadelphia. His tour with the Flyers was brief. He didn't even get a full season under his belt before he was packing his suitcase yet again. Following a stint in Tampa Bay, Sillinger had stopovers in Florida, Ottawa, and Columbus. Although he had signed with the Blue Jackets on his own terms as an unrestricted free agent in 2001 — for the first time in his career — Sillinger was not long for Columbus.

On July 22, 2003, the Blue Jackets shipped him and a second-round pick to the Stars for two-time all-star Darryl Sydor. But before Sillinger could even hop a flight to Dallas, he was traded again. Twice in one day. Instead of heading to the Lone Star State, Sillinger was on his way to Phoenix in exchange for veteran blueliner Teppo Numminen. Later that season, the Coyotes dealt Sillinger to the Blues, where he became just the third player in NHL history to play for 10 different teams. By the time he retired in 2009, Sillinger had played for two more clubs, the Predators and Islanders, and earned the distinction of being the only player in league history to score a goal for 12 different teams.

# JULY 23
## MAPLE LEAFS HIRE LOU LAMORIELLO, 2015

Many expected that Lou Lamoriello would retire as a Devil. He had been president and general manager of the club since 1987, making him the longest-tenured general manager with a single franchise in NHL history. Over his 27 seasons at the helm in New Jersey, Lamoriello had guided the team to 21 playoff appearances and had captured the Stanley Cup three times. A shrewd negotiator and a keen hockey mind, Lamoriello had been one of the most respected general managers around the league during his time in New Jersey. In 1999, long-time NHL executive Brian Burke told Michael Farber of *Sports Illustrated* that "Lou's a model for our business. This is not just the best run franchise in the NHL, it's the best run franchise in pro sports." But after the Devils failed to qualify for the post-season in three straight years, the organization stripped him of his general manager duties, appointing former Penguins general manager Ray Shero as the club's new GM in May 2015.

Although Lamoriello remained with the team as president, many believed his time with the organization was coming to an end. After all, he was 72 years old. After so much success in New Jersey, he could have retired with one of the best track records in NHL history. His resumé was sterling. There was nothing left to prove. Lou, however, was not done. He wanted one more challenge. On July 23, 2015, he abruptly resigned as president of the Devils and became the general manager of the Maple Leafs. At his first press conference, he told reporters how excited he was to take on the opportunity but understood it would be a difficult road ahead. "I've always said anything easy isn't worth it. Anybody can do it," he said. After three successful seasons in Toronto, Lamoriello joined the Islanders in May 2018, and it is now up to new general manager Kyle Dubas to end the Maple Leafs' Stanley Cup drought.

# JULY 24
## PANTHERS HIRE DOUG MACLEAN, 1995

After missing the playoffs by a single point in each of their first two NHL seasons, the Panthers made a coaching change behind the bench. After dismissing the club's inaugural coach, Roger Neilson, the team named Doug MacLean as his replacement on July 24, 1995. While Neilson was an NHL pioneer, he had drawn the ire of the organization for the conservative style of play he dictated and his reliance on veteran players. In his last season as coach, the Panthers finished with the fewest goals in the league. Although MacLean was stepping into his first NHL coaching role, general manager Bryan Murray believed he could turn things around. Before joining the Panthers organization as the director of player development, MacLean had served as an assistant coach under Murray in Detroit. Following two years on the Red Wings' bench, MacLean became the general manager of the club's American Hockey League affiliate in the Adirondacks, where he was chiefly responsible for acquiring Kris Draper from the Winnipeg Jets for $1 — one of the best deals in hockey history.

With the Panthers, the plan was that MacLean would infuse a more aggressive brand of hockey into the organization. At his introductory press conference, he acknowledged as much. "I think as you move into your third and fourth year, it's time to take another step," he said. With MacLean at the helm, the Panthers did just that. Relying on a mix of veteran players and youngsters such as defenceman Ed Jovanovski, whom the club had drafted first overall two years earlier, MacLean guided the team to its best finish and first playoff appearance in franchise history. In the post-season, the Panthers went on an improbable run to the Stanley Cup Final, captivating the hockey world with their play on the ice and the quirky rat-throwing tradition of the Florida faithful. Although they were swept by the Avalanche, it was an incredible story. MacLean would lead the Panthers to the post-season again the following season but was fired in 1997 after the club got off to a sluggish start.

# JULY 25
## MAPLE LEAFS HIRE ROGER NEILSON, 1977

Roger Neilson was a hockey innovator. While coaching the Peterborough Petes in the Ontario Hockey Association, he once brought his dog, Jacques, to practice to teach his players how to be patient on the forecheck. He would park his pup in front of the net, and no matter how many times Neilson moved to bring the puck out, Jacques didn't flinch. The lesson was that if his dog could wait for an opponent to make the first move, his players should be able to exercise that type of patience with the puck. During his seven seasons in Peterborough, Neilson also used his innovative approach to exploit weaknesses in the rulebook. During a game against the Toronto Marlboros on September 26, 1968, Neilson replaced his goaltender with defenceman Ron Stackhouse to stop a penalty shot. As soon as the Toronto player crossed the blue line, Stackhouse skated out from his crease and halted his opponent's progress. It was tactics like this that caught the eye of NHL general managers.

Following a season behind the bench of Toronto's minor-league affiliate in Dallas, Neilson was plucked by Maple Leafs owner Harold Ballard on July 25, 1977, to take over the club's vacant coaching position. Although he was in Toronto for only two seasons, his impact was far reaching. Over the next two decades, Neilson coached at the NHL level, and his innovative thinking changed the game. He continued to employ inventive tactics on the ice and became a pioneer in using video to scout opposing teams and players, earning him the nickname Captain Video. Beyond his duties as a bench boss, Neilson also inadvertently changed the atmosphere of the playoffs. While coaching for the Canucks, he was ejected from a 1982 post-season game after draping a white towel over a stick to protest the officiating. At the next Vancouver game, thousands of fans showed up with towels, turning Neilson's sign of surrender into a rallying cry. Since then, "towel power" has caught on elsewhere, and is now a hallmark of the NHL post-season.

# DUSTIN PENNER SIGNS OFFER SHEET, 2007

Offer sheets can be tricky. When a restricted free agent receives a qualifying offer from his team, general managers from other NHL clubs can tender an offer sheet to that player in an attempt to acquire his services. If the player accepts the offer sheet, his current NHL team has seven days to match the offer. If the team fails to do so, it is awarded draft picks as compensation — based on the average annual salary of the accepted contract — for the departed player. Although offer sheets can be utilized to pluck talented players away from teams that are tight against the salary cap and therefore unlikely to be able to match the proposal, they are rarely utilized in the league. General managers tend to shy away from offer sheets to avoid antagonizing their colleagues and potentially drawing their ire down the road with a comparable move.

Some offer sheets have nearly led to fisticuffs. On July 26, 2007, the Oilers tabled a five-year offer sheet worth $21.25 million to Ducks forward Dustin Penner. It was a significant upgrade from the $450,000 the 24-year-old Winkler, Manitoba, native earned the previous season with Anaheim. Penner, towering at six foot four and tipping the scales at 247 pounds, was coming off his first full NHL campaign with Anaheim, where he had scored 29 goals. Given his imposing frame and scoring ability, he was a player Edmonton general manager Kevin Lowe was eager to add to his roster. With the Ducks in a salary cap crunch following their Stanley Cup victory, general manager Brian Burke was unable to match the offer. After some heated words were exchanged between the two executives, the story goes that after Lowe challenged Burke to a fight in a radio interview, the Ducks' GM made plans to rent a barn for the occasion. But the barnyard brawl never came to pass. Once NHL commissioner Gary Bettman got word of Burke's plans, he threatened to suspend them both indefinitely if they proceeded.

## JULY 27
# FRANK ZAMBONI PASSES AWAY, 1988

Frank Zamboni changed hockey forever. Born to Italian immigrants in Eureka, Utah, in 1901, Zamboni never played hockey growing up. It was only after he and his brothers built the Iceland Skating Rink in the Los Angeles suburb of Paramount that his life begin to intersect with the game. Not long after the Iceland first opened its doors in 1940, Zamboni keenly recognized that even with a roof to protect the ice from the California sun, it was still incredibly difficult to keep the surface smooth for skaters. While flooding the ice was a relatively quick process, the procedure to prepare rinks for skaters was still quite rudimentary and time consuming. A tractor with a scraper attached to it would shave the ice, and then the excess would be shovelled up. Once the surface was cleaned of debris, it would be sprayed with fresh water, and the excess would once again be scraped off.

But Zamboni found a better way. In 1947, he built an ice resurfacing machine by attaching the front ends of two automobiles to a war-surplus Jeep engine and affixing a wooden bin to the frame. The idea was simple. The machine would shave the ice, gather the excess into its compartment, and spray the surface with water, all in one trip. Zamboni patented his machine in 1949, and in a few short years, it took the hockey and skating worlds by storm. In 1954, the Boston Bruins became the first NHL club to incorporate the machine into its operations. Although Zamboni lived long enough to see his name become synonymous with ice resurfacing machines, he passed away on July 27, 1988, before he was properly recognized for his contributions to the sport. He was posthumously inducted into the United States Figure Skating Hall of Fame in 2000, the World Figure Skating Hall of Fame in 2006, the United States Hockey Hall of Fame in 2009, and the United States Speed Skating Hall of Fame in 2013. Hopefully, one day, the Hockey Hall of Fame will add Zamboni to its pantheon of builders.

# MESSIER SIGNS WITH VANCOUVER, 1997

A s Mark Messier slipped the Canucks jersey over his head, it marked the beginning of a new era in Vancouver. On July 28, 1997, the six-time Stanley Cup winner signed a five-year deal with the Canucks worth $30 million. Although it had been just three years since Messier and his Rangers vanquished the Canucks in the Stanley Cup Final, he was given a hero's welcome. Bringing Messier to Vancouver sent a powerful message to the fans. His resumé spoke for itself. Six championships, six seasons of 100 or more points, and the third most playoff points in NHL history up to that point. Beyond those statistics, Messier also brought a well-established reputation as one of the league's consummate leaders. Although he was 36 years old, the belief was that Messier's presence would elevate the team, much like what he had done in New York in ending the Rangers' 54-year Stanley Cup drought.

While that was the hope, Messier's time in Vancouver proved to be a dark period. Although he maintained he had no aspirations of taking the captaincy away from Trevor Linden, shortly after his arrival, the incumbent, perhaps unwillingly, relinquished the C. In addition, while Messier had worn number 11 during his time with the Oilers and Rangers, it had been unofficially retired by the Canucks following Wayne Maki's tragic and unexpected death from brain cancer at the age of 29. Without consulting with the family, Messier insisted on resurrecting his old number, a move that was not well received by fans. Early into his tenure in Vancouver, general manager Pat Quinn and head coach Tom Renney were dismissed, which led to the hiring of Mike Keenan, Messier's former bench boss on Broadway. Their reunion fractured the team and led to the departure of fan favourites, including Linden. After three tumultuous seasons in Vancouver, in which Messier failed to lead the Canucks into the post-season, the club exercised an option in his contract and bought out his remaining two years.

# LUC ROBITAILLE IS TRADED TO THE PENGUINS, 1994

Despite scoring at least 44 goals in each of his first eight seasons with the Kings, Luc Robitaille was on the move. On July 29, 1994, Los Angeles traded the seven-time all-star left winger to Pittsburgh for Rick Tocchet and a second-round draft choice. After getting drafted 171st overall by the Kings in the 1984 NHL Entry Draft, Robitaille broke into the league in 1986 and potted 45 goals in his rookie season to win the Calder Trophy. Within two years, he would go from playing alongside future Hall of Famer Marcel Dionne to flanking the greatest of all time, Wayne Gretzky. Not bad company to keep.

Although Robitaille may have been overshadowed by the Great One's superstar status in Hollywood, he was an invaluable part of the team's success. When injury kept Gretzky out for most of the 1992–93 campaign, Robitaille admirably assumed the captaincy and racked up 63 goals and 125 points, establishing league records for a left winger. Nevertheless, after the Kings failed to make the playoffs in 1994 after advancing as far as the Stanley Cup Final in the previous post-season, the team felt a new direction was needed. Robitaille was thus dealt to Pittsburgh, but he would only play there for the lockout-shortened 1994–95 season before another trade sent him to New York. Three years later, Robitaille was back in Los Angeles. He was reacquired from the Rangers in exchange for Kevin Stevens. Following four more years with the Kings, Robitaille signed with the Red Wings, hoping to win the Stanley Cup. After capturing a championship in Detroit, he returned to Los Angeles in 2003 for his third tour of duty, nearly nine years to the day after he had initially left the Kings. After retiring from the NHL in 2006, Robitaille joined the Kings' front office, winning two more Stanley Cups, and became the team's president on April 10, 2017.

# SID THE KID GOES FIRST OVERALL, 2005

There was no question it would be Sid the Kid. After winning the draft lottery, the Penguins made it known in advance they would be taking Sidney Crosby, the consensus first overall pick, in the 2005 NHL Entry Draft. Everything after that was just a formality. On July 30, to no one's surprise, Pittsburgh used its top pick to select Crosby. The native of Cole Harbour, Nova Scotia, whose name had been uttered in the same breath as Mario Lemieux, was the most highly touted prospect in years. In 121 regular-season games with the Rimouski Océanic of the Quebec Major Junior Hockey League, Crosby scored 120 goals and 183 assists.

Even before he played his first NHL game, his ascension to the league had been a long time coming. From an early age, it was clear that Crosby was a hockey prodigy. He was peerless on the ice. His playmaking skills, ability to see the game, and puck control made him a difference maker. Off the ice, he seemed destined for stardom. He did his first interview with a reporter at the age of seven, and by 14, he was the subject of a nationally televised feature in Canada. Crosby was the complete package. For the Penguins, the timing could not have been any better. Although the franchise was just a little more than a decade removed from its last Stanley Cup, its on-ice product bore little resemblance to the championship-winning teams of recent memory. After losing to the Devils in the Eastern Conference final in 2001, the Penguins failed to qualify for the post-season for the next three years. As a result, attendance declined and the team struggled mightily at the gate. But Crosby had the potential to change all that. Something that Pittsburgh general manager Craig Patrick acutely recognized. "It's a very, very, very lucky day for our organization, our city and our fans worldwide," he told reporters after the draft. Four years later, Crosby guided the Penguins to a Stanley Cup. At the time, he was the youngest captain in NHL history to lead his team to a championship.

# MARTIN ST. LOUIS SIGNS WITH THE LIGHTNING, 2000

When Martin St. Louis signed a multi-year contract with the Lightning as a free agent on July 31, 2000, it was not headline news. The undersized winger was coming off two years in the Flames organization, playing 69 games in Calgary but spending the bulk of his time with the club's American Hockey League affiliate in Saint John. Despite a successful NCAA career at the University of Vermont and graduating from college as a three-time Hobey Baker finalist, St. Louis drew little interest from NHL teams and went undrafted. Although he was an offensive star with the Catamounts, he was five foot eight, and there were concerns that the diminutive forward would not be able to hack it in the big leagues. As a result, with no NHL offers forthcoming, he signed with the Cleveland Lumberjacks of the International Hockey League (IHL) in 1997.

While putting up solid numbers in the IHL, St. Louis caught the eye of the Flames. After splitting two years in Saint John and Calgary, St. Louis and the Flames parted ways at the end of the 1999–2000 season. Although he fielded offers from a few clubs, he opted to sign with the Lightning. In his first season in Tampa Bay, he scored 18 goals and 40 points. In his sophomore campaign, he was on pace for a career year, but a broken leg limited him to just 56 games that season. In 2003–04, lightning struck. St. Louis scored 38 goals and 94 points to lead the league in scoring, winning his first Art Ross Trophy and the Hart Trophy. St. Louis would spend the next nine seasons in Tampa Bay, where he would capture the Stanley Cup and another Art Ross. When he retired from the NHL in 2015, he was the Lightning's franchise leader in assists (588) and points (953). On January 13, 2017, the team raised St. Louis's number 26 to the rafters in a pre-game ceremony, making him the first player in club history to have his jersey retired.

# RANGERS SIGN ROD GILBERT, 1961

The Rangers had had their eye on Rod Gilbert for quite some time. As a member of the Guelph Royals, one of the Blueshirts' sponsored junior hockey clubs, Gilbert was a sure bet to make it to the Big Apple. In a one-game tryout with the Rangers on November 27, 1960, he picked up an assist against the Black Hawks but was sent back to junior for further development. He finished the season with 54 goals and 103 points in 47 games and was named the most valuable player in the Ontario Hockey Association.

That accomplishment, however, was overshadowed by a serious injury. In his final game with the Royals, Gilbert slipped on some debris that had been thrown onto the ice and awkwardly crashed into the boards, breaking his back. The Rangers sent him to the Mayo Clinic for a bone-grafting operation, and it could have been the end of his career. As part of the operation, surgeons removed bone from his leg in order to repair the damage to his spine. But during the first attempt at the delicate procedure, things did not go as planned. Gilbert's left leg began to hemorrhage, and the doctors had seriously considered amputation before they were able to stop the bleeding. After the medical team got things under control, the procedure continued and the spinal fusion was deemed successful. As a result, while Gilbert went through a lengthy recovery process, the Rangers signed him to his first NHL contract on August 1, 1961. Following his recovery, he spent much of the season with the Kitchener-Waterloo Beavers of the Eastern Professional Hockey League before joining the Blueshirts in the post-season against the Maple Leafs. Gilbert would become a full-time regular with the Rangers the next year and would go on to have a Hall of Fame career on Broadway, scoring 406 goals and 1,021 points. Following his retirement in 1978, the Rangers raised his number 7 to the rafters, making him the first player to have his jersey retired by the organization.

# BLACKHAWKS SIGN WENDEL CLARK, 1999

Wendel Clark wasn't ready to retire. After finishing the 1998–99 season with the Red Wings, he was hoping to continue his career in Detroit. But he wasn't the dominant force he had once been. Although he scored 32 goals that season while splitting time with the Lightning and Red Wings, his sixth campaign of 30 or more goals, he was 32 years old and had a long history of injuries. As a result, Detroit passed on re-signing Clark, making him a free agent. While the Red Wings felt he wasn't a good fit for their organization, Clark was confident he'd find his way onto another NHL roster. As the summer wore on, however, he still hadn't been signed and was understandably nervous about his future. In his book *Bleeding Blue*, he wrote, "I wasn't ready to retire yet, and I was willing to play just about anywhere, in any role, if it meant I got to keep lacing up my skates."

On August 2, 1999, he finally got the opportunity. On that day, Clark signed a one-year contract with the Blackhawks, his fourth team in two years. He was excited to continue his career in the Windy City, but early into training camp he pulled his groin. To avoid jeopardizing his position with the team, he kept the injury to himself and rehabilitated it on his own time. While his groin healed, Clark continued playing for the Blackhawks, but given his condition, his performance on the ice was not measuring up. As a result, Chicago put the veteran winger on waivers on November 15, 1999. When no other team claimed him, the Blackhawks terminated his contract. It looked as though his career was over, but then he was given an opportunity to go back to where it all began. On January 9, 2000, Clark signed a one-year deal with the Maple Leafs, the team that had drafted him first overall in 1985. It was his third tour of duty in Toronto. Clark played 20 games in blue and white that season before hanging up his skates for good.

# AUGUST 3
## THE FLYERS ARE BORN, 1966

Philadelphia had been granted an NHL franchise as part of the league's bold expansion plans, but needed a name. In July 1966, team president Bill Putnam announced the organization would hold a contest to name the team. Over the next 10 days, there was no shortage of ideas. Fans had mailed in upward of 11,000 ballots, with more than 500 different names, for the organization to choose from. As the team sifted through the ballots, they found proposals that included everything from the Lancers to the Royals and the Pioneers to the Raiders. One individual reportedly submitted as many as 63 suggestions. Plenty of fans had some fun at the expense of the organization, offering up names such as the Ice Picks, Philly-Billies, Croaking Crickets, and Scars and Stripes. Some of the other names such as Penguins, Sabres, and Flames landed on the cutting room floor; they would later be adopted by other NHL clubs.

There were some submissions that hearkened back to Philadelphia's history and early hockey heritage. Although Liberty Bells would be a nod to the city, the team felt it wouldn't convey the ferocity they were looking for on the ice. Others wanted to resurrect Quakers, which had been the name of Philadelphia's ill-fated NHL franchise in 1930 that lasted only a season. But Putnam was superstitious and wanted to avoid conjuring up any bad omens. While the Liberty Bells and Quakers proved to be quite popular in the ballots, there was only one suggestion that resonated with the ownership group. On August 3, 1966, Putnam announced that when Philadelphia's NHL team hit the ice for its inaugural season, it would be known as the Flyers. The name had received more than 100 votes and had actually been one of the suggestions from Ed Snider's sister-in-law, Phyllis. But since it wouldn't have been proper to crown the owner's sister-in-law as the contest winner, the club gave the bragging rights, and a new television set, to nine-year-old Alec Stockard, who had also submitted the name, only he had spelled it *Fliers*.

# AUGUST 4
# CURTIS JOSEPH IS TRADED TO THE OILERS, 1995

After reportedly falling out of favour with head coach Mike Keenan, Blues goaltender Curtis Joseph was left packing his bags. On August 4, 1995, St. Louis traded his rights, along with prospect Mike Grier, to Edmonton in exchange for two first-round picks. Joseph, who had joined the Blues as a free agent following his collegiate career at the University of Wisconsin, had backstopped St. Louis for five solid seasons and had even finished in the top three for consideration for the Vezina Trophy, as the league's best goaltender, in 1993. But after struggling in the 1995 post-season, he drew the ire of thorny head coach and general manager Mike Keenan, who was just finishing his first year with the club. As a result, Joseph was no longer part of Keenan's long-term vision for the franchise, and he was out the door.

Edmonton would give Joseph a fresh start, but first he would need a contract. At the time, he was what was known as a Group 2 free agent, a classification reserved for the league's players under the age of 32. Unlike unrestricted free agents, who could pursue negotiations with any club, Group 2 free agents were restricted to whichever team held their rights. But as training camp approached, Joseph and the Oilers still hadn't struck a deal. Complicating the matter was that the team had recently signed goaltender Bill Ranford to a one-year deal, which left many, including Joseph, thinking he would be traded. Nevertheless, he continued practising with Edmonton. When the NHL season started, however, and he had still not inked a deal, Joseph began playing with the Las Vegas Thunder of the International Hockey League. Finally, months later, CuJo and the Oilers agreed to terms on a new deal. He made his Edmonton debut on January 13, 1996, picking up an overtime victory over the Sabres.

# AUGUST 5
# RED WINGS SIGN RAY SHEPPARD, 1991

The Red Wings initially raised eyebrows when they signed free agent Ray Sheppard. On August 5, 1991, Detroit signed the 25-year-old winger to a three-year deal that reportedly paid him upward of $500,000. There was no question Sheppard could put the puck in the net, having previously scored 38 goals in his rookie season with the Sabres, but ever since his junior hockey days there had always been a knock on his skating. Red Wings coach and general manager Bryan Murray acknowledged as much when he announced the signing. "He's not a great skater, but he's got real good hands and he's good around the net. I think he has a real chance to complement our centre icemen," he told the *Detroit Free Press*.

Before joining the NHL, Sheppard had racked up 81 goals and 142 points with the Cornwall Royals of the Ontario Hockey League to lead the league in both categories. But after a solid rookie season with the Sabres, he reportedly had a falling out with coach Rick Dudley and spent his sophomore season relegated to the fourth line with other players who had fallen out of the coach's good graces. After an ankle injury limited him to just 18 games the following year, he was traded to the Rangers for future considerations. Sheppard played 59 games in New York before signing with the Red Wings after the 1990–91 season. In Detroit, he would live up to Murray's expectations. After putting up back-to-back seasons of 30 or more goals with the Red Wings, Sheppard exploded for 52 goals in the 1993–94 campaign, skating alongside captain Steve Yzerman. Although Sheppard found individual success in the Motor City, the team was still searching for its first championship since 1955. Early in the 1995–96 season, the Red Wings traded him to the Sharks in exchange for Igor Larionov. After leaving Detroit, Sheppard would continue to light the lamp. On February 21, 1999, he became the first player in NHL history to score 20 or more goals in a season for six different teams.

# AUGUST 6
## PREDATORS HIRE TROTZ, 1997

When newly minted Nashville general manager David Poile looked to fill the position behind his team's bench, he brought in a familiar face. On August 6, 1997, he hired Barry Trotz to serve as the club's inaugural coach. Five years earlier, when Poile had been at the helm in Washington, he named Trotz head coach of the team's American Hockey League affiliate in Baltimore. At the end of his first year as bench boss, the Skipjacks moved to Portland, Maine, and were rebranded as the Pirates. Trotz made the trip up north and guided the buccaneers to a Calder Cup championship in 1994. Portland advanced to the finals again two years later but fell to the Rochester Americans in a hard-fought seven-game series.

Given his success at the AHL level and his familiarity with Poile, Trotz seemed like a logical fit behind the bench in Nashville, even if he lacked NHL experience. With the city's still unnamed franchise not hitting the ice for another year, Trotz was heavily involved in the expansion process, taking on a significant role in scouting and building the team. He made his NHL coaching debut in Nashville against Florida on October 10, 1998, but the Panthers spoiled the party, shutting out the Predators 1-0. Three nights later, he picked up his first coaching victory as Nashville defeated the Hurricanes to capture the first win in franchise history. Trotz would go on to coach 1,196 games for the Predators over the course of 15 seasons. On April 14, 2014, it was announced that Trotz would not be back behind the bench. His time with Nashville made him the longest tenured coach with one team in NHL history. But he wasn't out of work for long. A month later, he returned to the organization where his coaching career began when he was named head coach of the Washington Capitals. In 2015–16, after guiding the team to a sterling 56-18-8 finish in the regular season, Trotz was awarded the Jack Adams Award as the league's best coach.

# AUGUST 7
## BLACKHAWKS TRADE HASEK, 1992

The Blackhawks knew goaltender Dominik Hasek had potential; they just didn't believe there was a fit for him in the organization. After advancing to the 1992 Stanley Cup Final, backstopped by rising star Ed Belfour, Chicago cemented its commitment to the Eagle by tapping him as the franchise goaltender. Moreover, with 22-year-old backup Jimmy Waite also on the depth chart, the team had a surplus in net. As a result, on August 7, 1992, the Blackhawks traded Hasek to the Sabres in exchange for goalie Stephane Beauregard. Not long after acquiring Beauregard, however, Chicago dealt him to Winnipeg — the team had had actually traded him just a couple of months earlier to avoid losing him for nothing in the expansion draft — for winger Christian Ruuttu.

Meanwhile, in Buffalo, the Sabres believed they had landed their goalie of the future. According to general manager Gerry Meehan, Hasek would be given the opportunity to become the team's starting goaltender, a position that would have been unavailable to him if he remained in Chicago as Belfour's understudy. "We've liked Hasek for a long time. We've been trying to get the trade done since February or March," Meehan told reporters at the time of the deal. During his first season in Buffalo, Hasek shared the net with veteran netminders Daren Puppa and Grant Fuhr, but the next year, after Fuhr suffered a knee injury in November, Hasek took the reins. With his unorthodox but effective style in the crease, Hasek posted seven shutouts in the 1993–94 season and became the first goaltender in 20 years to finish a campaign with a goals-against average of less than two. His performance led the Sabres to the playoffs, and he continued to dazzle in the post-season, stopping all 70 shots he faced in a thrilling quadruple overtime duel against Martin Brodeur and the Devils. For his efforts that year, Hasek was awarded the Vezina Trophy as the league's best goaltender, a distinction he would earn five more times in Buffalo.

## AUGUST 8
## GLENN HEALY SIGNS WITH TORONTO, 1997

After Maple Leafs goaltender Felix Potvin faced a barrage of 2,438 shots over the course of the 1996–97 season, an NHL record at the time, the club needed to get him an insurance policy. On August 8, 1997, Toronto signed veteran backup Glenn Healy. An undrafted goaltender out of college, Healy broke into the league when he signed with the Kings organization in the late 1980s. After establishing himself as a competent backup in Los Angeles, he went on to spend the better part of a decade in New York, backstopping both the Islanders and the Rangers, which included a Stanley Cup victory with the Blueshirts in 1994.

Signing with Toronto made sense for Healy. It was close to his hometown of Whitby, Ontario, and therefore an ideal location to wind down his career. For the Maple Leafs, however, the signing was curious. Although Healy was an established backup, he was 35 years old, and with a three-year contract worth $3.9 million (USD), the team had paid above market value for his services. While the team may have been able to scoop up another understudy at a reduced rate, the belief was that Healy would not only help push Potvin forward but also be able to reliably shoulder the workload of a backup goaltender. On October 4, 1997, he made his first start for the Maple Leafs, backstopping the club on the road against one of his former teams, the Islanders. He would start 17 games that season, taking some of the burden away from Potvin, but with little support in front of him at times, he finished with a .883 save percentage, one of the worst in the league. In the off-season, the Maple Leafs signed veteran goaltender Curtis Joseph, signalling the team was going in a new direction in net. While Potvin waited to be traded, Healy was banished to the International Hockey League. Following a deal that sent Potvin to the Islanders in exchange for defenceman Bryan Berard, Healy returned to the big club and served as backup to Joseph for two seasons before retiring.

# AUGUST 9
## THE TRADE, 1988

t turned the hockey world upside down. On August 9, 1988, the Edmonton Oilers traded Wayne Gretzky to the Los Angeles Kings. *Sold* is probably a better word, as money was at the heart of the deal. Gretzky, the greatest player in the world, was coming off his fourth Stanley Cup in Edmonton and his eighth straight Hart Trophy as the league's most valuable player. But Oilers owner Peter Pocklington was cash strapped, and trading the Great One would fetch a king's ransom. In return for sending Gretzky, along with Marty McSorley and Mike Krushelnyski to Los Angeles, Edmonton received Jimmy Carson, Martin Gelinas, three first-round draft picks, and $15 million.

Given Gretzky's iconic status both in the NHL and in Canada as its greatest athlete and most beloved son, when the news hit, there was understandable outrage. Irate and disgruntled fans jammed the Oilers' phone lines seeking answers. Gretzky's teammates in Edmonton were exploring the possibility of staging a strike or walk-out to protest Pocklington's move. There were even calls for the prime minister to intervene as Gretzky's departure was likened to the loss of a national treasure. New Democratic Party leader Nelson Riis issued a tongue-in-cheek press release that referred to Gretzky as "a national symbol like the beaver" and argued that Pocklington "may have sent Wayne to the moon as send him to L.A. Everybody knows that Los Angeles isn't a hockey town — they wouldn't know a puck from a beach ball." But that soon changed. With Gretzky's arrival in Los Angeles, the league's brightest star brought the game to Hollywood and put it on the biggest stage. The Great One's celebrity in Los Angeles increased hockey's popularity in the United States and helped the league expand into new markets. While not all these moves were successful, the Gretzky trade caused a transformational shift on the hockey landscape that still reverberates to this day.

# NEW BENCH BOSSES IN NEW YORK AND VANCOUVER, 1994

The day after the Rangers announced that Colin Campbell would become the team's new head coach, the Canucks made a similar move behind the bench. On August 10, 1994, Vancouver president and general manager Pat Quinn announced he was stepping down as head coach and turning over the duties to his assistant Rick Ley. Both moves came just months after the Rangers and Canucks battled for the championship in a hard-fought seven-game series that saw New York take home Lord Stanley's mug for the first time in 54 years. Rangers head coach Mike Keenan was hailed as a hero for bringing hockey's Holy Grail back to Broadway, but just a month later he became the villain. On July 15, he abruptly resigned from the organization and declared himself a free agent because of a contract dispute. Just days later, he bolted for St. Louis to become general manager and coach, leaving the Rangers' bench vacant.

Campbell, who joined the organization as an assistant in 1990 and ran the gauntlet to the Stanley Cup, was a logical successor. Meanwhile, on the West Coast, Ley, who had picked up some head coaching experience in Hartford before joining the Canucks as an assistant in 1991, was adamant he would be an NHL head coach for the upcoming season, even if that meant leaving Vancouver. After the heartbreaking loss to the Rangers, Quinn had announced his intentions to quit coaching, and promoting Ley made the most sense. While Quinn focused on managing the team, Ley led the Canucks back to the playoffs in the 1994–95 lockout-shortened season. The next year, Quinn dismissed his former protege with just six games remaining in the regular season and took over behind the bench. The two would be reunited again in 1998 in Toronto when Quinn brought in Ley to once again serve as his assistant coach.

# THE REAPER RETURNS, 1998

The Mighty Ducks didn't fear the reaper. On August 11, 1998, Anaheim reacquired heavyweight fighter Stu Grimson, also known as the Grim Reaper, along with Kevin Haller, from the Hurricanes in exchange for defenceman David Karpa and a future fourth-round draft pick. Towering at six foot five and packing 240 pounds into every punch and bone-crunching bodycheck, Grimson was one of the most formidable enforcers in the game. Opponents feared him. Fans loved him. In 504 career NHL games, Grimson had racked up 1,528 penalty minutes with five different clubs, including an earlier stint with the Mighty Ducks, where he and Todd Ewen intimidatingly patrolled the ice.

But after Hurricanes general manager Jim Rutherford refused to renegotiate his contract, a disgruntled Grimson wanted out of Carolina. The timing proved optimal for a return to Anaheim. Earlier in the off-season, Mighty Ducks all-star Paul Kariya reportedly felt the team was in need of some protection on the ice. Heeding his superstar's words, general manager Pierre Gauthier brought in the Grim Reaper as an insurance policy to safeguard Kariya and Teemu Selanne. In the first game of the 1998–99 season, Grimson lived up to those expectations. After Washington's Craig Berube gave Kariya a bump, Grimson took exception. The very next shift, he got into a fight with Berube and promptly dropped him to the ice. Following the game, Grimson spoke of his duty to defend his teammates. "Same situation takes place with another guy on my team, I plan to respond the same way," he said. A few games later, Grimson put his hands to a different use and registered his first multi-goal performance, including the game-winner, as the Mighty Ducks defeated the Lightning. In two seasons with Anaheim, Grimson racked up 274 penalty minutes, which included 32 major infractions. After retiring from the NHL in 2002, Grimson became a lawyer before working for a few years as a television analyst for the Nashville Predators.

# AUGUST 12
## SERGE SAVARD RETIRES, 1981

After patrolling Montreal's blue line in three different decades, defenceman Serge Savard was hanging up his skates. On August 12, 1981, the defenceman announced his retirement from the NHL. There were no tears shed at the press conference, however. Instead, Savard told the room full of reporters he had done his crying after the Canadiens were summarily eliminated by the Oilers in the post-season. It was at that point he knew his hockey days were over. In his first two full seasons with the Canadiens, Savard led the club to back-to-back championships. For his efforts, he was awarded the Conn Smythe Trophy as the most valuable player in the playoffs, becoming the first defenceman to win the award. Despite being one of the top defencemen of his era, Savard never took home the individual awards that had been bestowed upon many of his peers. While his name was never on the Norris Trophy, it was engraved eight times on the Stanley Cup.

When Savard announced his retirement, it was believed he was heading for a career in the stock market. He had reportedly enrolled in a stockbroking course and had already demonstrated his business acumen during his time with the Canadiens, making a fortune on real estate and horse racing off the ice. But Winnipeg Jets general manager John Ferguson had something up his sleeve. A former teammate of Savard's, Ferguson would select the newly retired defenceman in the league's annual re-entry draft on October 5, 1981, plucking his rights from the Canadiens after the team mistakenly failed to put him on the voluntary retirement list. Ferguson gambled that he could coax Savard out of retirement. The move paid off when, after months of persuasion, Savard played his first game for the Jets on December 20, 1981. He spent two seasons in Winnipeg before retiring for good in 1983. Not long after stepping away from the game, Savard became general manager of the Canadiens. He would preside over their championships in 1986 and 1993.

# BLUES HIRE RON CARON, 1983

f anybody could have given you examples of what happened on this day in hockey history, it would have been Ron Caron. Known as the Professor, Caron had an exceptional memory and uncanny knack for recalling historical details. On August 13, 1983, he was introduced as the general manager of the Blues. Prior to his arrival in St. Louis, he had served as the chief scout of the Montreal Canadiens for 15 years, where his keen eye for talent kept the club's cupboard stocked and was an integral part of its run of championships. Caron brought a unique perspective to his role with the Canadiens, as he hadn't travelled the typical route of his peers. Although he played hockey as a youngster growing up in Hull, Quebec, he was never good enough to dream he would have an NHL career.

After earning a bachelor of arts degree from the University of Ottawa in 1954, Caron became a teacher. He landed his first gig at a high school in Rouyn, Quebec, where he taught French and English. As part of his extracurricular duties, he coached hockey. After taking a position at St. Laurent College in Montreal, Caron continued to coach hockey, and it increasingly became his passion. In 1957, he had become a part-time scout with the Canadiens, and not long after, he became the chief scout for the Montreal Junior Canadiens. After being a part of two Memorial Cup championships with the team, he was promoted to chief scout with the big club in 1968, a position he held until he was dismissed by the organization in April 1983. Enter the St. Louis Blues. During his time at the helm in St. Louis, Caron presided over a number of critical moves that propelled the club to reach levels of success they hadn't achieved in years. Most notably, in 1988 Caron dealt Rob Ramage and goaltender Rick Wamsley to the Flames for Brett Hull and Steve Bozek. Hull, of course, went on to become the franchise goal-scoring leader, racking up 527 tallies in more than 10 seasons with the Blues.

# AUGUST 14
## JARI KURRI SIGNS WITH THE MIGHTY DUCKS, 1996

Jari Kurri would not be reuniting with Wayne Gretzky for a second time. On August 14, 1996, the Finnish right winger announced he had signed a one-year contract with the Mighty Ducks. Kurri, who had been drafted by the Oilers in 1980, had formed a dynamic partnership with the Great One in Edmonton, where the two had won four Stanley Cups together. Following Gretzky's trade to the Kings in 1988, Kurri stuck around in Alberta for another three years, winning another championship, before he also wound up in Los Angeles. With the pair reunited in Hollywood, Kurri scored 87 points in his sophomore season with the Kings as he and Gretzky guided the club to the Stanley Cup Final. A few years later, with the Kings in the midst of a rebuilding process, Gretzky was dealt to the St. Louis Blues before the 1996 trade deadline. Not long after, Kurri was shipped to the New York Rangers, along with Marty McSorley and Shane Churla, in exchange for Ray Ferraro, Ian Laperriere, Nathan LaFayette, and Mattias Norstrom. The crafty winger finished the season with five points in 14 games before adding eight more points in the playoffs.

Following his brief campaign with the Blueshirts, Kurri drew plenty of offers as a free agent. He was pursued by the Canucks, who had been interested in acquiring him earlier in the season, and the Rangers also looked to retain his services after they landed his former teammate, the Great One, in July. Instead, Kurri decided to sign with the Mighty Ducks, spurred by the prospect of playing with Paul Kariya and fellow Finlander Teemu Selanne. Although many expected Kurri would score his 600th career goal in Anaheim in the upcoming season, the 36-year-old was relegated to a smaller role with the club, finishing the year with just 13 goals and 35 points, his lowest career output in a full season. He eventually scored that milestone with the Avalanche the next year, during his final NHL season.

# AUGUST 15
## VANCOUVER HIRES ALAIN VIGNEAULT, 2005

After a two-year sabbatical coaching junior hockey, Alain Vigneault returned to the professional ranks when he was hired by the Manitoba Moose, Vancouver's American Hockey League (AHL) affiliate, on August 15, 2005. Vigneault had previously coached the Montreal Canadiens for three years before he was dismissed early in the 2000–01 season. After stepping away from the bench for two years, he joined the Prince Edward Island Rocket (now the Charlottetown Islanders) of the Quebec Major Junior Hockey League. Following two seasons with the Rocket, he was scooped up by the Canucks organization to replace Randy Carlyle, who had taken a position with the Anaheim Mighty Ducks, as the head coach of the Moose. Vigneault would guide Manitoba to a sterling 44-24-12 finish in the 2005–06 campaign before being promoted to the big club for the following season.

In just his first season behind the bench in Vancouver, he presided over a franchise-record 49 wins. For his efforts, he earned the Jack Adams Award, given annually to the league's best coach, as determined by the National Hockey League Broadcasters' Association. Over the next six seasons with the Canucks, Vigneault eclipsed his own franchise record for most wins in a season, as Vancouver finished the 2010–11 campaign with 54 victories, capturing its first ever Presidents' Trophy. In the playoffs, the Canucks would knock off the Blackhawks, Predators, and Sharks before losing a hard-fought seven-game series to the Bruins in the Stanley Cup Final. Although it was a disappointing end to an extraordinary season, Vancouver shook off defeat and finished atop the league standings for the second straight year. Although Vigneault guided the club to five consecutive division titles, he was fired by the Canucks on May 22, 2013. Less than a month later, he was hired to coach the Rangers, filling the vacancy left by John Tortorella, who coincidentally wound up being Vigneault's replacement in Vancouver.

# AUGUST 16
## RED WINGS AND BRUINS MAKE
## BLOCKBUSTER DEAL, 1949

ollowing a second straight loss to the Maple Leafs in the Stanley Cup Final, the Red Wings shook up their roster. On August 16, 1949, Detroit sent all-star defenceman Bill Quackenbush and forward Pete Horeck to Boston in exchange for wingers Pete Babando and Jimmy Peters and defencemen Clare Martin and Lloyd Durham. It was not an easy decision for Red Wings general manager Jack Adams to make. Quackenbush had been a fixture on Detroit's blue line since 1943 and was regarded as one of the best rearguards in the league. While other defenceman often relied on physicality to shut down opponents, Quackenbush was remarkably disciplined. During the 1948–49 campaign, he never incurred a penalty. As a result, it was not difficult to award him the Lady Byng Trophy that year for personifying sportsmanship and gentlemanly conduct on the ice. Moreover, in addition to admirable tactics, Quackenbush was one of the premier puck-moving defencemen of his era and had little difficulty evading opponents as he rushed up the ice.

Nevertheless, despite everything Quackenbush brought to the Red Wings, Adams knew that if he wanted to improve the positioning of the team up front, he'd have to part with his all-star defenceman. "We want the Stanley Cup…. We have defencemen. We don't have forwards. You can be sure I hate to lose Quackenbush," he told reporters. While Adams lamented the loss, he looked ahead to the future. "I have watched Peters and Babando since their junior hockey days and they are two players I always have felt would be valuable assets to the Wings," Adams said. He couldn't have been more right. On April 23, 1950, in double overtime in Game 7 of the Stanley Cup Final against the Rangers, Babando scored the championship-clinching goal to give Detroit its first Stanley Cup in seven years. Meanwhile, in Boston, Quackenbush continued his dominant play. He was inducted into the Hockey Hall of Fame in 1976.

# STEVE SMITH MAKES A COMEBACK, 1998

Steve Smith hopped off the bench and back onto the ice. On August 17, 1998, Smith announced he was leaving his position as a member of the Flames' coaching staff to make an NHL comeback with the team. A 12-year veteran of the league, he had patrolled the blue line for the Oilers and Blackhawks before a back injury forced him to retire after he was limited to just 21 games with Chicago in 1996–97. While he won three Stanley Cups with the Oilers, the most indelible image of Smith's time in Edmonton was when he scored on his own goal in Game 7 of the Smythe Division final against the Flames, on his birthday no less. Early into the third period, deep in his own zone, Smith made an errant pass that bounced off his goaltender, Grant Fuhr, and into the net. It proved to be the deciding goal and Calgary went on to eliminate the Oilers from the post-season. Although the three championships he later added to his trophy case undoubtedly made up for the rookie mistake, Smith could not get away from that moment, especially when he joined the Flames' coaching staff as an assistant nearly a decade later.

Being behind Calgary's bench gave Smith a new perspective on the game, but it also made him realize he wasn't ready for a career in coaching just yet. He still had some game left in him. His back had healed and he was ready to return to the ice. During his first season with the Flames, Smith played in 69 games and picked up 15 points. After he suited up for just 33 games over the next two campaigns, he decided he was finally ready to retire. After hanging up his skates for good, he joined the Blackhawks as a scout, winning the Stanley Cup with the club in 2010. Following his stint in Chicago, Smith returned to Edmonton where he served as an assistant coach for four years. The 2017–18 campaign was his fourth season as an assistant coach with the Carolina Hurricanes.

# KILLER GETS THE C, 1994

Doug Gilmour had some big shoes to fill. Following the departure of Maple Leafs team captain Wendel Clark in a blockbuster trade with the Nordiques on June 28, 1994, Toronto had a leadership vacancy heading into the upcoming season. Clark, who had been drafted first overall by the Maple Leafs nearly a decade earlier, was the heart and soul of the club. While Gilmour's style was different from Clark's crash-and-bang style of play, he also became a favourite of the Toronto faithful. After joining the Maple Leafs in 1992, Gilmour quickly endeared himself to the fans with how he approached the game. Despite being an incredible playmaker, he still played every game as if he were trying to earn a roster spot each and every night. Although he was unquestionably a star, he had a dogged work ethic that kept him grounded and made him a fan favourite. Even after he scored 127 points in 1992–93, setting a Maple Leafs franchise record for most points in a single season, he was still Doug, a regular guy. As a result, he was the perfect candidate to replace Clark.

On August 18, 1994, Toronto named Gilmour as the team's new captain. Although he reportedly wanted to keep the announcement low key, the Maple Leafs had none of that. Instead, Gilmour was presented his captain's sweater during a luncheon at the Hockey Hall of Fame, surrounded by some of the greatest leaders in team history. Looking on proudly as he received the captaincy were a pantheon of former captains that included Red Horner, Bob Davidson, Sid Smith, George Armstrong, Darryl Sittler, and Rob Ramage. For Gilmour, it was an incredible honour. In reflecting on the moment in his book *Killer* with Dan Robson, he wrote, "I was so proud to wear the *C* on the blue and white sweater." Gilmour captained the team for nearly three seasons before he was traded to New Jersey.

# HOWE ABOUT A TRADE FOR THE RAT, 1982

Despite scoring 92 points with the Flyers in 1981–82, a career high, Ken Linseman found himself on his way out of Philadelphia. On August 19, 1982, in a three-way deal between the Flyers, Whalers, and Oilers, Linseman ended up in Edmonton, along with Don Nachbaur from Hartford, as part of a package that saw six players swap locations. The deal saw Philadelphia acquire defenceman Mark Howe while the Whalers received Greg Adams and a first-round draft pick from the Flyers, along with Risto Siltanen and prospect Brent Loney from Edmonton. Although Linseman had piled up the points and led the team in scoring, the Flyers had grown weary of his propensity to take undisciplined penalties that often hurt the team. While he had begun making a career out of agitating his opponents, the organization felt he needed to mature his game more.

Known throughout the league as the Rat for his hunched-over skating style — a moniker reportedly given to him by Flyers' captain Bobby Clarke — Linseman's nickname also could have been reflective of the way he relentlessly pestered the opposition. The only problem was that he often stirred up trouble he couldn't finish. As a result, the Flyers — who had drafted him seventh overall in 1978 — decided to cut bait with the rat. Although there were knocks on Linseman's game, Oilers general manager Glen Sather believed the intensity and aggressiveness he brought to the ice could be just what his team needed. In Edmonton, Linseman clicked skating on a line with Glenn Anderson and Mark Messier, and the trio were integral in knocking off the Islanders in 1984 to capture the franchise's first Stanley Cup. Meanwhile, in Philadelphia, Howe became a fixture on the Flyers' blue line. Over the next decade, he developed into one of the most dependable rearguards in the game, finishing runner-up in Norris Trophy voting three times to fellow future Hall of Famers Rod Langway, Paul Coffey, and Ray Bourque.

# RANGERS ACQUIRE ERIC LINDROS, 2001

t took only nine years, but the Rangers finally got their man. On August 20, 2001, New York acquired Eric Lindros from Philadelphia in exchange for young forwards Pavel Brendl and Jan Hlavac, defenceman Kim Johnsson, and a conditional third-round draft pick. Back in 1992, when it was clear Lindros was not going to be suiting up for the Nordiques, Quebec had traded him to both the Flyers and the Rangers. In order to solve the dilemma, an arbitrator was brought in. After a week at the negotiation table, it was determined that Lindros's rights would be awarded to Philadelphia. Had the ruling gone the other way, New York would have reportedly sent the Nordiques' James Patrick, Tony Amonte, Alexei Kovalev, John Vanbiesbrouck, Doug Weight, Sergei Nemchinov, draft picks, and upward of $20 million. But it wasn't meant to be. With the Flyers, Lindros lived up to his billing. He won the Hart Trophy in the 1994–95 lockout-shortened season and followed up that campaign with a 115-point performance the following year.

But it wasn't always sunny in Philadelphia. As Lindros battled a string of concussions that kept him out of the lineup, his relationship with Flyers general manager Bobby Clarke became strained. Clarke stripped him of the captaincy and publicly criticized his play and character, even going as far as casting doubt on the veracity of Lindros's injuries. As the situation deteriorated, the two were not even on speaking terms. When Lindros entered restricted free agency in 2001, he rejected the club's qualifying offer and demanded a trade. Although he initially envisioned himself going to Toronto, he was excited about the new opportunity in New York. "This is a real special day for me. I know what I can accomplish," he said. In his first campaign on Broadway, Lindros racked up 73 points. Although he played his first injury-free season the following year, his production declined precipitously. Following the 2004–05 lockout, Lindros signed with the Maple Leafs as a free agent.

# NORTH STARS TRADE KEN HODGE JR., DRAFT JERE LEHTINEN, 1990

After the North Stars were unable to work out a deal with Ken Hodge Jr., who had spent most of his time in the organization with the team's International Hockey League affiliate in Kalamazoo, Michigan, they traded him to the Bruins for future considerations on August 21, 1990. Hodge had been drafted 46th overall by Minnesota in 1984, but after wrapping up his collegiate career at Boston College he only managed to suit up for a handful of games with the North Stars. Heading back to Boston gave Hodge the opportunity to play for the same team his father, Ken Sr., had helped win two Stanley Cups. In his rookie season with the Bruins, Hodge Jr. scored 30 goals in 70 games and finished as a finalist in voting for the Calder Trophy. While the move gave Hodge the chance to become a full-time NHL regular, it worked out even better for the North Stars. The future considerations Minnesota acquired in the trade turned out to be a fourth-round pick in the 1992 NHL Entry Draft, which the team used to draft Jere Lehtinen.

After the franchise relocated to Dallas, Lehtinen established himself as one of the league's best two-way players. He finished the 1996–97 campaign with 43 points, but his strong play on both sides of the puck made him a finalist for the Frank J. Selke Trophy, awarded annually to the league's best defensive forward. The crafty Finnish winger ended up capturing the Selke over two straight seasons (1997–98 and 1998–99), making him just the third player in NHL history to win the award in back-to-back years. He would add another to his trophy case in 2003. Capturing three Selkes is no small feat, especially as a winger. Recipients are predominantly centres, and as of the end of the 2017–18 NHL season, Lehtinen is still the last winger to win the award. For his exceptional play in Dallas, the Stars raised his number 26 jersey to the rafters in a pre-game ceremony on November 24, 2017.

# AUGUST 22
## RED WINGS SIGN BRETT HULL, 2001

ooking to make another run at a championship, the Red Wings added some firepower. On August 22, 2001, they signed Brett Hull to an incentive-laden two-year contract worth $9 million in base salary. Although the Red Wings had won back-to-back Stanley Cups in 1997 and 1998, the club had struggled to get beyond the second round of the playoffs in each of the next three seasons. Adding Hull to their arsenal was part of a reloading project that off-season, which included acquiring goaltender Dominik Hasek and Luc Robitaille, all in an effort to take another shot at a title.

Hull was just coming off a 39-goal campaign with the Stars, the ninth time in his career he posted a season of 30-plus goals. Although he had just turned 37, he was one of the most prolific scorers in the game. At the time, he was second among active players with 649 career goals, just two behind Mark Messier. As a result, when the Stars declined to exercise the option on Hull's contract, making him a free agent, his services were heavily sought by other clubs. Although he received more lucrative offers from the Canadiens, Canucks, and Rangers, he chose Detroit because he believed it gave him the best chance to drink from Lord Stanley's mug one last time. With the addition of Hull, the team's roster read more like a Hockey Hall of Fame induction list. Along with the veteran sniper, the Red Wings boasted an all-star cast that included Steve Yzerman, Luc Robitaille, Sergei Fedorov, Brendan Shanahan, Nicklas Lidstrom, Igor Larionov, Chris Chelios, and Dominik Hasek. Unsurprisingly, Detroit made short work of their opponents that season, finishing atop the standings with 51 wins. In the playoffs, Hull led the league in goal-scoring as Detroit went on to capture the Stanley Cup. The next year, Hull scored his 700th career goal with the Red Wings, becoming just the sixth player in NHL history to reach the milestone.

# AUGUST 23
# NORTH STARS AND CANUCKS SWAP GOALTENDERS, 1976

Cesare Maniago had been with the North Stars since their beginning. When Minnesota entered the league in 1967, the goaltender had been the club's first selection in the expansion draft. For the next nine years, he was the North Stars' last line of defence, valiantly backstopping the club, often against a battery of shots from the opposition. But after nearly a decade of his being a fixture in the crease, Minnesota was ready for a change in net.

On August 23, 1976, the North Stars traded Maniago to the Canucks in exchange for goaltender Gary Smith. For Maniago, it was a great move. He was 37 years old and was looking to wind down his career. Moreover, the native of Trail, British Columbia, was happy to finish his playing days in Vancouver, the ideal retirement location. Canucks manager and coach Phil Maloney believed Maniago's leadership and experience would be invaluable to the team, as the veteran could mentor the organization's younger goaltenders. Bringing in Maniago also alleviated the problem between Maloney and Smith. The two had been at loggerheads since February 8, 1976, when the goaltender was pulled after allowing five goals in 32 minutes in a game against the Penguins. Smith skated off the ice and disappeared. It turned out he actually left the rink in full gear and drove home. He later told the *Vancouver Province*, "It's tough driving in your skates." Afterward, the Canucks handed Smith a five-game suspension for the stunt before he returned to the net. As a result, it was only a matter of time before he was on his way out. When the trade happened, Smith wasn't even contacted by the team. Instead, he heard the news from a reporter. Although he initially didn't want to go to Minnesota, Smith eventually welcomed the change of scenery, but he ended up backstopping the North Stars for just one season before he was traded to the Capitals. Meanwhile, Maniago played two seasons in Vancouver before retiring and serving as the club's goaltending coach.

# AUGUST 24
# HALL OF FAME INDUCTION CEREMONY, 1972

Ted Lindsay didn't attend his Hockey Hall of Fame induction. When the former Detroit star received the honour in 1966, he declined the invitation because, at the time, the ceremonies were a stag affair and families were not included. Lindsay felt it was unfair that his wife and family wouldn't be able to share in the moment with him. "They sacrificed a lot through my career and went through a lot of inconveniences. They deserve it as much as I do," he told the *Globe and Mail*. At the time, some felt he was snubbing hockey's highest honour. But for him, it was just the right thing to do. Lindsay, who was no stranger to taking stands — he had been a driving force behind the establishment of the first players' association in the late 1950s — hoped his position would effect a change. "Maybe my reaction at this time will prevail on them to change their policy in the future," he noted. Six years later, when Lindsay's former teammate Gordie Howe got the nod, the Hall of Fame changed its protocol.

On August 24, 1972, Howe accepted his induction into hockey's pantheon, with wife Colleen, daughter Cathy and sons Marty, Mark, and Murray proudly looking on, marking the first time women and families were able to attend the ceremonies. Bernie "Boom Boom" Geoffrion was also inducted that day, but his wife, Marlene, who was the daughter of the league's first superstar, Howie Morenz, was unable to attend because she was recovering from surgery. During his speech, Geoffrion acknowledged her absence and lamented that she wasn't there to "see my kisser beside her old man in d'Hall of Fame." Although Lindsay was unable to have that moment himself, his protest helped ensure that future players and builders would have their families by their sides as they were enshrined into hockey greatness.

# MONTREAL MAROONS SUSPEND OPERATIONS, 1938

And then there were seven. On August 25, 1938, the NHL announced that the Montreal Maroons would suspend operations for a year, reducing the number of teams in the circuit to seven. The club had joined the league in 1924 as an expansion outfit alongside the Boston Bruins. Although the Maroons had success early on, winning the Stanley Cup in 1926 and capturing another in 1935, they struggled mightily on and off the ice during the Great Depression. Following the club's second championship, Montreal encountered early playoff exits in the next two years and finished in the cellar of the Canadian Division at the end of the 1937–38 campaign with just 12 victories. In addition, gate receipts precipitously dropped as the economic recession worsened, and the Maroons hemorrhaged cash.

In an effort to stop the bleeding, the club petitioned the league for a one-year hiatus to get its finances in order to get back on the ice. For NHL president Frank Calder, although it reduced the number of teams in the loop, it was a better option than transferring the franchise to St. Louis. A proposition from the Reconstruction Investment Company in that city had offered to run the moribund Maroons in Missouri, with the option of purchasing the team in three years. Although the NHL had operated a club, the Eagles, in St. Louis in 1934–35, it had been a disastrous campaign and the team shuttered after just a season. Given the challenges that had plagued the Eagles, Calder did not see much promise in the offer. Instead, the Maroons would be dormant. A few weeks later, key players were sold off to the crosstown rival Canadiens and the Black Hawks, all but sealing the club's fate. While the Bruins, who had entered the league at the same time as the Maroons, hoisted the Stanley Cup in 1939, there was no return in sight for the inactive Montreal club. It would never play another NHL game.

# AUGUST 26

## BOBBY ORR BECOMES NHL'S FIRST MILLION-DOLLAR MAN, 1971

During the 1970–71 season, it was estimated that Bobby Orr's salary was between $35,000 and $40,000. That was quite the bargain for the league's premier player who was just coming off a 139-point campaign in which he established league records for most points by a defenceman and most assists by a player. Moreover, he had just bagged his fourth consecutive Norris Trophy, as the league's top rearguard, and picked up his second straight Hart Trophy, as the NHL's most valuable player. Since breaking into the league in 1966, Orr had taken the Bruins from perennial cellar-dwellers to Stanley Cup champions. The Parry Sound, Ontario, native had scored the championship-clinching, and gravity-defying, goal a year earlier to bring Lord Stanley's mug back to Boston for the first time since 1938. Given his impressive resumé, the superstar defenceman was due for a significant raise.

On August 26, 1971, Orr inked a five-year contract with the Bruins worth an estimated $1 million. Although the financial terms were not announced at the time of the signing, the lucrative pact made Orr the league's highest-paid player. Alan Eagleson, Orr's financial advisor and executive director of the NHL Players' Association, always believed his client would be a millionaire by the time he turned 30 years old. At age 23, he was already there. Orr would certainly earn his big payday. In the next four seasons, he racked up 144 goals and 331 assists in 293 games. He finished top three in league scoring during those years, and nobody scored more points than him in the 1974–75 season. In 1972 Orr led the post-season in scoring and notched the Stanley Cup–winning goal against the Rangers. By the 1975–76 campaign, however, knee injuries had begun taking their toll on the eight-time Norris Trophy winner and he was limited to just 10 games that year, his last as a Bruin.

# RED WINGS ACQUIRE DANNY GRANT, 1974

t was not hard to spot Henry Boucha on the ice. The Red Wings forward and fan favourite sported a headband to keep his flowing black
hair out of his eyes. In an era before helmets, Boucha's style certainly
distinguished him from his peers. Selected 16th overall by the Red Wings
in the 1971 NHL Amateur Draft, he joined the club at the tail end of
the 1971–72 season, after representing the United States at the Winter
Olympics in Sapporo, Japan. But after two solid seasons in Detroit,
Boucha and his trademark headband were on their way to Minnesota.

On August 27, 1974, the Red Wings traded him to the North
Stars in exchange for former Calder Trophy–winner Danny Grant.
Although Boucha was a serviceable forward during his time in
Detroit, bringing in Grant added some firepower to the Red Wings'
lineup. Grant, who scored 34 goals in his rookie season in Minnesota
in 1968–69, had established himself as a dependable sharpshooter.
In Detroit, he found himself riding shotgun on a line with captain
Marcel Dionne. Flanking the superstar centre, he set career highs,
scoring 50 goals and racking up 87 points, in his inaugural season
with the Red Wings. But that off-season, Dionne was traded to Los
Angeles. Following Dionne's departure, Grant became the club's new
captain but would never revisit the offensive numbers he put up in his
first campaign with the Red Wings. Over the next few years, he sustained a series of serious leg injuries that consistently kept him out of
the lineup. Meanwhile, in Minnesota, Boucha was given a hero's welcome. Born and raised in Minnesota, he was immediately embraced
by the North Stars faithful. But early into his homecoming, Boucha
suffered a fractured right eye socket in a game against the Bruins. He
was never the same after the injury and it ultimately ended his career.
While he did return to professional hockey the next season, playing
for the Minnesota Fighting Saints of the World Hockey Association,
Boucha hung up his skates in 1977 after a brief return to the NHL.

## CAMPBELL LIFTS SUSPENSIONS, 1970

After 22 years of banishment from the NHL, Billy Taylor and Don Gallinger had their suspensions lifted. On August 28, 1970, league president Clarence Campbell announced he had rescinded the former players' lifetime ban for gambling on games, handed down on March 9, 1948. At the time of the offences, Gallinger was 22 years old and playing for the Bruins, while Taylor, who had been roommates with Gallinger during his time in Boston, had just been traded to the Rangers. Over the course of the 1947–48 season, the duo had begun gambling on NHL games, including some wagers against their own team. According to Campbell, Gallinger had placed a bet against the Bruins in one contest but played so well he lost his wager.

The betting continued, sometimes by as much as $1,000 per game, but the league only found out about the pair's nefarious activities by accident. It turned out that Gallinger and Taylor were placing bets with a Detroit bookmaker, James Tamer, who was under surveillance by the police department. One of the wiretapped conversations implicated the two NHL players, and it somehow made its way to the media. The story made front-page news, hearkening back to the 1919 Black Sox Scandal, in which eight players of the Chicago White Sox were accused of intentionally throwing the World Series against the Cincinnati Reds. Against that backdrop, Campbell took action. He suspended Gallinger indefinitely and banned Taylor from the league for life. The punishment effectively ended both players' hockey careers, as they were also unable to suit up for any amateur squads during their NHL moratorium. Over the next two decades, Gallinger attempted to have the ban lifted, but his efforts were unsuccessful. When Campbell finally ended the punishment in 1970, Taylor returned to the league as a scout for the Pittsburgh Penguins, but Gallinger never rejoined the NHL.

# AUGUST 29
## LEMIEUX STEPS AWAY FROM THE GAME, 1994

Mario Lemieux was stepping away from hockey. On August 29, 1994, the Penguins superstar announced he would miss the entire upcoming season. After battling Hodgkin's lymphoma for two years and a series of back injuries that had kept him out of the lineup, Lemieux needed a respite. Although he had defeated the cancer, the radiation treatments had weakened him considerably, and he was suffering from anemia. With the first part of the 1994–95 season already wiped away by the lockout, Lemieux decided to take the year to regain his strength with the hope of getting back on the ice in the future. "I still love the game of hockey," Lemieux said at the press conference. "This is not a hockey issue. This is a health issue. I feel my health at this time is a lot more important than playing hockey," he added. While Lemieux's hiatus was to be temporary, there were concerns within the hockey world that he might never play again. Acknowledging the possibility that he might never be healthy enough to return to the NHL, he said, "If I feel I'm not able to go out on the ice at close to 100 percent, another decision will have to be made."

But there would be no need for another solemn press conference. On October 7, 1995, Lemieux returned to the ice, racking up four assists in an 8-3 rout of the Maple Leafs. Later that month, on the road in a game against the Islanders, he scored his 500th career goal as part of a three-goal effort — his 32nd career hat trick — to power his club to victory. He reached the milestone in just his 605th career game, faster than anyone else in NHL history except for Wayne Gretzky, who accomplished the feat in 30 fewer games. Lemieux's comeback tour continued all season long. He scored 69 goals and added 92 assists to lead the league in scoring, picking up his fifth Art Ross Trophy and nabbing his third Hart Trophy.

# CAPITALS HIRE DAVID POILE, 1982

David Poile had his work cut out for him. On August 30, 1982, he accepted an offer to become the Capitals' new general manager, replacing Roger Crozier. At age 33, Poile was the youngest general manager in the league, but he had grown up in the hockey business. A month before he was born, his father, Bud, was traded from the Bruins to the Maple Leafs. When Bud became the first general manager of the Flyers, a teenaged David picked up a gig as a trainer at Philadelphia's inaugural training camp. Not long after graduating from Northeastern University in Boston, where he had a successful collegiate hockey career, Poile joined the upstart Atlanta Flames as an administrative assistant. He stayed with the organization for a decade, working his way up to assistant general manager in Calgary before joining the Capitals.

In Washington, he was tasked with ending eight years of futility. Since entering the league in 1974, the Capitals had never qualified for the post-season. Poile was up to the task. Within a week of taking the job, he pulled the trigger on a franchise-altering trade. On September 9, Poile pried the heart of the Canadiens defence corps — Rod Langway and Brian Engblom — along with Craig Laughlin and Doug Jarvis, out of Montreal in exchange for Ryan Walter and Rick Green. It was a veritable coup for the Capitals. Langway, who would be referred to as the Secretary of Defence by Capitals fans, would become the backbone of Washington's blue line for years to come. Following the trade, Poile said, "It was the kind of deal I dreamed about making when I took the job here." It immediately paid off. In Poile's first year on the job, Washington clinched a playoff berth for the first time in franchise history and qualified for the post-season for the next 14 straight years.

# AUGUST 31
## BRIAN BELLOWS IS TRADED TO MONTREAL, 1992

No one had scored more goals as a member of the North Stars than Brian Bellows. But after 10 years and 342 goals in Minnesota, the franchise's all-time leading scorer was off to Montreal. On August 31, 1992, the North Stars traded Bellows to the Canadiens for Russ Courtnall. Although Bellows racked up seven 30-or-more-goal seasons playing in Minnesota, the organization, particularly newly minted general manager Bob Gainey, felt he was a one-dimensional player who was unwilling or unable to play a more well-rounded game. Gainey, who had won four straight Selke trophies during his playing days in Montreal, was regarded as one of the best defensive forwards of his era. He believed Bellows was responsible for some of the North Stars' recent struggles, despite being just a year removed from an appearance in the Stanley Cup Final.

As a result, Gainey brought in his former Canadiens teammate Russ Courtnall, who lacked Bellows's scoring touch but was a much stronger defensive player. While the move may have addressed a perceived need in the North Stars organization, it was criticized in the hockey world. Even before either player took to the ice for his new team, most had declared Montreal as the clear-cut winner in the deal. Minnesota fans were incensed. One letter to the Minneapolis *Star Tribune* offered some simple advice to the North Stars' general manager. It read: "If Gainey wants to coach the Montreal team, perhaps it is simpler for him to go to Montreal instead of trying to trade for Montreal players. Bring Brian Bellows back!" In the 1992–93 season, Bellows would score 88 points for Montreal and played an integral role in capturing the Stanley Cup that year. Meanwhile, Courtnall notched career highs in points during his time with the North Stars franchise, while Bob Gainey would go on to engineer the team's 1999 championship in Dallas.

# SEPTEMBER 1
# LEMIEUX BECOMES THE EMPEROR PENGUIN, 1999

Mario Lemieux had been the superstar centre for the Penguins for years, but on September 1, 1999, he added a new position to his NHL resumé. On that day, the league accepted Lemieux's plans to own the team, making him the first player in North American sports history to own the team he had once played for. In his final years before retiring in 1997, the Penguins had been a financial disaster. After years of hemorrhaging cash, the organization was forced to declare bankruptcy in November 1998. Although the Penguins continued playing that season, the future of the team was in jeopardy, with many speculating it was only a matter of time before the franchise relocated or shuttered and dispersed its players.

Lemieux, however, had a plan. Pittsburgh owed him more than $30 million in deferred salary. Instead of trying to recover his lost wages, he proposed the idea of converting the bulk of his owed earnings into an equity stake in the Penguins, one that would give him a controlling interest. Along with a group of investors that included supermarket mogul Ron Burkle, Lemieux battled through federal bankruptcy court for months before he was awarded the team. Following the NHL's approval of his ownership plan, Lemieux assumed the positions of president, chairman, and CEO of the Penguins. Focusing on the team's business operations, he faced the difficult long-term task of transitioning the club out of bankruptcy and making the team viable and competitive, but for now he had saved his former team from the brink of disaster and kept the Penguins in Pittsburgh. But after just a year in his new ownership position, Lemieux still had unfinished business on the ice. He came out of retirement on December 27, 2000, becoming the first playing owner in modern major professional sports.

# SEPTEMBER 2
## CANADA FALLS OFF THE SUMMIT, 1972

Even before the first game of the Summit Series between the Soviets and Team Canada had been played, much of the hockey world had already crowned the Canadians as victors. Although the Soviets had dominated amateur competition for years, they were now going up against the NHL's star players, and few gave them much of a chance. Before the puck had even dropped, *Globe and Mail* columnist Dick Beddoes proclaimed that the Canadians would finish the tournament undefeated. "So, make it Canada 8 games to 0. If the Russians win one game, I will eat this column shredded at high noon in a bowl of borscht on the front steps of the Russian embassy," he wrote on August 29, 1972. Four days later, Beddoes would literally eat his words.

On September 2, 1972, before a full house at the Montreal Forum, the Canadians were trounced 7-3 by the Soviets. The nation was in disbelief. Hockey was Canada's game, and it was unfathomable that the best players in the world could have been bested by a group of players from a country that had only started playing organized hockey just a half-century earlier. Moreover, at the height of the Cold War, the battle on the ice represented not only a clash of two styles of hockey but also a collision of political ideologies. There was much more than hockey on the line. Despite so much being at stake, Team Canada went into the tournament brimming with confidence, but its players were physically unprepared to take on an opponent that trained and conditioned year-round. Once the game began, the Soviets controlled the tempo of the match by countering the Canadians' grinding style of play with a creative game that focused on passing. When the final buzzer sounded, a nation was in shock. Although it was just the first game in an eight-game series that would later shift to Moscow, Canada's myth of hockey superiority had been shattered.

# SEPTEMBER 3
# SCOTT STEVENS IS AWARDED TO
# THE DEVILS, 1991

After the Blues pried restricted free agent Brendan Shanahan out of New Jersey, they owed the Devils compensation. Under the collective bargaining agreement, the typical remuneration for signing restricted free agents from other clubs was forking over draft picks. But St. Louis's first-round picks in the near future were already spoken for. Just a year earlier, the Blues had signed all-star defenceman Scott Stevens from the Capitals to a five-year deal, forcing them to send five first-round draft picks back to Washington. Because of the unusual situation, the Blues offered New Jersey goaltender Curtis Joseph, Rod Brind'Amour, and two draft picks, but the Devils declined. Instead, they wanted Stevens. Given the steep price St. Louis had paid for the blueliner, they were unwilling to part with their captain. As a result, the matter went to arbitration.

On September 3, 1991, Judge Edward Houston sided with New Jersey and awarded the club Scott Stevens. While the Blues mourned, the Devils celebrated. New Jersey general manager Lou Lamoriello was delighted that he would be adding one of the league's hardest-hitting and effective defenceman. Although St. Louis added Shanahan, who was only 22 years old at the time and a rising star, they had lost their captain and a player for whom they had paid dearly. Meanwhile, Stevens was initially disheartened about the prospect of going to the Devils. He had chosen, after all, to sign with the Blues, and he and his family envisioned him retiring in St. Louis. After initially not reporting to camp, Stevens arrived in New Jersey. Over the next 13 years he became an integral part of the team's defensive corps and a driving force behind its three Stanley Cups. Although it wasn't where Scott and his wife, Donna, had envisioned him winding down his career, Stevens's years in New Jersey cemented his status as one of the league's all-time best defenceman.

# SEPTEMBER 4
# CLARENCE CAMPBELL BECOMES PRESIDENT, 1946

Within months of becoming assistant to NHL president Mervyn "Red" Dutton, Clarence Campbell was thrust into the big chair. On September 4, 1946, it was announced that Dutton had resigned from his position and that the league had approved Campbell as his successor. Dutton, who had been at the helm for only three years, was leaving his post to attend to personal business matters, which included trying to resurrect the Brooklyn Americans, the team for which he had previously played during his NHL career. Although Campbell was known in hockey circles, his appointment was still a surprise. A practising lawyer, he had been an NHL referee from 1936 to 1939 but had spent the next six years serving in the Canadian military during the Second World War. Campbell rose to the rank of lieutenant colonel and was made a member of the Order of the British Empire, and following the conflict he was part of the team that prosecuted Waffen-SS major general Kurt Meyer for war crimes.

Not long after returning to Canada, Campbell returned to the NHL and took the job with Dutton. His apprenticeship certainly progressed faster than he had anticipated. "It was my original understanding and my personal hope that Mervyn Dutton would have continued in the office of president for the ensuing years and at least for a few months," said Campbell's statement to the press. Although the league's new president may have been inexperienced, he did not show it. Over the next few years, Campbell would have a significant impact on the NHL, increasing the number of regular-season games and implementing the All-Star Game. His greatest legacy, however, was presiding over a period of tremendous growth. In 1967, Campbell was the architect behind the league's ambitious expansion plan that saw it double in size. By the time he retired in 1977, after more than three decades as president, the league had tripled in size and hockey had never been more popular.

# SEPTEMBER 5
# ALEXEI YASHIN SIGNS WITH THE ISLANDERS, 2001

A lexei Yashin was the first player the Senators ever drafted. In 1992, Ottawa used their second overall selection to nab the Russian centre. After wrapping up another season with Dynamo Moscow, Yashin joined the Senators for the 1993–94 campaign. He had an immediate impact in Ottawa, scoring 79 points as a rookie, eclipsing the play of fellow neophyte Alexandre Daigle, who was the number one draft choice in 1993. Yashin's future in Ottawa looked bright, but a series of contract disputes made for a tumultuous tenure with the Senators. After he racked up 94 points in 1998–99 and finished runner-up in Hart Trophy voting as the league's most valuable player, the situation reached its nadir when he refused to play out the final year of his contract unless he was given a significant raise.

When Ottawa declined to renegotiate his deal, he requested a trade. With the Senators unwilling to give in to his demands, Yashin refused to report to the team for the upcoming season. When he still hadn't join the team by November 1999, the Senators suspended him for the remainder of the season. After sitting out the entire year, Yashin returned for the 2000–01 campaign after an arbitrator ruled he owed the club a year's worth of services. The saga finally came to a close when Ottawa traded Yashin to the New York Islanders on June 23, 2001, for defenceman Zdeno Chara, Bill Muckalt, and the second overall selection in the draft. The Senators promptly used the pick to take Jason Spezza, who would go on to score 687 points in 686 games with the club. On Long Island on September 5, 2001, the Islanders inked Yashin to a 10-year deal worth $87.5 million, the biggest contract in league history at the time. While Spezza flourished in Ottawa, Yashin's production precipitously declined in New York after his first season with the team. In 2007, the Islanders bought out his contract, which only recently came off the club's books in 2015.

# DOUG WILSON LANDS IN SAN JOSE, 1991

Doug Wilson found himself in uncharted waters. After finishing the 1990–91 campaign atop the league standings with the Blackhawks, the all-star defenceman would be starting the upcoming season with the Sharks. On September 6, 1991, San Jose acquired Wilson from Chicago in exchange for Kerry Toporowski and a second-round draft pick. Wilson, who had been drafted sixth overall by the Hawks in 1977, had spent his entire NHL career with Chicago, becoming a fixture on the team's blue line. After racking up 85 points in 1981–82, he won the Norris Trophy as the league's best defenceman. He continued to be a stalwart player on Chicago's back end, finishing as a Norris finalist in 1989–90 and establishing all-time club records in points for a defenceman along the way. The arrival of general manager and coach Mike Keenan, however, changed things for Wilson in Chicago.

As tension developed between the two, Wilson's performance declined. "The relationship I had with Mike Keenan I don't think was conducive for me being happy or playing good hockey," he said. As a result, after 14 years with the Blackhawks, he found himself with a new NHL club for the first time in his career. Although the expansion Sharks struggled mightily in their inaugural season in the league, Wilson's pedigree brought credibility to the fledgling team and buoyed it through rough waters. In his two years in San Jose, Wilson served as the club's first captain and its first representative in the All-Star Game. After scoring 48 points in 86 games with the Sharks, he retired from the NHL. Twelve years after he first joined the team as a player, he was appointed as its new general manager. As of the end of the 2017–18 season, the Sharks have missed qualifying for the playoffs only once during Wilson's tenure and advanced as far as the Stanley Cup Final in 2016.

# SEPTEMBER 7
# NHL ADJUSTS TO PEACETIME, 1945

As the NHL headed into its first season after the conclusion of the Second World War, it did so without any significant rule changes on the ice. On September 7, 1945, at the semi-annual meeting of the league's board of governors, no noteworthy changes were instituted that would affect how the game was played. Following the end of the Second World War, league president Red Dutton lifted the restriction that prevented players serving in the armed forces or engaging in essential war work from playing in the NHL. As a result, many players who had served in the Canadian and United States military rejoined their squads, but plenty had difficulty adjusting to returning to the ice. Besides transitioning the league back to playing in peacetime, the board of governors agreed that for the first time in the history of hockey, the rules maintained and adopted by the NHL would become standardized in all organized hockey, from the amateur up to the professional circuits.

By the time of the meeting, the league had already inked agreements with the United States Hockey League and the Canadian Amateur Hockey Association to ensure that all players coming through their ranks were playing under the same system that governed players at the highest level. The move guaranteed standardization and consistency among the NHL's partner leagues and ensured that the NHL set the standard for the hockey world. While it was easy for the league's governors to agree on the adoption of universal rules, there was some discussion over how many assists should be awarded on goals. At the meeting, there was a proposal to restrict the number of assists to one on any goal scored, but it was decided to continue with the league's two-assist system when warranted. Even today, there still remains some debate in hockey circles about the utility and necessity of awarding secondary assists.

# SEPTEMBER 8
## PHIL ESPOSITO'S SPEECH, 1972

t was a moment that is engrained in the minds of a generation of Canadians. Following another dispiriting loss to the Soviets on home soil, a sweaty, winded Phil Esposito made an impassioned speech to the country during an interview with CTV's Johnny Esaw. "For the people across Canada: We tried. We gave it our best. For the people who booed us, geez ... all of us guys are really disheartened and we're disillusioned and we're disappointed in some of the people. We cannot believe the bad press we've got, the booing we've got in our own buildings. Every one of us guys, thirty-five guys who came out to play for Team Canada, we did it because we love our country. If the fans in Russia boo their players like some of the Canadian fans — I'm not saying all of them — some of them booed us, then I'll come back and apologize to each and every one of the Canadians," he said.

Heading into the Summit Series tournament, the Canadians were heralded as the unquestioned favourite. But after a stunning defeat by the Soviets at the Montreal Forum, Canada was reeling. Humbled by the opening loss, Team Canada rallied in the second game to even the series, but after a deflating tie in the third contest, the nation's confidence was shaken. Following another defeat in Vancouver on September 8, 1972, the Canadians were booed throughout the game, on and off the ice, by the 15,570 patrons at the Pacific Coliseum. For Esposito and his compatriots, the jeers stung more than the loss. It was certainly not the send-off they had been hoping for. After addressing the nation, Esposito and the Canadians were off to Moscow to continue the series. With the Soviets returning home holding the advantage, Esposito could only hope his words had a galvanizing effect on his teammates and his countrymen.

# GORDIE HOWE RETIRES, 1971

t was a difficult decision, but Mr. Hockey was calling it quits. On September 9, 1971, after 25 years in the National Hockey League with the Red Wings, Gordie Howe was retiring. He had actually made it known to the local media in Detroit the night before that he was hanging up his skates, but the official announcement came the next day. With his beloved wife, Colleen, by his side, he told reporters he was stepping away from the game. Howe, who was coming off the most unproductive season of his storied career after being hampered by a series of injuries, including an arthritic wrist, conceded it was time to retire because he felt he could no longer play to the level he wanted. "I could play one more year and play very badly, but what good would that do when it could undo 25 years of work," he said.

Instead, Howe had accepted a front-office job with Detroit, where he would serve as vice-president. In his first year away from the rink, the Red Wings organized an elaborate jersey retirement ceremony. On March 12, 1972, with United States vice-president Spiro Agnew in attendance, Howe's number 9 was raised to the rafters. It proved to be one of the few highlights during his time in the front office. When he first accepted the job, he thought it would be a great opportunity to effect change in the organization, but he quickly learned that his role was limited and largely symbolic. Unhappy with his situation, Howe was lured out of retirement by the opportunity to play with his sons Marty and Mark for the Houston Aeros of the World Hockey Association (WHA). In his first season in Houston, with his wrist healed, he racked up 100 points and won the league's most valuable player award. After six productive seasons in the WHA, Howe returned to the NHL in 1979 with the Hartford Whalers, where he registered 41 points as a 51-year-old, before calling it quits for good at the end of the season.

# SEPTEMBER 10
## ARTURS IRBE SIGNS IN CAROLINA, 1998

ollowing a tumultuous season backstopping the worst defensive team in the league, Latvian goaltender Arturs Irbe still said he wanted to return to the Canucks. Even though he had been given an incredibly short leash by tyrannical head coach Mike Keenan — Irbe was unceremoniously yanked from his net seven times in just 27 outings that season — he still wanted to stay in Vancouver if it gave him the opportunity to become a starting goaltender again. Although he had spent most of the year as an understudy to colleagues Kirk McLean and Sean Burke, neither of whom finished the season in Vancouver, the Latvian performed admirably despite a barrage of shots and frequent roster turnover.

After becoming the starting netminder in San Jose in 1993–94, Irbe had led the Sharks to a stunning first-round upset over the Red Wings in the playoffs. In the off-season, however, his career almost came to an end. Back home in Latvia, Irbe was bitten by his dog Rambo, sustaining a fractured finger and significant nerve damage to the digit on his left hand. While doctors believed the injuries were not career-threatening, his subsequent play in San Jose declined, culminating with the team's decision to release him in 1996. After stints as a backup for Dallas and Vancouver, Irbe was ready to prove he could be a starting goaltender again. On September 10, 1998, he signed a one-year deal with the Hurricanes worth $550,000. It turned out to be one of the biggest bargains of the season. Irbe had a resurgence in Carolina, usurping the starting job from Trevor Kidd, setting a career high in shutouts, and finishing the 1998–99 campaign with one of the best save percentages in the league. The Latvian's renaissance continued over the next three years with the Hurricanes. In 2000–01, he started all but six of Carolina's games and finished the season with 37 wins. The next year he backstopped the franchise to its first ever Stanley Cup Final appearance, turning in a valiant performance against the eventual champion Red Wings.

# SEPTEMBER 11

# NHL ANNOUNCES ANOTHER ROUND OF EXPANSION, 1969

After a successful expansion drive in 1967 doubled the size of the NHL, the league was keen to continue growing. On September 11, 1969, it announced it would be adding two more teams for the 1970–71 season. At the time of the announcement it was not clear where the two franchises would be going, but Vancouver was tapped as one of the top locations. After missing out on the NHL's first round of expansion, NHL president Clarence Campbell noted how important it was to ensure a Canadian city would be included in the league's next growth plan. "We could not carry on goodwill in Canada, a country which has contributed so much to the sport, unless we added a Canadian team," he said.

With Vancouver all but confirmed, other cities would have the opportunity to bid for a franchise leading up to the league's deadline of December 1. Before the expansion process had truly kicked off, the NHL noted it had already received informal applications from six locations in the United States, namely Atlanta, Baltimore, Buffalo, Cleveland, Kansas City, and Washington. At the top of the heap were Buffalo and Baltimore. Both cities had missed the cut two years earlier, with Baltimore coming narrowly close. In February 1966, when the NHL announced its previous expansion locations, many expected Baltimore to be included on the list. Instead, St. Louis had been awarded the sixth franchise. The NHL had chosen the city known as the Gateway to the West partly because of its geographic location but chiefly because the Wirtz family, who owned the Black Hawks, also owned the dilapidated St. Louis Arena and was keen to have an expansion partner take on the costs of the crumbling building. But it wasn't meant to be for Baltimore this time around, either. On December 1, 1969, the NHL announced that franchises had been awarded to Vancouver and Buffalo.

# OILERS ACQUIRE MARTY MCSORLEY, 1985

n Pittsburgh, Marty McSorley was a hard-hitting defenceman, but in Edmonton, he would become the protector of the Great One. On September 12, 1985, the Oilers acquired McSorley, along with Tim Hrynewich, from the Penguins in exchange for goaltender Gilles Meloche. In his first season in Edmonton, McSorley moved up front and scored 23 points in 59 games but racked up 265 penalty minutes intimidating and countering the opposition who dared take a run at Wayne Gretzky. Although he was primarily brought in to complement Dave Semenko's bodyguard duties, there was more nuance to McSorley's game. He had keen hockey instincts and could play both forward and defence. In his book *99: Stories of the Game*, Gretzky recalls how, when McSorley was playing on a line with Kevin McClelland and Dave Semenko in Edmonton, they were incredibly skilled at constraining the opposition and preventing them from advancing up the ice, all without touching the puck.

With the Oilers, he played a key role in winning back-to-back championships in 1987 and 1988, all while keeping a close eye on Gretzky. During his time in Edmonton McSorley forged a close relationship with his teammate on and off the ice. So much so that when Gretzky received word he would be traded to the Kings in August 1988, he specifically requested that McSorley, along with Mike Krushelnyski, accompany him to Los Angeles. As a member of the Kings, McSorley continued his protective duties but also played an integral part in the team's run to the Stanley Cup Final in 1993. Despite his play, McSorley was traded to the Penguins that off-season, but it was not long before he was back in Los Angeles. In February 1994, he was reacquired by the Kings and reunited with the Great One. Just over a month later, he would be a part of hockey history when he assisted on Gretzky's 802nd career goal to surpass Gordie Howe on the NHL's all-time list.

# SEPTEMBER 13
## LONDON CALLING, 1992

ondon called the NHL. On September 13, 1992, the league concluded a two-game exhibition series played between the Blackhawks and Canadiens at Wembley Arena in London. Looking to promote the league outside North America, the NHL hoped to establish a foothold in Great Britain, much as the National Football League had when it began playing its American Bowl exhibition series at Wembley Stadium in 1986. Although it marked the first time in 33 years an NHL matchup was played in London, the Blackhawks and Canadiens did not receive much fanfare. For the first game of the series, only 7,830 fans showed up to watch Montreal edge Chicago 3-2. The poor turnout, however, was not the only disappointment.

Even before the puck had dropped on the series, the NHL had encountered hostility from the British Ice Hockey Association. According to the *New York Times*, David Pickles, general secretary of the British Association, said, "Thanks very much, but we don't really need the NHL's exposure, especially if they are looking to sell their particular style of violent play." Despite the cool welcome from Britain's governing hockey body, the series continued, with the final game ending in a dramatic finish. After 60 minutes of play, the Blackhawks and Canadiens were tied 4-4. When overtime solved nothing, a shootout was held to break the deadlock. Chicago ended up winning the game, but with the series now tied at a game apiece, another shootout was held to determine the champion. The Blackhawks' snipers, backstopped by goaltender Jimmy Waite, who stopped eight of nine attempts by the Canadiens, took the second shootout to clinch the series. It would be another 13 years before the league adopted the shootout to break stalemates during the regular season. The NHL returned to London the following year with the Maple Leafs and Rangers, and in 2007, the Ducks and Kings went to London and played the league's first regular-season games in Europe.

# SEPTEMBER 14
## WORLD CUP OF HOCKEY, 1996 AND 2004

With a flurry of late goals, the United States defeated Canada to win the inaugural World Cup of Hockey. On September 14, 1996, with just four minutes remaining in the deciding game of the tournament, the United States exploded for four goals to take a 5-2 victory over their Canadian rivals. For years, Canada had dominated the Canada Cup, an eponymous international tournament sanctioned by the NHL and the International Ice Hockey Federation, before it was supplanted by the World Cup of Hockey in 1996. After Canada defeated the United States in the first game of the championship series, many expected the result would be similar to previous tournaments, but the Americans would not go down without a fight. They rallied in the second game to even the series, and before the championship-clinching game, head coach Ron Wilson pumped up his team by playing a motivational video that included their highlights from the tournament interspersed with clips from *Rocky II*. It worked. Just when it seemed as though the United States was down for the count, Brett Hull scored the tying goal, his second of the game, before Tony Amonte notched the decisive marker with just over two minutes remaining to give the Americans the first World Cup of Hockey.

Canada would redeem themselves eight years later to the day when they defeated Finland in the second installment of the tournament. It proved to be a bittersweet moment for the players and fans. With the NHL lockout looming, it ended up being the last game featuring the league's best players for another year. Following a 12-year hiatus, the World Cup of Hockey returned in 2016. Although Canada successfully defended its title, the star of the tournament was Team North America. Made up of the best 23-and-under players from across the continent, including Connor McDavid, Auston Matthews, and Mark Scheifele, it might have been the most fun hockey team ever assembled.

# SEPTEMBER 15
# CANADA WINS THE CANADA CUP, 1976

Streaking down the left side of the ice, his curly hair flowing with each stride, Darryl Sittler entered the Czechoslovakian zone with nine minutes remaining in overtime. As he approached the net, goaltender Vladimir Dzurilla, who was known for aggressively challenging opponents, came way out of his crease to halt Sittler's advance. But the 26-year-old Maple Leafs centre juked to his left and slipped the puck into the yawning cage. Canada had just won the inaugural Canada Cup. The tournament began 13 days earlier and featured the best players from Canada, the United States, the Soviet Union, Czechoslovakia, Sweden, and Finland. It was hockey's first true best-on-best competition.

While many expected Canada to square off against the Russians for the title — hearkening back to the Summit Series from four years earlier — Dzurilla stood on his head during the opening round-robin play, earning Czechoslovakia a berth against the Canadians in the final series. Although Canada starched their opponents 6-0 in the opening game, the Czechs were just two minutes away from tying the series in the second contest before Bill Barber scored the equalizer to send the game into overtime and the crowd at the Montreal Forum into bedlam. It proved to be a nail-biter. It was the first time Czechoslovakia had played sudden death at the international level, and a series of disallowed Canadian goals, and brilliant play in net, kept the Czechs alive until the second half of the first period of extra time. For Sittler, who was coming off a 10-point performance in the regular season and a five-goal game in the playoffs, that championship-clinching tally proved to be his biggest goal. "That was my highlight. I was never fortunate to be on a Stanley Cup team, so to be on a championship team with the best players from Canada in 1976 was my highlight," he later said.

# SEPTEMBER 16
## WAYNE GRETZKY'S FIRST
## TRAINING CAMP, 1978

When Wayne Gretzky set out onto the ice in Indianapolis on September 16, 1978, it marked the first time the hockey phenom attended a professional training camp. Earlier that summer, the 17-year-old Brantford, Ontario, native turned heads when he opted to forgo his final years of junior hockey and turn pro with the Indianapolis Racers of the World Hockey Association. High above the clouds, aboard the private jet of Nelson Skalbania, Gretzky signed a seven-year personal-services contract worth $1.75 million with the Racers' owner, as they flew from Edmonton to Vancouver. When they landed, Gretzky was a Racer and his dream of becoming a professional hockey player had come true.

Ever since he had scored 378 goals in the Brantford Atom League as an 11-year-old, Gretzky had been earmarked as a hockey prodigy. As he rose through the hockey ranks, scouts had begun referring to him as the next Bobby Orr. Although many of those same scouts had reservations about his size, after Gretzky scored 70 goals and racked up 112 assists in his first season in junior with the Sault Ste. Marie Greyhounds, it was clear he seemed destined for greatness. On October 20, 1978, he scored his first professional goal and added another in a losing effort to the Oilers. Too young to start his NHL career, Gretzky should have been a boon to the Racers, but his time in Indianapolis was fleeting. After just eight games, Gretzky, along with Peter Driscoll and goaltender Eddie Mio, was sent to Edmonton for $850,000. On his 18th birthday, not long into his tenure with the Oilers, Gretzky signed a 21-year personal-services contract worth upward of $5 million with Edmonton owner Peter Pocklington. The following season, after the WHA was absorbed by the National Hockey League, Gretzky began his NHL career with the Oilers, where he would win four Stanley Cups before Pocklington sold him to the Kings.

# SEPTEMBER 17
# MONTREAL TRADES ANDREW CASSELS, 1991

Andrew Cassels wanted out of Montreal. Dissatisfied with his ice time during his first full season with the Canadiens, the disgruntled centre sat out the team's training camp the following year. Drafted 17th overall by Montreal in 1987, Cassels had previously won the Emms Family Award, presented annually to the Ontario Hockey League's top rookie. He continued his junior hockey career with the Ottawa 67's, scoring 48 goals and racking up 151 points in 1988 to win the league's player of the year award. Following another campaign in Ottawa, Cassels joined the Canadiens organization in 1989–90 but spent most of the season in Sherbrooke in the American Hockey League. Although he became a full-time regular with the Canadiens the following year, he found himself in a limited role, playing behind Guy Carbonneau, Stephan Lebeau, and Denis Savard. As a result, the rookie was dismayed about his situation.

On September 17, 1991, he was traded to the Whalers for a second-round draft pick. In his second season in Hartford, Cassels would dish out 64 assists and finish with 85 points. Meanwhile, in Montreal the Canadiens used the return to select Valeri Bure in the 1992 NHL Entry Draft. Much like his older brother Pavel, the speedy Russian winger had a nifty set of hands and was known for his playmaking abilities. Undersized by NHL standards at the time, during his time in Montreal Bure formed part of Montreal's Smurf Line with Saku Koivu and Oleg Petrov, who were also deemed diminutive. Despite Bure's skills, his size was always a knock against him. On February 2, 1998, with the Canadiens looking to add muscle to the team, Bure was traded to Calgary in exchange for Zarley Zalapski and Jonas Hoglund. In just his third game with the Flames, Bure scored his first career hat trick. By his second full season with the club, he had proved he was not simply a wispy player. In the 1999–2000 campaign, he scored 35 goals and 75 points to lead the team in both offensive categories.

# SEPTEMBER 18
## CULLEN'S COMEBACK, 1998

A day after scoring a goal against the Whalers on March 27, 1997, John Cullen was diagnosed with non-Hodgkin's lymphoma. At the time, the Lightning forward was third in team scoring with 18 goals and 55 points, but he was forced to step away from the game to battle the disease. For the next year, the former all-star underwent gruelling chemotherapy sessions and radiation treatments that left him weakened and frail. Following a bone marrow transplant, he developed pericarditis, an inflammation of the sac surrounding the heart. The condition almost killed him after it stopped his heart for about a minute. But Cullen beat the odds. He had defeated the cancer, and after regaining his strength, he signed a one-year contract worth $500,000 with the Lightning.

Nine days after inking the deal, on September 18, 1998, Cullen was with his Tampa Bay teammates in Innsbruck, Austria, for an exhibition game against the Sabres. As he stepped out onto the ice, he was overcome with emotion. In his first NHL contest in 18 months, Cullen made a triumphant return, even notching the game-winning goal, his first tally since his diagnosis. His comeback continued into the regular season, but after four games with Tampa Bay it was apparent that, after battling cancer for nearly two years, he was no longer the player he once was. As a result, instead of demoting him to the minors, the Lightning offered him a position as an assistant coach, but Cullen wanted to continue playing and accepted the assignment to the Cleveland Barons of the International Hockey League. After six games with the Barons, including one contest in which he scored seven points, he decided that, for the sake of his health and family, he should hang up his skates. Although his comeback was shorter than he had hoped, its significance was not lost on the league. At the end of the 1998–99 season, Cullen was awarded the Masterton Trophy as the player who best exemplified perseverance, sportsmanship, and dedication to hockey.

# SEPTEMBER 19
## LINDROS FACES THE NORDIQUES, 1992

I t could not have been scripted any better. Eric Lindros's first taste of NHL action was against the team he had shunned just over a year earlier. On September 19, 1992, in a pre-season exhibition game, Lindros and the Flyers took on the Nordiques in Philadelphia. When Lindros had been drafted first overall by Quebec in 1991, he made it clear he would never slip a Nordiques sweater over his head. Citing issues around the team's economics and Quebec's language and culture, Lindros returned to junior and suited up for the Canadian national team the following year, hoping to force a trade. Following a deal that made him both a member of the Flyers and the Rangers, an arbitrator was brought in to determine where the phenom would actually land. After a week, it was ruled that Lindros would begin his professional career in Philadelphia, closing the chapter on a tumultuous ascendancy to the NHL.

But everything came full circle when Lindros skated out onto the ice to face off against a band of foes who should have been his teammates. In his first appearance, he demonstrated the range of his skill set, playing 25 minutes, killing penalties, working the power play, scoring a goal, and setting up the game-winner. Although Lindros encountered no issues against the Nordiques, the Flyers' brass decided to keep him in Philadelphia the next day rather than send him to Quebec City to accompany the team in a rematch. Given the reception he was expected to receive at le Colisée, management wanted to postpone that experience until the Flyers travelled to Quebec for their first regular-season matchup. During his first game against the Nordiques, on October 13, 1992, Lindros encountered a chorus of boos and jeers and no shortage of theatrics from fans who had mockingly attended the game wearing diapers and sporting pacifiers. If it bothered Lindros, you couldn't tell. He rifled off seven shots on Quebec's net and found the twine twice.

# SEPTEMBER 20
## THE NHL RETURNS TO OHIO, 2000

After more than two decades, the National Hockey League returned to Ohio. On September 20, 2000, the Columbus Blue Jackets played their first game — a pre-season exhibition contest — in Nationwide Arena against the Red Wings. The NHL had first landed in the Buckeye State in 1976 when the league relocated the California Golden Seals to Cleveland, where they became the Barons. But after just two seasons and abysmal attendance numbers, the Barons merged with the Minnesota North Stars and ceased operations. After Ohio was iced out of the league for the next 19 years, the NHL came back on June 25, 1997, following the announcement that Columbus had been awarded an expansion franchise along with Nashville, St. Paul, and Atlanta.

Although Columbus would not begin playing until the 2000–2001 season, it did not take long for the locals to start thinking about what the new franchise should be called. Following a formal naming contest, it came down to the Blue Jackets or the Justice. On November 25, 1997, the team announced that, in homage to the city's valiant role in the Civil War, the franchise would be known as the Blue Jackets. After three years of waiting, the club hit the ice for the first time in the newly completed Nationwide Arena. Although it was just an exhibition game, the sold-out crowd of 18,126 could barely contain its excitement. Following a long ovation as the Blue Jackets were introduced, the crowd rose to its feet again to celebrate Jamie Heward's opening goal, the first scored in Nationwide, which gave the home team an early lead over the Red Wings. Columbus defeated Detroit 5-2 and, fittingly, picked up its first regular-season home victory against the Red Wings just over a month later. The Blue Jackets finished their inaugural NHL campaign with a record of 28-39-9-6.

# SEPTEMBER 21
## CANUCKS ACQUIRE SAMI SALO, 2002

The Canucks took a shot on Sami Salo. On September 21, 2002, Vancouver acquired the Finnish defenceman from Ottawa in exchange for left winger Peter Schaefer. Salo, who had been drafted 239th overall by the Senators in 1996, established himself as a regular on the team's defence corps. With one of the hardest slapshots in the league, he had the potential to be lethal from the point on the power play. During his time in Ottawa, he reportedly went through 400 sticks in one season, turning them into tinder with his cannonading shot. Much to the delight of the Senators, a perpetually cash-strapped organization, Salo abandoned his lumber and switched to a composite model. By his fourth year in Ottawa, however, he was taken off the team's power play and relegated to a reduced role on the back end. With a seeming glut of talent on the blue line and young Russian rearguard Anton Volchenkov waiting in the wings, Salo was deemed expendable.

As a result, after qualifying him to a one-year deal worth $800,000, the Senators shipped him to Vancouver for Schaefer, who had actually spent the previous season playing for Salo's hometown team in Finland in the SM-liiga. The trade gave Salo the opportunity to solidify himself as a top-four defenceman with the Canucks. In Vancouver, he began logging heavy minutes and put his thundering shot to good use. During the 2011 Stanley Cup Playoffs, while on a five-on-three power play, Salo set a team record for fastest two goals when he rifled off two quick markers from the point in a span of 16 seconds. While he was an integral part of Vancouver's back end for nearly a decade, he was often hampered by injuries. Although his ailments in Vancouver, which affected his Achilles tendon, groin, knee, back, and shoulders, weren't as strange as the snakebite that caused him to miss some games with the Senators, they plagued his time with the Canucks and limited his effectiveness. Salo retired after the 2013–14 season following a two-year stint with the Tampa Bay Lightning.

# SEPTEMBER 22
## SUMMIT SERIES RESUMES IN RUSSIA, 1972

After a disappointing start for the Canadians against the Soviet Union, the Summit Series resumed in Moscow on September 22, 1972. While Canada was hoping to battle back from two disheartening losses on home soil, some members of the team had already seen enough. Before Canada took to the ice for the fifth game of the tournament, Vic Hadfield, Rick Martin, Jocelyn Guevremont, and Gilbert Perreault all packed up their bags and headed home. Although Hadfield, an all-star left winger for the Rangers, chiefly cited the lack of playing time he was receiving, following his departure he also noted that the reception the team received in Canada had really stung him. While the squad carried on in the wake of the defections, it was also missing Wayne Cashman. Before the team arrived in Moscow, Canada had played two exhibition games in Sweden. During a stick altercation with Ulf Sterner, Cashman's tongue was seriously lacerated. It took more than 50 stitches to close the wound, and the Bruins forward would not suit up for another game during the tournament, although he remained with the team for the duration. Despite the notable absences on the roster, there was still plenty of talent available for the remaining four games.

While Canada may have been in enemy territory, it certainly didn't feel that way before the puck dropped on the fifth game. As Team Canada was introduced to the Soviet crowd, they received a chorus of friendly cheers from the 3,000 Canadians who made the trip to Moscow. When Team Canada held a commanding 4-1 lead in the game, chants of "go Canada go" echoed throughout the ice palace. The Canadian revelry, however, quickly turned to silenced disbelief after the Soviets scored four unanswered goals late in the third period to win the game. Canada would now need to be flawless for the remaining three contests if it hoped to salvage the tournament. They did not disappoint. Guided by Paul Henderson's heroics, they won the final three games to take the series and return home to Canada as champions.

# SEPTEMBER 23
# MANON RHEAUME'S NHL DEBUT, 1992

When Manon Rheaume wasn't stopping pucks, she was breaking down barriers. Even from an early age, the goaltender
from Lac-Beauport, Quebec, was challenging hockey's gendered landscape. While backstopping her peewee team, Rheaume had
the opportunity to play in the world-renowned Quebec International
Peewee Tournament, becoming the first girl to participate in the competition. As she continued to refine her skills in net, she started practising
with the Trois-Rivières Draveurs of the Quebec Major Junior Hockey
League. Although she started the 1991–92 season with the Louisville
Jaguars in a lower junior tier, she was recalled by the Draveurs in
November after the team's starting goaltender sustained an injury. While
Rheaume initially served as the backup, she was thrust into action on
November 26, 1991. She served in relief for only 17 minutes, but her
appearance marked the first time a woman had suited up for a game in
the QMJHL. Less than a year later, Rheaume made history again.

On September 23, 1992, she played a period of an exhibition game
for the Lightning, becoming the first woman to play in the National
Hockey League. Prior to making her NHL debut with the Lightning,
she led Canada to a gold medal at the women's world championship
in 1992. In her historic outing with the Lightning, she stopped seven
of the nine shots she faced. Less than two months later, the ground-
breaking goalie signed a contract with the Atlanta Knights of the
International Hockey League, the first woman to sign a professional
hockey contract. On December 13, 1992, she played her first game
with the Knights, becoming the first woman to play a regular-season
professional hockey game. Rheaume went on to win another world
championship and backstopped Canada to the silver medal at the
1998 Nagano Winter Games. While Rheaume's brush with the NHL
was brief, her appearance was not simply another game. It inspired a
generation of young girls and women to follow their hockey dreams.

# SEPTEMBER 24
## NHL INTRODUCES ICING, 1937

Halfway through the third period of a game between the Americans and Bruins on December 8, 1931, patrons at Boston Garden began hurling pennies and bottles at the ice from the gallery above. They had been frustrated by the defensive style of play the New York team had employed for most of the game. Holding a two-goal advantage in the final frame of the game, the Americans, rather than putting further pressure on the Bruins, continuously batted the puck the length of the ice out of their zone in an effort to protect their lead. Although the Americans abandoned their choking defensive tactics in the final minutes of the match, it still unnerved the Bruins and their spectators. Boston owner Charles Adams publicly criticized the Americans' defensive brand of hockey and said his team would retaliate when the clubs played a rematch a month later. He wasn't bluffing. Sure enough, when the Bruins squared off against their opponents in New York on January 3, they gave the Americans a taste of their own medicine.

In just the first period, Boston heaved the puck down the ice at least 40 times. By the time the game ended in a scoreless draw, the Bruins had reportedly dumped the puck nearly 90 times. In response, John S. Hammond, president of the New York Rangers, said the Bruins should be fined for their antics. While NHL president Frank Calder did not necessarily agree with the team's defensive style of play, there was nothing in the league's rulebooks to prevent such action. The NHL finally addressed the issue on September 24, 1937, when it introduced a new rule known as icing to prevent such defensive measures. Moving forward, when playing at even strength, teams could no longer "ice" the puck the length of the playing surface when hemmed into their own zone. If they did, the referee would blow the play dead, and a faceoff would be held at the point from where the puck was iced.

# SEPTEMBER 25
## NHL ADMITS CHICAGO, DETROIT, AND NEW YORK, 1926

t was a big day for the NHL. On September 25, 1926, at the league's annual meeting in Montreal, teams in Chicago, Detroit, and New York were admitted, increasing the number of clubs in the circuit to 10. Looking to capitalize on the early success of the league's expansion into Boston and Pittsburgh, the NHL continued to carve out a place for hockey in the United States. To accommodate the entry of the new clubs, two divisions were established. The eastern grouping consisted of the league's existing clubs in Canada and New York (the Americans), and it soon became known as the Canadian Division because of its composition. The western leg was made up of the Boston Bruins, the Pittsburgh Pirates, and the new teams in Chicago, Detroit, and New York; unsurprisingly, it was referred to as the American Division or the International Division, depending on where you were reading your newspaper.

While New York already had an NHL team in the Americans, there was plenty of room in the Big Apple for more hockey. Given the popularity of the Americans on the ice, George Lewis "Tex" Rickard, president of Madison Square Garden, was keen to bring another team to Broadway. Before the new Manhattan squad had formally adopted a name, reporters had begun referring to the team as Tex's Rangers, a nod to Rickard's nickname, and it soon became the club's official name. Sporting blue sweaters with the word *Rangers* emblazoned diagonally across the front, the team quickly stood out from their New York peers, the Americans, who wore star-spangled jerseys with horizontal lettering. The Rangers played their first game at Madison Square Garden on November 16, 1926, shutting out the Montreal Wanderers 1-0 to pick up their first victory. The Rangers finished their inaugural campaign atop their division, and the following year, just their second in the league, they won the Stanley Cup, becoming the first NHL team from the United States to capture the trophy.

# SEPTEMBER 26
## JORDAN LEOPOLD IS TRADED TO THE FLAMES, 2000

Jordan Leopold's NHL career was bookended by trades. Before he even had the chance to play for the team that had drafted him, he was on the move. On September 26, 2000, Anaheim dealt the bourgeoning defenceman to Calgary in exchange for Andrei Nazarov and a second-round draft pick. Leopold, who had been selected 44th overall by the Mighty Ducks in the 1999 NHL Entry Draft, was just coming off his second year with the University of Minnesota. After finishing his collegiate hockey career, he won the Hobey Baker Award as the top player in U.S. college hockey. Although Leopold never got the opportunity to suit up for the Mighty Ducks, he made his NHL debut with the Flames on October 19, 2002. In his second year with Calgary, he was an integral part of the Flames' improbable run to the Stanley Cup Final. During the post-season, the blueliner contributed 10 assists as Calgary finished just a couple of goals shy of a championship.

Although Leopold was quickly establishing himself as one of the league's top young defencemen, the Flames dealt him to Colorado on June 24, 2006, in exchange for Alex Tanguay. Despite his stellar play on the back end, Leopold frequently found himself changing teams. Early into the 2014–15 season, with his career winding down, he was dealt for the seventh time. With his family back home in Minnesota, Leopold packed his bags for Columbus. While he patrolled the blue line for the Blue Jackets, his 10-year-old daughter Jordyn penned an impassioned letter to the coaching staff of the Minnesota Wild. In her handwritten note, she described how much she missed her dad and hoped the Wild could acquire him. "Can you please, please, please ask the Jackets if you guys can get him," she wrote. Jordyn's heartfelt plea made national headlines, and before long, her father was traded for the eighth, and final, time in his career. On March 2, 2015, Leopold was acquired by the Wild and reunited with his family.

# SEPTEMBER 27
## OUTDOOR GAME IN LAS VEGAS, 1991

Playing an outdoor game in Las Vegas was a gamble, but the NHL rolled the dice. On September 27, 1991, amid the desert heat, the Rangers and Kings squared off in an exhibition matchup outside Caesars Palace hotel and casino. Although NHL teams had participated in outdoor games before — in 1954 the Red Wings travelled to Marquette Branch Prison to take on a squad of inmates — this was the first outdoor exhibition game featuring two clubs from the league. Marketing a desert showdown with New York and Los Angeles on the marquee was easy enough; the challenge was engineering an outdoor ice surface in the sweltering heat. In order to pull it off, the league trucked in three huge refrigeration units, three times the normal size of ice power for a standard NHL game. In the week leading up to the game, a technical staff painstakingly tested the ice to make sure there would be no issues once the game commenced. While a reflective blanket protected the ice from the sun's glare and the 35-degree Celsius heat during the day, just hours before the game, rain turned the playing surface into a soupy mess. But with time to spare, technicians deployed the Zamboni and utilized the massive refrigeration units to return the ice to game condition.

When the puck dropped, the matchup went off without a hitch. Well, almost. Although there were some minor issues with the ice that were easily attended to by players and officials during stoppages, the game was interrupted by ... locusts. According to Rangers goaltender John Vanbiesbrouck, teammate Tie Domi, who was not known for his hands unless he was using them in a bout of fisticuffs, joked he would have scored on a breakaway had he not tripped over one of the pesky insects. Twenty-six years after Wayne Gretzky, the greatest hockey player in the world, played outside under the Las Vegas skies, not far from the neon glow of the Strip, the NHL returned to Sin City when the expansion Vegas Golden Knights began their inaugural season.

# NHL INTRODUCES THE FORWARD PASS, 1929

n an effort to bring more scoring and excitement to hockey, the NHL changed the rules. On September 28, 1929, at the league's semi-annual meeting, it introduced the forward pass for the upcoming season. Although earlier leagues such as the Pacific Coast Hockey Association had adopted forward passing, the NHL had been slow to change the rules and continued to limit its players to lateral routes with the puck. In order to introduce the forward pass, the league divided the ice into three sections: the defending zone, neutral zone, and attacking zone. When teammates were skating in the same zone, they were permitted to make forward passes in these areas but were still restricted from making breakout plays (e.g., passing the puck from the defending zone out to a player waiting in the neutral zone). In addition to encouraging offence through the adoption of the forward pass, the league also instituted a rule that limited teams to keeping no more than three players, including the goaltender, in its defensive zone when the puck was elsewhere.

The NHL believed these new changes, largely the forward pass, would make for a more exciting product for the fans by speeding up the game and creating more offensive opportunities. The results were immediate. In 1928–29, the season prior to the rule change, Ace Bailey led the league in scoring with 22 goals. The following year, Cooney Weiland potted 43 goals, while Dit Clapper and Howie Morenz both reached the 40-goal plateau, marking the first time in league history that multiple players scored at least 40 goals in a campaign. Team scoring also increased considerably. In 1928–29, the Bruins led the league with 89 goals for, but the following year, Boston found the back of the net 179 times, and none of the league's 10 clubs scored fewer than 100 times. The introduction of the forward pass revolutionized the league, and the adoption of the centre red line 14 years later brought the NHL into the modern era.

# RANGERS ACQUIRE PAT LAFONTAINE, 1997

When Pat LaFontaine was traded for the second time in his career, he still didn't need to change his licence plate. On September 29, 1997, LaFontaine was acquired by the New York Rangers from the Buffalo Sabres in exchange for a second-round draft pick and future considerations. It was his third NHL club since breaking into the league with the Islanders in 1984, giving him the distinction of being one of the few players in league history to suit up for all three teams located in New York State. "I've never been one to stand in motor vehicle lines. So, this has been great," he told reporters when the trade was announced. Originally drafted third overall by the Islanders in 1983, LaFontaine spent eight seasons on Long Island, where he established himself as one of the game's premier scorers, racking up four consecutive campaigns of 40 or more goals.

After being traded to the Sabres in 1991, he scored 53 goals and 148 points with Buffalo in the 1992–93 season, good enough to finish runner-up to Mario Lemieux in league scoring. Following that incredible performance, which set team records and a new league benchmark for American-born players, a series of injuries kept LaFontaine out of the lineup for much of the next two seasons. Although he returned to form for the 1995–96 campaign, scoring 91 points, he missed most of the next season after sustaining a concussion. LaFontaine and his doctors believed he had recovered enough to start the 1997–98 season with Buffalo, but the Sabres' medical staff disagreed. While his team did not believe he was medically fit to play, LaFontaine still had two years left on his contract and was not ready to retire. As a result, following rancorous debate with the Sabres, he was traded to the Rangers. After scoring 23 goals and 62 points in his first 67 games with the Blueshirts, he suffered another concussion and missed the rest of the regular season and the following year. He never played another game in the NHL.

# MAPLE LEAFS NAME MATS SUNDIN CAPTAIN, 1997

The new letter on Mats Sundin's sweater didn't just mark his new role with the Maple Leafs; it also signified the globalization of hockey. On September 30, 1997, Toronto announced it had named the Swedish centre the club's new team captain, making him the first non-Canadian to earn the honour. With the captaincy, Sundin joined fellow Swedes Lars-Erik Sjoberg and Alexander Steen as the only other Swedish players to captain an NHL team. Sjoberg had led the Jets during their inaugural season in the league in 1979–80, and Steen had piloted the Jets in 1990–91. For Sundin, it was a sign his teammates and management valued his leadership and contributions to the team, but it meant much more than that. Although Alexander Mogilny served as captain in Buffalo during the 1993–94 season while Pat LaFontaine recovered from injury, leadership roles in the NHL at that time were still largely reserved for Canadians.

Sundin's coronation, however, attested to the change that was taking place. Maple Leafs assistant general manager Anders Hedberg, a Swedish player who turned heads with the Jets in the World Hockey Association in the 1970s, understood the importance of Sundin's role. "It's proof that nationality doesn't count, it's personality," he said. Associate general manager Mike Smith, who was at the helm in Winnipeg when Steen was captain, echoed his colleague's sentiment. "The C has traditionally been for Canadians, but this is indicative of the global process our game has gone through in the past 20 to 25 years," he told reporters. While Sundin led the Maple Leafs for the next decade, more European players ascended to leadership positions with teams across the league. In 2008, more than half the captaincies in the NHL were filled by European players, including Sundin. Moreover, that year, the Red Wings' Nicklas Lidstrom made history when he became the first European captain to lead his team to a Stanley Cup.

# OCTOBER 1
## OILERS RETIRE GRETZKY'S 99, 1999

Nearly two decades after Wayne Gretzky made his NHL debut with the Oilers, the team honoured him by retiring his number 99 jersey in a touching pre-game ceremony on October 1, 1999. As Gretzky trucked out onto the ice to greet the raucous crowd at the Skyreach Centre in Edmonton, it marked the first time in 21 years he wouldn't be suiting up for a game as a player. Gretzky began his career in Edmonton back in the Oiler's World Hockey Association days. When the team joined the NHL in 1979–80, he was still a teenager. Over the next two decades, he would evolve into the greatest player the game has ever known. When he hung up his skates in April 1999, he had 61 NHL records to his name, four Stanley Cups, and a bulging trophy case that included 10 Art Ross trophies and nine Hart trophies.

With his wife, Janet, and children Trevor, Paulina, and Ty by his side, Gretzky fought back tears as the Oilers raised his jersey to the rafters. It was an emotional moment, particularly when Rod Phillips, the Oilers' long-time announcer, got choked up when he exclaimed, "Ladies and gentlemen, we'll now say these words for the last time ever in this building. Hockey fans, tonight's first star, number 99, Wayne Gretzky." A few months later, the Great One's banner was once again raised, this time at the Air Canada Centre in Toronto before the All-Star Game. Although no one other than Gretzky had worn the number 99 since 1982 — the Maple Leafs' Wilf Paiement was the last — this signified that no NHL player, on any team, would ever be allowed to wear 99 again. It is still the only number to be retired across the league, but Gretzky thinks it should have some company. Following the death of Gordie Howe, Gretzky's boyhood idol, in 2016, the Great One told ESPN he believes the NHL should retire Howe's jersey for all his contributions to the league and the sport of hockey.

# OCTOBER 2
## VILLE KOISTINEN'S HOMECOMING, 2009

t was a fitting end to an incredible homecoming. On October 2, 2009, Finnish defenceman Ville Koistinen scored the deciding goal in a shootout to give the Panthers a victory over the Blackhawks in the first regular-season NHL game played in Finland. Koistinen delighted the crowd of 12,056 at Hartwall Arena in Helsinki not once but twice that game. Halfway through the third period, the blueliner notched a goal to tie the score. After Chicago and Florida traded goals again, the matchup went to a shootout after overtime, solving nothing. Although not known for his scoring prowess, Koistinen was tapped to be the Panthers' second shooter. Given where the game was being played, it was a no-brainer for head coach Peter DeBoer to give his Finnish rearguard the rare opportunity to impress his home crowd. Koistinen did not disappoint. After skating in on Blackhawks goaltender Cristobal Huet, the defenceman lifted a high backhand shot that held up as the game-winner.

Following the contest, Koistinen was incredulous. "This is quite unbelievable, to do this in a game before a home crowd in my home country," he said. When reporters pressed him about his shootout technique that fooled Huet, he joked, "It's the only move I have." But the biggest thrill for Koistinen during his homecoming tour was arguably the Panthers' exhibition game a few nights earlier in his hometown of Tampere against Tappara, the bitter rival of his former Finnish club, Ilves. Before making the jump to North America in 2006, Koistinen had played six seasons in the SM-liiga. After he led the Finnish league in scoring by a defenceman with 34 points, he signed with the Nashville Predators organization and joined the Panthers as a free agent three years later. Now he was playing in the NHL and squaring off against former rivals in the same arena that, as a boy growing up in Tampere, he had dreamed about playing in.

# OCTOBER 3
## BIG IN JAPAN, 1997

The NHL broadened its horizons to start the 1997–98 season. On October 3, 1997, the Mighty Ducks and Canucks squared off in Tokyo, Japan, marking the first regular-season NHL game to be played outside North America. With the Winter Games being held in Nagano that upcoming February, it provided the league with a tremendous opportunity to market its athletes and grow the game in Japan in the months leading up to the Olympics. As part of the festivities, the Stanley Cup travelled to Japan and was the premier showcase of a league-organized event, HockeyFest, held outside Yoyogi Arena. A huge lineup of fans showed up to view hockey's Holy Grail. For Tomonori Tahara, who was quoted in the *New York Times*, "It's like a dream come true to see the Stanley Cup."

Inside Yoyogi, the sold-out crowd of 10,500 watched the Mighty Ducks and Canucks duel to a tight 3-2 finish, with the edge going to the Canucks. Vancouver's Scott Walker scored the first regular-season goal outside North America, and Pavel Bure potted the game-winning goal. The only thing missing from the game was Paul Kariya. The Mighty Ducks star did not travel to Japan with his team because of a contract dispute, which disappointed the local fans who were hoping to see him in action. Kariya, whose father was Japanese-Canadian, would have been a big draw for Japan's hockey patrons. While much of the Japanese contingent focused on the absence of Kariya, the rest of the hockey world zeroed in on Trevor Linden and Mark Messier. Just days before the game, Linden surrendered Vancouver's captaincy to Messier in a move that would rankle fans for years to come. When the Canucks signed Messier just a few months earlier, many anticipated he would get the C. Even though Linden had been serving in the role for six years and management had no plans to make a change in leadership, Linden relinquished the position and Messier played his first game as Canucks captain in Japan.

# OCTOBER 4
## RANGERS ACQUIRE MESSIER, 1991

n the 51 years since the Rangers' last championship in 1940, New York had come up empty-handed three times in the Stanley Cup Final, while Mark Messier had captured Lord Stanley's mug five times with the Oilers. Looking to draw from his proven track record and ability to elevate a team, the Rangers brought in Messier in advance of the 1991–92 season. On October 4, 1991, the Blueshirts acquired him from the Oilers in exchange for Bernie Nicholls and prospects Steven Rice and Louie DeBrusk. At the time, Messier had two more years remaining on his contract with Edmonton, but after requesting a contract renegotiation in the spring following his fifth championship with the club, it seemed his days with the Oilers were numbered. Although the team had tabled a significant raise, Messier declined the offer, noting that after playing in Edmonton for 12 years, he was going to leave sooner rather than later.

As a member of the Oilers, Messier had been an integral part of their first four championships, including a Conn Smythe performance in 1984 as the most valuable player in the post-season. Following Gretzky's departure in 1988, Messier emerged from the Great One's shadow, guiding the team to a fifth Stanley Cup in 1990 and winning his first Hart Trophy that year. Given everything he had accomplished in Edmonton, he felt as though he would be starting over in New York. "I'm starting a second career," he told reporters. "I have every confidence that my second career will be every bit as good as the first," he continued. Messier certainly lived up to his words. In his first season with the Rangers, he racked up 107 points, picking up his second Hart Trophy, as he led the Blueshirts to their first Presidents' Trophy, awarded to the team that finished the NHL regular season with the most points. Although the Rangers faltered in the playoffs, Messier made up for it, and then some, two years later when he guided the club to its first Stanley Cup since 1940.

# OCTOBER 5

## HAROLD BALLARD NEARLY SELLS
## MAHOVLICH FOR $1 MILLION, 1962

As dinner turned into drinks, Maple Leafs owner Harold Ballard and Black Hawks owner James Norris chatted about their respective teams. As the two NHL executives continued to imbibe late into the evening, they struck an extraordinary deal. On the night of October 5, 1962, Norris offered to purchase Maple Leafs star Frank Mahovlich for $1 million. While Mahovlich was a fan favourite in Toronto and coming off a 48-goal campaign, it was an unprecedented sum for an athlete. Nevertheless, satisfied with the incredibly bold transaction, Norris and Ballard clinked glasses, shook hands, and outlined the terms of the deal on a stationery pad from the Royal York Hotel, which included both of their signatures.

The next morning, while the pair were presumably shaking off the cobwebs from the night before, news of the transaction made headlines after Chicago's Tommy Ivan arrived at Maple Leaf Gardens with a cheque for $1 million. Although Norris and Ballard thought they had consummated the deal during their night out, Toronto president Stafford Smythe thought otherwise. Incensed by the tentative deal Ballard had made behind his back, and without his consultation, Stafford told reporters, "We can't consider a deal of that nature without going to the board of directors." But even in the cold light of day, Norris and Ballard remained committed to inking their deal. In issuing a statement to reporters, the Chicago owner said, "I have made the offer. One million dollars is my offer. I made it last night and we shook hands on it. As far as I am concerned it is a deal." Moreover, Ballard agreed and attested to having $1,000 in his pocket as a down payment. Meanwhile, fans began arriving at Maple Leaf Gardens to protest the potential sale of the former Calder Trophy winner. In the end, Smythe nixed the deal, and Mahovlich went on to win four Stanley Cups with the Maple Leafs.

# OCTOBER 6
# GRETZKY MAKES HIS HOLLYWOOD DEBUT, 1988

Under the bright lights of Hollywood, the Great One made his regular-season debut for the Kings. On October 6, 1988, Wayne Gretzky appeared in his first game as a King when Los Angeles hosted the Red Wings at the Forum. Just a couple of months earlier, Gretzky had been celebrating his fourth Stanley Cup and his marriage to wife, Janet, when the Oilers dealt him to the Kings in the biggest trade in NHL history. Although Gretzky was sad to leave Edmonton, the city where he evolved from a teenager to legend, shattering records and amassing a significant trophy case along the way, he quickly embraced his new life in Tinseltown. The feeling was mutual.

With the arrival of the Great One, the popularity of hockey in Los Angeles reached a fever pitch. Even outside the rink, he was unquestionably a star. After years of struggling, the future finally looked bright for the Kings. Heading into the 1988–89 campaign, for the first time in franchise history, the Kings sold out their season-opening game. As the Great One stepped onto the ice for the first time in a Kings uniform, he was greeted to thunderous applause from the crowd. On just his first shot of the game, he wired one past Detroit goaltender Greg Stefan to pick up his 584th career goal. But the Great One wasn't done there. He picked up three assists as Los Angeles trounced the Red Wings 8-2 in his debut. Hollywood could not have scripted it any better. Less than two weeks later, Gretzky returned to Edmonton for the first time. Skating onto the ice of the Northlands Coliseum for the first time as a member of the opposition, Gretzky received a four-minute standing ovation from the Oilers faithful. Although his return was not as spectacular — the Kings lost 8-6 — it was an incredible homecoming for the player who had guided the franchise to its first four Stanley Cups.

# OCTOBER 7
# JAROMIR JAGR'S FIRST GOAL, 1990

ate in the third period against the Devils, the Penguins scored four goals in two minutes and 27 seconds. The barrage vaulted them to a 7-4 victory over their New Jersey rivals. Amid that offensive flurry was the first tally from newcomer Jaromir Jagr. On October 7, 1990, Jagr notched his first career NHL goal. Less than a minute after Bryan Trottier tied the game, Jagr banged in a rebound from close range. The Devils never recovered, and the rookie's goal held up as the game-winner.

Jagr, a native of Czechoslovakia, began his NHL career differently from his predecessors. Following the collapse of the Iron Curtain in his home country in 1989, he was able to become the first Czechoslovakian player to join the NHL without needing to defect. Moreover, when the Penguins selected him fifth overall in the 1990 NHL Entry Draft in Vancouver, he was actually able to attend the event in person. Just a year earlier, when fellow countryman Bobby Holik had been drafted 10th overall by the Hartford Whalers, his sister, Andrea, stood in for him at the draft because he had not yet defected from Czechoslovakia. After moving to Pittsburgh, Jagr suited up for the Penguins in their pre-season exhibition games but still remained under contract with his Czechoslovakian club. Just days before he was scheduled to make his NHL debut, Pittsburgh general manager Craig Patrick negotiated a settlement with his former team, freeing him up to play in the NHL. The rest is history. After an NHL career that spanned three decades, Jagr trails only Wayne Gretzky and Gordie Howe for the most goals. While his time with the Calgary Flames in 2017–18 ended unceremoniously, he hasn't officially retired from the NHL, and there's still a long-shot possibility he could return to chase down the 800-goal mark (he stands at 766). Whenever Jagr does finally hang up his skates, however, he will do so as the league's all-time leader in game-winning goals.

# OCTOBER 8
## ANTTI NIEMI SPOILS THE KINGS' PARTY, 2014

Antti Niemi spoiled the party. It was supposed to be the Kings' night, but he had other plans. On October 8, 2014, the Sharks goaltender stopped all 34 shots he faced, shutting out Los Angeles at the Staples Center. It was the Kings' home opener and was supposed to be a celebration of their recent Stanley Cup victory, their second in three years. In an elaborate ceremony before the game began, the Stanley Cup was carefully lowered from the Staples Center's scoreboard. Once Lord Stanley's mug touched down, the Kings gathered around the trophy at centre ice as the team raised another championship banner to the rafters.

Meanwhile, the Sharks remained firmly positioned in their dressing room. And for good reason. Although visiting teams are not present during season-opening celebrations for the reigning Stanley Cup champions, the Sharks wouldn't have been caught dead out on the ice. When the 2014 post-season began, the two teams had squared off in the opening round of the Western Conference quarter-final series. After winning the first three games, the Sharks were just one victory away from defeating the Kings. But following an epic collapse, San Jose lost four straight games, and Los Angeles became just the fourth team in NHL history to recover from a 3-0 deficit to win a series. The Sharks were devastated. As they struggled to put the memories of the playoffs behind them, the season-opening rematch loomed large on their calendars. Although defeating the Kings wouldn't change what had happened, spoiling the party would have provided the Sharks with a semblance of retribution. As the clock ticked down, even with a two-man advantage in the final minutes of the third period, the Kings could not find the back of the net. When the final buzzer sounded, Los Angeles was scoreless, giving Niemi the distinction of being the first goaltender to shut out the defending Stanley Cup champions in their season opening game since the Maple Leafs' Turk Broda accomplished the feat against the Bruins on November 8, 1941.

# OCTOBER 9
## KINGS "TRADE" RAY BOURQUE, 1978

After Rogie Vachon signed with the Red Wings as a free agent, the Kings needed reinforcements in net. On October 9, 1978, Los Angeles acquired goaltender Ron Grahame from the Bruins in exchange for the Kings' first-round pick in the 1979 draft. Grahame was just coming off his first NHL campaign in Boston. He served as the team's starting goaltender during the regular season, racking up 26 victories. Before signing with the Bruins in 1977, he had turned professional with the World Hockey Association (WHA) following his collegiate career at the University of Denver. In his first full season with the Houston Aeros, Grahame was awarded the Ben Hatskin Trophy as the league's top goaltender. In the 1974 playoffs, he backstopped the club to a league championship, capturing the Avco World Trophy. For his efforts, he was named the most valuable player in the playoffs.

Although Grahame enjoyed considerable success in the WHA, his dream was to play in the NHL. As a result, with the Aeros struggling financially, he made the jump to the NHL and inked a deal with the Bruins. But after a solid inaugural season with Boston, Grahame struggled mightily with the lowly Kings. After less than three seasons in Los Angeles, the Kings sold him to the Nordiques. He suited up for eight games with Quebec before he was sent down to the minors and subsequently retired. While the trade to the Kings did not work out the way Grahame might have envisioned it, the Bruins made out like gangbusters. Using Los Angeles's first-round pick, Boston nabbed defenceman Ray Bourque with the eighth overall selection. Bourque went on to a Hall of Fame career with the Bruins that included five Norris trophies. He spent more than two decades with Boston, becoming the franchise's all-time leader in games played, assists, and points.

# IRON MAN DOUG JARVIS'S STREAK COMES TO AN END, 1987

Doug Jarvis never missed a day of work in his NHL career. After making his debut for the Montreal Canadiens on October 8, 1975, the resilient centre went on to play in an incredible 964 consecutive games. Originally drafted by the Maple Leafs in 1975, he was promptly sent to the Canadiens in exchange for defenceman Greg Hubick. While Hubick played only 77 NHL games for Toronto and Vancouver before fading into obscurity, Jarvis was an integral part of four Stanley Cups in Montreal.

After playing 560 straight games for the Canadiens, prior to the start of the 1982–83 season, he was part of a transformational trade that also sent Rod Langway, Brian Engblom, and Craig Laughlin to the Capitals. In Washington, Jarvis continued to establish himself as a rugged shutdown checker, winning the Frank J. Selke Trophy in 1984 as the league's best defensive forward. On December 6, 1985, the Capitals traded him to the Whalers for left winger Jorgen Pettersson. At the time, the NHL still played only 80-game seasons, but because of a quirk in the scheduling, Jarvis suited up for a combined 82 games between both teams that season. Heading into the 1986–87 campaign, he was zeroing in on Garry Unger's record for consecutive games (914). Given his uncanny ability to stay in the lineup, most figured it wasn't a question of whether he would catch Unger but when. After Jarvis surpassed Unger's milestone on December 26, 1986, his "ironman" streak continued until he played his 964th consecutive game on October 10, 1987. The next day, however, it ended when an injury kept him out of the lineup. He never played another NHL game. Since then, no other NHL player has challenged Jarvis's incredible achievement. Steve Larmer, who played 884 straight games for the Blackhawks and Rangers, came the closest, but unlike Jarvis, his streak didn't start at the beginning of his NHL career.

# OCTOBER 11
## SUPER MARIO'S FIRST GOAL, 1984

O n his first shot of his first shift in his first game, Mario Lemieux scored his first NHL goal. Lemieux, who had been selected first overall by Pittsburgh in the 1984 NHL Entry Draft, was heralded as the saviour who would lead the Penguins out of the abyss. For years, the team had struggled, both on the ice and financially, but with Lemieux entering the fray, the hope was that the hulking centre from Montreal with hands as smooth as silk would turn things around. Early in his first game, on October 11, 1984, he lived up to his billing. As Bruins all-star defenceman Ray Bourque attempted to set up a play in the Penguins' zone, Lemieux intercepted the pass and was off to the races. With a clear breakaway from the red line, the rookie sensation was all alone on Boston goaltender Pete Peeters. Lemieux faked him out and slipped the puck behind his right pad with a backhander. He added an assist on a goal by Warren Young during the second period, but Bourque spoiled his coming-out party, scoring the game-winner late in the third period to hand the Penguins the defeat.

As the season continued, despite missing seven games, Lemieux scored 42 more goals and finished the campaign with 100 points, capturing the Calder Trophy as the league's top rookie. Although the Penguins wouldn't qualify for the post-season for the first four years that Lemieux was with the club, his remarkable skill and playmaking abilities rejuvenated the failing franchise. In 1988, he racked up 168 points to win his first Art Ross and Hart trophies. The following season, he came within a single point of reaching the 200-point milestone, a feat only Wayne Gretzky has accomplished. In 1991, guided by Lemieux's brilliant play, the Penguins won their first of back-to-back championships.

# OCTOBER 12
## AUSTON MATTHEWS'S DEBUT, 2016

Maple Leafs fans should have this date circled on their calendar. On October 12, 2016, Auston Matthews made his NHL debut against the Senators. After Toronto had selected the highly touted prospect first overall, just a few months earlier, the Maple Leafs faithful eagerly awaited his first NHL game. Although fans had gotten a sneak peek of what Matthews could do against NHL competition, when he was draped in black and orange for Team North America in the World Cup of Hockey, it was just not the same. Matthews's first regular-season game in a Maple Leafs sweater was going to be special. And while we knew the day was coming, nothing could have prepared us for what transpired.

Less than halfway through the first period, Matthews scored his first NHL goal, a fine start to his career, but then he scored again, and again, and again. The hockey world was in disbelief. Even Auston's mother, Ema, could barely believe her eyes. Standing in the Canadian Tire Centre in Ottawa, she was overcome with emotion as she watched her son, a boy who had grown up in Scottsdale, Arizona, make National Hockey League history. Although a handful of players had scored hat tricks in their NHL debuts, no one in the modern era had ever scored four goals in his opening game. It was an incredible performance that somehow exceeded the lofty expectations. For an organization long mired in despair and frustration, Matthews's debut truly felt as though it was the start of a new era in Toronto. For Maple Leafs fans, it has already entered into the lore of "Where were you when it happened?" I know I'll never forget; I was at home with my wife and two-week-old daughter, Zoe. Although Zoe slept through the whole game in her tiny Maple Leafs pajamas, holding her in my arms as we shared an unforgettable moment in hockey history is something I will cherish forever.

# OCTOBER 13
## PIRATES PACK IT IN, 1930

The Pirates were packing it in. After five seasons in the National Hockey League, the Pittsburgh club announced on October 13, 1930, that it was transferring its operations to Philadelphia. After joining the league, the Pirates found success early on, qualifying for the post-season twice in their first three years. In their inaugural season, they were a part of NHL history when they and the New York Americans combined for 141 shots on goal on December 26, 1925. Although the New Yorkers defeated the Mighty Steel City Sextet 3-1, picking up their first victory in Madison Square Garden, Pirates goaltender Roy "Shrimp" Worters valiantly turned away 70 of the shots he faced in the record-setting barrage.

While the Pirates performed admirably on the ice, financial problems plagued the team, and by its fourth campaign, these issues were compounded by the fact that Pittsburgh's play began to suffer. A change in ownership did little to stop the bleeding, and with the onset of the Great Depression in 1929, attendance declined significantly. When the team made the announcement it would be moving to Philadelphia, the reason given was that Pirates president, James F. Callahan, felt Duquesne Gardens was not a suitable arena for the club. The relocation was supposed to be only a temporary measure while the team made other arrangements. In fact, it was initially believed the Pirates would loop back into the league during the next round of expansion in a few years, but it never happened. Instead, Pittsburgh went without an NHL franchise until the Penguins joined the league as part of the 1967 expansion. In Philadelphia, the franchise didn't fare much better. Rebranded as the Quakers, the club finished its inaugural season with an abysmal record of 4-36-4 and did not ice a team for the 1931–32 season. Ironically, Philadelphia, too, would go without another NHL team until the Flyers' arrival in 1967.

# OCTOBER 14
# GRETZKY'S FIRST PRO GAME, 1978

When Wayne Gretzky skated out onto the ice at Market Square Arena in Indianapolis on October 14, 1978, he was not yet the Great One. At the time, he was just 17 years old and suiting up for his first professional hockey game with the Racers of the World Hockey Association. He didn't get on the scoresheet in the 6-3 loss to the Winnipeg Jets, but it marked the beginning of a brilliant pro hockey career. Although Gretzky had been touted as a hockey prodigy since he was a boy and had racked up 182 points in junior with the Sault Ste. Marie Greyhounds, entering the 1978–79 season the sentiment was that, even with all his skill, he wouldn't be able to turn around the struggling Racers franchise. On October 21, 1978, Gretzky netted two goals, but Indianapolis still fell 4-3 to visiting Edmonton, still searching for that elusive first home win of the season.

But his time with the Racers was brief. With the team struggling financially, he was sold to the Oilers, along with left winger Peter Driscoll and goaltender Eddie Mio. Following the transaction, Gretzky expressed disappointment in the move. "I don't like it, but I'm like a puppet on a string. I want to play and I have to go where they will send me," he told the *Globe and Mail*. Although he was initially upset, the move proved to be fortuitous. After just 25 games that season, the Racers folded. Meanwhile, Gretzky finished his first pro campaign with 110 points. After the Oilers, along with the Whalers, Nordiques, and Jets, merged with the National Hockey League, Gretzky made his NHL debut on October 10, 1979, picking up an assist in a 4-2 loss to the Black Hawks. Four nights later, exactly a year after making his professional hockey debut, he scored his first NHL goal and added an assist as the Oilers played to a 4-4 tie against the Canucks at home. He would go on to score 893 more regular-season goals in the NHL.

# OCTOBER 15
# THE GREAT ONE BECOMES THE GREATEST, 1989

Just 10 years into his NHL career, the Great One became the greatest. On October 15, 1989, Wayne Gretzky picked up his 1,851st career point to pass his boyhood idol, Gordie Howe, on the NHL's all-time scoring list. Just 12 years earlier, Gretzky was 11 years old and had been given the opportunity to meet Howe. Mr. Hockey offered the young phenom just one piece of advice: "Work on your backhand." Gretzky certainly took the counsel to heart. Fittingly, it just so happened that the point that vaulted Gretzky ahead of his hockey hero was a backhander. With just 53 seconds remaining in a game against the Oilers, Gretzky flipped the puck up past goaltender Bill Ranford to enshrine himself into the record books. The crowd at Northlands Coliseum in Edmonton went into bedlam.

The record-setting point couldn't have happened at a more perfect place. Gretzky had begun his NHL career with the Oilers in 1979, shattering league records and guiding the team to four Stanley Cups before he was unceremoniously sold as part of a blockbuster trade to Los Angeles in 1988. As the sold-out crowd honoured its former captain with a raucous standing ovation, the game was halted in order to properly mark the significance of the milestone. At centre ice, Gretzky was greeted by his father, Walter; wife, Janet; Howe; Mark Messier; and NHL president John Ziegler. Messier, who had succeeded Gretzky as captain of the Oilers, presented his former teammate with a gold bracelet with 1.851-carats worth of diamonds — one for each point — while the Kings gave him a crystal hologram engraved with his image. But the greatest gift for Gretzky was accomplishing the feat in front of his idol and family, in the building where he had forged his legacy as the greatest player in the game's history. As the Kings' Dave Taylor, who set up the record-setting goal, later reflected, "I don't know who writes his script, but it was just perfect."

# OCTOBER 16
# MAPLE LEAFS ACQUIRE
# TOM KURVERS, 1989

Hoping to shore up their porous blue line, the Maple Leafs made a deal with the Devils. On October 16, 1989, Toronto acquired defenceman Tom Kurvers from New Jersey in exchange for a first-round pick in 1991. At the time, it made sense for both sides. Kurvers, who led the Devils in scoring the year before, would strengthen the Maple Leafs' back end, while New Jersey cashed in on its defensive surplus. Despite being an important part of the Devils' 1988–89 campaign, Kurvers found himself as the odd man out heading into the following season. The emergence of Bruce Driver as the team's premier blue-line gunslinger and the off-season acquisitions of Slava Fetisov and Reijo Ruotsalainen conspired against him, forcing Kurvers to watch most of the Devils' games from the press box to start the season.

Heading to Toronto would give him the opportunity to return to the ice, but he initially refused to report to the club. The Maple Leafs expected he would be in the lineup the next night to take on the Penguins, but he was actually in Detroit meeting with his agent, Bob Goodenow. A Minneapolis native, Kurvers was unhappy with his situation and was hoping to force a trade to Minnesota, St. Louis, or Chicago in order to play closer to home. After a tense few days, especially for Toronto general manager Floyd Smith, who had no protection on the first-round pick if Kurvers failed to report, Kurvers made his Maple Leafs debut against the Capitals on October 21, 1989. Although he had a good campaign with Toronto that year, the following season the team got off to a sluggish start, and Kurvers was dealt to Vancouver for forward Brian Bradley. The Maple Leafs ended up finishing in the cellar of the Norris Division that year, and the Devils used their first-round selection to grab Scott Niedermayer third overall. Niedermayer went on to enjoy a Hall of Fame career, winning three Stanley Cups with New Jersey before guiding the Ducks to a championship in 2007.

# OCTOBER 17
## JARI KURRI SCORES 500, 1992

t might not have been how he envisioned it in his mind, but Jari Kurri took his 500th career goal all the same. On October 17, 1992, with just 54 seconds remaining in a game against the Bruins, he stripped the puck from defenceman Ray Bourque and charged down the ice. Trailing 7-6 to the Kings as the clock ticked down, the Bruins had already pulled their goaltender for an extra attacker. Outracing Bourque and another Boston defender, Kurri charged toward the vacant net and shot the puck into the yawning cage to pick up the landmark goal. In reflecting on the milestone after the game, Kurri confessed he imagined the moment a little differently. "I definitely hoped that Wayne [Gretzky] would have passed me the puck for that goal," he told reporters. "He's been in on a lot of goals in my career," he added.

For nearly a decade, he had flanked the Great One in Edmonton, where Kurri scored 397 goals and won four Stanley Cups. After Gretzky was traded to the Kings in August 1988, Kurri racked up another 77 goals with the Oilers, along with another championship, before the two were reunited in Los Angeles in 1991. Kurri, however, wasn't riding shotgun with Gretzky on that memorable night in Inglewood. Instead, Gretzky was on the shelf with a back injury and wouldn't play his first game for the Kings that season until January 6, 1993. Meanwhile, Kurri, naturally a right winger, had valiantly accepted a position change in order to fill the void in Gretzky's absence. For the newly converted centre, who had been stuck on goal number 499 for a little while, getting the goal eased his mind. "I had a lot of chances and they didn't seem to go in," he told the *Los Angeles Times*. But with an open net, Kurri made no mistake. With his 500th career goal, he became the first European-trained player in league history to reach the milestone.

# OCTOBER 18
## CROSBY RECORDS HIS 500TH ASSIST, 2014

Sidney Crosby recorded his first NHL assist on October 5, 2005, in a lopsided loss to the Devils. Just over nine years and 553 games later, on October 18, 2014, Crosby earned his 500th career assist in a 3-1 victory against the Islanders, becoming the sixth fastest player in NHL history to reach the milestone. Only Wayne Gretzky, Mario Lemieux, Peter Stastny, Bobby Orr, and Peter Forsberg needed fewer games to accomplish the feat.

Heading into that game against the Islanders, Crosby was just a couple of helpers shy of reaching the 500-assist plateau. With time winding down in the second period, he charged into the Islanders' zone. Eluding the opposition as he raced toward the net, he drew a penalty as New York's Cory Conacher draped his stick around him in an effort to slow him down. On the ensuing power play, the Penguins caught another break when the Islanders were penalized for too many men on the ice. With Pittsburgh gearing up to take full advantage of a five-on-three power play, Crosby, now recuperated from the initial play that sparked the sequence, returned to the ice. As the Penguins cycled the puck against the hapless Islanders, Crosby spotted Evgeni Malkin across the ice and made a quick pass. In anticipation of the shot, Islanders defenceman Brian Strait dropped to the ice to make the block, but it was too late. Malkin had already released the puck and beat goaltender Jaroslav Halak on the short side. Crosby returned to the bench with his 499th career assist. With less than two minutes remaining in the game, the Islanders pulled their goaltender for the extra attacker in an effort to tie the game. As the clock ticked down, Crosby cleared the puck from his zone, leading to a late-frame insurance goal from Patric Hornqvist, to collect his 500th career assist. It was a fitting end to the game. Crosby, selected first overall in 2005, picked up the milestone assist on a play finished by Hornqvist, who happened to be the last player taken in the NHL Entry Draft that year.

# OCTOBER 19
## ROCKET REACHES 500, 1957

As the red light flashed and Maurice Richard leapt into the outstretched arms of Jean Beliveau, the Montreal Forum erupted into mayhem. The 14,405 fans who filled the Forum on the night of October 19, 1957, had just witnessed history. Richard had scored his 500th career goal, becoming the first player in National Hockey League history to reach the milestone. After Chicago's Ian Cushenan was sent to the penalty box for holding just before the 15-minute mark of the first period, Montreal's lethal power play went to work. As the Canadiens converged around the Black Hawks' net, Beliveau made a nifty pass to Richard, and the Rocket blasted the puck by goaltender Glenn Hall. While Richard and Beliveau celebrated, the Forum erupted into raucous acclaim. Programs and other debris littered the ice while the fans honoured their goal scorer with a noisy two-minute standing ovation.

In the days leading up to the matchup, it seemed to be a foregone conclusion that Richard would reach the milestone at home when the Canadiens hosted the Black Hawks. Two nights earlier, Richard had potted two goals against the Maple Leafs, bringing him up to career goals 498 and 499 and moving him within striking distance of 500. In addition, Chicago had not won a contest since their season-opening draw against Toronto, and the team seemed like easy prey for Richard, who was no stranger to scoring milestone goals on the Black Hawks. Nearly three years earlier, on December 18, 1954, he made history against Chicago by becoming the first player in NHL history to score 400 career goals. Richard would retire after the 1959–60 season, and it wasn't until March 14, 1963, that another player, Gordie Howe, joined him in the 500-goal club.

# OCTOBER 20
## GRETZKY VS. GRETZKY, 1993

When Wayne Gretzky made his NHL debut, his younger brother Brent was just seven years old. While Wayne collected Art Ross trophies and Hart trophies with the Oilers, Brent honed his hockey skills as a youngster, hoping that one day he would get the opportunity to square off against his big brother. On October 20, 1993, it finally happened. On that day, the Gretzky brothers faced each other for the first time in an NHL game. It was a special moment for the family. Although Keith Gretzky had been drafted by the Buffalo Sabres in 1985, he had never suited up for an NHL game. So when Brent was drafted 49th overall by the Tampa Bay Lightning in 1992, it renewed the possibility of a family showdown.

Following the draft, the Lightning held a press conference for Brent, and one of the reporters asked him how it would feel to play against Wayne. "He's been avoiding me for 10 years," he said. "I can't wait to get at him." While Brent's tongue-in-cheek response hinted at a sibling rivalry, the reality was that Wayne had left the family home at an early age and, therefore, spent much of life away from his youngest brother. Although hockey might have inadvertently kept them apart for all those years, it had finally brought them back together. As Brent headed out toward the ice in the ThunderDome in St. Petersburg that evening, he later told reporters he had experienced some pre-game jitters. "Coming up the ramp, somebody mentioned Wayne and my legs went funny," he said. But when the puck dropped, it was all business. Although Brent came close to notching his first NHL goal, wringing a shot off the post, the Great One got the better of his younger brother. He scored a goal and assisted on two others as the Kings defeated the Lightning. It proved to be the only time the Gretzkys would face off. Brent would play just 11 more games in the NHL. Nevertheless, with four points, Brent would add to Wayne's 2,857 career total, giving them the record for the most combined points by two brothers.

# OCTOBER 21
# JORDAN STAAL, SHORT-HANDED STAR, 2006

When Jordan Staal arrived at the Penguins' training camp in 2006, some thought the 18-year-old might be sent back to junior, but the six-foot-four Thunder Bay, Ontario, native exceeded expectations. Drafted second overall by Pittsburgh just a few months earlier, Staal impressed the club's top brass at training camp, particularly with his skills on the penalty kill, and made the team as a rookie. Early in the season, Staal continued to demonstrate why the Penguins had made a smart choice in keeping him around. On October 21, 2006, in a 5-3 victory over the Blue Jackets, Staal potted two short-handed goals, giving him the distinction of becoming the first NHL rookie in nearly a quarter-century to score each of his first three goals short-handed. Bill Gardner had last done it with the Black Hawks in 1981–82.

Although it was an impressive achievement for Staal, it was overshadowed by the brilliant play of another Penguins rookie, Evgeni Malkin. Malkin, who was drafted second overall by Pittsburgh in 2004, had scored in each of his first three NHL games, becoming the first rookie to accomplish this feat since Jan Caloun did it with the Sharks in 1995–96. While Malkin continued turning heads, finding the back of the net in each of his first six games, including a two-goal performance on the road against the Kings, Staal also continued to make a case for himself as one of the league's top rookies. Before the NHL's holiday break, the penalty-killing specialist had added two more short-handed goals to bring his league-leading total to five. In February 2007, Staal told the Canadian Press that he tries "to jump on my opportunities when [opponents] least expect offence" on the penalty kill. He certainly made the most of those chances. Staal finished the season with seven short-handed goals, setting an NHL record for the most short-handed tallies by a rookie.

# BOBBY HULL'S FIRST GOAL, 1957

Although Montreal's Bernie "Boom Boom" Geoffrion was one of the first to use the slapshot in the NHL, it was Bobby Hull who took the cannonading release to the next level in Chicago, racing in on goaltenders and winding up in full stride as he blasted the puck into the back of the net. Hull's shot was more lethal than his predecessor's because he and teammate Stan Mikita also introduced the curved blade to their arsenal. While Cy Denneny had adopted a curved blade, colloquially referred to as a banana blade, in the 1920s, it was Hull and Mikita who started regularly using bowed sticks to give their shots more velocity and accuracy. Combined with his speed and power, Hull's slapshot, which was reportedly clocked at 190 kilometres per hour, came to terrify NHL goaltenders.

As a result, he quickly established himself as one of the league's premier snipers, and on March 12, 1966, he became the first player in NHL history to score more than 50 goals in a season, surpassing the benchmarks set by Geoffrion and Maurice Richard. He'd finish the year with 54 markers and followed up the performance with a 52-goal campaign the next year, becoming the first player in league history to register back-to-back 50-goal seasons. Although Hull's NHL career was forever linked to his booming shot and penchant for goal-scoring, his first career tally was inconspicuous. In fact, it wasn't even a goal at all. On October 22, 1957, Hull, playing in his seventh game with the Black Hawks, was credited with his first NHL marker. The goal, however, belonged to Bruins defenceman Jack Bionda. Hull had rifled a shot at goaltender Don Simmons, who made the save, but Bionda, in an errant attempt to protect the puck, accidentally slipped into the open net with it. As a result, since Hull was the last Chicago player to touch the puck, he was awarded the goal. Although it was an unceremonious way to notch a first NHL goal, Hull would go on to score 609 more over the next two decades.

# OCTOBER 23
## RICH SUTTER JOINS THE FLYERS, 1983

When Brian Sutter made his NHL debut for the St. Louis Blues in 1976, it was not long before his five younger brothers followed in his footsteps. Darryl joined the Black Hawks in 1979, and Duane and Brent suited up for the Islanders just a couple years later. In 1982, twins Ron and Rich were taken just six spots apart in the NHL Entry Draft, going to Philadelphia and Pittsburgh, respectively. Both had played junior together in Lethbridge, and while they'd be starting their NHL career as rivals, it was not long before they were reunited.

On October 23, 1983, the Penguins traded Rich to the Flyers in exchange for Ron Flockhart, Mark Taylor, Andy Brickley, and a first-round draft pick. It had been well known that Rich was unhappy in Pittsburgh, unable to find a regular place in the Penguins' lineup, and the Flyers had been trying to pry him out ever since the draft. The organization hoped that reuniting the twins would be a catalyst for Philadelphia, similar to the combination that Brent and Duane had formed on Long Island. It did not take long for the Flyers to get a return on their investment. In his first game with Philadelphia, just hours after he was traded, Rich played on a line with his twin brother and scored his first NHL goal, making the Sutters the first family in league history to have six brothers score goals. Ron fittingly picked up the primary assist on Rich's first goal. Joining the brothers on the ice that night was Darryl Sittler, flanking Ron down the left side. Following the game, he told reporters how impressed he was with their play. "They have good bloodlines and I'm sure they're going to be a large part of our future," he said. Sittler noted just one issue: "The hardest part is telling them apart."

## OCTOBER 24
# BOBBY ORR REACHES 900, 1976

After missing a few games with a sore knee, Bobby Orr returned to the Black Hawks' lineup on October 24, 1976. He powered Chicago to a convincing 7-2 victory over the Blues, scoring two goals to pick up his 900th career point in just his 638th NHL game. But the more noteworthy goal that evening may have come from Cliff Koroll, who also netted a pair. Five minutes after scoring his first goal of the night, Koroll was taken down on a breakaway by Chuck Lefley. Referee Bruce Hood whistled down the infraction and promptly awarded Koroll a penalty shot. Skating in alone on Blues goaltender Ed Johnston, Koroll made no mistake and found twine again, becoming the first Black Hawk to score on a penalty shot since Joe Cooper accomplished the feat against the Canadiens on December 4, 1941.

Thirty-five years later, after revolutionizing the role of the defenceman in Boston with his dizzying end-to-end rushes, Orr was starting a new chapter in Chicago. Although he no longer had the fantastical speed he once possessed — his knees had begun betraying him long before — he was still peerless when it came to carrying the puck and breaking out of his defensive zone. While Orr's return to the lineup and his two-goal performance gave a flicker of hope that he was returning to form, he missed most of November as he battled a bad left knee. He wouldn't score another goal for the Black Hawks that season until January 12, 1977. It would prove to be his last tally of the campaign. In early February, Orr announced he would take the rest of the year off, unable to play in his current condition. After undergoing another surgery, Orr sat out the following season before returning to the team's roster on October 11, 1978. He would score his last NHL goal on October 28, just days before announcing he would be hanging up his skates for good.

# OCTOBER 25
# BOURQUE BECOMES HIGHEST ALL-TIME SCORING DEFENCEMAN, 2000

After racking up points from the Bruins' blue line for more than two decades, Ray Bourque continued his play as one of the league's top-scoring rearguards with the Avalanche. Traded to Colorado, along with Dave Andreychuk, on March 6, 2000, in an effort to take one last shot at capturing the Stanley Cup in the twilight of his career, Bourque missed out on the championship that post-season but had another opportunity the following year in his first full campaign with the Avalanche. In addition to seeking out Lord Stanley's mug, Bourque was also chasing down some history.

Although he had piled up the points in Boston, he always trailed Paul Coffey as the league's highest-scoring defenceman. But even as Bourque's career was coming to a close, it seemed only a matter of time before he passed Coffey. On October 25, 2000, Bourque did just that. In a game against the Predators, he set up two goals, including the overtime winner by Peter Forsberg, to vault himself ahead of Coffey. Heading into the 2000–01 season, Bourque was just seven points behind his rival, who was now suiting up for Bourque's former team, the Bruins, his fourth club in four years. Going to work on the Colorado blue line, Bourque quickly closed the gap. He picked up seven points in his first eight games to draw even with Coffey, who was sitting idle with the Bruins, unable to find the scoresheet in his first six contests with his new club. After the Avalanche and the Predators were held scoreless through two periods, Bourque picked up his 1,528th career point with a game-tying assist to take possession of the top spot. As the clock ticked down in overtime, he wired a slapshot at Nashville goaltender Mike Dunham that was tipped in by Peter Forsberg, creating more space between him and Coffey on the all-time list. By season's end, Bourque easily solidified his position as the league's all-time leading scorer among defenceman, finishing the campaign with 59 points.

# OCTOBER 26
## LEMIEUX SCORES 500, 1995

After sitting out the entire 1994–95 lockout-shortened season to rest his ailing back and regain his strength from radiation therapy to treat his cancer, Mario Lemieux returned with a vengeance. When he initially announced he was taking a sabbatical from the game on August 29, 1994, many were worried he might never come back. But Lemieux erased every one of those doubts when he returned to the ice on October 7, 1995, picking up four assists in an 8-3 rout over the Maple Leafs. The Penguins superstar continued his torrid comeback, racking up 13 points in his first five games back with Pittsburgh.

When the Penguins travelled to Long Island on October 26, 1995, Lemieux continued to put any concerns about his back to rest. Playing in his 605th NHL game, he recorded his 32nd career hat trick, notching his 500th career goal in the process to become just the 20th player in league history to reach the milestone. Only Wayne Gretzky did it faster, needing just 575 games when he accomplished the feat nearly 10 years earlier. While Lemieux's landmark goal moved him into some pretty illustrious company, it also made him the first player in franchise history to score 500 goals as a member of the Penguins, a distinction he still holds as of the end of the 2017–18 NHL season. The milestone moment happened with less than three minutes remaining in the matchup. With two goals already under his belt that evening, Lemieux once again beat Islanders goaltender Tommy Soderstrom to reach the 500-goal plateau and clinch the game for the Penguins. Following the contest, Lemieux told reporters how important it was for him to reach the milestone. "I knew I needed one more. It's important for me to score 500. It's a mark great players go out and achieve," he said. Lemieux would finish his comeback season with 69 goals and 161 points to capture his fifth Art Ross Trophy as the league's leading scorer, and he also nabbed his third Hart Trophy as the NHL's most valuable player.

# THE RUSSIAN FIVE, 1995

The Red Wings had been quietly building their own Red Army. The final piece was acquired on October 24, 1995, when Detroit brought in Igor Larionov from San Jose in exchange for sharp-shooter Ray Sheppard. Larionov complemented the Red Wings' suite of Russian players, which already included Sergei Fedorov, Vyacheslav Kozlov, Vlad Konstantinov, and Slava Fetisov, all of whom had previously played for CSKA Moscow, the famed Red Army team of the former Soviet Union. For Larionov, it felt like a reunion of sorts. "It's great to play with Russian guys again. I can't describe my feelings," he told reporters following the trade. A few days later, head coach Scotty Bowman acted on Larionov's feelings.

On October 27, 1995, the Red Wings made NHL history when they deployed an entire five-man unit made up of Russian players. Less than two minutes into a game against the Flames, the Russian revolution hit the ice. In their second shift of the game, the Russian Five, as they came to be known, combined to open the scoring, with Kozlov getting a goal with help from Fedorov and Konstantinov. Later in the third period, Larionov notched his first as a Red Wing, with another assist from Fedorov, as Detroit snuffed out the Flames 3-0, limiting them to just eight shots in the matchup. Although Bowman varied the line combination over the years, the Russian Five became a driving force on the Red Wings, particularly in capturing the Stanley Cup in 1997. But the unit's dominance was cut short by tragedy following the championship victory in June when Konstantinov, Fetisov, and team masseur Sergei Mnatsakanov were involved in a car accident. Although Fetisov escaped relatively unscathed, Konstantinov and Mnatsakanov suffered debilitating injuries. Konstantinov never played again. While he remained in hospital, Fetisov, Larionov, and Kozlov travelled to Moscow with the Stanley Cup. Before bringing the trophy to Red Square, Fetisov said, "It's a great moment in my life and in the life of Russian fans."

# MADDEN AND MCKAY SCORE FOUR GOALS EACH, 2000

ohn Madden and Randy McKay pulled off something that had not been done in a National Hockey League game in nearly eight decades. On October 28, 2000, the Devils forwards each scored four goals in an 8-0 trouncing of the Penguins. The last time two NHL teammates scored four goals in the same game was on January 14, 1922, when brothers Odie and Sprague Cleghorn guided the Montreal Canadiens to a 10-6 victory over the Hamilton Tigers. Madden's and McKay's feat also marked the first time a pair of Devils scored hat tricks in a game since Brendan Shanahan and Pat Verbeek did it in an 8-1 rout of the Maple Leafs on February 13, 1989.

Their achievement was even more special because neither Madden nor McKay was known for his scoring prowess. It was the first NHL hat trick for Madden, who had signed with New Jersey as an undrafted free agent in 1997. McKay, an 11-year veteran of the league, had previously recorded two career hat tricks, his last on March 24, 1998. In reflecting on their extraordinary achievements after the game, both players were still in disbelief. "I was just happy to score one," Madden said. McKay chalked it up to just being one of those nights where every time he touched the puck it went in. It made him feel like a kid again. "I have to go back to high school for the last time I did this," he said. But for McKay, the best part about it all was seeing his teammates' reaction to what was happening on the ice. "Guys on the bench couldn't believe it. Bobby Holik was shaking his head every time we went to the bench after a goal," McKay said. It would prove to be his last NHL hat trick. He would play three more seasons before hanging up his skates in 2003. While Madden had the early offensive outburst to start the 2000–01 campaign, by the end of the season he had established himself as one of the league's top defensive forwards, winning the Frank J. Selke Trophy.

# DETROIT MILESTONES, 1970

t was a landmark evening for a pair of Red Wings veterans. On October 29, 1970, in a game against the Bruins, Detroit captain Alex Delvecchio potted two goals, including his 400th career marker, becoming just the sixth player in league history to reach the milestone. Delvecchio joined Maurice Richard, Bobby Hull, Jean Beliveau, Bernie Geoffrion, and teammate Gordie Howe as the only other NHL players to accomplish the feat. Meanwhile, Howe notched a goal of his own late in the third period and also picked up two helpers, including his 1,000th career assist.

The Red Wings, who had been listless to start the season, picking up just two victories under rookie coach Ned Harkness, needed to make a statement against the defending Stanley Cup champions. Boston had not been defeated since the start of the season and was riding a 16-game unbeaten streak that extended back into the playoffs when they travelled to Detroit to take on the struggling Red Wings. Heading into the matchup, Harkness, who was coaching in his first NHL season after making the jump from the collegiate ranks at Cornell University, threatened his team with a major shakeup if they didn't turn things around. He had already started the 42-year-old Howe on defence to open the season, so there was no telling what the neophyte coach might do if his team picked up another loss. The bench boss's menacing words proved to be unnecessary. Early in the game, Delvecchio stripped the puck from superstar defenceman Bobby Orr at centre ice and had a clear breakaway on goaltender Gerry Cheevers. After his captain wired his 400th career goal past Cheevers, Frank Mahovlich scored another goal three minutes later. Although the Bruins tied the game before intermission, the Red Wings added three more goals to defeat Boston 5-3 and pick up their first victory in five games.

# OCTOBER 30
# GLENN HALL STARTS 500 STRAIGHT GAMES, 1962

Since becoming a full-time NHL goaltender with the Red Wings in 1955, Glenn Hall never took a night off. On October 30, 1962, then with the Black Hawks, Hall started in his 500th consecutive regular-season game. To celebrate the amazing feat, before the contest began, Chicago president Gene Metz presented the netminder with a gold stick. Although Hall didn't take the commemorative stick into his crease, he still had the Midas touch. He made 24 saves as the Black Hawks picked up their third straight win, moving them just one point behind the league-leading Red Wings.

Just over a week later, Hall made his 552nd straight start, including playoffs, but left the game midway through the first period with a back injury. During practice a day earlier, he had reportedly pinched a nerve in his back while he was trying out some new equipment. According to the netminder, the stiff pads caused him to move unnaturally, resulting in the injury. Although he had initially complained of some pain, he felt up to the challenge when the Black Hawks hosted the Bruins on November 7, 1962. But after allowing a goal from Boston forward Murray Oliver, it was clear Hall wasn't himself. As he headed to the Chicago dressing room, it was the first time in more than a decade he had been forced to leave a game with an injury. The last time it happened, he was playing in the junior ranks and had to vacate his crease after taking a puck to the face. Hall never returned to the game, and the Black Hawks settled for a 3-3 tie against the Bruins. The following day, it was announced that, after conferring with the team doctor, Hall would not accompany the Black Hawks on their upcoming road trip. It would be the first time Chicago would be without their goaltender since 1957. No other NHL goaltender has started 500 consecutive games, and it's doubtful the feat will ever be matched. Hall's incredible streak remains as one of the league's most unassailable records.

# OCTOBER 31
# MARCEL DIONNE SCORES
# HIS 700TH, 1987

t was all tricks and no treats for the Rangers on Halloween in 1987. Playing against their crosstown rivals, the Islanders, the Blueshirts put on a ghoulish performance at Nassau Coliseum. After just 40 minutes of play, the Isles had scored five goals, including three in a span of 10 minutes in the second period. When things seemed as though they couldn't get any worse, the Rangers allowed three more goals in the first seven minutes of the final frame. It was 8-0. It was a horror show.

The Blueshirts simply had no answers for the Islanders, who were coming off a deflating loss to the Maple Leafs earlier in the week in which head coach Terry Simpson had glued three of the team's younger players to the bench during the final period. The controversial decision sent shockwaves through the locker room, but the team, now galvanized, took out any residual frustration on their visiting opponents. Lost in the dreadfulness of the Rangers' performance was that, in the final minute of the game, Marcel Dionne scored his 700th career goal. While it was a meaningless tally as far as the outcome of the game was concerned, it was still a historic moment. Dionne, who had been traded to the Rangers after spending more than a decade with the Kings, joined Gordie Howe and Phil Esposito as the only players in NHL history at the time to reach that milestone. Esposito, who spent most of his career with the Black Hawks and Bruins, also happened to get his 700th career goal with the Blueshirts seven years earlier, in 1980, as his career was coming to a close. Dionne's landmark goal was the one bright spot on an otherwise dark Halloween for the Rangers. When he retired a year later, Dionne had 731 career goals to his name. As of the end of the 2017–18 season, he ranks fifth in NHL all-time goal-scoring.

# NOVEMBER 1
# JACQUES PLANTE PUTS
# ON THE MASK, 1959

J acques Plante changed the game. On November 1, 1959, after taking a puck to the face from Rangers forward Andy Bathgate, the Canadiens goaltender retired to the dressing room to get medical repairs. After he was stitched and bandaged up, he returned to his crease with a different look: he was wearing a fibreglass mask. Although he had sported a protective face covering from time to time during practices, it was the first time he had worn a mask during an NHL game. Although Plante is often credited with being the first goaltender to don a mask, others had adopted facial protection — albeit briefly — before his fateful night.

In 1927, Elizabeth Graham wore a fencing mask in a game while tending goal for the Queen's University women's hockey team, and at the NHL level, Montreal Maroons goaltender Clint Benedict briefly wore a leather face shield after his nose had been broken in a game against the Canadiens in 1930. While these were merely temporary measures, Plante was truly a trailblazer. Following that first game with the mask, he continued to wear it, becoming the first goaltender in the NHL to wear facial protection on a regular basis. His decision, however, was not without controversy. His colleagues, such as Rangers netminder Gump Worsley, felt the protective gear was unnecessary. His biggest critic, however, was his head coach, Toe Blake. The Canadiens' bench boss despised the mask, but since Plante continued to perform well behind his new protective accessory, Blake gradually came around. Plante's courageous move to adopt the mask revolutionized hockey for goaltenders. Now mandatory equipment, masks have significantly reduced injuries and have also become a means for netminders to showcase their personalities through the addition of unique designs.

# NOVEMBER 2
## HOWIE MORENZ MEMORIAL GAME, 1937

As Howie Morenz Jr. stepped out onto the ice, he received a roaring ovation from the crowd and players at the Montreal Forum. Skating among his father's peers during the warm-up, the youngster certainly did not seem out of place. He and his family were there as part of a memorial game to honour his late father, who had tragically passed away following complications from breaking his leg during a game against the Black Hawks.

Morenz, also known as the Stratford Streak, was arguably the league's first bona fide superstar. His speed and goal-scoring ability dazzled fans. Over the course of 11 seasons with the Canadiens, he captured the Hart Trophy three times as the most valuable player to his team and was part of three Stanley Cup victories. On November 2, 1937, players from the Maroons and Canadiens teamed up to take on a squad of NHL all-stars to pay tribute to Morenz and raise money for his family. Even King Clancy, the former Maple Leafs star and current coach of the Maroons, came out of retirement to play defence for Montreal. Although the NHL all-stars narrowly edged the mighty Montreals 6-5, the on-ice results didn't matter. The matchup was about Howie Morenz, his wife, and his children. Before the game commenced, in a touching ceremony, the Canadiens retired his number 7; this marked the first time in franchise history that a player had been honoured in this fashion. All proceeds from the game went to Morenz's family, including the gate receipts from the 8,653 patrons who turned out to pay tribute. Moreover, during the game, souvenirs and memorabilia were auctioned off in support of the fund. Joe Cattarinich, former part-owner of the Canadiens, bought Morenz's uniform and equipment and promptly presented them to Howie Jr. All told, the game raised more than $20,000 for the Morenz family.

# NOVEMBER 3
## AL ARBOUR RETURNS TO THE BENCH, 2007

When Al Arbour stepped away from the Islanders' bench following the 1993–94 season, he retired with a sterling resumé. The spectacled coach had been with the club from nearly the beginning, arriving on Long Island for the team's second season in the league. Over the next two decades, he took the Islanders from being a newly minted expansion club to being a dynasty. From 1980 to 1983, New York won four straight championships, the last NHL club to accomplish the feat. When it was all said and done, Arbour had four Stanley Cup rings, a Jack Adams Award, given annually to the league's best coach, and 739 career victories with the Islanders.

Despite his illustrious career on Long Island, there was still something that had eluded Arbour. Although he logged the most games behind the bench in Islanders history, he was one contest shy of 1,500. While that missed milestone was not likely something that had weighed on him after leaving hockey, 13 years later it was on the mind of then Islanders head coach Ted Nolan. Knowing how close Arbour was to the monumental benchmark, Nolan couldn't help but think how wonderful it would be if the Islanders could bring back their storied coach for just one more game, so he could bookend his career with the franchise with a nice round number. Team owner Charles Wang and general manager Garth Snow wholeheartedly agreed. So on Arbour's 75th birthday, he signed a one-game deal with the Islanders. The next day, on November 3, 2007, Arbour returned to his position behind the Islanders' bench for the first time in 13 years. Not only did he reach the 1,500-game milestone, but with New York's 3-2 defeat of Pittsburgh, he added another victory to his name, too. Following the contest, in a touching moment, members of Arbour's championship-winning teams presented him with a banner with the number 1,500 on it, and it was raised to the rafters to a chorus of cheers from the Nassau Coliseum faithful.

# THE GREAT ONE GETS 1,000 HELPERS, 1987

Wayne Gretzky beat Marcel Dionne to the punch. Heading into a matchup on November 4, 1987, both players were sitting at 998 career assists. With the Oilers hosting the Rangers that evening, Gretzky and Dionne were squaring off in person with the milestone on the line. There was no question that either player could easily reach the mark in that game, so it was just a matter of who would get there first. Within fewer than five minutes of puck drop, Jari Kurri scored the opening goal with some help from Gretzky and Esa Tikkanen. One down, one to go. By the time the first period ended, Gretzky was no closer to the 1,000-assist mark, but he had picked up two goals. Not long after the second period commenced, he ripped one by Rangers goaltender John Vanbiesbrouck to complete the hat trick.

After 40 minutes of play, Gretzky had three goals and an assist, while Dionne had yet to find the scoresheet with his team trailing 6-0 to the Oilers. Early in the final frame, the drama was over. After New York's John Ogrodnick ruined Grant Fuhr's shutout bid and got the Rangers on the board, Tikkanen found the back of the net, with a little help from Gretzky, to restore Edmonton's six-goal lead. With that assist, he punched his membership in the 1,000-assist club, joining his childhood idol, Gordie Howe, as the only two players in league history to reach the milestone. The duel between Gretzky and Dionne proved to be anticlimactic that evening. There were only 15,936 spectators at the Northlands Coliseum, the smallest Edmonton crowd in five years, and Gretzky completely stole the show with a five-point performance. Nevertheless, Dionne did get a little bit closer to the benchmark in the final moments of regulation. He assisted on another futile goal by Ogrodnick to bring his career assist total up to 999. Fittingly, three nights later, Dionne would get his 1,000th assist against his former team, the Kings.

# NOVEMBER 5
## JEAN BELIVEAU'S POWER-PLAY HAT TRICK, 1955

As Montreal's premier power-play unit took to the ice, the scorekeeper may have just as well left the goal lamp lit the whole time. When head coach Toe Blake deployed five future Hall of Famers, Jean Beliveau, Maurice Richard, Bert Olmstead, and defencemen Doug Harvey and Tom Johnson, Boston knew they were in trouble. At that time, players who served minor penalties were required to stay in the penalty box until their full sentence had expired, regardless of how many goals the opposing team scored. As a result, during this decade, the Canadiens feasted on the league's other clubs when prowling on the power play. Montreal's reputation for prolific punishment with the man advantage had become so well established in the 1950s that the league had already begun considering a rule change in order to mitigate the damage the Canadiens could inflict.

On November 5, 1955, with Montreal on the power play, Beliveau notched three goals in a span of just 44 seconds. The crowd at the Montreal Forum showered the ice with a flurry of programs and debris. Meanwhile, Boston's bench boss, Milt Schmidt, was incensed. While Beliveau's power-play hat trick was emblematic of the predatory nature of the Canadiens' power play during the 1950s, that particular performance was the last straw for the league's five other clubs. Later that year, the NHL amended its rules so that penalties would end after the opposition scored. Canadiens general manager Frank Selke was furious. He was, unsurprisingly, the lone voice of dissent on the vote to change the rule. Citing Detroit's dominance on the power play in previous years, Selke argued it was unfair that Montreal was now the focus of a rule change when there had been no proposals to alter gameplay when the Red Wings had been preying on opponents. Although Selke begrudgingly accepted his defeat, he left his colleagues with a few choice words. "Go get a power play of your own," he barked.

# NOVEMBER 6
## THE WIZARD IS CLAIMED OFF WAIVERS, 1997

When Ray Whitney signed with the Oilers in advance of the 1997–98 season, it was a dream come true. As a youngster, Ray and his brother, Dean, served as stick boys for the club, and now he had a chance to be on the other side of the bench in Edmonton. Although he had signed a one-way deal worth $300,000, things did not go as planned. Just nine games into his tenure with the Oilers, Whitney found himself on waivers. He was devastated. His father, an Edmonton police officer who occasionally worked security for the team at Northlands Coliseum, was equally upset. He said his son's dream was to play for the Oilers, not to watch them. At the time, Whitney was 25 years old and was just a season removed from a 41-point campaign with the Sharks, the club that had drafted him 23rd overall in the 1991 NHL Entry Draft. As a result, while he may not have fit into the Oilers' plans, he could still bring value to a team, something the Panthers shrewdly recognized.

On November 6, 1997, Florida claimed him off waivers. While the move ended Whitney's boyhood dream of playing for the Oilers, the move to South Beach gave him the opportunity to establish himself as a bona fide NHLer. By the Christmas holidays that year, he had recorded 12 goals and 12 assists in his first 24 games with the Panthers. Although he played only 68 games in his inaugural season in Florida, he finished the campaign as the team leader in scoring, with 32 goals and 61 points. Whitney would make the most of his opportunity in Florida, establishing himself as a premier playmaker and earning the nickname the Wizard for his nifty passes and playmaking abilities. One of the greatest waiver pickups in league history, he'd go on to win the Stanley Cup with the Hurricanes in 2006 and finished his NHL career with 1,064 points. Not bad for a former stick boy.

# NOVEMBER 7
## FIRST PARTITIONED PENALTY BOX, 1963

t's hard to believe but prior to 1963, opposing players used to share the same penalty box. After battering each other on the ice with their sticks and fists, bruised and bloodied players would retire to the same confined space to serve their infractions. Given how heated hockey can be, it's difficult to imagine how some of that chaos didn't spill over into the sin bin more often. All those years of sharing the box, however, came to a grinding halt following an altercation between Toronto's Bob Pulford and Montreal's Terry Harper. On October 30, 1963, the two were engaged in a skirmish in front of the Canadiens' bench. After Pulford dropped Harper with a fierce right, the two were promptly sent to the penalty box at Maple Leaf Gardens. Within seconds of sitting down on the bench, Pulford got up and began pummelling Harper. Given that NHL president Clarence Campbell was sitting just a few seats away, the penalty box slugging match caught the league's attention.

Following the brawl, Maple Leafs president Stafford Smythe commented on the situation. "It's ridiculous to ask two guys who've been trying to knock each other's heads off to sit quietly side by side. We've tried policemen, but that didn't work out too well. Linesmen are supposed to go in and break it up, but they didn't do it here," he said. The Canadiens took Smythe's words to heart. Before the team hosted the Black Hawks on November 7, 1963, the Forum staff divided the penalty box into two sections with steel piping. It marked the first time an NHL arena featured a partitioned penalty box. Two nights later, Maple Leaf Gardens debuted its newly revamped penalty box. Although Toronto did not have a physical barrier between the two players — instead a timekeeper sat between them — it had installed two entrances for further separation. The league eventually backed the initiative and suggested that all teams adopt separate penalty boxes. Even the evolution of the penalty box has its own moment in hockey history.

# BOBBY ORR RETIRES, 1978

ighting back tears, Bobby Orr made a difficult announcement. On November 8, 1978, the eight-time Norris-winning defenceman declared he was retiring from the NHL. Orr, who broke into the NHL in 1966 as an 18-year-old, revolutionized the way defencemen played the game. His dizzying end-to-end rushes, blistering speed, and smooth playmaking abilities defied the conventions of the day and what a player could bring to the blue line. Early in his tenure with the Bruins, it was easy to see why the team had gone to the lengths it did to sign the Parry Sound, Ontario, native as a 14-year-old. Orr was rewriting the record books. In 1970, he became the first defenceman in NHL history to score 100 points in a season. In addition, he was running out of shelf space for all the hardware he was collecting. By the end of his fourth season in Boston, Orr had already racked up three straight Norris trophies, his first Hart, the Stanley Cup, and the Conn Smythe for the most valuable player in the playoffs.

Following his dazzling goal that won the championship for the Bruins over the Blues in 1970, St. Louis coach Scotty Bowman reportedly said, "They say the Bruins started rebuilding when Orr signed. I don't believe it. I think they started rebuilding in 1948 the year he was born." That's how much he meant to his team and the sport of hockey. Much to everyone's loss, Orr's career was cut short by chronic knee injuries. After signing with the Black Hawks as a free agent in 1976, he was limited to just 20 games in his first season in Chicago. Following another surgery on his left knee, Orr took the next year off to recover. When he returned the next season, he felt as though he was ready to play again, but just six games into the campaign, his damaged left knee had given out on him again. He was just 30 years old when he hung up his skates for the last time.

# NOVEMBER 9
## CRAIG MACTAVISH SCORES FINAL
## HELMETLESS GOAL, 1996

t would mark the end of an era. On November 9, 1996, Blues forward Craig MacTavish scored on Flames goaltender Rick Tabaracci. At the time, it wasn't necessarily a noteworthy goal. It wasn't a milestone marker for MacTavish, nor did it change the outcome of the game. It would, however, prove to be his final career NHL goal, and as a result, it ended up being the last goal scored by a helmetless player. For years, it was easy to spot MacTavish on the ice. He was one of the league's few players who did not sport a helmet. By 1996, he was the last player to suit up for an NHL game without a bucket. Following a collegiate hockey career at the University of Lowell, MacTavish was drafted by the Bruins in 1978. Just a few months before he made his NHL debut, the league had decreed in August 1979 that any player who had signed a contract after June 1, 1979, would need to wear a helmet when they entered the league. MacTavish, who had inked his first contract with the Bruins prior to that cut-off date, was exempted from the new regulation.

In the league's earlier days, team ownership often encouraged players not to wear helmets so they would be more recognizable to the fans. After the tragic death of Bill Masterton in 1968, however, more and more players began wearing helmets, but it remained optional. When the NHL made its safety announcement 11 years later, 70 percent of its players had worn head protection the previous season, but the minority were eligible to be grandfathered if they signed a waiver. Although MacTavish wore a helmet during his early days in Boston, he later discarded the head protection for the remainder of his career. When he retired on April 29, 1997, after an NHL career that spanned nearly two decades, MacTavish was asked why he never wore a helmet all those years. "It was just a comfort thing for me," he said.

# NOVEMBER 10
## FIRST NHL PENALTY SHOT, 1934

When the NHL introduced the penalty shot for the 1934–35 season, it was thought to be a "sniper's delight." In the depths of the Great Depression, it was seen as a way to inject some additional excitement into hockey games. Pushed forward by the Patrick brothers, who had previously introduced the concept in the Pacific Coast Hockey Association during the 1920s, it ushered in a new wave of exhilaration at the hockey rink. The original penalty shot, however, would be unrecognizable from what we see in today's NHL. Back then, players made the shot 38 feet out from the net while staying within a circle that was 10 feet in diameter. You could either take the shot from a stationary position or skate with the puck, provided you did not leave the designated area. While it was marketed as a "sure goal," under these regulations goaltenders still had a significant advantage.

On November 10, 1934, following a trip on Canadien Georges Mantha, after much deliberation, Armand Mondou was selected to take the penalty shot for Montreal. Mondou was a curious choice. He had scored only five goals the previous season but now had a chance to enshrine himself into hockey lore by scoring on the first penalty shot in NHL history. However, it was not meant to be. Shooting from a stationary position, his shot never left the ice, and the puck slid easily into the outstretched glove of George Hainsworth. While Mondou was not able to convert his opportunity, three nights later, Ralph "Scotty" Bowman fared much better. In another game featuring a Montreal team (the Maroons), the St. Louis Eagles were awarded a penalty shot in the second period. Bowman slipped the puck past goaltender Alec Connell to tie the game. Although St. Louis ended up losing that game in overtime, Bowman became the first NHL player to score a penalty shot goal. More would follow. In 1941, the league amended its rules by adding minor and major penalty shots. The latter allowed players to skate up to the goaltender in a one-on-one situation, which led to more thrills and goals.

# BOBBY SMITH NETS SEVEN POINTS, 1981

The stars aligned in Minnesota on November 11, 1981. That night, the North Stars lit up the Winnipeg Jets for 15 goals in the biggest offensive outing in franchise history. At the centre of the starburst was Bobby Smith, who scored four goals and added three assists in a stellar performance. Three years earlier, he had been drafted first overall by the club following an astral campaign in the Ontario Hockey League, where he put up 69 goals and 123 helpers in his final year, establishing league records for assists and points. After notching 74 points in his rookie year in Minnesota, Smith was awarded the Calder Trophy as the league's top newcomer. He proved he was not just a shooting star, following up his rookie season with 83- and 93-point performances.

But early into that memorable game against the Jets, there was no indication that Smith or the North Stars would have such a galactic game. At the first intermission, Minnesota was only leading by a score of 2-1 and Smith had an assist. During intermission, head coach Glen Sonmor reportedly told his players to take the game over. They certainly did. The North Stars fired 27 shots and scored eight goals against the Jets in the second period. During that frame, Smith potted two goals and added two more assists to his column on the scoresheet. In the final period, he found the back of the net two more times as the North Stars added five goals in the first 15-goal team performance in a game since the Red Wings shellacked the Rangers 15-0 on January 23, 1944. Moreover, Minnesota was just one goal shy of the all-time record set by the Montreal Canadiens on March 3, 1920, when they trounced the Quebec Bulldogs 16-3. Although the Stars are now playing under the skies in Dallas, those single-game benchmarks by the team and Smith remain franchise records.

# NOVEMBER 12
## SWEET 16, 1942

Although Armand "Bep" Guidolin was too young to enlist for military service, he was old enough for the Boston Bruins. On November 12, 1942, the 16-year-old Timmins, Ontario, native suited up for his first NHL game, becoming the youngest player in league history to take the ice. Guidolin had attended the Bruins' training camp in Montreal in October, and had even laced up his skates in an exhibition game against an Army team in Cornwall, but he returned to his junior hockey club in Oshawa. A season earlier with the Generals, he had been part of the team that won the Ontario Hockey Association championship and went on to compete for the Memorial Cup, Canada's junior hockey crown. But early into his sophomore season in Oshawa, he signed a contract with the Bruins.

During the Second World War, NHL clubs experienced roster shortages due to players enlisting for military service. As a result, players like Guidolin were given opportunities to crack big-league rosters in order to alleviate the lack of available talent. A day after Bruins general manager Art Ross inked him to a contract, the undersized Italian Canadian made his NHL debut against the Maple Leafs. He slotted in on a line with fellow teenagers Bill Shill and Don Gallinger, forming a trio that would be known as the Sprout Line. Although Guidolin did not make the scoresheet in his first game, 12 days later in a matchup against the Black Hawks, he scored his first NHL career goal, making him the youngest player in league history to light the lamp, a distinction he will always hold now that the league has minimum age restrictions. Following a 10-year NHL career, Guidolin went on to play in the minor leagues for nearly another decade. After he retired from hockey, he stepped behind the bench of his former junior team, the Generals, where he first coached Bobby Orr. Guidolin and the superstar defenceman would be reunited years later when he became the bench boss for the Bruins, guiding the team to the Stanley Cup Final in 1974.

# NOVEMBER 13
## SIGNALLING THE GOAL, 1947

After Billy Reay scored the opening goal in a game against the Black Hawks, he raised his stick. It was not, however, a spontaneous celebration. Instead, it was at the behest of league officials, who had adopted a new proposal from Frank Patrick, one of the game's most renowned trailblazers. Patrick, a former player who helped found the Pacific Coast Hockey Association with his brother Lester, would pioneer a number of innovations in the sport that included the forward pass, the blue line, the penalty shot, numbered jerseys, and artificial ice, just to name a few.

In addition to these initiatives, Patrick had also petitioned the NHL for players to raise their sticks after they score a goal as a gesture to spectators and a signifying move to the officials and scorekeepers. Moreover, more than simply signing to the crowd, Patrick had actually suggested that players skate upward of 40 feet with their stick upraised to the rafters. After the idea received the blessing of league president Clarence Campbell, it was implemented in a matchup between the Canadiens and the Black Hawks on November 13, 1947. Reay was the first to make the signal, and he did so again on his second tally of the game, but the orchestration of the move was not as well choreographed by other players that evening. According to the *Globe and Mail*, after Montreal's Toe Blake scored a goal, he was "so hemmed in by players in the goal scramble he couldn't get his stick up." When he scored again later that game, he didn't make the signal because he simply forgot. As a result, the gesture didn't receive the fanfare the league anticipated, but President Campbell said they would continue to push the initiative. Today, goal-scoring celebrations are ubiquitous and they can be as unique as the players themselves. It's incredible to think that an act so engrained in hockey now started off as a league directive.

# NOVEMBER 14
## CAPS HIRE GREEN, 1979

At just 26 years old, you could say the Capitals' new head coach was green. On November 14, 1979, Washington named Gary Green as the club's new bench boss, replacing Dan Belisle, who had been dismissed a day earlier. With the promotion, Green, who had been coaching the team's American Hockey League affiliate in Hershey, became the youngest coach in NHL history, eclipsing the distinction previously held by Claude Ruel, who was 31 when he coached the Montreal Canadiens a decade earlier.

Prior to joining the Capitals organization, Green had been behind the bench of the Peterborough Petes of the Ontario Hockey League. He guided the team to back-to-back league championships and a Memorial Cup victory in 1979 before he was snatched up by Washington. Coaching the Capitals would not be easy. Since joining the league in 1974, the team had never qualified for the post-season. Although it was daunting, Green seemed up for the challenge. "It's a big challenge but coaching in the NHL is something I always wanted to do," he told reporters. He made his NHL coaching debut the next day, but the Bruins spoiled the occasion with a 3-2 victory over Washington. Green was considered one of the brightest up-and-coming minds in hockey, but even he could not turn around the fledgling Capitals. Although the team improved to 23-30-13 in his first campaign behind the bench, Washington missed the playoffs yet again. The next year, the club racked up 70 points, the best performance in franchise history up to that point, but it still could not crack the post-season. After starting the 1981–82 season on an 11-game losing streak, Green was dismissed by the organization. While he was still two years away from his 30th birthday, Green said his experience in Washington aged him. "I feel like I'm 48 years old…. After two years with the Caps, I guess that can happen," he said.

# NOVEMBER 15

## DAVE ANDREYCHUK'S POWER-PLAY RECORD, 2002

D ave Andreychuk was a punisher on the power play. Using his big frame, he would park himself in front of the opposing team's net and bang in rebounds and loose pucks. Although his goals were not always the flashiest, he certainly made the most of his opportunities on the man advantage. Growing up in Hamilton, Ontario, Andreychuk brought the blue-collar spirit from Canada's largest steel-producing city to his NHL career. Both of his parents were steelworkers, so he understood the importance of developing a strong work ethic and brought those values to his game. After getting drafted 16th overall by the Buffalo Sabres in 1982, Andreychuk went on to play in the league for more than two decades. His durability and scoring touch, particularly on the power play, became hallmarks of his career. Of course, it helped that, in addition to possessing a smooth set of hands, he was also six foot four and weighed 225 pounds. As a result, combined with his steadfast determination, few could move him away from the front of the net, where he did most of his damage.

By his 21st season in the league, Andreychuk, who was then with the Tampa Bay Lightning, was chasing down the NHL record for the most power-play goals. On November 15, 2002, he made history. Halfway through the first period, he shovelled home a loose puck to rack up his 250th career power-play goal, passing Phil Esposito on the all-time list. Funnily enough, Esposito, who was a radio broadcaster for the Lightning, was in the building that evening and saw the goal from the press box. A week later, against one of his former teams, the Devils, Andreychuk potted his 600th career NHL goal. For good measure, he would go on to add 24 more power-play goals to widen his lead on the league's all-time list. On November 13, 2017, he was inducted into the Hockey Hall of Fame.

# NOVEMBER 16
## FLAMES ACQUIRE
## MIIKKA KIPRUSOFF, 2003

With too many Sharks swimming around in San Jose's net, it was only a matter of time before the team cut bait with one of its goaltenders. On November 16, 2003, the Sharks traded Miikka Kiprusoff to the Calgary Flames in exchange for a second-round pick in 2005. Drafted 116th overall by San Jose in 1995, Kiprusoff was coming off his second full NHL campaign as the club's backup. The Finnish netminder, however, struggled down the stretch of the 2002–03 season and lost his backup job to colleague Vesa Toskala. Since neither goaltender was going to usurp Evgeni Nabokov's full-time position between the pipes, the Sharks had to decide which netminder was expendable. With Kiprusoff starting 2003–04 as the odd man out, he was sent to Calgary.

In the Flames' net, Kiprusoff's game caught fire. He finished the season in Calgary with a sterling 24-10-4 record and the best save percentage in the league. More incredible was that, in his 38 appearances that season, he allowed only 65 goals against, giving him a 1.69 goals-against average, the lowest ever in the NHL's modern era. In the 2005–06 season, his remarkable play in Calgary's crease continued. He racked up 42 victories and posted 10 shutouts to win the Vezina Trophy. Over the better part of the next decade, Kiprusoff established himself as one of the NHL's premier netminders and endeared himself to the Flames faithful. When he hung up his pads in 2013, he held franchise records for the most wins (305) and shutouts (41), benchmarks that should stand the test of time for quite a while. Given all of Kiprusoff's success in Calgary, it would be easy to say that San Jose lost the trade, but the Sharks still made out well. In 2005, they used the second-round pick to select Marc-Edouard Vlasic 35th overall. Since then, Vlasic has been a stalwart player on the San Jose blue line and has been regarded as one of the league's top rearguards.

# NOVEMBER 17
## GRETZKY VS. HOWE, 1979

n 1972, a young Wayne Gretzky met his idol, Gordie Howe. As the two posed for a picture, Mr. Hockey playfully put his stick up against the young prodigy's neck as if he were giving him one of his famous hooks. Seven years later, they were peers. On November 17, 1979, Wayne Gretzky and Gordie Howe squared off in their first of four NHL matchups. The showdown between hockey's elder states-man and its newest phenom represented the passing of a torch from one career that spanned five decades to another that would be the greatest of all time.

But truth be told, it wasn't their first meeting. Howe and Gretzky had encountered each other before in the World Hockey Association (WHA). A year earlier, Howe was with the New England Whalers and was starting the final leg of a six-year sabbatical in the WHA. Meanwhile, Gretzky, who was only 17 years old at the time, was just beginning his professional career. Too young to join the NHL, the Brantford, Ontario, native signed his first contract with the Indianapolis Racers. A year later, both players were in the NHL. The WHA had merged with the league, and Gretzky found himself with the Edmonton Oilers after being traded there for magic beans a season earlier, while Howe was still with the Whalers. Heading into that game in Hartford on November 17, 1979, Gretzky was still a few months away from the legal drinking age in Ontario and Howe was approaching his 52nd birthday. When the buzzer sounded after 60 minutes of play, the edge went to Gordie, as the Whalers shut out the Oilers 4-0. Howe picked up an assist while Gretzky was, obviously, absent from the scoresheet. Given the 34-year age difference between the two, we shouldn't have ever expected to see them play against each other in the NHL. The fact that we did, even if it was just for four games, makes it a truly special part of hockey history.

# NOVEMBER 18
# ART DUNCAN LEADS THE COUGARS, 1926

The Detroit Cougars couldn't have picked a better man than Art Duncan to lead them into battle for their first NHL game. A veteran of the First World War, Duncan was no stranger to taking charge in pressure situations. As a captain in the Royal Flying Corps, he was credited with shooting down 22 enemy aircraft, for which he was awarded the Military Cross. At the end of the war, he stayed on with the Royal Air Force for another year before trading in his aviator goggles for a hockey stick. He played eight seasons on the blue line in the Pacific Coast Hockey Association with the Vancouver Millionaires and Vancouver Maroons. In 1925, he moved into the Western Hockey League (WHL), where he served as a player-manager for the Calgary Tigers.

Following the purchase of the WHL by the National Hockey League in 1926, Duncan headed eastward with many of his colleagues to continue playing. After the Victoria Cougars officially became the property of Detroit hockey interests, he was brought in to act as the manager-player-coach of the club. On November 18, 1926, the Detroit Cougars made their NHL debut, taking on the Bruins at Border Cities Arena in Windsor, Ontario. The game, however, was all but over just after the puck dropped. Boston scored two goals within the first three minutes, and the Cougars spent the rest of the matchup chasing them, only to be shut out before the capacity crowd of 6,000. Although the game ushered in the NHL era in Detroit, it would be another year before the league truly arrived in the Motor City. When the 1926–27 season started, construction on the Olympia wasn't complete, so the Cougars played all their home games across the river in Windsor. By the time the Cougars got to Detroit, Duncan had moved on to the Maple Leafs. With Toronto, Duncan would see his former team rebrand as the Falcons in 1930 before becoming the Red Wings in 1932.

# DEFENCEMEN LIGHT THE LAMP, 1929

The *Pittsburgh Post-Gazette* referred to it as more exciting than "a rodeo, grid setto, a fistic encounter, and a wrestling match combined." Those were the terms used to describe the matchup between the Toronto Maple Leafs and the Pittsburgh Pirates on November 19, 1929. Highlighted by the work of two dynamic defencemen, the contest gave the Duquesne Gardens' patrons plenty of action. While many people in Canada and the United States were withdrawing funds from their bank accounts as the economy inched closer to the precipice of an unprecedented recession, blueliners Hap Day and Johnny McKinnon were making deposits into the back the of the net.

Less than a minute after puck drop, Toronto's Day scored the opening goal. Twenty-five seconds later, the Maple Leafs scored again. The Pirates were not off to a great start. Halfway through the first period, Day's counterpart on the Pirates, McKinnon, got the buccaneers on the board with a marker of his own. When play resumed for the middle stanza, Day scored another early goal to add to Toronto's lead, but McKinnon answered a few minutes later to cut the deficit to one. After Pittsburgh's Harold Darragh tied the game, the Pirates scored three more goals in the next seven minutes, including two more from McKinnon. With the Pirates leading 10-3 with 10 minutes remaining in the third period, Hap Day scored two goals in one minute as he attempted to will his team to a comeback. Although McKinnon's Pirates got the better of Day's Maple Leafs, both rearguards scored four goals apiece. It was the first, and only time, an NHL game has been punctuated by two defencemen posting four-goal performances. No small feat considering that neither player was known for his scoring prowess. Day's effort represented more than half his season output, while McKinnon would score only six more goals in 39 more games that year.

# NOVEMBER 20
## END OF REGULAR-SEASON OVERTIME, 1942

During the Second World War, NHL overtime came to a grinding halt. On November 20, 1942, the league announced it had placed a moratorium on extra time during the regular season because of wartime travel restrictions. In order for teams to catch their respective trains on time, and not exacerbate sensitive travelling schedules and resources during the conflict, regular-season games that ended in deadlocks after regulation would be ruled draws. Previously, if teams were tied after 60 minutes of play, a 10-minute period of overtime would be played to break the stalemate.

When the league first introduced overtime for the 1928–29 season, it did not include a sudden-death provision. Instead, the supplementary period was played just as straight time. Teams could score any number of goals in the additional frame, and games would still end in a draw if neither team potted a goal or scored the same number of goals in the extra 10 minutes. On January 16, 1934, Toronto's Ken Doraty capitalized on this regulation when he scored three goals in extra time against Ottawa, becoming the first, and only, player in NHL history to score a hat trick in overtime. Although the NHL scrapped overtime during the regular season, it was still in place during the playoffs. During the post-season, if teams were at an impasse after regulation, they would continue to play full periods in the sudden-death format until the deadlock was broken. Later that season in Detroit, on March 23, 1943, the Leafs and Red Wings battled through four periods of overtime until Detroit's Jack McLean mercifully ended the game after they had played more than 130 minutes of hockey. Regular-season overtime wouldn't return to the NHL for more than four decades. When the league reintroduced it for the 1983–84 season, it consisted of a five-minute sudden-death period. On October 8, 1983, with the Islanders and Capitals tied 7-7 in Washington, New York's Bob Bourne scored the NHL's first regular-season sudden-death goal.

# NOVEMBER 21
## SIDNEY CROSBY RETURNS, 2011

ollowing more than a 10-month absence, Sidney Crosby made his triumphant return to the NHL. On November 21, 2011, the Penguins superstar played in his first game since January 6, after battling back from a series of concussions. During the 2011 Winter Classic at Heinz Field, Crosby suffered a concussion when he was hit by Washington's David Steckel, but he finished the game and suited up four days later for Pittsburgh's next contest against the Lightning. During that matchup, he sustained another hit. Although it appeared to be far less jarring, combined with the previous impact, it was enough to keep him out of the lineup for nearly the next 11 months.

While Crosby took the time to recover from his concussion-related injury, the hockey world collectively held its breath. He was just 23 at the time and the league's brightest star, but his career was already being limited by head trauma. As his absence turned from days to weeks and weeks to months, there were growing concerns about Crosby's future on and off the ice. When he finally returned, it was if he had never left. On his first shot of the game, he scored a nifty backhand goal to give the Penguins an early lead. It was his first goal since December 28, 2010. He would add another marker and pick up two assists as Pittsburgh cruised to a 5-0 victory over the Islanders. While the hockey world exhaled, the relief was short-lived. Just eight games into his return, his concussion symptoms reappeared and he did not play again until March 15, 2012. After rejoining the lineup, Crosby racked up 25 points in the Penguins' final 14 games of the season. Following his comeback, he went on to lead the league in scoring in 2013–14 and in goals in 2016–17, along with leading the Penguins to back-to-back Stanley Cups and winning the Conn Smythe Trophy twice. While it appears as though Crosby has made a full recovery from his injuries, the concussion issue in hockey still looms large for the NHL and its players.

# HERITAGE CLASSIC, 2003

The NHL returned to hockey's roots. On November 22, 2003, the Montreal Canadiens and the Edmonton Oilers played an outdoor game, known as the Heritage Classic, that hearkened back to hockey's early beginnings on frozen ponds and rivers. Although the league had orchestrated outdoor games before, such as when the Los Angeles Kings and the New York Rangers duelled in an exhibition contest at Caesars Palace in Las Vegas in 1991, the Heritage Classic was the first regular-season game to count toward the standings.

Despite the frigid temperatures in Edmonton that day, a record-setting 57,167 fans filled Commonwealth Stadium. Many of them braved bone-chilling weather all day, arriving early to catch an afternoon alumni game between some Oilers and Canadiens legends, including Wayne Gretzky and Guy Lafleur. Even Mark Messier, still an active member of the New York Rangers, participated in the festivities. He received permission from his general manager, Glen Sather, who happened to be behind the bench for the Oilers' alumni team, to suit up for the game. When the puck dropped for the official game that evening, it was even colder. While the fans froze in their seats, it wasn't much better on the ice. Between periods, Canadiens' goaltender Theodore, who had stretched a wool toque over his mask for the game, guzzled tea and hot chocolate to keep warm, but it didn't help. "My hands were really cold and my leg muscles really tightened up. With the cold, all my equipment and pads got so stiff it was just hard to keep your focus," he told Rick Westhead after the game. But in the end it was worth it. Theodore and the Canadiens picked up the victory over the Oilers. The scene of players skating around outside, their breath visible in the frigid November air, was beautifully reminiscent of childhood memories on backyard rinks and frozen ponds. The NHL has since tried to recapture that nostalgia each year as part of its Winter Classic and Stadium Series outdoor games, but the ubiquity of those spectacles has dulled their charm.

# WAYNE GRETZKY SCORES HIS 600TH CAREER GOAL, 1988

t should have been a night of celebration, but instead a black cloud hung over it. On November 23, 1988, Wayne Gretzky scored his 600th career NHL goal, becoming just the fifth player in league history to reach the benchmark. He also added five assists that game as the Kings defeated the Red Wings 8-3 at Joe Louis Arena. It was Gretzky's first milestone with his new team, and while he always downplayed his personal achievements with modesty, this time it was different. Following the game, Keith Gave of the *Detroit Free Press* asked Gretzky why he had a long face after such an incredible performance. The Great One responded simply, "Just tired, that's all."

But there was something else going on behind the scenes. With the end of the second period nearing, Gretzky was having himself a night. He had already scored his monumental goal and bagged four assists, but as the middle frame came to a close, the puck slipped by him and the Red Wings' Steve Yzerman scored a goal. Upset with his mistake, Gretzky slammed his stick against the crossbar. As the Kings adjourned for intermission, coach Robbie Ftorek, displeased with Gretkzy's emotional outburst, informed his superstar player that he would be benching him to start the third period. Ftorek was still a relatively new coach in the NHL, and he flouted convention by wearing sweaters behind the bench instead of suits, but benching the Great One was just something you didn't do. After being stapled to the bench for nearly the first eight minutes of the third period, Ftorek finally signalled for Gretzky to hit the ice. Following the game, Gretzky kept his emotions to himself, but he was livid about the situation. It did not take long for the story to make its rounds throughout the league. On a night when everyone should have been toasting the Great One, the topic of conversation was Ftorek's coaching gaffe. He didn't make that mistake again.

## OH, BROTHER! 2003

Mathieu Biron wasn't known for putting the puck in the back of the net. As a hulking six-foot-six defenceman, his skill set was better suited toward executing thunderous body checks as opponents tried to enter his zone. Through his first 149 NHL games, Biron found twine just five times. But on November 24, 2003, in a game against the Sabres, he scored the biggest goal of his career. It not only held up as the game-winner for the Panthers but also gave him family bragging rights. Mathieu had scored on his older brother Martin, a first since Phil Esposito scored on his younger brother Tony in 1980.

Of course, in a much smaller league, the Esposito brothers had played each other upward of 50 times, and Phil bragged he had lost count of the goals he scored on Tony. For the Biron brothers, however, it was only their fifth encounter, and Martin had stymied Mathieu in each of their previous meetings. But with their parents in attendance, Mathieu finally came out on top. Late in the first period, as Florida drove to the Buffalo goal, Mathieu fired a puck that completely fooled his sibling. Martin didn't get a clear look at the shooter, but after he fished the puck out of his net, he saw Mathieu grinning from ear to ear. It was his first goal of the season — and he had scored it on his older brother. "He was jumping in the air with his teammates like it [was] Game 7 of the Stanley Cup and I said to myself, 'oh no, that just happened,'" Martin later recalled. As much as Martin was upset he had been scored on, he was happy for Mathieu. "He was ecstatic, so I did have that part of me that was glad and really happy for him. Did I want my team to score two goals so we could win 3-2? Absolutely," he told VICE Sports. Mathieu scored six more goals in his NHL career, but no more against Martin. As of the end of the 2017–18 season, no other player has scored on his sibling.

# NOVEMBER 25
## MOE ROBERTS GOES IN GOAL, 1951

When Moe Roberts replaced injured Bruins goaltender Doc Stewart on December 8, 1925, Roberts was just days away from his 20th birthday, making him the youngest goaltender at the time to play in the NHL. In relief, Roberts backstopped Boston to the victory, earning himself a start three nights later. Afterward, he was sent back to the minor leagues, where he tended twine for another five years before returning to the NHL, making just a handful of appearances for the New York Americans in the 1930s. Following three years of service in the United States military during the Second World War, Roberts returned to hockey. He played for the Washington Lions of the Eastern Amateur Hockey League, but at the end of the 1945–46 campaign, he retired. Five years later, he was working for the Black Hawks as an assistant trainer and practice goaltender.

During a game against the Red Wings on November 25, 1951, goaltender Harry Lumley was injured and Chicago found itself without his services. Although Roberts had played his last NHL game nearly two decades earlier, he bravely set out for the net. At that point in the contest, the game already seemed well out of reach for the Black Hawks, as they trailed the Red Wings 5-2. Nevertheless, Roberts performed admirably in relief. He turned aside every shot he faced in the final frame, but Chicago still fell to Detroit. With Roberts just weeks away from his 46th birthday, his third-period performance made him the oldest goaltender to appear in an NHL game. Nearly 20 years later, Johnny Bower played his final game with the Maple Leafs just a month after turning 45, but Roberts still remains the oldest goaltender to see NHL action.

# NOVEMBER 26
## THE NHL IS FOUNDED, 1917

After four days of meetings in the Windsor Hotel in Montreal, Quebec, the National Hockey League was born. On November 26, 1917, it was announced that the National Hockey Association (NHA), made up of teams in Montreal, Quebec, Ottawa, and Toronto, had suspended operations and established a new national league. The disbandment was partly spurred by the strained relationship between Toronto owner Eddie Livingstone and the rest of the NHA. Known for his combativeness, Livingstone had been a thorn in the side of colleagues for years. A couple of years earlier, the situation had worsened considerably. Prior to the 1915–16 season, he purchased a second Toronto club, the Blueshirts, from Frank Robinson. At the time, Livingstone also owned the Shamrocks, but rather than operating two teams in the city, he essentially merged the two clubs, leaving Toronto with just one NHA franchise. The other owners were furious, as it now made their trips to the Ontario capital costlier with just one team on the docket. The association soldiered on, but the relationship with Livingstone only got worse. Finally, in 1917, the other owners took drastic action.

Unable to remove Livingstone from the NHA, as per the association's constitution, they did the next best thing; they ceased operations and formed a new league without him. Instead, a new four-team league was formed that included the Canadiens, Wanderers, and Senators from the NHA, along with a new franchise in Toronto that would be operated by the Toronto Arena Company. Although Quebec would not operate during the league's inaugural season, it remained on the directorate of the new syndicate and would return to action a few years later, fielding a team for the 1919–20 campaign. With Livingstone out of the picture, a new era of professional hockey took shape in Canada. Less than a month later, on December 19, the first pucks were dropped and the NHL began.

# GORDIE'S MILESTONE DAYS, 1960, 1965, 1969

Gordie Howe was no stranger to scoring milestone goals in Montreal. At the Forum, he had scored his 100th and 400th career goals and had also notched his 544th and 545th goals, which tied and broke the mark set by beloved Canadien Maurice "Rocket" Richard. On November 27, 1965, Howe found himself in a familiar setting but was peerless in his feat. That evening, he scored his 600th career goal, becoming the first player in NHL history to reach the milestone. Even the faithful Montreal crowd could not help but cheer Howe's significant achievement. After he scored his landmark goal, the fans littered the ice with newspapers and programs. Of course, the applause didn't last very long. Just a few moments later, Howe elbowed Canadiens defenceman J.C. Tremblay to a chorus of jeers. It turns out that on the other end of Howe's history-making marker was Canadiens goaltender Gump Worsley, who had been in net for two of Mr. Hockey's other milestone goals. That's one way to get yourself into the record books.

But that was far from the only memorable November 27 Howe had in his incredible 26-year NHL career. Rewind to five years earlier, and he had actually made history on the same day. On November 27, 1960, he picked up two assists in a game against the Maple Leafs to become the first player to rack up 1,000 career points. Nine years later, he was at it again. On November 27, 1969, in his penultimate season with the Red Wings, Howe recorded two assists in a 5-1 victory over the visiting Kings. Following his helper on Pete Stemkowski's goal, the crowd of 12,886 thunderously applauded the play, as it was Howe's 1,700th career point. This achievement once again moved him into the record books as the only NHL player at the time to reach the milestone.

# BILLY SMITH GETS CREDIT FOR A GOAL, 1979

arly in the third period in a game against the Rockies, the Islanders incurred a delayed penalty. As Colorado looked to capitalize on the situation by pulling goaltender Bill McKenzie for an extra attacker, something unexpected happened. Deep in the Islanders' zone, Rockies rookie defenceman Rob Ramage attempted to set up a play, but his pass missed the mark and slid the length of the ice into the vacant net. Since New York goaltender Billy Smith was the last Islander to touch the puck, having blocked a shot before Ramage's errant pass, he was awarded the goal, becoming the first goaltender in NHL history to be so credited. Years later, when Smith reflected on that moment, he couldn't help but chuckle. "That was just a little bit of a fluke," he said.

The blunder almost cost the Rockies a critical win. Before Ramage scored on his own goal, Colorado was just 20 minutes away from capturing the first franchise victory against the Islanders. Since 1974, when the club joined the league as the Kansas City Scouts, they had been unable to crack the Islanders. Even after the move to Denver in 1976, the change of scenery did little to improve their fortunes, and the team was 0-13-2 against New York heading into that contest. Luckily for Ramage, his teammates scored three unanswered goals in the final frame to secure the victory. While Smith was the first NHL goaltender to be credited with a marker, it was another eight years before Ron Hextall became the first goaltender in league history to score a goal by shooting the puck into the net.

# BJORN SKAARE MAKES HIS
# NHL DEBUT, 1978

At just 16 years of age, Bjorn Skaare had cracked the roster of Furuset Ishockey, one of the most prestigious hockey clubs in Norway. The following year, he continued his professional development, suiting up for Färjestad BK in the Swedish Hockey League. But after just a season in neighbouring Sweden, Skaare made a big move, heading to Canada to play junior hockey for the Ottawa 67's in the Ontario Hockey Association. After a successful campaign in Ottawa, where he scored 42 points in 38 games, the Scandinavian was selected 62nd overall by the Red Wings in the NHL Amateur Draft. Following his first training camp with Detroit at the beginning of the 1978–79 season, he was frustrated with not making the opening-day roster, reportedly quitting the team for a few days. But after a few days to process the situation, he reported to the Red Wings' Central Hockey League (CHL) affiliate club in Kansas City. After an admirable start to the season in Missouri, Skaare was recalled by Detroit.

On November 29, 1978, in a game against the Colorado Rockies, he made his National Hockey League debut, becoming the first Norwegian player to suit up for a game in the NHL. He was held off the scoresheet but fired a shot in what would turn out to be his only appearance for Detroit. Just a few months after returning to Kansas City, he decided to pack it in with the Red Wings. Back in Norway, Skaare returned to Furuset, where his career had begun, and guided the club to a league championship. After representing Norway at the 1984 Winter Olympics, he made a brief return to the CHL, playing a handful of games for the Tulsa Oilers, but once again returned home. Tragically, he was killed in a car accident on June 21, 1989. He was just 30 years old. Almost 20 years after Skaare made his NHL debut, Anaheim's Espen Knutsen scored a goal against the Senators, becoming the first Norwegian player to record a goal in the NHL.

# JOE THORNTON IS TRADED, 2005

Joe Thornton thought he would be a Bruin for a long time. In 1997, Boston selected him first overall in the NHL Entry Draft. Within five years he would become team captain and the cornerstone of the franchise. But after a sluggish start to the 2005–6 season, the Bruins abruptly changed direction. On November 30, 2005, Boston traded Thornton to San Jose in exchange for Brad Stuart, Marco Sturm, and Wayne Primeau. Thornton felt blindsided. Although the Bruins were sitting in the basement of the Northeast Division at the time of the trade, their captain was leading the team in scoring with 33 points in 23 games. As a result, despite Thornton's performance, some felt the Boston brass had scapegoated the star centre for the team's slow start. Thornton certainly felt as much. "Who knows? Hindsight's 20-20. I came here to win. We're not winning. Whose fault that is, I'm not sure. But right now, I'm out of here. So, it must be mine," he said.

While the acquisition of Stuart, Sturm, and Primeau shook up the Bruins roster, it did little to improve their fortunes in the short term. Boston missed the post-season for the next two years before squeaking into the playoffs in 2008. Although the Bruins would win the Stanley Cup in 2011, they did so without Stuart, Sturm, and Primeau, who had all been shipped out of the organization by that point. Meanwhile, in San Jose, Thornton flourished. He finished out the 2005–06 campaign with the Sharks, racking up 92 points with his new team to win the Art Ross Trophy as the league's leading scorer, becoming the first player in league history to capture the award following a midseason trade. In addition, for his efforts that year, he was awarded the Hart Trophy as the league's most valuable player. Thornton scored his 1,000th career point with the Sharks on April 8, 2011, and as of the end of the 2017–18 season, he is the all-time franchise leader in assists by a country mile.

DECEMBER

# DECEMBER 1
## FIRST NHL GAME IN THE UNITED STATES, 1924

Seven years after the National Hockey League was founded, it arrived in the United States. On December 1, 1924, the Boston Bruins hosted the Montreal Maroons at Boston Arena. Both clubs were newly minted expansion teams, but the buzz was unquestionably around the Bruins, which was the first American representative in the NHL at the time. Despite being the hottest new ticket in Beantown, the Bruins' first game was hardly a sellout. The fans in attendance got to see a close game against the Maroons. Although the home team trailed 1-0 after the first period, the Bruins rallied in the second frame, scoring two goals en route to defeating their fellow expansion team 2-1. While the results may have looked good on paper, it was anything but on the ice. The team was not yet in high-performance condition, and as the season unfolded, things only got worse.

Unfortunately for the Boston faithful, that first win over the Maroons was just one of a handful the Bruins recorded that season. The club didn't pick up another victory until the following year. Well, to be fair, 1925 was only a month away, but still. Following that first game, the Bruins dropped 11 straight contests. Over the course of that losing streak, Boston played more like teddy bears than bruins, posting a goal differential of -41, before picking up a second win on January 10, 1925, against the Canadiens. Boston finished the season with an abysmal record of 6-24-0 and, unsurprisingly, did not make the post-season. The next year, the Bruins would be joined by the Pittsburgh Pirates and New York Americans as the league continued its push into the United States. By 1926–27, the NHL had expanded to 10 teams, with more than half of those clubs hailing from the United States.

# DECEMBER 2
# PATRICK ROY PLAYS LAST GAME FOR MONTREAL, 1995

Patrick Roy was incensed. After allowing nine goals on 26 shots to the Red Wings, the Canadiens netminder was finally, and mercifully, pulled from his crease. During the course of his shelling, Roy seemingly blamed his defence corps for some of the miscues, and when the goaltender received a sarcastic cheer from the crowd for making a routine save, he responded with a mocking gesture of his own. As Roy made his way down the Canadiens' bench, he brushed by Mario Tremblay, his fiery gaze firmly fixed on his head coach, before turning back toward the seat of club president Ronald Corey. In the brief exchange that followed, Roy supposedly told Corey, "That's my last game in Montreal." And that was it. December 2, 1995, was Roy's last game as a Canadien.

Not long after the incident, the team suspended him for his gesture to the crowd and placed him on the trading block. There was no going back. Although he had been with the club for nearly a decade, earning three Vezina trophies along the way as the league's top goaltender and leading the Canadiens to two championships with his superb playoff performances, which also earned him two Conn Smythe trophies, they had reached an impasse. In the days that followed, Roy addressed the media, acknowledging that his time in Montreal had come to an end. "My career is taking a new turn. It's not easy and it's too bad how this whole situation turned out," he told reporters. And so, on December 6, 1995, the Canadiens announced they had concluded a trade with the Avalanche. Roy, along with Mike Keane, was going to Colorado in exchange for goaltender Jocelyn Thibault, Martin Rucinsky, and Andrei Kovalenko. While it was not the way Roy wanted to leave Montreal, in Colorado he cemented his place as one of the league's greatest goaltenders. Backstopping a star-studded Avalanche squad, Roy picked up two more Stanley Cups and a third Conn Smythe before hanging up his pads in 2003.

# DECEMBER 3
# BRUINS RETIRE PHIL ESPOSITO'S JERSEY, 1987

When Ray Bourque found out the Bruins were going to retire Phil Esposito's number 7, he immediately offered to make the switch to another number. Bourque, who had been sporting 7 since he broke into the league with Boston in 1979, was willing to part with it out of deference to Esposito and everything he had accomplished with the franchise. But Esposito declined the move, saying it wasn't necessary. Bourque, however, wouldn't take no for an answer.

On December 3, 1987, in a pre-game ceremony before hosting the Rangers, the Bruins sent Esposito's jersey to the rafters. But before the banner raising took place, Bourque skated out to meet Esposito and presented him with his jersey. As Esposito held it in his hands, the black and gold stitching bringing back memories of two Stanley Cup championships during his near decade with the Bruins, Bourque pulled his own number 7 jersey over his head, revealing another sweater underneath. As the Bruins captain slyly did a turn in front of Esposito and the crowd, it became clear that he was wearing the number 77. The Garden faithful roared approvingly as the significance of the gesture became apparent. Bourque had decided that, despite Esposito's initial response, he would switch numbers. It made for a touching ceremony. Neither Esposito nor the crowd knew Bourque had been planning to adopt a new number. Prior to the celebration, newspapers reported he would continue to wear his familiar number 7. But Bourque knew that giving up his jersey was the right thing to do, and the sentiment was not lost on Esposito. Even through grainy footage, the genuine look of surprise and appreciation on Esposito's face is unmistakable. As Esposito's sweater ascended to the top of the Boston Garden, Bourque proudly looked on, sporting his number 77 jersey that he would wear for the remainder of his NHL career.

# DECEMBER 4
## HOWE SCORES HIS 700TH, 1968

On December 4, 1968, Gordie Howe became the first player in National Hockey League history to score 700 regular-season goals. When asked about scoring 800, he said, "It depends on how my legs stand up." Howe was already in a league of his own. Three years earlier, he had become the first player to rack up 600 regular-season goals; his 700th put him 156 ahead of Maurice Richard, who had retired in 1960 with 544 goals to his name. When the Rocket hung up his skates, many believed his benchmark would stand for decades, but Howe made short work of his record, surpassing it just three years later before moving into uncharted territory.

Howe's 700th came on the road in a game against the Penguins. Just before the halfway mark of the first period, he blasted a 30-foot shot past Pittsburgh goaltender Les Binkley to tie the game 1-1. While Howe celebrated with his teammates, the officials stopped the game to retrieve the puck and give it to Mr. Hockey as the crowd showered him with applause. Following the game, reporters pressed him for his thoughts on reaching the next milestone, but Howe was reticent in his response. "I have to admit it's getting tougher," he said. He wasn't sure how much longer he would be able to play but noted that "as long as you're scoring goals, though, it's easier." After finishing the 1970–71 season, his 25th campaign in the NHL, Howe announced his retirement. At the time, he had 786 career regular-season goals, and it looked as though number 800 would elude him. But after taking a front-office job with the Red Wings, he was lured out of retirement by the opportunity to play with his sons in the World Hockey Association (WHA). Following six seasons in the rebel league, a 51-year-old Howe returned to the NHL in 1979 with the Hartford Whalers and closed out his incredible career with his 801st regular-season goal on April 6, 1980, against, fittingly, the Red Wings. The record stood for 14 years before Wayne Gretzky, who idolized Howe as a youngster, toppled it.

# DECEMBER 5
## ESPOSITO VS. ESPOSITO, 1968

Starting in his first NHL game, Canadiens goaltender Tony Esposito faced off against a familiar adversary: his older brother Phil. On December 5, 1968, the Esposito brothers suited up for their first National Hockey League encounter. Tony had gotten his first taste of NHL action just a week earlier when he accompanied the Canadiens on a road trip after goaltender Gump Worsley, who loathed airplane travel, was given a month off by the team for refusing to accompany the club on a flight to Oakland. With Gump grounded, Esposito served as Rogie Vachon's backup and was called into relief in a game against the Seals on November 29, 1968. Phil, on the other hand, was a five-year veteran of the NHL and playing in his second season with the Bruins following a trade from the Black Hawks in 1967.

On that notable night, he did not take it easy on his little brother. Less than eight minutes into the game, Phil slipped a puck past Tony to open the scoring for the Bruins. After the Canadiens took a 2-1 lead with goals from Bob Rousseau and Yvan Cournoyer, Tony was just 10 minutes away from recording his first career NHL victory when Phil, once again, got the better of his younger sibling. With the clock winding down in the third period, Phil wired a shot from 45 feet out to tie the game. Neither team would score again, and the matchup ended in a 2-2 draw. It wasn't the first time a brother had spoiled a party in the NHL. Three decades earlier, on December 21, 1937, Boston's Cecil "Tiny" Thompson was in line for a shutout when his younger brother Paul scored a goal with nine seconds remaining in the game. It marked the first time an NHL player had scored on his brother. The Espositos continued their NHL battles for nearly the next two decades. After claiming he had scored upward of 42 goals against his younger brother in their matchups over the years, Phil tallied his final goal against Tony on November 5, 1980.

# MIKE MURPHY PERFECT IN ONLY LOSS, 2011

M ike Murphy was in the wrong place at the wrong time. Although the Hurricanes goaltender stopped both shots he faced in relief of Cam Ward in a game against the Flames, he was still charged with a loss. On December 6, 2011, he became the first goaltender in league history to record a loss without allowing a goal against. Murphy, who had been drafted by the Hurricanes in the sixth round in 2008, spent the start of his professional career with the club's American Hockey League affiliates, first in Albany and then in Charlotte, before being recalled to accompany Carolina on a road trip through western Canada while regular backup goaltender Brian Boucher nursed a lower-body injury.

As the Hurricanes squared off against the Flames, Murphy intently sat on the bench for his first NHL contest. With Ward starting the game, Murphy did not anticipate seeing the ice unless Ward succumbed to injury or had a bad outing. After surrendering six goals to Calgary, the former Conn Smythe Trophy winner was pulled from the game with less than 10 minutes remaining. As he mercifully skated toward the bench, Murphy suited up and prepared for his first taste of NHL action. Not long after taking his place in the crease, Carolina captain Eric Staal scored a goal to cut the deficit to two. With the clock ticking down, the Hurricanes pulled Murphy for an extra attacker. With Murphy back on the bench, Calgary's Jarome Iginla scored an empty-net goal to extend the lead again. Down by three goals with just over a minute remaining, the game seemed well out of reach for the Hurricanes. But Chad LaRose potted a goal to bring his team within two. Thirty seconds later, and with just five seconds remaining in the contest, Staal scored again. When the final buzzer sounded, Calgary had defeated Carolina 7-6. Since Jarome Iginla scored the game-winning goal, Murphy was charged with the loss because he was the goaltender of record at the time of the deciding tally.

# TORONTO CHANGES ITS NAME TWICE, 1919

Toronto's NHL club did not officially have a name during the league's inaugural season. Operated by the Toronto Arena Company, it was simply known as the Arena Gardens Hockey Club of Toronto, but as time passed, the squad was colloquially embraced as the Arenas. Although the team won the Stanley Cup in 1918, defeating the Vancouver Millionaires in a playoff series for the right to hoist the silver mug, the Arenas struggled mightily the following campaign, winning just a handful of games over the course of a split-season schedule. Moreover, the club also encountered legal troubles when Eddie Livingstone, the former owner of Toronto's National Hockey Association club who had been shut out by his colleagues when the NHL was founded in 1917, brought forward a lawsuit against the Toronto Arena Company over the use of his former players. With the company bogged down in litigation, a new owner was sought so the hockey club could operate unencumbered from the legal action brought by Livingstone.

As a result, on December 7, 1919, manager Charlie Querrie changed the team's name to Tecumseh as the Toronto Arena Company prepared to sever itself from operating the club. The moniker, however, was short-lived. The following day, negotiations were concluded with a new group of owners consisting of Querrie and members of Toronto's amateur hockey ranks, who took over the club and christened it the St. Patricks Hockey Club. Frank Heffernan, who had played for the St. Patricks in the Ontario Hockey Association, was tapped as the team's new manager. For the next six years, the St. Pats represented Toronto at the NHL level, winning the Stanley Cup in 1922. The club wouldn't win another championship for five more years, but by that point, following another change in ownership in early 1927, when the franchise celebrated the victory, it did so under the banner of the Maple Leafs.

# DECEMBER 8
## HEXTALL SCORES, 1987

With a two-goal lead in the final minutes of the third period against the Bruins on December 8, 1987, Flyers goaltender Ron Hextall made history. With Boston's net empty, Hextall fired a shot from just outside his crease, becoming the first NHL goalie to score a goal by shooting the puck into the opponent's net. For Hextall and his teammates, what transpired that game was just something that seemed bound to happen. During his time in the NHL, Hextall was regarded as one of the most proficient puck-handling goaltenders in the league, and perhaps of all time.

Leading up to that night in December, the fans and his teammates were getting on his case about when he was going to score. Reflecting on that moment many years later with VICE Sports, Hextall, then the general manager of the Flyers, said he had been waiting for the perfect moment. "With a two-goal lead, the right situation just presented itself. The puck came to my left side and I set it up and was fortunate that it hit the net," he said. After the puck landed near the Bruins' blue line and glided into the net, Hextall was immediately mobbed by his teammates. He recalls that scoring a goal wasn't high on his list of career aspirations, but it was an immensely significant moment for him and the Flyers. "The thing I remember most is my teammates coming off the bench," he said. "The way the guys were yelling and screaming it was almost like we won a playoff series, so that made it really special for me." Since Hextall became the first goaltender to score a goal by shooting the puck, there have been only four other netminders to accomplish the feat during the regular season. Detroit's Chris Osgood did it in 1996, Montreal's Jose Theodore pulled it off in 2001, San Jose's Evgeni Nabokov did it in 2002, and, most recently, Mike Smith did it with the Coyotes in 2013.

# DECEMBER 9
## NHL'S BOLD EXPANSION PLAN, 1989

n between rounds of croquet and soaking up the sun in Palm Beach, Florida, the NHL's board of governors got down to business. On December 9, 1989, the league's representatives agreed to an expansion plan that would see the number of teams grow to 28 by 2001. It was a bold move for the league, the first round of expansion in more than a decade. The NHL had not grown since absorbing four World Hockey Association clubs — the Edmonton Oilers, Winnipeg Jets, New England Whalers, and Quebec Nordiques — in advance of the 1979–80 season. According to the ambitious plan, the league would add at least one and a maximum of three teams to the circuit no earlier than the 1992–93 campaign. Following the meetings, the focus immediately shifted toward tapping into new markets.

In the coming years, the shape of the NHL and the hockey landscape would change dramatically. On May 9, 1990, the league granted approval for the Gund brothers to sell the Minnesota North Stars in exchange for the rights to an expansion franchise in the San Francisco Bay Area. In September 1990, the NHL announced it had awarded the first franchise to the Gunds, known as the Sharks, to begin playing in time for the 1991–92 season. Other franchises followed. With Gary Bettman taking office as the league's first commissioner on February 1, 1993, the NHL soon embarked on pushing deeper into larger markets in the United States with the intention of landing its first U.S. network television deal in decades. By the start of the 1996–97 campaign, the league had added new teams in Ottawa, Tampa Bay, Miami, and Anaheim, along with relocations to Denver, Phoenix, and Raleigh. By 1999, expansion had continued with developments in Nashville and Atlanta, putting the league at 28 teams, two years ahead of schedule.

# DECEMBER 10
## JOHNNY BOWER'S LAST NHL GAME, 1969

Maple Leafs coach John McLellan had a hunch that Johnny Bower would do well against the Canadiens on December 10, 1969. For the most part, McLellan was right. Through the first 40 minutes of play, the 45-year-old Bower stopped nearly everything that came his way. In the final frame, however, the Maple Leafs defence cratered and Bower was shelled for 15 shots, giving up four goals in a 6-3 loss to Montreal. It would prove to be Bower's last NHL game. Just over two weeks later, he was sporting a full leg cast after tearing some ligaments in his right knee during practice. It was a big loss to a Maple Leafs roster that had already been decimated by injuries that season. Coach McLellan had hoped to start Bower in the next few games in order to give Bruce Gamble a respite, but with Bower out indefinitely, the club had to soldier on in his absence.

Bower had been a minor-league goaltender for most of his professional career, except for a full campaign with the Rangers in 1953–54, until he joined the Maple Leafs as a 33-year-old in 1958 after being claimed in the Inter-League Draft. In Toronto, he established himself as a premier NHL goaltender, winning the Vezina Trophy as the league's top netminder in 1961 and 1965 and backstopping the Maple Leafs to four Stanley Cups. While Bower recovered from his injury, he took up scouting assignments for the team, even travelling to Phoenix while still wearing a cast to check out the talent on the Roadrunners, Toronto's Western Hockey League affiliate. When the cast came off, he continued his scouting duties but hung up his goalie pads. Although he announced his retirement on March 19, 1970, Bower wasn't ready to step away from the game completely. Instead, he joined the Maple Leafs as a scout and goaltending coach. For nearly the next five decades, even after retiring, the affable Bower was forever linked to the organization, serving as the club's most beloved ambassador. A Maple Leaf forever, he passed away on December 26, 2017.

# DECEMBER 11
# KATE SMITH'S "GOD BLESS AMERICA" IS PLAYED AT THE SPECTRUM, 1969

The Flyers broke with tradition. Instead of playing the national anthem before hosting the Maple Leafs on December 11, 1969, the team's vice president Lou Scheinfeld had Kate Smith's rendition of "God Bless America" played over the loud speakers at the Spectrum. Although some were critical of the decision, calling it unpatriotic, they couldn't argue with the results that followed. After Smith's voice echoed through the building, the Flyers, powered by a hat trick from Andre Lacroix, doubled up the Maple Leafs 6-3. Although Smith's song did not completely supplant "The Star-Spangled Banner" in Philadelphia, over the next three seasons the Flyers were a sterling 19-1-1 when "God Bless America" was played. By the start of the 1973–74 campaign, the team's record had improved to 29-3-1 under Smith's rendition, leading the Flyers to bring the exuberant singer in for a live performance.

On October 11, 1973, fittingly, in a game against the Maple Leafs, against whom the tradition had begun, the Flyers faithful welcomed Smith to the Spectrum for her first live performance of "God Bless America." As she emphatically belted out the final note of the song, the 17,007 patrons gave her a thunderous ovation. Under the lights of the Spectrum, the power of her live performance seemingly galvanized the team, as the Flyers blanked the Maple Leafs 2-0. She continued her live performances throughout the season, but none was more special than in Game 6 of the Stanley Cup Final against the Bruins on May 19, 1974. Before puck drop, the piano-organ was moved out onto the ice. The simple sight of it confirmed that Smith would be making an appearance and was enough to electrify the building. Following her performance, the power of "God Bless America" continued. The Flyers went on to shut out the Bruins 1-0 to capture the first championship in franchise history.

# RICK MARTIN RETIRES, 1981

After playing in just three games with the Kings that season, 30-year-old Rick Martin retired on December 12, 1981. Martin, who was selected fifth overall by the Sabres in the 1971 Amateur Draft, was one of the league's premier scorers. For the better part of a decade, he was a member of Buffalo's famed French Connection line with Gilbert Perreault and Rene Robert. The trio, highlighted by Martin's potent slapshot, Robert's lightning speed, and Perreault's nifty playmaking abilities, was one of the most prolific scoring lines in the league. During the 1973–74 campaign, Martin became the first Sabres player to rack up 50 goals in a season, a feat he repeated the following year. Over the next nine years, no one scored more goals in Buffalo than Martin. The sniping winger's career, however, came to a grinding halt on November 9, 1980, in a game against the Capitals. Martin sustained a serious knee injury. While he recovered, Sabres general manager Scotty Bowman went in a different direction.

On March 10, 1981, as the NHL's trade deadline approached, Martin, along with Don Luce, was dealt to the Kings in exchange for a first-round pick. Bowman, who had joined the organization just two years earlier, was keen to move on from the club's aging stars in order to start building toward the future. Although Martin was the franchise's leading goal scorer and a fan favourite in Buffalo, he quickly embraced the move to Los Angeles, even as he awaited medical clearance. He played his first game as a King on April 4, 1981, scoring a goal and assisting on another in a 5-5 tie with the Colorado Rockies. The following season, Martin wrestled with his damaged knee, suiting up for only three games with the Kings before announcing his retirement. Meanwhile, in Buffalo, Bowman used the first-round pick from the trade to select goaltender Tom Barrasso in the 1983 draft. Barrasso would backstop the Sabres for the better part of six seasons, winning the Calder and Vezina in his rookie year.

# DECEMBER 13
## WAYNE GRETZKY'S MILESTONE DAY, 1983–89

t should have been Wayne Gretzky's night. On December 13, 1983, playing in just his 350th NHL game, Gretzky racked up his 300th career goal. The Oilers captain's feat, however, was overshadowed by the handiwork of New York's Butch Goring, who scored four goals and powered the Islanders to an 8-5 victory. Before scoring his milestone marker, Gretzky assisted on a Willy Lindstrom goal to pick up a point in 31 straight games, breaking his own league record for longest consecutive point streak. But the accolades and records brought little consolation to Gretzky, who was dismayed by his team's performance.

Gretzky and the Oilers would do much better two years later on the same night when they defeated the Jets 6-3 in Winnipeg. In that contest, Gretzky scored twice in the final minutes of the third period as Edmonton downed the Jets to pick up their second consecutive road victory. Two nights earlier, Gretzky picked up seven assists — tying Billy Taylor's record for most assists in a road game — in Chicago as the Oilers ravaged the Black Hawks 12-9 in the highest-scoring game since the introduction of the red line in 1943. In Winnipeg, Gretzky continued serving up assists, adding two helpers as he reached the 1,200-point milestone in just his 504th career game. Four years later, December 13th continued to be another great day for the Great One. In a game against the Whalers, Gretzky tied an NHL record by earning an assist for the 17th straight game. The Kings captain had actually established the record as a member of the Oilers in 1983–84 and saw the mark equalled two years later by teammate and defenceman Paul Coffey. Over the course of his streak in Los Angeles, Gretzky racked up 35 assists in 17 games before he was limited to just a goal against the Devils on December 15, 1989. He finished that season with 102 helpers to lead the league in assists for the 11th straight year.

# DECEMBER 14

# BOBBY ORR SCORES HIS FIRST NHL HAT TRICK, 1968

Although Bobby Orr had been turning heads since he broke into the NHL as a rookie in the 1966–67 season, he may have turned in the finest performance of his young career on December 14, 1968. In a home game against Chicago, the Bruins' superstar defenceman, just two years removed from his Calder Trophy victory, scored his first career NHL hat trick and put up two assists as Boston humbled the Black Hawks in a 10-5 rout. While Orr had undergone knee surgery over the summer, he continued to put any doubts about his health to rest that evening.

Early in the matchup, he completed a dazzling rink-long dash, deking through Chicago's defence corps before wiring a wrist shot past goaltender Dave Dryden to even the score. Five minutes later, the 20-year-old blueliner scored again to give the Bruins the lead. From there, they never looked back. By the time the first period ended, Boston was winning 5-2 and Orr already had two goals and two assists. Although the Black Hawks scored two goals six minutes into the middle frame, closing the deficit to just one, Orr completed the hat trick at the halfway mark of the period to put the game out of reach for Chicago. It was a splendid performance for the young defenceman, who was just getting started that year. On March 20, 1969, celebrating his 21st birthday, he scored his 21st goal of the season, becoming the highest-scoring defenceman in a single season, surpassing the mark set by Detroit's Flash Hollett in 1944–45. Less than a week earlier, he had established a new record for most points in a season by a defenceman when he picked up his 60th point of the campaign in a game against the Maple Leafs. Orr, of course, would shatter his own records in just a few short years. In 1970–71, he racked up 139 points, and in 1974–75, he lit the lamp 46 times. Although Paul Coffey broke the goal-scoring record in 1985–86 with 48, Orr's 139-point season remains the gold standard for NHL defencemen.

# DECEMBER 15

## DERON QUINT TIES THE RECORD FOR TWO FASTEST GOALS, 1995

Winnipeg's rookie defenceman Deron Quint didn't need much time to light the Oilers up like a Christmas tree. On December 15, 1995, just before the halfway mark of the second period, the Jets had a 2-1 lead and were on a power play that was just about to expire. With five seconds remaining on the man advantage, the 19-year-old blueliner wired a shot from just inside the blue line. On its way to the net, the puck deflected off Edmonton forward Scott Thornton and went by goaltender Joaquin Gage. So with the Jets now up 3-1, the puck went back to centre ice for the faceoff. Winnipeg won the draw and Quint took possession of the puck. After carrying it up to the red line, he lobbed it deep into Edmonton's zone. As it headed for the glass, Gage moved behind his net to position himself for an easy recovery. Instead, with the crease vacant, the puck bounced off the glass and into the net, giving the Jets a three-goal lead, all in the span of four seconds.

Edmonton's defence couldn't believe what had happened. Neither could the game's colour commentators. According to John Garrett, "These old buildings, when goalies play in here a lot, you realize you can't take the chance, you never commit. Well Joaquin Gage has never played in here. He doesn't know the Winnipeg Arena." But Garrett's words weren't entirely accurate. Gage had actually played there before on November 26, 1995, when he surrendered three goals on 23 shots. Quint's quick offensive flurry tied an NHL record originally set by Nels Stewart, who accomplished the feat some 64 years earlier. On January 3, 1931, Stewart and his Maroons were taking on the Boston Bruins. Early in the period, Montreal was trailing by a goal, but two quick markers from Stewart put the Maroons ahead, and they held on for a 5-3 win. Quint and Stewart still share the record for the fastest two goals in NHL history.

# DECEMBER 16
## THE NHL'S LONGEST SHOOTOUT, 2014

After 60 minutes of play, the Capitals and Panthers were tied 1-1. When overtime failed to break the deadlock, the two teams headed to the shootout. Eric Fehr shot first for Washington, but Florida goaltender Roberto Luongo made the save. After Jonathan Huberdeau was unable to get a shot off, Nicklas Backstrom lifted a backhander that was snared by the Panthers netminder. Next up was Florida's leading goal scorer, Nick Bjugstad; surely he could break the stalemate. Negative. He rung it off the post. After Evgeny Kuznetsov and Brad Boyes were each stopped on their respective efforts, Washington's Alex Ovechkin got the Capitals on the board with the first goal of the shootout. Jussi Jokinen needed to score in order to keep the Panthers alive, and he did, tucking the puck behind Braden Holtby with just one hand on his stick.

After Troy Brouwer hit the post on his attempt, Tomas Kopecky came up short as well. Following Luongo's save on Michael Latta, Aleksander Barkov had the chance to send everybody home, but he failed to get a shot off and the puck was easily kicked aside by Holtby. Opening the seventh round of the shootout, Brooks Laich tucked a backhand between Luongo's pads. Needing to score, Dave Bolland sped in on Holtby and wired the puck past the weary Capitals goaltender to keep the exhibition going. After Washington's Marcus Johansson failed to sneak the puck over Luongo's outstretched right pad, Tomas Fleischmann had a great opportunity, but mishandled the puck. Nate Schmidt was then stopped on a backhand attempt, as was Scottie Upshall. After Joel Ward and Derek MacKenzie each scored in the 10th round, John Carlson and Sean Bergenheim also found the back of the net. Seventeen more attempts followed. It seemed as though the shootout would never end. Finally, after 39 shooters and 10 goals, Bjugstad stepped up for the second time and scored the deciding goal in the 20th round, ending the longest shootout in NHL history.

# DECEMBER 17
# MICHAL ROZSIVAL'S GOALS, 2008

"A penalty shot doesn't happen every day, especially for a defenceman," was what Michal Rozsival told reporters after a game against the Kings. On December 17, 2008, the Rangers blueliner was awarded a penalty shot with less than eight minutes remaining in the second period. With the game tied 1-1, it was a tall order for a defenceman who was not known for his scoring prowess. Since breaking into the league with the Penguins in 1999, Rozsival scored 46 goals in his first seven seasons. Then in his fourth campaign with the Rangers, after joining the club as a free agent in 2005, he had struggled offensively in the early part of the season, finding the back of the net just two times in 34 contests. When the referee called a penalty on Drew Doughty, after the rookie defenceman shattered Jarret Stoll's stick, sending debris into the pathway of Rozsival, the veteran blueliner did not expect to be awarded a penalty shot. "It happened so quick. I'm not used to this. I made up my mind that I was going to go in on a direct line and go to the backhand," he was quoted as saying after the game.

As Rozsival skated in on Kings goaltender Jason LaBarbera, who had originally been drafted by the Rangers in 1998, Rozsival stuck to his plan and lifted the puck up over the netminder's stick side to give the Blueshirts a 2-1 lead. But Rozsival wasn't done just yet. After Los Angeles's Dustin Brown tied the game early in the third period, the two teams needed extra time. With time winding down in overtime, Rozsival fired a one-timer at LaBarbera, this time beating him high glove side. Rozsival not only doubled his season goal total that game but also became the second player in NHL history, since the league reintroduced overtime in 1983, to score on a penalty shot and notch the game-winning goal in overtime. Steve Thomas first did it with the Mighty Ducks on April 1, 2003.

# DECEMBER 18
## TRIPLE HAT TRICK, 1965

H at tricks abounded between the Rangers and Maple Leafs on December 18, 1965. In what proved to be a highly offensive affair, three different players recorded hat tricks in the Maple Leafs' 8-4 rout of the struggling Rangers. After opening the scoring for Toronto less than three minutes into the matchup, Dave Keon notched a pair of goals to start the second period and record his first regular-season NHL hat trick. Not to be outdone by his opponent, New York's Earl Ingarfield, who netted two goals in the first frame, completed his hat trick just 20 seconds after Keon had accomplished the feat and tied the game 4-4.

Punctuating the offensive performances from Keon and Ingarfield was the pugilistic presentation put on by Toronto's Eddie Shack. In the second period, a pair of Rangers, Rod Gilbert and Phil Goyette, were attempting to mount an offensive attack when Shack dropped them both. As Gilbert advanced into the Maple Leafs' zone, Shack drilled him with an elbow to the cheekbone, which caused him to collapse to the ice, where he hit his head and was knocked unconscious. After levelling Gilbert, Shack then cross-checked Goyette in the back of the neck, sending him to the ice as well. According to the *Globe and Mail's* recount of the game, Goyette suffered a pinched nerve in his neck and was momentarily paralyzed while he was sprawled on the ice. The dust-up had happened so quickly that when play advanced out of Toronto's zone, officials and the Maple Leafs faithful were surprised to see the pair of Rangers prostrate on the ice. Somehow, Shack avoided being penalized. When the game resumed for the third period, the rough stuff continued between Vic Hadfield and Wally Boyer, but it was Toronto's Bob Pulford who stole the show, scoring two goals late in the frame to complete his own hat trick, the third of the evening.

# DECEMBER 19
## THE NHL'S FIRST GAMES, 1917

t was the dawn of a new era. On December 19, 1917, the first National Hockey League games were played. Less than a month after the league was formed at the Windsor Hotel in Montreal, the pucks dropped for the first matchups. In Montreal, the Wanderers hosted the Toronto Hockey Club. The game went off with a bang. Just a minute into the contest, Montreal's Dave Ritchie scored the opening goal, becoming the first player ever to score in the NHL. When the first period had closed, the Wanderers led 5-3, bolstered by a hat trick from Harry Hyland and a two-goal performance from Harry Cameron. Although the *Globe* reported that Toronto "had the better of the argument for most of the game," it was let down by its goaltending. When play resumed for the second period, Toronto made a change in net, replacing Sammy Hebert with Art Brooks. But the change did little to alleviate the situation. Brooks allowed five goals in the remaining 40 minutes as Toronto fell 10-9 to Montreal in its inaugural matchup.

Meanwhile, in Ottawa, the Canadiens and Ottawa Hockey Club faced off. Scheduled to start at 8:30 p.m., 15 minutes later than the first game in Montreal, the matchup was delayed by 15 minutes as Ottawa hammered out last-minute contracts for Jack Darragh and Hamby Shore. With the details sorted out play began, but Darragh and Shore were not able to get out onto the ice until the second period. By that point, it was too late. The game was nearly out of reach. Guided by the play of Joe Malone, the Canadiens led 3-0 after the first period. Although Ottawa got on the board early in the second period to cut the deficit to two, Malone scored back-to-back goals, recording his first NHL hat trick, to extend the lead even further. When the dust settled, Malone had scored five goals and the Canadiens handily defeated Ottawa 7-4.

# DECEMBER 20
## DOUG SMAIL'S FASTEST GOAL, 1981

J ust five seconds after the opening faceoff, Winnipeg's Doug Smail made NHL history. On December 20, 1981, after the Jets won the draw against the Blues, Smail cruised in on the left side and wired a wrist shot at the St. Louis net. Goaltender Paul Skidmore, who was playing in his very first NHL game, mishandled the puck, giving the Jets the lead with just five seconds off the clock. Smail's tally established a new league record for the fastest goal to start a game, surpassing the previous mark of six seconds set by the North Stars' Henry Boucha in a matchup against the Canadiens on January 28, 1973.

It didn't take long, however, for someone to match Smail's feat. On March 22, 1984, in a game between the Islanders and Bruins, New York's Bryan Trottier won the opening draw against Boston's Steve Kasper. As the puck bounced behind Bruins defenceman Mike O'Connell, Trottier blew by him on the left side and blasted a slap-shot past goaltender Doug Keans, matching Smail's mark. Although Trottier's goal got the Islanders off to an early head start, they soon had to overcome a 3-1 deficit, which they did with goals from Mike Bossy in the second and final frames, to draw the Bruins to a 3-3 tie. Five years later, on October 5, 1989, Alexander Mogilny made his NHL debut with the Sabres. Just 20 seconds into his first shift, the Soviet rookie scored his first career goal, establishing a league record for the fastest goal by a player making his NHL debut. Although it wasn't as fast as Smail's or Trottier's, it was a preview of things to come. Almost 10 years to the day that Smail made NHL history, Mogilny matched the accomplishment, on December 22, 1991, when he stole the puck from the Maple Leafs' Michel Petit and scored five seconds into the game. As of the end of the 2017–18 NHL season, no one has lit the lamp quicker to start a game than Smail, Trottier, and Mogilny.

# DECEMBER 21
## ROB ZEPP MAKES HIS NHL DEBUT AT 33, 2014

R ob Zepp travelled a long, winding road to get to the NHL. After being selected 99th overall by the Atlanta Thrashers in 1999, the Newmarket, Ontario, goaltender returned to his duties in the Ontario Hockey League, backstopping the Plymouth Whalers, with the hope that one day he would get the call from Atlanta. But that call never came. The Thrashers never signed Zepp to a contract, making him eligible once again for the NHL Entry Draft. In 2001, he was taken 110th overall by the Hurricanes, but he spent much of the next four seasons toiling in the East Coast Hockey League, with little hope of cracking a big-league roster. With his dream of playing in the NHL seemingly getting further out of reach, he decided to pursue options in Europe. After two seasons in the Finnish Elite League, Zepp joined Eisbären Berlin of the Deutsche Eishockey Liga. But after tending goal for Berlin for the next seven years, including leading the club to five league championships, he returned to North America for one last shot at the NHL.

On July 1, 2014, he signed a two-way contract with the Flyers. After starting the season with the Lehigh Valley Phantoms, Philadelphia's American Hockey League affiliate, Zepp got the call he had been waiting for all his life. On December 19, 2014, he was recalled by the Flyers on an emergency basis. With the team playing back-to-back games that weekend, it seemed as though Zepp was going to get the opportunity to be in net for an NHL team. Finally, on December 21, 2014, Zepp, then 33 years old, made his NHL debut against the Winnipeg Jets. After making 25 saves in a 4-3 overtime victory over the Jets, Zepp became the oldest goaltender to win his NHL debut since 41-year-old Hugh Lehman accomplished the feat with the Black Hawks on November 17, 1926. Zepp started nine more games for the Flyers that season, a testament to his patience and perseverance.

# BRETT HULL SCORES HIS 500TH GOAL, 1996

A cheer rose up in the Kiel Center in St. Louis as Brett Hull scored his 500th career goal. Heading into the contest against the Kings on December 22, 1996, Hull was sitting at 497 markers, and after piling up two goals already that evening, it looked as though he had completed the hat trick and reached land-mark territory. Less than a minute into the third period, with the Blues leading 5-3, he fired a shot at Kings goaltender Stephane Fiset. After hitting the netminder's stick, the puck found the back of the net. Hull's teammates mobbed him in celebration while the Blues faithful erupted into applause and showered the ice with hats. Hull, however, didn't actually score. While the goal was initially awarded to Hull, officials later determined that Stephane Matteau had actually deflected the puck past Fiset. Despite the raucous ovation, Hull would have to wait.

But it didn't take too long. Ten minutes later, following a pass from Pierre Turgeon, Hull wired a one-timer past Fiset to officially notch his 500th career goal, becoming the 24th player in league history to reach the milestone. Moreover, with the landmark goal, Hull and his father, Bobby, became the only father-son duo in NHL history to each record 500 goals. Bobby, who had spent 15 seasons with the Black Hawks, where he became the first NHL player to score more than 50 goals in a season, racked up 610 career goals over the course of his time with Chicago and later with Winnipeg and Hartford. Scoring the goal in St. Louis, in what would be the Blues' first home victory in more than a month, was a fitting end to a tumultuous week for Hull. After publicly feuding with general manager and head coach Mike Keenan all season long, the Blues had sided with their goal scorer and dismissed Keenan on December 19. Hull would finish the campaign with 42 goals to lead the team in scoring for the ninth consecutive year.

# DECEMBER 23
## BRYAN TROTTIER'S BIG PERIOD, 1978

B ryan Trottier gave Islanders fans an early Christmas present they could cheer about. On December 23, 1978, in a game against the Rangers, the Islanders centre — who broke into the league just three years earlier with a 95-point rookie campaign that set club records — racked up six points in the second period in a 9-4 victory over their crosstown rivals. Trottier's performance in the middle frame, three goals and three assists, established an NHL record for the most points in one period. He eclipsed the mark of five points initially set by the Rangers' Bill Cook on March 12, 1933, a feat that had since been matched four times by four different players over the next four decades before Trottier rewrote the record book.

Although he opened the scoring with less than seven minutes to go in the first period, when the New York clubs adjourned for intermission, the game was tied 1-1 and there was little indication that the contest was going to turn into a rout when play resumed. Just over a minute into the second period, Trottier set up Mike Bossy for the first of five straight Islanders goals in the span of 10 minutes. When the dust settled, Trottier had added another goal and three assists to his opening marker, and he added two more tallies to close the period. But Trottier wasn't done just yet. Before the halfway point of the final stanza, he scored what would end up being his fifth goal of the game. When the matchup actually finished, Trottier had been credited with only four goals, but after officials reviewed footage from the game, he was awarded a goal that had initially been attributed to teammate Stefan Persson. Trottier's six-point outburst in the second period was the talk of the town, but the crafty centre also finished the game with five goals and three assists, setting Islanders records for most goals and points in a game.

# THE NHL'S FIRST CHRISTMAS EVE GAME, 1919

As the Quebec Bulldogs skated out onto the ice on December 24, 1919, to square off against the Canadiens, they were missing a few players. In the NHL's first Christmas Eve matchup, Montreal certainly had the advantage on the bench, with eight skaters compared with Quebec's six. Before long, the Bulldogs were overwhelmed by their provincial counterparts. Just 30 seconds into the contest, Montreal's Newsy Lalonde opened the scoring, and by the time the first period came to a close, he had a hat trick and the Canadiens were leading 5-0. Although Montreal added another quick goal to start the second period, a marker that proved to be the nail in the coffin, the overmatched Bulldogs posted a better performance that frame, mustering up two goals and heavily outplaying their opponents. The two clubs exchanged goals to open the third period, but Montreal added five more in the final five minutes to bury the Bulldogs 12-5.

The NHL's first Christmas Eve game was in the books, but the holiday tradition never really caught on. Over the next six decades, the league played only 29 more games intermittently on December 24. In 1971 the NHL announced it was scrapping Christmas matchups so that players could spend more time with their families over the holidays, and the league's final Christmas Eve contests were played the following year. On December 24, 1972, Rangers goaltender Eddie Giacomin stopped all 24 shots he faced from the Red Wings to record the last Christmas Eve shutout. For his efforts, he earned a $100 bonus from head coach Emile Francis. Later that evening, the Kings' Serge Bernier powered Los Angeles to a 5-3 victory over the Golden Seals, but it was his teammate, Juha Widing, who had the distinction of scoring the NHL's final Christmas Eve goal.

# DECEMBER 25
# THE NHL'S LAST CHRISTMAS GAME, 1971

Gerry O'Flaherty has no doubt about the greatest Christmas gift he ever received. Drafted 31st overall by the Maple Leafs in 1970, O'Flaherty started his professional career with the Tulsa Oilers, Toronto's Central Hockey League affiliate. After beginning the 1971–72 season in Oklahoma, the 21-year-old right winger received a call he would never forget. On December 24, 1971, Maple Leafs general manager Jim Gregory informed him he would be an emergency replacement for the big club, filling in for Paul Henderson, who was out with a knee injury. Not only would he be making his NHL debut, but he would be doing it on Christmas when Toronto hosted the Red Wings.

Making the moment even more special was that O'Flaherty and his wife Mary were both from Toronto. The young newlyweds would get to surprise their families for Christmas, and Gerry would get to suit up for his first game as a Maple Leaf in front of his family and friends. In reflecting on that special moment, O'Flaherty told VICE Sports that it was the best Christmas gift he had ever had. "I fulfilled a lifetime dream and played in the NHL, which is what I had really wanted to do my whole life," he said. That night, O'Flaherty skated on a line with Norm Ullman, who would lead the team in scoring that season, as the Maple Leafs defeated the Red Wings 5-3 in one of the league's last Christmas contests. While other professional leagues such as the NBA and NFL still play games on Christmas, the NHL's cessation of operations over the holidays sets it apart. Although O'Flaherty made his NHL debut on Christmas, he says it's important for players to spend that time with their families. "I think it's really special for all the players who have families. It's a special day, and I think it should be treated as a special day," he said.

# DECEMBER 26
## SERGEI FEDOROV'S BOXING DAY BLOWOUT, 1996

After a sluggish start to the 1996–97 season, recording just five goals in his first 25 games, Sergei Fedorov scored seven goals in 10 games leading up to the holidays. When NHL contests resumed after the Christmas break, Fedorov turned in a Boxing Day performance for the ages. On December 26, 1996, he scored five goals in a game against the Capitals, becoming the first player in NHL history to score all five goals in his team's victory. Although the speedy Russian had had an immediate impact since breaking into the league in 1990–91, he wasn't exactly known for scoring in bunches. While he had recorded 33 career multi-goal efforts leading up to that memorable evening, he didn't record his first career NHL hat trick until the tail end of his fourth season, and the only other time he potted three or more goals was when he put four past Los Angeles on February 12, 1995.

Nevertheless, everything seemed to be clicking that night for Fedorov. Whether he was acting as the trigger man on some silky passing between Igor Larionov and Vladimir Konstantinov or making it happen by himself on a breakaway, Fedorov put the Red Wings on his back that night. Not only did he tie the game to force overtime, but after receiving another elegant dish from Konstantinov halfway through the extra frame, he ripped a wrist shot past Capitals goaltender Jim Carey to secure the Red Wings victory. Although he had made NHL history and was the first Red Wings player to score five goals in a game since Syd Howe accomplished the feat on February 3, 1944, against the Rangers, Fedorov offered few words after his incredible performance. In speaking humbly with reporters, he acknowledged his accomplishment but simply said, "I don't want to spoil it by talking all about it."

# DECEMBER 27
# MARIO LEMIEUX RETURNS AS
# PLAYER-OWNER, 2000

Just a few months after becoming owner of the Penguins, Mario Lemieux added some new duties to his job description. Complementing his roles as president, chairman, and CEO, Lemieux added the position of first-line centre. On December 11, 2000, he announced he would be making a return to hockey, becoming the first player-owner in the modern era of major professional sports. Lemieux, who had spent his entire NHL career with the Penguins, winning two Stanley Cups and a collection of individual trophies, had originally retired following the 1997 playoffs.

Although his new responsibilities with the Penguins off the ice certainly kept him busy, after a few years away from the game, it was clear he still had some hockey left in him. In preparation for his comeback, the 35-year-old Lemieux began training behind the scenes with trainer and former teammate Jay Caufield. He officially came out of retirement on December 27, 2000, when the Penguins hosted the Maple Leafs. Much like his very first NHL game, in which he scored his first goal on his first shot of his first shift, Lemieux wasted no time in his return. Just 33 seconds into the contest, he set up Jaromir Jagr to open the scoring for the Penguins, much to the delight of the sold-out crowd of 17,148 at Mellon Arena, who had not witnessed Lemieux's nifty playmaking abilities for nearly four years. In the second period, Jagr returned the favour, dishing Lemieux a beautiful pass that he promptly fired into the back of the net, scoring his first regular-season goal since April 6, 1997. He finished the game with three points, adding another assist, and afterward told reporters he was satisfied with his performance despite being off for so long. It certainly didn't seem as though Lemieux had lost a step because of his time away. In his first eight games back, he racked up 19 points, and he finished the campaign with 76 points in just 43 games.

# DECEMBER 28
## SUPER SERIES '76, 1975

n 1972, Team Canada — made up of the NHL's premier Canadian players — took on the Soviets in the highly politicized and game-changing Summit Series, but just three years later, the Russians invaded again. On December 28, 1975, the Rangers squared off against the indomitable Soviet Red Army team, the top club in the USSR, in the first contest of Super Series '76, a midseason exhibition tournament that pitted eight NHL clubs against the Red Army and the Soviet Union's second-best squad, the Wings. With the Rangers taking on the Red Army in the first matchup, they became the first NHL club to play against a touring Soviet team. For those Rangers players who had suited up in the Summit Series, especially Phil Esposito, they knew not to take the contest lightly.

In advance of the matchup against the Red Army, Esposito, who had been acquired just a month earlier by the Rangers in a blockbuster trade with the Bruins, told Robin Herman of the *New York Times*, "It was a traumatic experience. I never want to go through that again." In 1972, Esposito had been incredibly vocal when Team Canada had been booed off the ice in Vancouver after losing a second game on home soil. Although the Canadians came back to win the series in Russia, the country's faith in its hockey superiority had been shattered by the nimble play of the Soviets — along with the incredible performance of goaltender Vladislav Tretiak. Three years after turning the Summit Series on its head in the opening games, the Russians did it again when the Red Army defeated the Rangers 5-3 at Madison Square Garden. Highlighted by the play of Tretiak and some exceptional skating, particularly from Valeri Kharlamov, whose speed was compared to Montreal's Yvon "Roadrunner" Cournoyer, the Soviets deftly kept the puck away from the Blueshirts. In the games that followed, the Red Army tied the Canadiens and defeated the Bruins before finally giving up their only loss to the hard-nosed Flyers.

# DECEMBER 29
## BRODEUR'S LAST SHUTOUT, 2014

After 21 seasons with the Devils, highlighted by a Calder Trophy, four Vezinas as the league's top goaltender, and three Stanley Cups, Martin Brodeur was moving on from the only organization he had ever known. Drafted 20th overall by New Jersey in 1990, Brodeur would become a fixture in net for the Devils over the next two decades, backstopping the club to its first championship in franchise history. Following the 2009–10 season, however, in which he led the league in wins and shutouts, his play began to decline. After the conclusion of the 2013–14 season, with his contract set to expire, it was clear his time with the Devils was coming to an end. Although he had just turned 42 years old, Brodeur believed he still had more game in him and announced he would test the free-agent market for the first time in his career.

While he may have been the NHL's all-time leader in victories and shutouts, the job offers were not as forthcoming as he might have anticipated. After failing to ink a contract in the summer, an opportunity presented itself early in the new season when Blues goaltender Brian Elliott sustained a lower-body injury that would keep him on the shelf for weeks. On November 26, 2014, the Blues signed Brodeur to a professional tryout contract to test his services, and a week later, on December 2, they signed the goaltender to a one-year deal. The three-time Vezina winner got his first start with St. Louis on December 4. Two days later, he recorded his first career victory with the club when he relieved Jake Allen in a game against the Islanders and salvaged the win. After a few more appearances, Brodeur turned in his most memorable performance on December 29, 2014, when he stopped all 16 shots he faced against the Avalanche to record his 125th career shutout. But with Elliott nearing a return from injury, and Allen anointed as the franchise's goaltender of the future, it proved to be Brodeur's final shutout. On January 29, 2015, after a record-setting career, he officially announced his NHL retirement.

## 50 IN 39, 1981

After scoring 45 goals in the first 38 games of the 1981–82 season, it wasn't a question of whether Wayne Gretzky would become the first player to score 50 goals in fewer than 50 games, but when he would do it. While the hockey world knew it was only a matter of time before the Great One eclipsed Maurice Richard and Mike Bossy, the only two players in league history who scored 50 goals in 50 games, Gretzky shattered those expectations on December 30, 1981, when the Oilers hosted the Flyers. That evening, before the capacity crowd of 17,490 at the Northlands Coliseum, Gretzky made NHL history when he racked up five goals to reach the 50-goal mark in just his 39th game of the season.

Even his parents, Walter and Phyllis, weren't expecting their son to stage such an incredible and record-setting performance that evening. They were still at home in Brantford, Ontario. Following the game, Gretzky told reporters his parents had been planning on travelling to Vancouver the next day in the hope they would catch him break the record when the Oilers took on the Canucks. He lamented that he probably disappointed his parents by making history in their absence, but he said that "if you're going to break a record the best place to do it is at home." After scoring his fourth goal of the game five minutes into the third period, it seemed as though Walter and Phyllis had made the right call; Gretzky would finish the contest with 49 goals and they'd get to see their son break the record in Vancouver. But after the Flyers scored two quick goals in the final frame to cut Edmonton's lead to just one, Gretzky made history with just three seconds remaining on the clock. With Philadelphia's net empty, he shot the puck into the yawning cage and the Coliseum crowd erupted. Fifty goals in 39 games. It's an NHL record that will likely stand the test of time.

# MARIO'S FIVE GOALS, FIVE WAYS, 1988

t was one of the most magnificent performances in NHL history. On New Year's Eve 1988, Mario Lemieux did it all. In a game against the Devils, the Penguins captain scored five goals, five different ways. He scored at even strength. He scored short-handed. He scored on the power play. He even scored on a penalty shot. Finally, just for good measure, he scored an empty-net goal. Not a bad way to close out the year. After New Jersey's Jim Korn opened the scoring early in the first period, Lemieux responded by streaking down the right side and eluding a pair of Devils defencemen to even the score. Just over three minutes later, with the Penguins killing a penalty, Lemieux evaded blueliner Aaron Broten to score his seventh short-handed goal of the season and give his team the lead. But he was just getting warmed up. Three minutes later, with the game knotted 2-2 and Pittsburgh on a power play, he wired a shot from the point, beating goaltender Bob Sauve to complete the hat trick. And that was all just in the first period. After assisting on two goals in the middle frame, Lemieux was awarded a penalty shot after goaltender Chris Terreri, who had mercifully replaced Sauve, threw his stick at Lemieux while he had possession of the puck. He made no mistake on the attempt and picked up his fourth goal. Finally, with just a second remaining on the clock, he scored into an empty net to cap his magnificent evening.

Nearly three decades later, as part of the NHL's centennial celebrations in 2017, fans voted on the greatest moment in league history and overwhelmingly selected Lemieux's five goals, five different ways, as the top event. When Lemieux officially received the honour on December 16, 2017, during the NHL 100 Classic between the Canadiens and Senators, he told the crowd, "You think of all the great moments in the NHL over the last 100 years, for the fans to pick my five goals is something special." Only time will tell which moments will captivate the imaginations of hockey fans in the next century.

# ASSISTS

Putting *Hockey 365* together was truly a team effort.

I would like to first thank my agent, Arnold Gosewich, for putting this together and connecting me with the wonderful people at Dundurn Press. I owe a debt of gratitude to Dominic Farrell and Kathryn Lane for their help throughout the project and to Elena Radic for steering it to its conclusion.

A big stick tap to my good friend and colleague Mark Kuhlberg. He's been reading and editing my words for years and always finds a way to get the best out of my work to set me up for a one-timer. He played a big part in getting *Hockey 365* on the ice.

Although they say you shouldn't judge a book by its cover, I'm fine if you did that with *Hockey 365* because the cover artwork is beautiful. Thanks to Laura Boyle at Dundurn Press for conceptualizing the idea and to Ron Beltrame, for taking the pass from her and scoring a big goal with the final design.

I would also like to thank Bob Borgen and Jen Conway, aka @NHLhistorygirl, for helping me nail down some of the dates and information for the book, along with members of the Society for International Hockey Research.

Thank you to Chris Toman from VICE Sports and Mike Cormack from Sportsnet. Before this book was even a possibility, they gave me the opportunity to bring my hockey history writing to a broader audience.

As much as I would love to be a full-time hockey writer one day, for now I still have a great day job at Cambrian College. I would be remiss if I didn't thank my colleagues at work, Emile, Steve, and James (Chebby), for all their insights, laughs, and title suggestions.

Thank you to my parents, Patti and Tony, for always believing in me and supporting me in my passions. You were by my side when I completed my Ph.D. in environmental history and you've continued to cheer me on in this new arena. Mom, you're still my longest-tenured editor. Thanks for all your help.

To my sister, Kyleigh, thanks for keeping me grounded while still being my biggest champion. Thank you to my brother-in-law, Sam. I'm counting on you to introduce *Hockey 365* to the Australian market.

Thank you to my in-laws, Moe and Sue. You have both been incredibly supportive of my work and I appreciate everything you do for me. I would also like to thank my brother-in-law, Andre, and his partner, Ashley. Andre always finds the best deal, but I know that even he will pay full price for this book.

And thank you to my wife, Chantal. You are my all-star, my coach, and my general manager. As with much of this book writing process, I am writing these words while you are sleeping. Thank you for your unrelenting patience and encouragement throughout this journey. You had to go to sleep alone a lot while I finished the book, but you always kept my side of the bed warm. I love you.

Finally, to my Zoe. You light up my life. You are the best thing that's ever happened to the Commito team. Your mother and I couldn't have asked for a better franchise player. Thank you for being such an amazingly beautiful, funny, and inquisitive girl. I can't wait to read some of these pages to you when you're older.

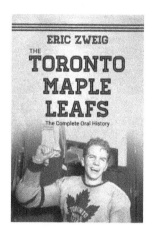

**THE TORONTO MAPLE LEAFS**
The Complete Oral History
Eric Zweig

**A complete history of the Toronto Maple Leafs, as told by the players, coaches, and reporters.**

On December 19, 1917, the Toronto Arenas took to the ice for the first NHL game ever played. Over the next hundred years, the franchise changed names twice, home rinks twice, and won thirteen Stanley Cups on its way to becoming one of the most successful and storied franchises in NHL history.

*The Toronto Maple Leafs: The Complete Oral History* gives the most comprehensive record of the team from its formation to the present day. With first-hand accounts of some of the biggest names ever to play the game — Syl Apps, Darryl Sittler, Mats Sundin — as well as coaches, managers, and commentators, Eric Zweig gives readers the full insider history of Canada's most iconic team.

**BLUE MONDAY**
The Expos, the Dodgers, and the
Home Run That Changed Everything
Danny Gallagher

**Blue Monday: one of the most unforgettable
days in Canadian baseball history.**

Danny Gallagher leads readers up to that unforgettable day in October 1981 when Rick Monday of the Los Angeles Dodgers hit a home run off of Montreal Expos pitcher Steve Rogers in the ninth inning, giving the Dodgers a berth in the World Series. Readers will be taken back to 1976 when a five-year plan for winning the National League championship was set in place by the Expos with the hiring of experienced manager Dick Williams. Gallagher examines old narratives about Blue Monday and talks to all the key players involved in the game, unearthing secrets and stories never before told.